DATE DUE

JY 30 '98			
AG 9 07			

DEMCO 38-296

Psychoanalytic Perspectives on Developmental Psychology

Psychoanalytic Perspectives on
Developmental
Psychology

Edited by Joseph M. Masling and Robert F. Bornstein

American Psychological Association • Washington, DC

Copies may be ordered from
APA Order Department
P.O. Box 92984
Washington, DC 20090-2984

In the United Kingdom and Europe, copies may be ordered from
American Psychological Association
3 Henrietta Street
Covent Garden
London WC2E 8LU
England

Typeset in Palatino by EPS Group, Inc., Easton, MD

Printer: Braun-Brumfield, Inc., Ann Arbor, MI
Cover and jacket designer: Berg Design, Albany, NY
Technical/production editor: Valerie Montenegro

Volumes 1, 2, and 3 of the series Empirical Studies of Psychoanalytic
Theories, edited by Joseph Masling, were published by The Analytic Press,
Hillsdale, NJ.

Library of Congress Cataloging-in-Publication Data
Psychoanalytic perspectives on developmental psychology / edited by
      Joseph M. Masling and Robert F. Bornstein.
          p. cm. — (Empirical studies of psychoanalytic theories ; vol. 6)
      Includes bibliographical references and index.
      ISBN 1-55798-385-2 (casebound : acid-free paper)
          1. Psychoanalysis. 2. Developmental psychology. I. Masling,
      Joseph M. II. Bornstein, Robert F. III. Series.
      BF175.45.P78   1996
      155—dc20   96-30399
                                                                                  CIP

British Library Cataloguing-in-Publication Data
A CIP record is available from the British Library.

Printed in the United States of America
First edition

Psychoanalytic Perspectives on Developmental Psychology

Contents

Contributors

Sidney J. Blatt is Professor of Psychiatry and Psychology at Yale University and a faculty member at the Western New England Institute of Psychoanalysis. Blatt was Sigmund Freud Professor of Psychoanalysis and Senior Fulbright Foundation Research Fellow at the Hebrew University of Jerusalem (1988–1989). He has published widely on psychoanalytic theory, research, and treatment, and he recently received the Society for Personality Assessment's Lifetime Achievement Award and an award for Distinguished Contributions to Research from the Association of Medical School Professors of Psychology.

Robert F. Bornstein is Professor of Psychology at Gettysburg College. Bornstein has written numerous articles on perception without awareness and has published widely on the dynamics of dependent personality traits. Bornstein wrote *The Dependent Personality* (1993), coedited (with Thane Pittman) *Perception Without Awareness: Cognitive, Clinical and Social Perspectives* (1992), and recently received the Society for Personality Assessment's 1995 Walter Klopfer Award for Distinguished Contribution to the Literature on Personality Assessment.

Bertram J. Cohler is William Rainey Harper Professor of Social Sciences in the Departments of Psychology (Committee on Human Development), Psychiatry, and Education at the University of Chicago. Cohler is also on the faculty at the Institute for Psychoanalysis, Chicago.

Yeates Conwell is Associate Professor in the Departments of Psychiatry and Oncology at the University of Rochester Medical Center, where he is Director of the Laboratory of Suicide Studies and Director of the Psychiatry Residency Education Program.

David S. deBoer is a doctoral student in the Department of Psychology (Committee on Human Development) at the University of Chicago.

Paul R. Duberstein is Assistant Professor of Psychiatry and Oncology at the University of Rochester Medical Center, where he is also Associate Director of the Laboratory of Suicide Studies. A recipient of a National Institute of Mental Health Academic Career Award focusing on personality and stress in late life, Duberstein has published widely on suicide.

Morris N. Eagle is Professor of Psychology at the Derner Institute of Advanced Psychological Studies, Adelphi University. He is the author of *Recent Developments in Psychoanalysis: A Critical Evaluation* (1984) and coeditor (with James Barron and David Wolitzky) of *The Interface of Psychoanalysis and Psychology* (1992). Eagle is currently president of the Division of Psychoanalysis (Division 39) of the American Psychological Association (APA).

Ruth Feldman is Lecturer in the Department of Psychology at Bar-Ilan University, Israel. She has been the Rothschild Post-Doctorate Scholar at the Yale University Child Study Center. Feldman's research interests include the development of play and symbol across cultures, and the relations of psychophysiological and emotional development in infants at risk.

Rachel Karliner is a doctoral student in clinical psychology at the Derner Institute of Advanced Psychological Studies, Adelphi University. She is currently completing her predoctoral internship at Kings County Hospital in Brooklyn, NY. Her research interests include the roles of language, interpretation, and action in psychoanalytic play therapy with children. Before entering the field of psychology, Karliner taught second grade in Brooklyn, New York.

Lisa Sandow Lyons is a Fellow of Psychology in Psychiatry at Cornell University Medical College. She holds a postdoctoral fellowship in Personality Disorders and Community Psychiatry sponsored by the Office of Mental Health of the State of New York. Her research interests include cognitive changes associated with attachment style, clinical applications of attachment theory, outcome of relapse prevention programs for the severely mentally ill, and treatment of borderline personality disorder. Lyons has received research awards from the Science Directorate of the APA and from APA Division 39, Section VI (the Psychoanalytic Research Society).

Joseph M. Masling is Emeritus Professor of Psychology at the State University of New York at Buffalo. Masling has written numerous articles on interpersonal and situational variables influencing projective tests and has published widely on the empirical study of psychoanalytic concepts. Masling edited the first three volumes of the Empirical Studies of Psychoanalytic Theories series (1983, 1986, 1990) and coedited with Robert F. Bornstein *Psychoanalytic Perspectives on Psychopathology* (1993) and *Empirical Perspectives on Object Relations Theory* (1994).

Martin Mayman is Professor of Psychology at the University of Michigan and holds a faculty position at the Michigan Psychoana-lytic Institute. He has written numerous articles on early memories as reflections of current psychological functioning and manner of relating to others. Mayman developed the Early Memories Test, a widely used projective technique that allows clinicians and researchers to study an individual's sense of self, experience of others, and experience of the surrounding environment.

Sandra W. Russ is Professor and Chair of the Department of Psychology at Case Western Reserve University. She has published widely in the areas of children's play, creativity, and child psychotherapy. Russ is President of the Clinical Child Psychology Section of APA Division 12.

Larry Seidlitz is currently a Research Assistant Professor in the Department of Psychiatry at the University of Rochester Medical Center, where he is examining the role of emotion in psychopathology.

Jonathan Shedler has held positions at the University of California, Berkeley; the Derner Institute of Advanced Psychological Studies, Adelphi University; and Harvard Medical School. He has published widely on illusory mental health and adolescent drug use. Currently on leave from academia, Shedler teaches skiing and maintains a clinical practice in Aspen, Colorado.

Michael B. Sperling is Associate Professor of Psychology at Fairleigh-Dickinson University, as well as a Visiting Fellow of Psychology in Psychiatry at Cornell University Medical College. Sperling has conducted research on the assessment and treatment of adult interpersonal attachments and has written and edited volumes on adult attachment and on psychodynamics and managed care. He recently was awarded a fellowship in academic administration at Baruch College/City University of New York by the American Council on Education.

Ellen Katz Westrich is a doctoral student in clinical psychology at the Derner Institute of Advanced Psychological Studies, Adelphi University. She is currently completing her predoctoral internship at the Veterans Administration Medical Center, Brooklyn. Westrich's research interests include the somatic expression of psychological experience.

Introduction:
On the Empirical Testing of Psychoanalytic Concepts: Psychoanalysis as Developmental Psychology

Joseph M. Masling and Robert F. Bornstein

Few ideas have influenced Western thought as strongly as has psychoanalytic theory, even in the absence of empirically confirmatory evidence. In no other serious form of inquiry have the primary data been so unavailable to colleagues and the general scientific community as in the psychoanalytic process. No other field has been so limited to the voluntary release of selected data (the case history) by an agent who helped generate those data. In contrast, for 50 years nonpsychoanalytic psychotherapists, beginning with Rogers (1942), have made available to serious investigators the primary data of the psychotherapeutic session. It is incredible that so considerable an enterprise as psychoanalytic treatment could have remained so secret, so unavailable for public scrutiny, for so many years.

That this secrecy was maintained in the name of ethics and concern for the patient's privacy did not allay suspicions that empirically untested theories have a great deal to hide. A number of scholars, some rather open-minded about psychoanalysis and some obviously prejudiced and dismissive of the theory no matter what the evidence, have criticized it on three grounds. First, scholars have complained that the failure to share primary clinical data with other investigators has kept psychoanalysis from the same rigorous public scrutiny given other disciplines. Linked to this is a second objection, that psychoanalytic theory has been insufficiently tested empirically. Third, critics have claimed that those experimental results that do exist fail to support the theory's hypotheses.

The general attitude of many academic psychologists toward psychoanalysis is consistent with that of George Kelly, who observed that psychoanalytic theory may well have been as great a hindrance to the progress of psychology in the 20th century as it was a help in the 19th. Unfortunately, a great many academic psychologists have rejected psychoanalytic theory outright, without first becoming familiar with its propositions, tenets, and supporting empirical base. Consequently, in many academic settings, psychoanalytic theory tends to be viewed as a mildly interesting piece of ancient history—an all but extinct species that briefly dominated the psychological world and then vanished because of its inability, or perhaps unwillingness, to adapt to changing conditions. In many undergraduate departments (and even in many graduate training programs), psychoanalysis often is mentioned only as an example of what a personality theory should *not* be (i.e., tautological, sexist, refractory to operational definitions, largely untested, and accepted by its adherents as gospel truth).

Criticisms from those without psychoanalytic training and experience can be dismissed on several grounds, including the resistance to psychoanalytic ideas that Sigmund Freud discussed, but it is not as easy to dismiss criticism that comes from within the psychoanalytic establishment. In his presidential address to the American Psychoanalytic Association, Cooper (1984) warned that "our exciting debates will become arid if they are not sprinkled with new data. Even if we do not feel impelled by our scientific and theoretical curiosity, we might respond to the demands of a society that will not forever allow us to practice clinical psychoanalysis without evidence of its efficacy" (p. 259). Holt (1992) was more explicit, arguing that "American psychoanalysis is in a state of crisis in virtually every aspect. . . . Its status as a science is shaky at best and its prospects for improvement poor" (p. 375). Spence's (1994) position is similar: "This troubling lack of progress can be laid to two factors: reliance on an outmoded method of scientific data collection and a preference for fanciful argument over hard fact. . . . Most disturbing of all is the absence of data. Argument by authority stands directly in the way of the benefits, zealously guarded since the Renaissance, of an adversarial, critical, and dialectical tradition of investigation" (pp. 1–3).

It cannot be denied that the psychoanalytic treatment session has rarely been subjected to public scrutiny, both because psychoanalysts have been reluctant to allow others to inspect the psychoanalytic hour and because research on psychoanalytic transactions is extraordinarily difficult, labor-intensive, and expensive, requiring competence in both psychoanalytic treatment and research design. Nevertheless, a few researchers have managed to gain access to treatment protocols and have examined empirically the transactions that occur within the psychoanalytic session. Dahl (1983); Gill and Hoffman (1982); Gill, Simon, Fing, Endicott, and Paul (1968); Horowitz (1991); Luborsky and his colleagues (Luborsky, 1967, 1976; Luborsky, Graff, Pulver, & Curtis, 1973; Luborsky & Spence, 1978); Spence (1969, 1973, 1994); and Weiss and Sampson (1986a, 1986b) are among the handful of investigators who have had the opportunity, interest, facilities, and training to study psychoanalytic protocols. Given the long history of psychoanalytic treatment, this does not constitute a glorious record of empirical study.

The situation is made even worse by the almost total disregard of these few studies by most psychoanalytic clinicians. As Spence (1994) has carefully delineated, starting with Freud, "psychoanalytic literature tends to minimize evidence at the expense of conclusions and maximize argument at the expense of evidence" (p. 30). Indeed, Wolitzky (1990) has noted that of 200 references in a recent book by 16 analysts on treatment, only 6 referred to empirical work, and of these 6 citations, 5 were made by one author. In dramatic contrast, nonpsychodynamic forms of treatment rely heavily on empirical results. The literature on cognitive and behavioral therapies is filled with reports demonstrating the close interplay between treatment methods and research findings. The situation is so bad that Luborsky has commented that psychoanalysts who use experimental data in their presentations may actually forfeit their clinical status.

However, the criticisms of Cooper and others are egregiously incorrect in a larger sense in that psychoanalytic theories of personality have proven to be robustly heuristic. The critics who have been persistently predicting the imminent demise of psychoanalysis for the past 20 years or so could not have been more wrong. As L. Silverman (1976) declared, reports of the death of psychoanalysis "have been greatly exaggerated" (p. 621). The development of object relations theory and self psychology has produced an abundance of new and innovative perspectives on psychoanalytic theory and therapy (see Eagle, 1984; Greenberg & Mitchell, 1983). Moreover, there have probably been more well-designed empirical studies testing and extending psychoanalytic concepts during the past two decades than at any other time in the history of the discipline (Fisher & Greenberg, 1978, 1985, 1996; Masling, 1983, 1986, 1990; Masling & Bornstein, 1993, 1994; Shapiro & Emde, 1995). Indeed, it is quite likely that psychoanalytic theory has inspired more empirical research than has any other theory of personality. Fisher and Greenberg (1996), for example, estimated that more than 2,500 research articles have been inspired by psychoanalytic theory, an estimate that is probably quite conservative. If one criterion of the merit of a theory is that it be heuristic, psychoanalytic theory has more than satisfied this test. Furthermore, contrary to the assertions of many critics, a considerable number of psychoanalytic propositions have been found to be consistent with empirical results. There is much more scientific merit in psychoanalytic theories of personality than critics have granted.

Thus, contrary to the predictions (and perhaps desires) of some critics, psychoanalysis is not disappearing. Psychoanalytic ideas have influenced research programs in clinical, social, developmental, and cognitive psychology (see, e.g., Aronson, 1992; Bornstein, 1992; Bornstein & Pittman, 1992; Bowers & Meichenbaum, 1984; Erdelyi, 1985; Horowitz, 1988, 1991; Singer, 1990; Stern, 1985; Tabin, 1985; Uleman & Bargh, 1989). As Emde (1992) observed, many recent (and not so recent) stage theories of social and personality development are rooted in S. Freud's (1905/1954) psychosexual stage model. The same is true of recent theories regarding the development of the self-concept in infancy and early childhood (see Stern, 1985; Tabin, 1985). In cognitive psychology, many models of perception, cognition, and memory without awareness have been influenced by psychoanalytic theories of the unconscious (Bornstein & Pittman, 1992; Schachter, 1987). Similarly, cognitive research on mental representations and schemas has borrowed liberally from object relations theory and self psychology (Horowitz, 1991). Finally, social research on person perception and social cognition has been influenced by concepts and ideas from object relations theory (Westen, 1991).

The impact of psychoanalytic theories on psychological and psychiatric thinking has been nothing short of pervasive, its influence extending well beyond psychology and psychiatry. Psychoanalytic theory remains one of the most important scientific and intellectual ideas of this century, profoundly influencing not only the mental health disciplines and academic psychology but also anthropology, sociology, philosophy, literature, art, criminology, and even the physical sciences (Grunbaum, 1984; Holland, 1984). Furthermore, the influence of psychoanalytic theory reaches well beyond academia: Torrey (1992) has discussed in detail the myriad ways in which psychoanalytic theory has influenced political thought and social policy during the past 50 years.

Empirical Data and Clinical Evidence in Psychoanalysis

The question of whether psychoanalysis is a science and should be held to scientific accountability has occasioned long, contentious, and fruitless debates. To the present day, scholars have taken fiercely held positions on this issue (Grunbaum, 1984), with no resolution likely to occur within any reader's lifetime. Those psychoanalysts who disparage the relevance of empirical research base their objections on three grounds. First, such research has been criticized as *irrelevant* to the clinical theory of psychoanalysis. This view holds that what is truly psychoanalytic cannot be studied in the laboratory, and what can be studied in the laboratory is not truly psychoanalytic.

The second objection to empirical data is that they are *unnecessary* because clinical evidence is so compelling and convincing that no independent verification is needed. However, the ongoing controversy about Freud's "seduction theory" is ample evidence that clinicians' prior beliefs strongly influence perception and memory of patients' behavior (Loftus, 1993). Instead of systematically collecting data on reports of childhood sexual assaults, psychoanalysts have relied on dogma and authority. As Spence (1994) put it, "It is disturbing to recognize the power of Freud's authority and the way in which theory prevails over observation. . . . Evidence that does not support standard theory tends to be minimized or disparaged, and independent thinking tends to be discredited" (p. 4).

Finally, some psychoanalysts argue that empirical research represents a *misapplication of psychoanalytic concepts*. In this context, they contend that psychoanalysis is intended to be used to investigate intensively the psychological functioning of individuals and that the application of psychoanalytic theory to arbitrarily defined groups of people (e.g., hysterics, character-disordered persons, obsessives, victims of child abuse) is inappropriate and contrary to psychoanalytic principles. For these scholars, psychoanalysis should be confined to the description and analysis of one person and is misused when applied to the aggregates that compose the raw material of personality and clinical research.

These objections are invalid. To dismiss the entire enterprise of experimental testing of psychoanalytic hypotheses is as simple-minded and naive as it is to dismiss the case history method. Experiments need not twist psychoanalytic theory into unrecognizable shape, and most of those summarized in this volume and in the preceding five in the Empirical Studies series do not. The need for extra-clinical evidence to provide a more secure footing for psychoanalytic theory ought to be abundantly evident to anyone interested in the long-term welfare of psychoanalysis. Grunbaum's (1984) closely reasoned analysis of the philosophical and scientific assumptions underlying psychoanalytic theory makes explicit the great need for extra-clinical, empirical support of the theory. Perhaps Malcolm (1984) put the matter best: "Certainly the self-congratulatory clinical histories in the analytic literature cannot be accepted as evidence of anything beyond the writer's self-regard" (p. 18).

Ironically, the third objection to experimental treatment of psycho-analytic observations could have been made about Freud's own writings or those of most major psychoanalytic writers. Freud frequently generalized observations made from his treatment of one patient to the behavior of groups of people. It was Spence's (1994) contention that around 1900, when Freud began to minimize the importance of describing large numbers of cases, he started to "rely on choice specimens and favorite examples to make his point, he played down the importance of replication as a hedge against error, and he depended increasingly on arguments based on authority" (p. 1). Nevertheless, from a choice example or two he would generalize to larger populations. For example, from the case of Schreber he derived a general statement about the dynamics of the origins of paranoid thinking. Throughout the "Rat Man" and "Wolf Man" cases, Freud extrapolated from his observations about these and other patients and generalized about differences between hysterical and obsessive–compulsive disorders. In "Character and Anal Erotism," S. Freud (1908/1959) described a cluster of traits that he found in some people: "The people I am about to describe are noteworthy for a regular combination of the three following characteristics. They are especially *orderly, parsimonious, and obstinate*" (p. 20; emphasis in original).

S. Freud's (1908/1959) assertion can be viewed as a kind of informal research study—he observed groups of people and noticed that they differed in character traits. Experimenters do the same thing, but they do it better: Their methods are more explicit, their data gathering is more systematic, and the experiment is made public so that it is available for replication by others. If psychoanalysis were restricted to hermeneutics or were confined to the construction of a narrative based on a single person's life, it would be robbed of one of its greatest merits—its heuristic value. The extent to which psychoanalytic theory has inspired research has been astounding. (The quality of some of this research is another matter, but the base rate of good experimental design in research on personality is not very high, and the same caveat can be issued about many other areas of study in psychology.)

Clinical Evidence, Empirical Evidence, and the Self-Fulfilling Prophecy

Nothing in these remarks is intended to discredit or diminish the value of psychoanalytic treatment. We wish to distinguish here between treatment and the theory of personality that supports and explains it. All psychodynamic therapists have seen patients who improved considerably as a result of treatment, but the reason for behavioral and attitudinal changes may be independent of the therapist's personality theory. Indeed, the therapeutic successes that every school of psychoanalysis can point to suggest strongly that some nonspecific forces (e.g., the uncritical, accepting attitude of the therapist, the empathic therapeutic relationship) may be more relevant to change than is the therapist's theory.

Our comments speak to the wisdom of constructing a theory of personality based exclusively on material learned from the clinical interaction and to the belief of many clinicians that the words, dreams, recollections, and associations of the patient reflect only the patient's life and therefore reveal some basic psychological truths. Such a theory will help greatly in understanding a particular patient and might well reveal some general facets of human behavior. Indeed, as the volumes in this series demonstrate, many parts of psychodynamic theories are consistent with empirical evidence. However, to believe that everything a patient says or does originates from the patient without having been influenced in any way by the analyst is to ignore the important (but subtle, and frequently ignored) role of the therapist.

All therapists, of whatever therapeutic persuasion, carry a personality theory into the consulting room, a theory that instructs the therapist (and after a while, the patient as well) about which content is important and which is less consequential. Every intervention by the therapist results from the therapist's decision that what the patient has said or done (or not said or not done) warrants interpretation, clarification, or further discussion. Inevitably, the patient learns what the therapist considers important and what the therapist generally ignores. Before long, most patients know what will elicit a response and what will only produce silence. Thus, in a detailed analysis of the verbal interchange between a client and Carl Rogers, Murray (1956) demonstrated that Rogers' theory led him to intervene only for some categories of thematic material but not for others; in due time, the client talked only about the issues in which Rogers had demonstrated interest. This analysis by Murray (1956) was later confirmed by Truax (1966) for a second case of Rogers.

The subtle communication by therapist to patient is obviously not confined to Rogerian therapy. Marmor (as cited in Grunbaum, 1984) described how this might work in an analytic session:

> In face-to-face transactions, the expression of the therapist's face, a questioning glance, a lift of the eyebrows, a barely perceptible shake of the head or shrug of the shoulder all act as significant cues to the patient. But even *behind* the couch, our "uh-huhs" as well as our silences, the interest or the disinterest reflected in our tone of voice or our shifting postures all act like subtle radio signals influencing the patients' responses, reinforcing some responses and discouraging others. (p. 267)

There is nothing inherently improper about this kind of coaching by the therapist, who is, after all, being paid to help patients understand the events in their lives. Negative consequences of this process occur only if therapists are unable to acknowledge that the content of a patient's speech is partly the result of their implicit coaching. To believe that everything the patient says emerges untutored and un-shaped by the therapist is to mistake a mirror for a window. It is inevitable that the patient's words (and memories) sometimes reflect both therapist and patient. The controversy about recovered memo-ries of childhood sexual abuse demonstrates the ease with which therapists' beliefs may sometimes result in patient "recollections" (Loftus, 1993).

Grunbaum's (1984) comprehensive, sophisticated review of the philosophical bases of psychoanalytic theory concluded that

> the clinical use of free association features epistemic bases of selec-tion and manipulative contamination as follows: (1) the analyst *selects thematically* from the patient's productions, partly by inter-rupting the associations—either explicitly or in a myriad more sub-tle ways—at points of his or her own theoretically inspired choosing; and (2) when the Freudian doctor harbors the suspicion that the associations are faltering because of evasive censorship, he uses ver-bal and also subtle nonverbal promptings to induce the continuation of the associations *until* they yield *theoretically* appropriate results. (pp. 210–211; emphasis in original)

S. Freud (1937/1964), of course, was aware that this sort of criticism could be made about the psychoanalytic method and vigorously defended against it:

> The danger of our leading a patient astray by suggestions, by per-suading him to accept things which we ourselves believe but which he ought not to, has certainly been enormously exaggerated. An ana-lyst would have had to behave very incorrectly before such a mis-fortune could overtake him; above all, he would have to blame him-self with not allowing his patients to have their say. I can assert without boasting that such an abuse of "suggestion" has never occurred in my practice. (p. 262)

S. Freud's concern about the vulnerability of psychoanalytic practice to this criticism is amply warranted, but his reassurance is unconvincing.

The end result of this unintentional coaching of the patient has been described by Marmor (as cited in Grunbaum, 1984):

> Patients seem to bring up precisely the kind of phenomenological data which form the theories and interpretations of their analysts! Thus each theory tends to be self-validating; Freudians elicit mate-rial about the Oedipus Complex and castration anxiety, Jungians about archetypes, Rankians about separation anxiety, Adlerians about mas-

culine strivings and feelings of inferiority, Horneyites about idealized images, Sullivanians about disturbed interpersonal relationships, etc. (p. 289)

Modern-day psychoanalysis is marked by a large number of schools and theoretical orientations, each separated from the next by differences that are sometimes so minute that they can be observed only by vigilantes in opposing camps, and each begun by a charismatic, authoritative leader—Freud, of course, as well as Anna Freud, Melanie Klein, Reik, Kernberg, Kohut, Horney, Jung, Lacan, Winnicott, Adler, Reich, Mahler, and Fairbairn. The existence of so many schools and versions of psychoanalytic thought is clear evidence that adherents of each school somehow derive material from their patients that supports a particular view of the world (see Masling & Cohen, 1987). As is the case with competing religions, the ideas and experiences so compelling to one school are dismissed as unpersuasive by the others. One way out of this endless morass (and the fruitless arguments based on nothing more substantial than authority and the selective release of undocumented portions of case histories) is to agree to open the psychoanalytic session to scrutiny by qualified experts and to subject deeply held beliefs to rigorous experimental tests. "Sooner or later, the central concepts (of psychoanalysis) must be exposed to the test of the marketplace, subjected to the traditional cross-validation and replication expected of any empirical science" (Spence, 1994, p. 179).

Rather than discarding the case history method as corrupted by the unwitting shaping of the patient's behavior or dismissing the experimental method as inappropriate or redundant, the two methods of gathering data can—and should—be seen as complementary. "Psychoanalysts must begin to face the fact that their primary and typical form of research, the uncontrolled case study, is devoid of scientific value *except* as a source of hypotheses" (Holt, 1984, p. 13). Although the theme of these volumes strongly endorses the need to use empirical methods to investigate psychoanalytic theories, there should be no confusion about the relative contribution of experiment and case history method: Relatively few truly creative ideas have originated in laboratory studies of personality. The raw material of psychoanalytic thought, the good stuff, has come primarily through the analyst–patient interaction and the case method of presenting these ideas. Data derived from the experimental method can demonstrate the extent to which some psychoanalytic proposition is consistent with laboratory results. For example, S. Freud's observation of the anal triad has repeatedly been confirmed experimentally (Masling & Schwartz, 1979), as has his conjecture that some mental processes work below the level of conscious awareness (Bornstein, Leone, & Galley, 1987; Masling, 1992), but his observation that women are less satisfied with their bodies than are men has not (Fisher & Greenberg, 1985, 1996). Although a simple demonstration of the validity of psychoanalytic hypotheses is important, more valuable are those studies that extend the theory into previously unexplored areas. Most of the chapters in these volumes do this, for example those by Beebe (1986); Blatt and Lerner (1983); Greene and Rosencrantz (1986); Sackeim (1983); D. Silverman (1986); Wilson, Passik, and Faude (1990); Blatt, Quinlan, and Chevron (1990); Fisher and Greenberg (1993); Auerbach (1993); Bornstein (1993); Marcia (1994); and Tangney (1994), among others.

Psychoanalysis as Developmental Psychology

Psychoanalytic theory is in many respects a theory of human development. In fact, a fundamental tenet of psychoanalysis is the proposition that early experiences affect later personality dynamics. Moreover, many of the core elements of psychoanalytic theory (e.g., unconscious processes, ego defenses, fixation and regression) were created in part to explain how early life events can affect personality functioning years—or even decades—after these events take place. Without question, the shift from classical psychoanalytic theory to object relations theory and self psychology has altered the language of psychoanalysis. However, this shift has not altered its focus: Psychoanalysis remains, above all, a model that seeks to explain the processes that underlie normal and abnormal personality development.

Although developmental issues have considerably influenced psychoanalytic thinking for nearly 100 years, many important changes have taken place in psychoanalytic models of personality development and psychopathology since Freud's time. For example, the almost exclusive emphasis on infant development has given way to a more comprehensive life span perspective (Galatzer-Levy & Cohler, 1993). At the risk of oversimplifying this important theoretical shift, one might argue that it has taken place in four stages. Early in the history of psychoanalysis, when Freud's drive model was the centerpiece of the psychoanalytic movement, infancy and early childhood were regarded as the key periods during which important psychodynamic events took place (Greenberg & Mitchell, 1983). Anna Freud's seminal writings on adolescent personality development and dynamics (e.g., A. Freud, 1936) initiated a theoretical shift that caused psychoanalysts to attend more closely to the events that occurred during late childhood and beyond. Erickson's (1963, 1968) psychosocial stage model broadened the psychoanalytic view of development still further, helping clinicians and researchers to recognize that psychodynamically relevant events take place during every stage of life. With the delineation and refinement of object relations theory and self psychology, psychoanalysis has truly become a comprehensive, unified theory of life span development (Eagle, 1984; Galatzer-Levy & Cohler, 1993).

A second important theoretical shift in the developmental component of psychoanalytic theory involves the psychodynamic conceptualization of the infant–caretaker relationship. Early psychoanalytic writings tended to concentrate exclusively on the influence of parent on child, all but ignoring the possibility that parents and children influence each other reciprocally (Bornstein, 1992; Tabin, 1985). As research on parent–child interactions became more sophisticated, however, it became increasingly clear that children are not passive beings who wait quietly for the parent to act on them. Rather, the child is an active, striving entity whose temperament and behavior are important determiners of parental behavior (Beebe, 1986; Stern, 1985).

The recognition that children influence parents quite as much as parents influence children is paralleled in our evolving conceptualization of the patient–therapist relationship. Early psychoanalysts incorrectly viewed the therapist as an objective, unbiased observer who remained largely detached and unaffected by the behavior of the patient (Masling & Cohen, 1987), but as our previous discussion of patient–therapist mutual influence demonstrated, this early view was overly simple and incorrect. As the psychoanalytic conceptualization of human development has been influenced by empirical research on infant–mother interaction, the psychoanalytic understanding of patient–therapist dynamnics has shifted from a "unidirectional influence" model to a "bidirectional influence" model that emphasizes the complex interplay between patient and therapist behavior (Horowitz, 1991; Shapiro & Emde, 1995; Weiss & Sampson, 1986a, 1986b).

Without question, developmental research has profoundly influenced psychoanalytic theory. Increasingly, however, the reverse is also true. The past 25 years have seen considerable growth in the influence of psychodynamic thinking on developmental theory and research. For example, studies of infant–caretaker attachment have been strongly affected by object relations models of personality and psychopathology (Main, Kaplan, & Cassidy, 1985). Not surprisingly, as psychoanalytic theory has become more of a life span developmental theory, clinicians and researchers have increasingly emphasized attachment relationships in adulthood. We now know that early attachment patterns affect friendships, romantic relationships, and even the therapeutic relationship (Shaver & Clark, 1994; Sperling & Berman, 1991).

Studies of identity development and the construction of the self-concept have also been shaped by psychoanalytic thinking. Object relations theory has provided a language that many developmental psychologists use to describe the processes that underlie identity formation during childhood and adolescence (Emde, 1992; Marcia, 1994). Similarly, many recent advances in object relations theories of identity formation have been influenced by research on cognitive development and the socialization process (Guisinger & Blatt, 1994; Shapiro & Emde, 1995).

Finally, increasing interest in the psychodynamics of aging is emerging, as developmental researchers and psychoanalysts recognize that many developmental milestones occur long after adolescence. Psychoanalytic theory and developmental psychology have combined to reveal important aspects of the personality processes that influence marriage, child rearing, career development, and retirement (Galatzer-Levy & Cohler, 1993). Moreover, due in part to the influence of existential psychologists and philosophers (e.g., Boss, 1963; May, Angel, & Ellen-berger, 1958), psychoanalytic theorists and developmental psychologists no longer avoid discussing the psychodynamics of senescence and mortality. As the ensuing chapters will show, the events and transitions that occur late in the life cycle are beginning to receive attention from psychoanalytic investigators, helping to create a more balanced and comprehensive psychoanalytic model of life span development.

The Empirical Studies of Psychoanalytic Theories Series

This series of books was begun with the aim of contributing to the empirical base of psychoanalysis by presenting the best and most current experimental work inspired by psychoanalytic theories, thereby helping to fill a critical gap in the literature. A considerable amount of such work has already been completed and reviewed (see, e.g., Fisher & Greenberg, 1985, 1996; Kline, 1972; Masling, 1983, 1986, 1990; Masling & Bornstein, 1993, 1994; Masling & Schwartz, 1979). A scientific theory is expected to generate data that will force it to be revised and ultimately discarded. Most of the experiments reported in this series point to instances in which the theory must be modified to fit the data more closely. Because Freud did not have modern technology available when he wrote about the process of dreaming or about the way in which cognition can occur below the level of conscious awareness, his ideas on these topics were necessarily less complete, less detailed, and less accurate than are the results of research on dreaming reported by Levin (1990) or the results on subliminal presentation of stimuli reported by Bornstein (1990). This slow accretion of knowledge from scientific studies will suggest how psychoanalytic theories can be modified to accommodate current information. Investigators using psychoanalytic theories should be seen less as bank auditors looking for signs of fraud than as sympathizers eager to keep the spirit of psychoanalytic inquiry alive and consistent with systematically collected scientific data.

The Empirical Studies series is now more than a decade old. The present volume, number 6, is devoted to psychoanalytic models of development. Wherever possible, contributors to the series attempt to bring the research results they discuss to issues of diagnosis and clinical interventions. Future volumes will deal with gender differences in personality, the psychoanalytic unconscious, the psychodynamics of affect, and events within the psychoanalytic treatment session.

Volume 6 opens with Feldman and Blatt's chapter examining the precursors of relatedness and self-definition in mother–infant interaction. Their review of research on mother–infant mutual influence demonstrates how events that occur during the first year of life may affect later personality in predictable ways. The findings discussed in this chapter also offer strong support for Blatt's long-standing distinction between the introjective and anaclitic lines of development, a theoretical model that has influenced many psychoanalytic and nonpsychoanalytic research programs during the past 20 years.

Chapter 2, by Karliner, Westrich, Shedler, and Mayman, addresses the complex relationships among three important psychological variables: early memories of key life events and relationships, adult personality dynamics, and mental health. In addition to describing the development of a new psychometrically sound measure of early memories, this chapter also discusses the evolving concept of "illusory mental health," thereby helping to reduce the distance between informal clinical observation and objective assessment of psychopathology.

Russ's (chap. 3) discussion of the psychodynamics of creativity not only has implications for child and adolescent development but also helps connect psychodynamic theory and research with an ongoing controversy in cognitive and social psychology: the extent to which affective responses can occur with little or no intervening cognitive activity by the responder. The studies described in this chapter are part of a sophisticated, long-term, psychoanalytically inspired research program that touches a number of important issues in psychoanalytic theory and therapy.

Eagle (chap. 4) contrasts psychoanalytic theory and attachment theory, noting those issues that are treated more fully in one framework or the other. Of special interest is Eagle's discussion of early attachment experiences and later relationships, the intergenerational transmission of attachment patterns, and the role of internal working models in the etiology and maintenance of maladaptive relationships. Eagle also discusses the implications of patient attachment style for therapeutic strategies and interventions in psychodynamic treatment.

Cohler and deBoer's (chap. 5) thorough and insightful discussion describes the ways in which psychodynamic theories can act as a unifying framework that allows researchers to understand and investigate the processes underlying adult development. This chapter brings together several independent areas of research, allowing clinicians, theoreticians, and researchers to appreciate the ways that adult development is similar to, yet different from, development that takes place during infancy and early childhood.

Lyons and Sperling (chap. 6) combine empirical research and clinical data to illustrate how attachment theory can influence psychodynamically oriented clinical work. Beginning with the recognition that the therapeutic relationship is strongly influenced by earlier attachments, Lyons and Sperling go on to demonstrate convincingly that many aspects of psychotherapy—including transference and countertransference dynamics—reflect the recapitulation of these earlier relationships in various subtle (and not so subtle) ways.

Finally, Duberstein, Seidlitz, and Conwell (chap. 7) use psychoanalytic theory to examine recent research on completed suicides. The authors meticulously review relevant research on completed suicides, demonstrating how psychodynamic models of suicide have been heuristic and explanatory and showing where these models may need revision to make them more consistent with contemporary findings regarding the psychodynamics of suicidal, self-destructive behavior.

All contributors to this series, as well as its editors, seek to keep psychoanalytic theory alive and consistent with modern scientific canon. Our tasks are to continue to investigate the extent to which psychoanalytic theories of personality have a substantial scientific base, to indicate where the theories have been found to be inadequate and flawed, and to extend psychoanalytic thinking into new areas of inquiry—hoping thereby to help reinvigorate psychoanalytic scholarship, teaching, and practice. This work must continue in order to avoid Spence's (1994) gloomy prediction that if psychoanalysis does not alter its collection and use of data, "the enterprise Freud began with such promise [will end] up being fascinated with its own reflection—and seeing nothing else" (p. 203). As the chapters in this series demonstrate, more people are engaged in this effort than is commonly appreciated, and more progress is being achieved than is usually recognized. The work, however, is far from complete.

References

Aronson, E. (1992). *The social animal.* New York: Freeman.

Auerbach, J. S. (1993). The origins of narcissism and narcissistic personality disorders: A theoretical and empirical reformulation. In J. M. Masling & R. F. Bornstein (Eds.), *Empirical studies of psychoanalytic theories: Vol. 4. Psychoanalytic perspectives on psychopathology* (pp. 43–110). Washington, DC: American Psychological Association.

Beebe, B. (1986). Mother–infant influence and precursors of self- and object-representation. In J. Masling (Ed.), *Empirical studies of psychoanalytic theories* (Vol. 2, pp. 27–48). Hillsdale, NJ: Analytic Press.

Blatt, S. J., & Lerner, H. (1983). Investigations in the psychoanalytic theory of object relations and object representations. In J. Masling (Ed.), *Empirical studies of psychoanalytical theories* (Vol. 1, pp. 189–249). Hillsdale, NJ: Analytic Press.

Blatt, S. J., Quinlan, D. M., & Chevron, E. S. (1990). Empirical investigations of a psychoanalytic theory of depression. In J. Masling (Ed.), *Empirical studies of psychoanalytic theories* (Vol. 3, pp. 89–147). Hillsdale, NJ: Analytic Press.

Bornstein, R. F. (1990). Subliminal mere exposure and psychodynamic effects: Implications for the psychoanalytic theory of conscious and unconscious mental processes. In J. Masling (Ed.), *Empirical studies of psychoanalytic theories* (Vol. 3, pp. 55–88). Hillsdale, NJ: Analytic Press.

Bornstein, R. F. (1992). The dependent personality: Developmental, social, and clinical perspectives. *Psychological Bulletin, 112,* 3–23.

Bornstein, R. F. (1993). Parental representations and psychopathology: A critical review of the empirical literature. In J. M. Masling & R. F. Bornstein (Eds.), *Empirical studies of psychoanalytic theories: Vol. 4. Psychoanalytic perspectives on psychopathology* (pp. 1–41). Washington, DC: American Psychological Association.

Bornstein, R. F., Leone, D. R., & Galley, D. J. (1987). The generalizability of subliminal mere exposure effect: Influence of stimuli perceived without awareness on social behavior. *Journal of Personality and Social Psychology, 53,* 1070–1079.

Bornstein, R. F., & Pittman, T. S. (1992). *Perception without awareness: Cognitive, clinical and social perspectives.* New York: Guilford Press.

Boss, M. (1963). *Psychoanalysis and dasienanalysis.* New York: Guilford Press.

Bowers, K. S., & Meichenbaum, D. M. (1984). *The unconscious reconsidered.* New York: Wiley.

Cooper, A. M. (1984). Psychoanalysis at one hundred: Beginnings of maturity. *Journal of the American Psychoanalytic Association, 32,* 245–268.

Dahl, H. (1983). On the definition and measurement of wishes. In J. Masling (Ed.), *Empirical studies of psychoanalytical theories* (Vol. 1, pp. 39–68). Hillsdale, NJ: Analytic Press.

Eagle, M. (1984). *Recent developments in psychoanalysis.* New York: McGraw-Hill.

Emde, R. N. (1992). Individual meaning and increasing complexity: Contributions of Sigmund Freud and Rene Spitz to developmental psychology. *Developmental Psychology, 28,* 347–359.

Erdelyi, M. H. (1985). *Psychoanalysis: Freud's cognitive psychology.* New York: Freeman.

Erickson, E. H. (1963). *Childhood and society.* New York: Norton.

Erickson, E. H. (1968). *Identity, youth and crisis.* New York: Norton.

Fisher, S., & Greenberg, R. P. (Eds.). (1978). *The scientific evaluation of Freud's theories and therapy.* New York: Basic Books.

Fisher, S., & Greenberg, R. P. (1985). *The scientific credibility of Freud's theories and therapy.* New York: Basic Books.

Fisher, S., & Greenberg, R. P. (1993). Psychodynamics of spatial experience: Role in localization of somatic disorder. In J. M. Masling & R. F. Bornstein (Eds.), *Empirical studies of psychoanalytic theories: Vol. 5. Psychoanalytic perspectives on psychopathology* (pp. 253–280). Washington, DC: American Psychological Association.

Fisher, S., & Greenberg, R. P. (1996). *Freud scientifically reappraised: Testing the theories and therapy.* New York: Wiley.

Freud, A. (1936). *The ego and the mechanisms of defense.* Madison, CT: International Universities Press.

Freud, S. (1954). Three essays on the theory of sexuality. In J. Strachey (Ed. and Trans.), *The standard edition of the complete psychological works of Sigmund Freud* (Vol. 7, pp. 125–248). London: Hogarth Press. (Original work published 1905)

Freud, S. (1959). Character and anal erotism. In J. Strachey (Ed. and Trans.), *The standard edition of the complete psychological works of Sigmund Freud* (Vol. 9, pp. 167–176). London: Hogarth Press. (Original work published 1908)

Freud, S. (1964). Constructions in analysis. In J. Strachey (Ed. and Trans.), *Standard edition of the complete psychological works of Sigmund Freud* (Vol. 23, pp. 225–270). London: Hogarth Press. (Original work published 1937)

Galatzer-Levy, R. M., & Cohler, B. J. (1993). *The essential other: A developmental psychology of the self.* New York: Basic Books.

Gill, M. M., & Hoffman, I. Z. (1982). *Analysis of transference: Vol. 1. Psychological Issues Monograph 54.* Madison, CT: International Universities Press.

Gill, M., Simon, J., Fing, G., Endicott, N. A., & Paul, I. H. (1968). Studies in audio-recorded psychoanalysis: I. General considerations. *Journal of the American Psychoanalytic Association, 16,* 230–244.

Greenberg, J. R., & Mitchell, S. M. (1983). *Object relations in psychoanalytic theory.* Cambridge, MA: Harvard University Press.

Greene, L. R., & Rosencrantz, J. (1986). Idiosyncratic needs for fusion and differentiation in groups. In J. Masling (Ed.), *Empirical studies of psychoanalytic theories* (Vol. 2, pp. 199–217). Hillsdale, NJ: Analytic Press.

Grunbaum, A. (1984). *The foundations of psychoanalysis.* Berkeley, CA: University of California Press.

Guisinger, S., & Blatt, S. J. (1994). Individual and relatedness: Evolution of a fundamental dialectic. *American Psychologist, 49,* 104–111.

Holland, N. N. (1984). Freud, physics and literature. *Journal of the American Academic of Psychoanalysis, 12,* 301–320.

Holt, R. R. (1984, August). *The current status of psychoanalytic theory.* Paper presented at the 92nd Annual Convention of the American Psychological Association, Toronto, Ontario, Canada.

Holt, R. R. (1992). The contemporary crises of psychoanalysis. *Psychoanalysis and Contemporary Thought, 15,* 375–402.

Horowitz, M. J. (1988). *Psychodynamics and cognition.* Chicago: University of Chicago Press.

Horowitz, M. J. (1991). *Person schemas and maladaptive interpersonal patterns.* Chicago: University of Chicago Press.

Kline, P. (1972). *Fact and fantasy in Freudian theory.* London: Methuen.

Levin, R. (1990). Psychoanalytic theories on the function of dreaming: A review of empirical dream research. In J. Masling (Ed.), *Empirical studies of psychoanalytic theories* (Vol. 3, pp. 1–53). Hillsdale, NJ: Analytic Press.

Loftus, E. F. (1993). The reality of repressed memories. *American Psychologist, 48,* 518–537.

Luborsky, L. (1967). Momentary forgetting during psychotherapy and psychoanalysis: A theory and research method. *Psychological Issues Monograph 17/18.* Madison, CT: International Universities Press.

Luborsky, L. (1976). Helping alliance in psychotherapy. In J. Cleghorn (Ed.), *Successful psychotherapy* (pp. 92–116). New York: Brunner/Mazel.

Luborsky, L., Graff, H., Pulver, S., & Curtis, H. (1973). A clinical–quantitative examination of consensus on the concept of transference. *Archives of General Psychiatry, 29,* 69–75.

Luborsky, L., & Spence, D. P. (1978). Quantitative research on psychoanalytic therapy. In S. L. Garfield & A. E. Bergin (Eds.), *Handbook of psychotherapy and behavior change* (pp. 331–368). New York: Wiley.

Main, M., Kaplan, N., & Cassidy, J. (1985). Security in infancy, childhood and adulthood. *Monographs of the Society for Research in Child Development, 50,* 66–104.

Malcolm, J. (1984). *Psychoanalysis: The impossible profession.* New York: Random House.

Marcia, J. E. (1994). Ego identity and object relations. In J. M. Masling & R. F. Bornstein (Eds.), *Empirical studies of psychoanalytic theories: Vol. 5. Empirical perspectives on object relations theory* (pp. 59–104). Washington, DC: American Psychological Association.

Masling, J. (Ed.). (1983). *Empirical studies of psychoanalytic theories* (Vol. 1). Hillsdale, NJ: Analytic Press.

Masling, J. (Ed.). (1986). *Empirical studies of psychoanalytic theories* (Vol. 2). Hillsdale, NJ: Analytic Press.

Masling, J. (Ed.). (1990). *Empirical studies of psychoanalytic theories* (Vol. 3). Hillsdale, NJ: Analytic Press.

Masling, J. (1992). What does it all mean? In R. F. Bornstein & T. S. Pittman (Eds.), *Perception without awareness* (pp. 259–277). New York: Guilford Press.

Masling, J. M., & Bornstein, R. F. (Eds.). (1993). *Empirical studies of psychoanalytic theories: Vol. 4. Psychoanalytic perspectives on psychopathology.* Washington, DC: American Psychological Association.

Masling, J. M., & Bornstein, R. F. (Eds.). (1994). *Empirical studies of psychoanalytic theories: Vol. 5. Empirical perspectives on object relations theory.* Washington, DC: American Psychological Association.

Masling, J., & Cohen, I. S. (1987). Psychotherapy, clinical evidence, and the self-fulfilling prophecy. *Psychoanalytic Psychology, 4,* 65–79.

Masling, J., & Schwartz, M. (1979). A critique of research in psychoanalytic theory. *Genetic Psychology Monographs, 100,* 257–307.

May, R., Angel, E., & Ellenberger, E. H. (1958). *Existence: A new dimension in psychiatry.* New York: Basic Books.

Murray, E. J. (1956). A content–analysis method for studying psychotherapy. *Psychological Monographs, 70*(13, Whole No. 420).

Rogers, C. R. (1942). The use of electrically recorded interviews in improving psychotherapy. *American Journal of Orthopsychiatry, 12,* 429–434.

Sackeim, H. A. (1983). Self-deception, self-esteem and depression: The adaptive value of lying to oneself. In J. Masling (Ed.), *Empirical studies of psychoanalytic theories* (Vol. 1, pp. 101–158). Hillsdale, NJ: Analytic Press.

Schachter, D. L. (1987). Implicit memory: History and current status. *Journal of Experimental Psychology: Learning, Memory, and Cognition, 13,* 501–518.

Shapiro, T., & Emde, R. N. (1995). *Research in psychoanalysis: Process, Development, Outcome.* Madison, CT: International Universities Press.

Shaver, P. R., & Clark, C. L. (1994). The psychodynamics of adult romantic attachment. In J. M. Masling & R. F. Bornstein (Eds.), *Empirical studies of psychoanalytic theories: Vol. 5. Empirical perspectives on object relations theory* (pp. 105–156). Washington, DC: American Psychological Association.

Silverman, D. K. (1986). Some proposed modifications of psychoanalytic theories of early childhood development. In J. Masling (Ed.), *Empirical studies of psychoanalytic theories* (Vol. 2, pp. 49–72). Hillsdale, NJ: Analytic Press.

Silverman, L. H. (1976). Psychoanalytic theory: The reports of my death are greatly exaggerated. *American Psychologist, 31,* 621–637.

Singer, J. L. (1990). *Repression and dissociation.* Chicago: University of Chicago Press.

Spence, D. P. (1969). Computer measurement of process and content in psychoanalysis. *Transactions of the New York Academy of Science, 31,* 828–841.

Spence, D. P. (1973). Tracing a thought system by computer. In B. B. Rubenstein (Ed.), *Psychoanalysis and contemporary science* (Vol. 2, pp. 188–201). New York: Macmillan.

Spence, D. P. (1994). *The rhetorical voice of psychoanalysis: Displacement of evidence by theory.* Cambridge, MA: Harvard University Press.

Sperling, M. B., & Berman, W. H. (1991). An attachment classification of desperate love. *Journal of Personality Assessment, 56,* 45–55.

Stern, D. N. (1985). *The interpersonal world of the infant.* New York: Basic Books.

Tabin, J. K. (1985). *On the way to self.* New York: Columbia University Press.

Tangney, J. P. (1994). The mixed legacy of the superego: Adaptive and maladaptive aspects of shame and guilt. In J. M. Masling & R. F. Bornstein (Eds.), *Empirical studies of psychoanalytic theories: Vol. 5. Empirical perspectives on object relations theory* (pp. 1–28). Washington, DC: American Psychological Association.

Torrey, E. F. (1992). *Freudian fraud: The malignant effect of Freud's theory on American thought and culture.* New York: HarperCollins.

Truax, C. B. (1966). Reinforcement and nonreinforcement in Rogerian psychotherapy. *Journal of Abnormal Psychology, 71,* 1–9.

Uleman, J. S., & Bargh, J. A. (1989). *Unintended thought.* New York: Guilford Press.

Weiss, J., & Sampson, H. (1986a). Testing alternative psychoanalytic explanations of the therapeutic process. In J. Masling (Ed.), *Empirical studies of psychoanalytic theories* (Vol. 2, pp. 1–26). Hillsdale, NJ: Analytic Press.

Weiss, J., & Sampson, H. (1986b). *The psychoanalytic process: Theory, clinical observation & empirical research.* New York: Guilford Press.

Westen, D. (1991). Social cognition and object relations. *Psychological Bulletin, 109,* 429–455.

Wilson, A., Passik, S. D., & Faude, J. P. (1990). Self-regulation and its failures. In J. Masling (Ed.), *Empirical studies of psychoanalytic theories* (Vol. 3, pp. 149–213). Hillsdale, NJ: Analytic Press.

Wolitzky, D. L. (1990). Pathways to psychoanalytic cure. *Contemporary Psychology, 35,* 1154–1155.

1

Precursors of Relatedness and Self-Definition in Mother–Infant Interaction

Ruth Feldman and Sidney J. Blatt

Freud (1930/1957) identified a fundamental polarity in personality development when he noted that "the development of the individual seems . . . to be a product of the interaction between two urges, the urge toward happiness, which we usually call 'egoistic,' and the urge toward union with others in the community, which we call 'altruistic'" (p. 140). He also observed, "The man who is predominantly erotic will give the first preference to his emotional relationship to other people; the narcissistic man, who inclines to be self-sufficient, will seek his main satisfactions in his internal mental processes" (p. 140).

In contrasting the urge toward egoism with the urge toward union with others in the community, Freud (1930/1957) noted that these "two processes of individual and of cultural development must stand in hostile opposition to each other and mutually dispute the ground" (p. 141). He extended this polarity by distinguishing anxiety and guilt due to aggression and to the internalization of authority in the super-ego—both of which are related to the ego instincts and issues of mastery—from social anxiety that involves primarily the fear of the loss of love and contact with others. Freud (1914/1957, 1926/1959) also distinguished between object and ego libido and between libidinal instincts in the service of attachment and relatedness and aggressive instincts necessary for autonomy, mastery, and self-definition. Although there is no known citation for the comment, Freud also made the distinction between relatedness and self-definition in his often-quoted statement that the two major tasks of life are "to love and to work." Loewald (1962) was impressed with Freud's extensive use of this polarity and noted that Freud's exploration of

> these various modes of separation and union . . . [identify a] polarity inherent in individual existence of individuation and "primary narcissistic union"—a polarity that Freud attempted to conceptualize by various approaches but that he recognized and insisted upon from beginning to end by his dualistic conception of instincts, of human nature, and of life itself. (p. 490)

This chapter presents theoretical formulations that extend this fundamental psychoanalytic polarity between object and ego libido, between libidinal instinctual forces in the service of attachment (or relatedness) and aggressive instinctual forces in the source of self-definition. We discuss aspects of this polarity and how it defines the dimensions of a complex, fundamental, dialectic developmental process that is central to understanding normal personality development as well as a wide range of psychopathology.

The first half of this chapter summarizes a theoretical model of personality development and psychopathology that focuses on the complex intertwining of these two major dimensions (Blatt, 1991, 1995; Blatt & Blass, 1990, 1996; Blatt & Shichman, 1983). These theoretical formulations based primarily on adults guided us in further exploration of a data set that had been established to evaluate aspects of mother–infant interaction at 3 and 9 months and the relationship of aspects of the children's functioning at 2 years of age. Thus, the second half of this chapter presents further analyses of these data gathered on mother–infant interaction in an attempt to identify early precursors of relatedness and self-definition that appear to be central to personality development and psychopathology in adults.

A Model of Personality Development and Psychopathology

Personality development involves the evolution of (a) the capacity for reciprocal, mutually satisfying, intimate interpersonal relationships and (b) an essentially positive, realistic, well-differentiated, and integrated sense of self. These two dimensions, also referred to as *communion and agency* or *relatedness and identity*, are established in interpersonal interactions throughout the life cycle, beginning with the earliest experiences of the infant in the caring relationship with the mother. This development involves cognitive–affective schemas (or representations) of self and others and of their actual and potential interactions, established as the child matures and experiences various developmental demands. When developmental perturbations are age-appropriate and not severe, the child's existing cognitive schemas accommodate the experienced perturbations, thereby leading to the development of more comprehensive and mature representations of self and others.

Concepts of self and of others develop in a reciprocal or dialectic interaction so that further differentiation occurs in the representation of both self and others as well as the representation of the relationship between them. The emerging sense of self facilitates the development of more mature levels of interpersonal relatedness, and, conversely, new forms of relatedness facilitate the development of new levels in the sense of self. In normal development, these two lines of self-definition and relatedness emerge in a mutually facilitating and synergistic fashion throughout the life cycle, from infancy to senescence. This process usually unfolds in a natural, well-defined dialectical process: The consolidation of identity is contingent on establishing satisfying relationships, and the formation of increasingly mature interpersonal experiences depends on the formation of a more differentiated sense of self (Blatt, 1991, 1995; Blatt & Blass, 1990, 1996; Blatt & Shichman, 1983).

Psychoanalytic theorists other than Freud also have addressed this polarity. Bowlby (1969, 1973), from an ethological viewpoint, explored the two groups of instincts—libido and aggression—and how they create the emotional substrate for human personality as expressed in strivings for attachment and separation. Adler (1951) discussed social interest and self-perfection. He viewed neurosis as the consequence of a distorted overemphasis on self-enhancement in the absence of suffi-cient social interest. Pampering (overprotection, overindulgence, and overdomination) or rejection leads to feelings of inadequacy and self-ishness and a lack of independence. Rank (1929) also discussed self- and other-directedness and their relationship to creative and adaptive personality styles. Horney (1945, 1950) characterized personality as moving toward, moving against, or moving away from interpersonal contact. Balint (1959), from an object relations perspective, also dis-cussed the centrality of these two dimensions: a clinging or connect-edness (an ocnophilic tendency) as opposed to self-sufficiency (a philobatic tendency). Shor and Sanville (1978), based on Balint's for-mulations, discussed psychological development as involving a fun-damental oscillation between "necessary connectedness" and "inevitable separations," or between "intimacy and autonomy."

A number of nonpsychoanalytic personality theorists, using a variety of different terms, have also discussed relatedness and self-definition as central processes. Angyal (1941, 1951), for example, discussed sur-render and autonomy as two basic personality dispositions. Surrender for Angyal (1951) is the desire to seek a home, to become part of some-thing greater than oneself, whereas autonomy represents a "striving basically to assert and to expand . . . self-determination, [to be] an autonomous being, a self-governing entity that asserts itself actively instead of reacting passively. . . . This tendency . . . expresses itself in spontaneity, self-assertiveness, striving for freedom and for mastery" (pp. 131–132). Bakan (1966), similar to Angyal, defined *communion* and *agency* as basic aspects of personality development. Communion for Bakan (1966) is a loss of self and self-consciousness in a merging and blending with others and the world. It involves feeling a part of and participating in a larger social entity; being at one with others; feeling in contact or union; and experiencing a sense of openness, cooperation, love, and eros. Agency, in contrast, is a pressure toward individuation that Bakan believed permeates all living matter; it emphasizes being a separate individual and being able to tolerate iso-lation, alienation, and aloneness. The predominant themes in agency are self-protection, self-assertion, self-expansion, and an urge to master the environment and make it one's own. The basic issues are separa-tion and mastery.

Bakan's *communion* and Angyal's *surrender* both define a profound desire for union in which the person seeks to merge or join with other people and with the inanimate environment in order to achieve a greater sense of participation and belonging. Communion and surrender refer to a stable dimension of personality organization directed toward interdependent relationships with others. Themes of dependency, mutuality, and unity characterize this element of life.

Agency (Bakan) and *autonomy* (Angyal) both define a basic striving toward individuation—a seeking of separation from others and from an attachment to the physical environment, as well as a fuller differentiation within oneself. Agency and autonomy both refer to a stable dimension of functioning that emphasizes separation, individuation, control, self-definition, and autonomous achievement—the striving for uniqueness and the expression of one's own capacities and interests (Friedman & Booth-Kewley, 1987). Communion (or surrender)—the emphasis on connectedness, attachment, and a movement toward a sense of belongingness to and sharing with others (another person, group, or society)—serves as a counterforce to experiences of loneliness and alienation that can occur in agency and autonomy. Conversely, uniqueness and self-definition serve as a counterforce to experiences of a loss of individuality that can occur in surrender and communion.

Research investigators of personality development also have discussed similar phenomena. Gilligan (1982), for example, stressed the importance of including interpersonal responsibility as well as investment in individual rights and principles of justice as two dimensions of moral development. McAdams (1980) discussed motives for affiliation (or intimacy) and achievement (e.g., McClelland, 1986; McClelland, Atkinson, Clark, & Sowell, 1953) or power (Winter, 1973) as central dimensions of personality organization. In a series of studies of life narratives, McAdams (1985) identified two central themes or dominant clusters: (a) themes of intimacy (e.g., feeling close, warm, and in communication with others) and (b) themes of power (e.g., feeling strong and influential in one's environment). Individuals rated high on intimacy motivation spoke frequently of reciprocal, harmonious, interpersonal interactions and participation in social groups and express a "recurrent preference or readiness for experiences of warmth, closeness and communicative exchange" (McAdams, 1985, p. 76). He defined this intimacy motive as a "recurrent preference or readiness for experiences of warmth, closeness and communicative exchange" (p. 76). Individuals rated high on this motive often portrayed themselves as a helper, lover, counselor, caregiver, and friend. In contrast, people related high on power motivation spoke frequently of self-protection, self-assertion, and self-expansion. They separated themselves from the social context and expressed needs for mastery, achievement, movement, force, and action. McAdams (1985) defined this power motive as "a recurrent preference or readiness for experiences of having impact and feeling strong and potent vis-à-vis the environment" (p. 84). Individuals rated high on the power motive often spoke of themselves as a traveler, master, father, authority, or sage.

Wiggins (1991), an empirically based personality investigator, argued that agency and communion should serve as primary conceptual coordinates for the measurement of interpersonal behavior and as the fundamental coordinates of a trait language for describing personality functioning. Wiggins (1991) noted that the circumflex and five-factor models of personality that have been useful in the conceptualization and measurement of interpersonal acts, traits, affects, problems, and personality disorders are "derived from the metaconcepts of agency and communion" (p. 107). Although agency and communion may not by themselves capture the broad spectrum of individual differences that characterize human transactions, Wiggins (1991) concluded that they "are propaedeutic to the study of [the] . . . determinants of interpersonal behavior" (p. 109). Spiegel and Spiegel (1978) also discussed the importance of these two dimensions of intimacy and power (McAdams), communion and agency (Bakan), or surrender and autonomy (Angyal), and drew a parallel between these two personality dimensions and two fundamental natural forces—fusion and fission or integration and differentiation.

The Synergistic Developmental Dialectic Between Relatedness and Self-Definition

Consensus, from a number of theoretical positions, concludes that normal personality development involves the evaluation of two basic dimensions: a capacity for interpersonal relatedness and the development of self-definition (Stewart & Malley, 1987). However, personality development also involves an integration of these dimensions. Both Angyal and Bakan emphasized the simultaneous need for differentiation as well as integration and the need to establish a constructive resolution of these opposing polarities. Angyal (1951, pp. 135–136), like Bakan, stressed that the major task in life is to achieve a compromise and balance between these two forces so that both are represented fully in one's experiences. Increased autonomy, mastery, and a capacity to govern one's life and environment is best done not by force or violence but by understanding and respect for laws and rules of the social matrix—attitudes toward society similar to those involved in forming loving relationships. Similarly, a loving relationship requires not only a capacity for relinquishing one's autonomy and agency to some degree; it also requires a capacity for mastery of one's environment, resourcefulness, and self-reliance, without which a relationship is in danger of deteriorating into helpless dependency, exploitation, and possessiveness. Bakan (1966) discussed the importance of the individual's being able to maintain a *dynamic tension* between agency and communion, between surrender and autonomy. Kobasa, Maddi, and Kahn (1982) also discussed the blend of communion and agency, of intimacy and power needs, as central to the development of psychological well-being and hardiness. McClelland (1986) discussed the most mature form of power motive as being based on an essential integration of autonomy and affiliation. McAdams (1985) found that an integration of power and intimacy motivation in stories given to cards of the Thematic Apperception Test was correlated with a capacity to portray constructive action scripts that are future oriented and high on generativity. Power and intimacy are integrated by establishing a clear agential sense of self and also dedicating and devoting oneself to establishing intimate exchange with others. A mature identity according to McAdams (1985) is based on a sense of "sameness and continuity which provides unity and purpose" (p. 28). It requires both individuation and connectedness, an integration of identity formation and interdependence, and a continuity and a separation from one's past and one's environment, as well as a sense of the future and the capacity to establish new connections. According to Erikson (1982), "a mature sense of identity means a sense of being at one with oneself as one grows and develops; and it means, at the same time, a sense of affinity with a community's sense of being at one with its future as well as its history—or mythology" (pp. 27–28).

Shor and Sanville (1978) similarly discussed personality development as "oscillating between necessary connectedness and inevitable separateness . . . as a dialectical spiral or helix which interweaves the two dimensions of development, intimacy and autonomy. The pace and style of oscillation and the transitions between these two axes will vary for each person and map out his particular life history, his individual pattern of growth" (p. 121). They viewed the capacity for adult intimacy and love as a product "of an intense search to formulate one's individual identity and, once having formed it, to risk to suspend concern with oneself while focusing on the qualities of a potential mate" (Shor & Sanville, 1978, p. 121).

The importance of the interplay of interpersonal relatedness and self-definition in normal development is also seen in the developmental psychoanalytic formulations of Mahler and her colleagues and in the work of Stern. Stern (1985) presented a theory of the development of a sense of self but did so through describing children's emerging relatedness with the caring agent(s) with whom they develop a sense of empathic relatedness and intersubjectivity. The development of object relations (e.g., object constancy) was described by Mahler, Pine, and Bergman (1975) through the process of separation–individuation in periods of separation, practicing, and rapprochement. Both Mahler and Stern demonstrated how the sense of self and interpersonal relatedness develop as a complex dialectic process and are basic dimensions essential for psychological maturity. Thus, although these dimensions constitute two fundamental lines in personality development, the relationship between them goes well beyond parallel processes or a simple interaction or integration. Rather, the relationship involves a complex dialectical process throughout the life cycle in which progress along each line is essential for progress in the other (Blatt & Blass, 1990, 1992, 1996; Blatt & Shichman, 1983). Both of these developmental processes are expressed in unique ways at various points throughout the developmental process.

The dialectic synergistic development of the concept of the self and of the relationship with others can probably best be illustrated by an elaboration of Erikson's (1950) epigenetic model of psychosocial development. Erikson's model, although presented basically as a linear developmental process, implicitly indicates that normal personality development involves the mutually facilitating development of self-definition and interpersonal relatedness. If one includes in Erikson's model an additional stage of cooperation versus isolation (occurring around the time of the development of peer play and the initial resolution of oedipal crisis at about ages 4 to 6 years) and places this stage at the appropriate point in the developmental sequence between "initiative versus guilt" and "industry versus inferiority" (Blatt & Shichman, 1983), then Erikson's epigenetic model of psychosocial development illustrates the complex transaction between interpersonal relatedness and self-definition throughout the life cycle. Erikson initially emphasized interpersonal relatedness in his discussion of trust versus mistrust, followed by two stages of self-definition, autonomy versus shame and initiative versus guilt. This was followed by another stage of interpersonal relatedness, cooperation versus isolation, followed by two stages of self-definition, industry versus inferiority and identity versus role diffusion. The following stage, intimacy versus alienation, was again clearly a stage of interpersonal relatedness, followed by two more stages of self-definition, generativity versus stagnation and integrity versus despair (Blatt & Shichman, 1983).

This reformulation of Erikson's model (Blatt, 1991, 1995; Blatt & Blass, 1990, 1996; Blatt & Shichman, 1983) corrects the deficiency noted by a number of theorists (e.g., Franz & White, 1985) that Erikson's model tends to neglect the development of interpersonal attachment. The inclusion of a relational dimension as an integral aspect of personality development to complement the more usual emphasis on individuation and self-definition is consistent with the call by feminist theorists (e.g., Chodorow, 1978; Gilligan, 1982; Miller, 1976, 1984), who point out the failure to give equal status to the development of interpersonal relatedness in most theories of personality development. It is also consistent with the extensive research and theory of the past two decades that demonstrate the importance of attachment (e.g., Ainsworth, 1969; Bowlby, 1969, 1973), the processes of separation–individuation (e.g., Mahler et al., 1975), and the growth of the capacity for mutuality and empathy (e.g., Stern, 1985) in personality development.

The articulation of an attachment developmental line broadens Erikson's model and more clearly demonstrates the dialectic developmental transaction between relatedness and self-definition implicit in Erikson's model. Relatedness and individuality (attachment and separation) both evolve through a complex interactive process. The evolving capacities for autonomy, initiative, and industry in the individuality line develop parallel to a capacity for relatedness—to engage with and trust another; to cooperate and collaborate in activities with peers (e.g., play); to develop a close friendship with a same-sex chum; and eventually to experience and express feelings of mutuality, intimacy, and reciprocity in a mature, intimate relationship. Normal development involves a coordination between the evolving capacities along these two lines. For example, one needs a sense of basic trust to venture in opposition to the need-gratifying other in asserting one's autonomy and independence, and later one needs a sense of autonomy and initiative to establish cooperative and collaborative relationships with others. Although these two developmental lines interact throughout the life cycle, they remain relatively independent of each other through the early developmental years.

Relatedness and Self-Definition in Normal Personality Styles

Although *normality* can be defined ideally as an integration of interpersonal relatedness and self-definition, within normal limits most individuals place a relatively greater emphasis on one of these over the other. This relative emphasis on one versus the other delineates two basic personality configurations, each with particular experiential modes and preferred modes of cognition, defense, and adaptation (Blatt, 1974, 1990; Blatt & Shichman, 1983). As Bakan (1966) noted, individual differences in personality style and motivational disposition can be understood in part according to which of these two tendencies an individual gives priority (Maddi, 1980).

Based on these formulations of personality development, Blatt and his colleagues (Blatt, 1974, 1990, 1995; Blatt & Blass, 1990; Blatt & Shichman, 1983) proposed two broad, multidimensional personality styles : (a) an anaclitic or relational personality style in which the individual is primarily concerned about interpersonal relations and affectionate ties; is particularly vulnerable to feelings of abandonment, rejection, and loss; and uses primarily avoidant defenses (e.g., denial and repression) to cope with conflicts and difficulties; and (b) an introjective or self-definitional personality style in which the individual is primarily concerned about autonomy, power, self-control, self-worth, and identity; is particularly vulnerable to feelings of loss of control and of autonomy and to feelings of failure; and uses primarily counteractive defenses (e.g., reaction formation, intellectualization, and overcompensation) to cope with conflicts and difficulties.

Individuals with a relational as opposed to a self-definitional personality style not only are vulnerable to different types of stressors to which they respond with different types of coping strategies, but they also structure their environments in different ways. They select different environments in which to participate, they evoke different types of responses from others, and they interpret and transform their environments in unique ways (Buss, 1987). Individuals who are oriented toward relatedness are generally more figurative in their thinking and focus primarily on affects and visual images. Their thinking is usually characterized more by simultaneous rather than by sequential processing; it is much more intuitive and determined by feelings, affects, and personal reactions than by facts, figures, and other details. The emphasis is on reconciliation, synthesis, and integration of elements into a cohesive unity rather than on a critical analysis of separate elements and details (Szumotalska, 1992). In terms of cognitive style, these individuals tend to be repressors and levelers (Gardner, Holzman, Klein, Lipton, & Spence, 1959; Gardner, Jackson, & Messick, 1960), and their predominant tendency is to seek fusion, harmony, integration, and synthesis. They are primarily field dependent and are very aware of and influenced by environmental factors (Witkin, 1965). Their chief goal is to seek harmony, peace, and satisfaction in interpersonal relationships (Luthar & Blatt, 1995). Their principal instinctual mode is more libidinal than aggressive, and they value affectionate feelings and the establishment of close, intimate relationships (Blatt, Quinlan, Chevron, McDonald, & Zuroff, 1982; Blatt & Zuroff, 1992).

In individuals focused mainly on self-definition, thinking is much more literal, sequential, linguistic, and critical. They attend to issues of action, overt behavior, manifest form, logic, consistency, and causality rather than feelings and relationships. Emphasis is on analysis rather than synthesis, on the critical dissection of details and part properties rather than on achieving an integration and synthesis (Szumotalska, 1992). These individuals tend to be sensitizers or sharpeners and to be field independent (Witkin, 1965; Witkin, Dyk, Faterson, Goodenough, & Karp, 1962). Their experiences and judgment are determined primarily by internal appraisal rather than by environmental events. Their chief goals are self-assertion, control, autonomy, power, and prestige rather than relatedness. Their primary instinctual mode involves assertion and aggression in the service of differentiation and self-definition rather than affection and intimacy (Blatt & Blass, 1990, 1992; Blatt, Cornell, & Eshkol, 1993; Blatt & Shichman, 1983; Blatt & Zuroff, 1992).

Different types of psychological defenses or coping styles are also integral to these two basic personality types. Defenses can be discussed as specific mechanisms (e.g., denial, repression, isolation, intellectualization, reaction formation, and overcompensation), or individual defenses can be considered as specific examples of a more generic classification of avoidant versus counteractive defenses (Blatt & Shichman, 1983) or repression versus sensitization (Byrne, Barry, &

Nelson, 1963). Both avoidant and counteractive defenses attempt to keep aspects of painful and conflict-laden issues out of awareness, but in very different ways. Denial and repression are avoidant defenses; they seek to avoid recognizing and acknowledging the existence of conflict. In contrast, counteractive defenses (e.g., projection, intellectualization, reaction formation, and overcompensation) do not avoid conflicts; rather, they transform them into alternative, more acceptable form. Reaction formation or overcompensation are examples of counteractive defenses in which an impulse, often an aggressive one, is transformed into its opposite, thereby achieving partial expression or discharge of the underlying wish or impulse (Blatt & Shichman, 1983). Research by Byrne and his colleagues (e.g., Byrne et al., 1963) on repression and sensitization is an approximation of the distinction between avoidant and counteractive defenses.

The cognitive–affective processes inherent in the psychological defenses used to deal with psychological conflict are often the very same cognitive–affective styles that individuals use in general adaptation. People rely on the same basic cognitive–affective processes to cope with important situations, whether they are relatively neutral and impersonal or difficult, conflict-laden, personal situations. These two broad generic types of defense processes, avoidant and counteractive defenses, express particular modes of thinking, feeling, and behaving, and each is an integral part of an individual's personality or character style (Shapiro, 1965). Avoidant defenses, such as denial and repression, are typical of the character style that emphasizes interpersonal relatedness, whereas counteractive defenses, such as intellectualization, reaction formation, and overcompensation, are typical of the character style that emphasizes self-definition and identity.

The research of Byrne et al. (1963) on repression–sensitization offers support for the distinction between these two types of defenses and their relationship to two primary personality configurations. Repressors tend to be more concerned with interpersonal relations and tend to maintain a more positive and optimistic outlook about themselves and others. They tend to have a more global cognitive approach (Hamilton, 1983) and avoid contradiction and controversy. They have difficulty expressing anger and personal conflicts. Although they try to avoid conflict and interpersonal difficulties, they have more conflictual relationships (Graziano, Brothen, & Berscheid, 1980) and are less aware of feelings about themselves and others that might disrupt their relationships. They avoid conflictual themes and report few negative childhood experiences (Davis & Schwartz, 1987), but their speech has a greater frequency of disruptions than does speech of other groups. Although they report little awareness of contradiction and conflict (Beutler, Johnson, Morris, & Neville, 1977; Byrne et al., 1963; Rofe & Lewin, 1979; Tempone & Lamb, 1967), they are physiologically responsive to emotionally stressful situations (Epstein & Fenz, 1967; White & Wilkins, 1973). Thus, repressors have a marked discordance between their subjective experiences and their physiological responses. Although repressors report low levels of anxiety (Slough, Kleinknecht, & Thorndike, 1984; Sullivan & Roberts, 1969), they have high levels of physiological arousal (Weinberger, Schwartz, & Davidson 1979). Sensitizers, in contrast, are preoccupied with issues of self-worth, self-control, and identity, and are overly critical of themselves and others. They have more negative views of themselves and are more aware of contradiction and conflict. They are ruminative, autonomous, independent, less influenced by the judgment of others (Zanna & Aziza, 1976), introspective, and self-critical.

Spiegel and Spiegel (1978) presented a distinction similar to the anaclitic and introjective personality styles (Blatt & Shichman, 1983) in their discussion—deriving in part from Friedrich Nietzsche—of Dionysian and Apollonian personality styles. They describe Dionysians as sensitive to interpersonal issues, more distractable, intuitive, passive and dependent, emotional, naive and trusting, and focused more on feelings than on ideas. They are open to and easily influenced by new ideas and others, place greater value on tactile and kinesthetic experiences, and are more action oriented. They tend to suspend critical judgment, live primarily in the present rather than in the past and the future, and value interpersonal affiliation and relationships.

Apollonians, in contrast, are described as very cognitive, organized, and critical; they value control and reason over emotions. They are very steady, responsible and reliable, unemotional, highly organized individuals who use critical reason to plan for the future. Apollonians value their own ideas, use them as a primary reference point, and seek to have others accept and confirm their ideas. They dominate interpersonal relationships, seeking to be in control, and are often very critical about the ideas of others. They are very cautious and methodical, comparing and contrasting alternatives and evaluating ideas and situations piece by piece before they arrive at a final decision and take action. They often pride themselves on being extremely responsible and are hesitant about making commitments; once they make them, they feel obligated by them. They are highly reliable and steadfast, often able to stick by a decision, and relatively uninfluenced by others. They seek to make sure that things are carried out correctly, and they plan logically and systematically. Spiegel and Spiegel (1978) succinctly summarized the differences between these two personality or character styles by noting that Dionysians are oriented to and influenced by the heart, whereas Apollonians are organized and influenced by the head.

A similar, but more limited, distinction was made by Jung (1923) about extroverted and introverted personality styles. Extroverts seek contact with others and derive gratification and meaning from relationships, whereas introverts give priority to their own thoughts and experiences and maintain a clear sense of self-definition, identity, and uniqueness. Jung (1923), like Spiegel and Spiegel (1978), Blatt (1974), and Blatt and Shichman (1983), viewed these character types as independent of, but related to, concepts of psychopathology (e.g., hysteric and obsessive; Shapiro, 1965). Eysenck (1960a) extended the Jungian topology to discuss neuroticism in terms of both the hysteric and the obsessive. Research with the Myers-Briggs Type Indicator (e.g., McCaully, 1981; Myers, 1962) and Eysenck Neuroticism Scale (Eysenck, 1960b) provides empirical support for the importance of this differentiation of two basic character types and their relationships to neurotic psychopathology.

Relatedness and Self-Definition in Psychopathology

The modes of relatedness and self-definition (communion and autonomy, or anaclitic and introjective) evolve in normal development in an integrated form so that the individual develops both an active commitment to interpersonal relatedness and a viable sense of self. Biological predispositions and disruptive environmental events, however, can disturb this integrated developmental process in complex ways and lead to exaggerated emphasis on one mode at the expense of the other. As discussed above, mild deviations result in unique character styles that are within the normal range. More extensive deviations, that is, markedly exaggerated emphasis on one developmental line at the expense of the other, however, occur in psychopathology as a response to severe developmental disruptions. Thus, the differentiation of anaclitic and introjective personality configurations provides a basis for defining different types of psychopathology and for considering the relationships among them (Blatt & Shichman, 1983).

On occasion, severe and repeated untoward events disrupt the complex, normal, dialectic developmental process. Some individuals— depending on biological predispositions, cultural factors, gender, basic capacities and vulnerabilities, and cultural and family patterns— attempt to compensate for these serious developmental disruptions by exaggerating one developmental line, fixating either on relatedness or on the sense of self. The normal dialectic developmental process is disrupted somewhere in the life cycle, and, if no subsequent ameliorating circumstances and experiences occur, these patterns are continually repeated and become consolidated as distorted modes of adaptation. The earlier in the developmental process these disruptions occur and the more extreme the distortions, the more severe the psychopathology.

As a consequence of major disruption of the normal, dialectic developmental processes of relatedness and self-definition, some individuals, most often women, become excessively preoccupied with relatedness at the expense of development of the sense of self. If this developmental disruption occurs early in the life cycle, it can lead to the development of an infantile character, manifested as excessive concern for need gratification, such as constantly wanting to be held, cared for, fed, and attended to. If this disruption of the dialectic developmental process occurs somewhat later in the life cycle, a more organized kind of hysterical disorder can develop in which the person is concerned not only with being held, cared for, and loved, but also with being able to express as well as receive love. Some patients more often function at the infantile level, using denial as their primary defense; their concerns are primarily dyadic in structure, and they strive to be accepted and cared for, like the young child with his or her mother. Other patients are at the developmentally higher hysterical level, using repression as their primary avoidant defense; their primary concerns involve triadic configurations and oedipal themes—striving for the attention and love of one parent in competition with the other. At both the infantile level and the developmentally more advanced hysterical level, the issues relate primarily to libidinal attachment—concerns about being loved, intimate, and close. Infantile and hysteric disorders can occur in relatively pure form, but they are not isolated disorders or diseases. Rather, they represent relative end points on a continuum of anaclitic psychopathology (Blatt, 1991, 1995; Blatt & Shichman, 1983).

Some individuals, more often men, deal with severe disruption of the normal, dialectic developmental process by exaggerated attempts to consolidate a sense of self. In the extreme, this is expressed in disorders of paranoia, obsession–compulsion, guilt-ridden (introjective) depression, and phallic narcissism. These disorders all express preoccupations with the self ranging from primitive concerns in paranoia to more integrated concerns about the self in introjective depression and phallic narcissism. The paranoid patient is preoccupied with maintaining a rigid definition of self as distinct and separate from others. Paranoid patients struggle to prove that they exist as a separate entity and that they are not merged and fused in a symbiotic relationship with another (Blatt & Wild, 1976; Blatt, Wild, & Ritzler, 1975). They struggle to maintain a sense of self in a primitive form. All bad is placed onto the other, all good is attributed to the self, and an isolated and embattled distance is maintained from others. Obsessive–compulsive disorders express somewhat higher concerns about the self: concerns about mastery, autonomy, control, prerogatives, and possessions. At a still higher developmental level, individuals are more concerned about self-worth than about mastery. In introjective depression, the predominant concerns are about one's intent and one's value in comparison to an idealized value system, with the belief and feeling that one is a failure or that one has transgressed. Phallic narcissism is the reversal of introjective depression in which, through counteraction and overcompensation, the individual seeks to exhibit himself or herself and win endless accolades and approval to defend against intense feelings of guilt and shame, worthlessness, and humiliation.

The dynamics, conflicts, defenses, and cognitive–affective and interpersonal style of the various forms of psychopathology of the introjective configuration share a fundamental similarity. Paranoia, obsession–compulsion, introjective depression, and phallic narcissism all involve issues of self-reproach; guilt; and preoccupations with self-definition, self-control, and self-worth. Interest is directed primarily to things rather than to people, and there is a heightened emphasis on thoughts and accomplishments (deeds) rather than on feelings and interpersonal relations. In all the forms of psychopathology of the introjective configuration, defenses are essentially counteractive rather than avoidant. Projection, reversal, intellectualization, doing and undoing, reaction formation, introjection (or identification with the aggressor), and overcompensation all attempt, with varying degrees of effectiveness, to alter or transform impulses and conflicts rather than to avoid (deny or repress) them. Although each of the disorders in the introjective configuration can be viewed as independent and separate, they are interrelated disorders, and, most often, individual patients present a complex admixture of these various disorders (Blatt & Shichman, 1983).

Thus, two primary configurations of psychopathology are each defined primarily by exaggerations of the tasks of each of the two fundamental developmental lines. Exaggerated and distorted preoccupation about satisfying interpersonal relations, to the neglect of the development of concepts of self, defines the psychopathologies of the anaclitic configuration—the infantile and hysterical syndromes. Exaggerated and distorted concerns about the definition of the self, at the expense of establishing meaningful interpersonal relations, defines the psychopathologies of the introjective configuration—paranoid, obsessive–compulsive, introjective depressive, and phallic narcissistic disorders.

Each of these two configurations of psychopathology has several evolving levels of organization ranging from more primitive to more integrated attempts to establish meaningful interpersonal relations and a consolidated self-concept. The various levels of psychopathology within the anaclitic and the introjective configurations also define lines along which patients progress or regress. Thus, an individual's difficulties can be specified as being predominantly in one or the other personality configuration, at a particular developmental level, and with a differential potential to regress or progress to other developmental levels within the configuration. In this conceptualization, the various forms of psychopathology are no longer considered as isolated, independent disease entities but rather as interrelated modes of adaptation, organized at different developmental levels within two basic configurations.

Psychopathologies within the anaclitic configuration share a basic preoccupation with libidinal issues such as closeness and intimacy. There is a greater capacity for affective bonding and a greater potential for the development of meaningful interpersonal relations. Psychopathologies within the anaclitic configuration also have a similar defensive style with a predominant use of avoidant defenses such as denial, repression, and displacement. Psychopathologies in the introjective configuration share a basic focus on anger; aggression; and themes of self-definition, self-control, and self-worth. They also share a similarity in defensive style with the use of counteractive defenses such as isolation, doing and undoing, intellectualization, reaction formation, introjection, identification with the aggressor, and overcompensation. Cognitive processes are more fully developed, and there is greater potential for the development of logical, abstract thought. Although most forms of psychopathology are organized primarily around one configuration or the other, some patients may also have features from both the anaclitic and introjective dimensions, and their psychopathology derives from both configurations (Blatt & Shichman, 1983).

The Precursors of Relatedness and Self-Definition

The theoretical formulations about personality development and psychopathology presented above alerted us to the possibility that further analyses of data gathered in a detailed longitudinal study of mother–infant play should enable us to explore systematically some of the early developmental precursors or antecedents of relatedness and self-definition in the early mother–infant, face-to-face play patterns.[1] Our analyses of these data are based on several assumptions: (a) The precursors of relatedness and self-definition would each be uniquely associated with a distinct set of behavior in early mother–infant play; (b) a longitudinal sequential relationship would exist between relatedness and self-definition as a consequence of their dialectical development; and (c) specific expressions of relatedness and individuation in the early months of mother–infant play, at 3 and 9 months, would be differentially related to socioemotional adjustment and cognitive functioning at 2 years of age.

[1]Portions of these data were gathered by Ruth Feldman as part of her doctoral dissertation at the Hebrew University of Jerusalem. This research was supported in part by fellowships from the Smolin Foundation through the Sigmund Freud Center and from the Levin and Rothschild Foundations at the Hebrew University of Jerusalem. We wish to acknowledge the contributions of Professor Charles W. Greenbaum to the design and implementation of this study and of Dr. Nurit Yirmiya for her participation.

Before presenting the details of the research procedures and the results, we shall review briefly some of the literature on infant development that provided the basis for these assumptions and our further analyses of these data.

Indications of Relatedness and Self-Definition in Mother–Infant Interaction

Theory and developmental research suggest that relatedness and self-definition can be identified as two distinct developmental dimensions in infancy. Emde (1984, 1988) discussed two basic developmental tendencies in the emergence of the prerepresentational self: self-regulation and social fittedness. Self-regulation marks the first expression of the infant's autonomous self (Connell, 1990), whereas social fittedness develops in the security of the mother–infant dyad, which is later extended to include peers, intimate relationships, colleagues, and general social adaptability (Blatt & Blass, 1992, 1996). Stern (1985) proposed that early experiences of "self with other" (interpersonal feelings of intersubjectivity, mutuality, and harmony) and experiences of "self versus other" (experiences of self as a differentiated entity vis-à-vis the other) are two fundamental configurations that contribute to the establishment of the sense of self. These mechanisms of connectedness and separateness interact to form internal models of self and other and of their relationship (Behrends & Blatt, 1985; Pipp, 1990).

Development is a process of continuous transactions between the individual and his or her ever-changing environment. The individual and the environment constitute a unitary system whose inner structure is hierarchically organized. The complexity of this organization expresses the nature of the relationship between the individual and the surround and serves as an index of the system's maturity and competence. Thus, a dialectical relationship exists between self-defining and interactive interpersonal aspects of development: The self develops within, as well as is constrained by, interpersonal relationships (Emde, 1994; Fogel, 1993; Fogel & Thelen, 1987; Thelen & Smith, 1994).

Sander (1975, 1984, 1987), based on extensive home observations of early parent–child interactions, proposed that the adaptive integration of polarities accounts for developmental change. Autonomy and connectedness defines a central polarity that infants must integrate during the first 2 years of life. Sander delineated several phases in this integration during the early development, alternating between stages of self-definition and of relatedness: (a) the stage of "basic regulation" at 3 months, (b) "coordinated interaction" at 3 to 6 months, (c) "initiatory infant" activity at 6 to 9 months, and (d) "dyadic emotional regulation" from 9 months to 1 year, which leads to "autonomous action" at 1 year and self-constancy at 18 months.

Investigations of early mother–infant face-to-face interaction often view the mother–infant face-to-face exchange as a unitary social system. The intersystemic transactions between caregiver and infant during this intense social process become the primary focus of investigation. Thus, systemic concepts such as mutuality (Symons & Moran, 1987), reciprocity (Belsky, Rovine, & Taylor, 1984), bidirectional influence (Cohn & Tronick, 1988), interpersonal timing (Feldstein et al., 1994), or synchrony (Isabella & Belsky, 1991) become central constructs in the study of face-to-face interactions. The associations between levels of dyadic synchrony or maternal responsiveness in infancy and the child's later attachment security (Isabella, 1993; Smith & Pederson, 1988) and the relations between attachment security and social adaptability during the toddler's years (Sroufe, 1983) suggest that these systemic constructs assess a relatedness dimension in infancy and early childhood (Ainsworth, Blehar, Waters, & Wall, 1978).

Sensitive caregiving relationships also provide the basis for the emergence of self and affect regulation, antecedents of self-definition (Bretherton, 1987; Cassidy, 1994; Pipp & Harmon, 1987). Research on the infant's growing capacities as a separate entity emphasizes that cognitive development begins with the early ability to attend and perceive various properties of the environment. These abilities provide the basis for the development of higher cognitive functions such as symbolic thought, comprehension, and memory (e.g., Meltzoff, 1985, 1990). Infants' attention in early infancy has been shown to be a relatively stable quality (Rutter & Durkin, 1987) that predicts later cognition (Bornstein & Sigman, 1986; McCall & Carriger, 1993). Interactive patterns, including maternal regulation of stimulus intake (Gable & Isabella, 1992), maternal scaffolding (Findji, 1993), and verbal stimulation (Belsky, Goode, & Most, 1980) promote infant attention, encourage exploratory behavior, and facilitate cognitive development.

Mother–infant face-to-face interaction, emerging around the 3rd month of life, signifies the infant's first participation in a purely social interchange (Stern, 1974). Specific maternal and infant play patterns as well as the overall guiding principles of face-to-face interaction provide the foundation for the development of both self-definition and secure relatedness. Research has linked the typical face-to-face play patterns, such as mutual synchrony of gaze (Kaye & Fogel, 1980), simultaneous vocalizations (Feldstein et al., 1994), maternal acknowledgment of the infant's social communication (Mayes & Carter, 1990), and imitation and variations of the infant's movement and vocalization (Field, Goldstein, Vega-Lahr, & Porter, 1986) with affective (Malatesta, 1988; Stern, 1985) as well as with cognitive and linguistic development (Jasnow & Feldstein, 1986; Stern & Gibbon, 1978). The second-by-second match between mother's and infant's attentive–affective states during face-to-face interaction promotes the development of synchrony and intersubjectivity on the one hand and structures the interaction to facilitate the emergence of self-regulation and state control on the other (Cohn & Tronick, 1987, 1988; Lester, Hoffman, & Brazelton, 1985).

The early face-to-face play patterns advance the development of dyadic reciprocity and socioemotional adjustment but also contribute to the development of self-definition and cognitive growth. Predictable rhythmic oscillation between states of attention and nonattention enables mothers to adapt the level of stimulus input to infants' information-processing capacities (Lester et al., 1985). Repetition allows infants to develop expectations—the first expression of analytic and analogic thinking (Stern & Gibbon, 1978). Moreover, repetition, regulation, and rhythmicity, the guiding principles of the face-to-face interaction, facilitate the formation of rudimentary cognitive–affective structures, variously discussed as sensorimotor schemas (Piaget, 1954/1970), internal working models (Bowlby, 1969), or repeated interactions that have been generalized (Stern, 1985). These schemas not only promote information-processing subfunctions (e.g., attention, encoding, and retrieval) but also the sense of security and predictability in relationships, thus emphasizing the close tie between cognitive and affiliative systems in early infancy.

During the second half of the first year, both the relatedness and self-definitional dimensions of mother–infant face-to-face play undergo major transformations (Lamb, Morrison, & Malkin, 1987). The maternal eliciting style, which provides the foundation for secure relatedness through gaze synchrony, imitation, and elaboration of the infant's expressions, gives way to reciprocal affective sharing (e.g., intersubjectivity [Stern, 1985] or dyadic emotion regulation [Sander, 1975]). This development of dyadic reciprocity follows a major leap in affective development that occurs between 6 and 8 months of age, after which infants become capable of transmitting and sharing intentions and affects (Emde, 1984). At the same time, the self-definitional aspects—infant alertness, organized emotional expression, and focused attention—become organized around the infant's emerging capacity for initiation (Hoffmann, 1994). Both dyadic reciprocity and infant initiation develop within the context of a sensitive and responsive maternal style that facilitates curiosity and exploration and promotes affective sharing and the ability to engage in intimate relatedness. A lack of consistent maternal emotional availability may lead to a reduction in both interpersonal relatedness and exploratory behavior. Intrusive or unavailable maternal style, particularly at around 9 months of age, when initiation and reciprocity emerge, has been associated with later insecure attachment (Isabella & Belsky, 1991), increased dyadic asynchrony (Field, 1994), and diminished exploratory behavior (Belsky et al., 1980).

Research evidence suggests that distinct sets of face-to-face patterns are differentially related to interpersonal or exploratory modes of interaction. Bornstein and Tamis-LeMonda (1990) distinguished two prototypes of early interactive styles—"social," in which mother and infant are directed toward each other, and "didactic," in which mothers direct infant attention to the environment. These maternal interactive styles were found to be stable at 2 to 5 months. And the dyadic exploratory, directing maternal style at 5 months predicted the complexity of the child's symbolic play at 13 months (Tamis-LeMonda & Bornstein, 1989). Infants' social attention and object attention have been associated with distinct sets of facial, visual, vocal, and gestural configurations. These two configurations are associated with different emotional expression, that is, with joy and interest, respectively (Weinberg & Tronick, 1994). Thus, specific aspects of early mother and infant play behavior appears to be uniquely related to the development of mutuality and exploration, of relatedness and self-definition. Infant attention and exploratory orientation are linked to the development of cognitive capacities, whereas maternal responsiveness and dyadic reciprocity are related to attachment security and socioemotional adaptation.

On the basis of these theoretical formulations and research findings, we reexamined the data of the mother–infant interaction study to assess the relationships among maternal, infant, and dyadic interactive patterns at 3 and 9 months and their relationship to cognitive and socioemotional functioning at 2 years. Assessment at both 3 and 9 months had included evaluation of aspects of relatedness (the degree of maternal responsivity, acknowledgment, imitation and elaboration, constant gaze, and positive affect) and aspects of infant attentiveness to the environment (e.g., alertness and initiative) that are viewed as precursors to cognitive development and self-definition. We expected that at both 3 and 9 months, patterns of relatedness and self-definition would emerge as distinct and independent factors in mother–infant play and there would also be sequential relationships between dimensions of relatedness and self-definition. We expected a lagged correlation both between early expressions of relatedness and later infant attention and involvement and vice versa, because infant temperamental tendencies shape the nature of the maternal interactive style (van den Boom & Hoeksma, 1994). Finally, we expected that measures of infant alertness, attention, and initiative would be associated primarily with cognitive development, whereas maternal responsivity— in particular, the dimension of dyadic reciprocity at 9 months—would be associated with reduced socioemotional externalizing and internalizing symptomatology at 2 years.

Research Design

Mother–infant dyads, selected at random through well-baby clinics in Jerusalem, were screened for pre- and postnatal health complications, premature birth, or underweight (under 2,700 g). Mothers of infants without birth complications were recruited by phone to participate in a study of mother–infant play. Of 55 mothers approached, 41 agreed to participate, and 5 of these composed a pilot sample. The families who participated and those who declined did not differ significantly in paternal and maternal education, age, and income, or on child's birth order, birth weight, or Apgar score.

The infants were healthy, full-term gestation, first- and second-born boys and girls (the sample was equally divided for gender and birth order). They were between 12 and 14 weeks old ($M = 90$ days) at the first session, between 36 and 39 weeks old ($M = 264$ days) at the second session, and between 24 and 25 months ($M = 24.3$ months) at the third session.

Mothers were between 26 and 36 years of age ($M = 28.7$ years, $SD = 2.5$ years), had completed on average 14.2 years of education ($SD = 1.1$), and were currently married to the child's father, all of whom were employed in skilled or semiskilled positions. All families were considered middle class by Israeli standards (Harlap, Davis, Grower,

& Prywes, 1977). According to the records of the well-baby clinic, none of the mothers had suffered serious illness, psychopathology, or serious pregnancy complications.

Thirty-two infants were observed at 24 months. Two families had moved abroad, one could not be located, and one cited returning to work as the reason for not participating. No significant differences in demographic variables were found between those who returned for the 2-year assessment and those who did not. The final sample included 15 girls and 17 boys, 16 firstborn and 16 second-born children.

Participants were tested in a laboratory with two adjoining rooms. The studio was equipped with an infant seat mounted on a table, an adjustable stool for the mother, two video cameras, and a microphone. One camera was focused on the infant's face and another on the mother's. Both pictures were transmitted through a split-screen generator into a video recorder placed in the adjoining room that showed the infant's face on the left side of each frame and the mother's on the right.

On the first and second visits, mothers were greeted by an experimenter and interviewed regarding their personal adjustment, social support systems, and their child's early development, and they completed a variety of self-report measures. Thereafter, mother and infant entered the studio, and the baby was situated in the infant chair. The mother sat next to the infant on the stool and was instructed to play freely with her child for 10 min. At 9 months of age, an additional 10-min play episode was videotaped when mother and infant were playing on a carpeted floor with age-appropriate toys. At 24 months, mother and infant were filmed in a variety of play contexts. Verbal and visual IQ were assessed by the Stanford-Binet Intelligence Scale–Fourth Edition (Thorndike, Hagen, & Sattler, 1986) administered by psychology graduate students. Externalizing and internalizing disruptive behavior were assessed with the Child Behavior Checklist completed by the mother (Achenbach, 1992; Achenbach & Edelbrook, 1984).

Videotapes of the 3- and 9-month play sessions were rated for 12 global measures of maternal, infant, and dyadic play behaviors. Seven of these measures were adapted from the Rating Scale of Interactional Style (Clark & Seifer, 1983), a scoring system for dyadic interactions rated on a 5-step Likert scale. These were the maternal measures of Acknowledging, Imitating, Elaborating, Affect, Gaze, the infant measure of Gaze Aversion, and the dyadic measure of Reciprocity. Five measures were added to the present study and were scored in a similar way. These included the maternal measures of Adaptation and the infant measures of Alertness, Fatigue, Initiation, and Fussiness. The measures are described in the Appendix to this chapter.

Two coders scored each variable after viewing the entire interaction. At 9 months of age, separate coding was performed for the face-to-face and the toy interaction, and the two scores for each measure were averaged into a single score (Cronbach's $\alpha > .50$). Coders were trained for reliability on the pilot sample until 80% agreement was reached and disagreement did not exceed one scale point. Interrater reliability was estimated periodically on a random sample of 12 dyads at each age and play context. Mean reliability percentages were 94% for play ratings at 3 months and 91% for play ratings at 9 months.

Results

The first step in the data analysis was to examine mean-level changes between 3 and 9 months in maternal and infant play patterns. As suggested by Block (1971), the central tendency in the group provides the basis for understanding individual stability and change as it points to the direction of the developmental process during the period of observation. Table 1 presents the means, standard deviations, and F values of the repeated measure multivariate analysis of variance ($dfs = 1, 34$) with infant sex and birth order as the between-subjects variables.

The data reported in Table 1 indicate that the maternal play patterns of Imitating and Elaborating were significantly reduced between 3 and 9 months. Maternal Affect, Gaze, Adaptation, and Acknowledging of the infant communication remained unchanged. At the same time, infants' Alertness and Initiation increased, whereas their Fussiness, Gaze Aversion, and Fatigue decreased. Thus, infants' involvement and active participation in the interaction increased in concordance with the mothers' reduction of her eliciting play behavior. The level of Dyadic Reciprocity similarly increased between 3 and 9 months. Mothers seemed to reduce their active involvement to allow the child to take a more active role in the interaction, thereby facilitating a more balanced and reciprocal interaction between the participants. On the other hand, the maternal behaviors that provided the framework for the interaction—Positive Affect, constant Visual Attention, and Acknowl-

Table 1

Means and Standard Deviations of Maternal, Infant, and Dyadic Play Behaviors at 3 and 9 Months

	3 Months		9 Months		
Variable	M	SD	M	SD	F
Maternal play behaviors					
Acknowledging	2.75	1.25	3.06	1.19	ns
Imitating	2.81	1.23	1.51	0.78	36.08***
Elaboration	2.73	1.28	1.81	0.77	29.28***
Gaze	4.64	0.59	4.57	0.88	ns
Adaptation	3.14	1.36	3.40	1.39	ns
Affect	4.08	1.01	4.62	0.80	ns
Infant play behaviors					
Gaze Aversion	2.92	1.05	1.77	0.73	23.64***
Alert	2.56	1.46	3.87	0.92	24.74***
Fussy	2.31	1.35	1.11	0.52	38.14***
Initiation	1.72	1.72	2.72	1.04	26.85***
Fatigue	2.54	1.52	1.13	0.49	45.19***
Dyadic play behaviors					
Reciprocity	2.14	1.25	2.76	1.39	10.88**

**p < .01. ***p < .001.

edgment of the infant's social communication—remained equally high at 3 and 9 months.

Next we examined the factor structure of the 12 global measures of mother–infant interaction. A principal-components factor analysis with varimax rotation was applied separately to the 12 play behavior scales at 3 and at 9 months, and four factors were identified at each age with eigenvalues greater than 1.00.

As indicated in Table 2, the four factors cumulatively accounted for most of the variance at 3 and at 9 months (73.2% and 73.7%, respectively). The results confirm the initial hypothesis: At both 3 and 9 months, maternal and infant behavior each formed distinct factors. The first two factors at 3 months reflected maternal behavior and were termed (a) *Maternal Responsiveness*, with high loadings on Acknowledging, Imitating, Elaborating, and Dyadic Reciprocity; and (b) *Maternal Attentiveness*, with loadings on Maternal Adaptation, Maternal Gaze, and Maternal Affect. Two factors also emerged that

Table 2

Factor Loadings for Play Behaviors at 3 and 9 Months

Factor	3 Months				9 Months			
	1	2	3	4	1	2	3	4
Maternal Responsiveness								
Acknowledging	.90	−.08	.02	.06	.90	−.05	.05	−.03
Imitating	.87	.17	−.09	.02	.75	.23	.04	.22
Elaborating	.85	.15	−.11	.17	.92	−.07	−.07	.02
Dyadic Reciprocity	.80	.39	.05	.10	.78	.05	.19	−.26
Maternal Attentiveness								
Maternal Adaptation	.47	.58	.41	−.08	.53	−.16	.54	.41
Maternal Affect	.26	.67	.30	−.26	.54	−.15	.52	−.30
Maternal Gaze	.14	.82	−.13	−.04	−.06	.07	.91	.12
Infant Involvement								
Infant Alertness	.06	−.07	.93	−.02	.00	.84	.06	.10
Infant Fatigue	.27	.10	−.87	.01	.02	−.78	.08	.15
Infant Initiation								
Infant Initiation	.03	−.05	−.08	.92	.05	.77	.02	−.32
Infant Fussiness	−.44	.04	.18	.34	−.34	.02	−.03	.36
Gaze Aversion	.03	−.62	.19	.38	−.06	.00	.01	.87
Eigenvalue	3.27	1.66	1.29	1.09	4.33	2.05	1.32	1.12
% variance	32.80	16.70	12.70	11.00	36.10	17.20	11.00	9.40

pertained to the behavior of the infant and were labeled *Infant Involvement* and *Infant Initiation*. At 3 months, Infant Gaze Aversion had a moderate loading (−.62) on the second maternal factor (Maternal Attentiveness), which included Maternal Gaze and Affect. Infant gaze aversion in a social context at 3 months may be influenced more by the maternal interactive style (e.g., engaged or disengaged) than by the infant's own attentive capacities. For this reason, Infant Gaze Aversion may not have been associated with the two infant factors (Factors 3 and 4).

At 9 months, the first factor, Maternal Responsiveness, still had substantial loadings on Acknowledging, Imitating, Elaborating, and Dyadic Reciprocity but also medium loadings on Maternal Adaptation and Maternal Affect. The second factor concerns the infant's behavior, with high loadings on Alertness and Fatigue, but, unlike the factor at 3-months, Infant Involvement at 9 months also included Infant Initiation. The third factor, Maternal Attentiveness, contained loadings on

Table 3

Cross-Age Correlations Between Play Factors at 3 and 9 Months

	Factor at 3 months			
Factor at 9 months	Maternal Responsiveness	Maternal Attentiveness	Infant Involvement	Infant Initiation
Maternal Responsiveness	.47**	.17	.15	−.12
Maternal Attentiveness	.32*	.11	.36*	.33*
Infant Involvement	.33*	.13	.15	.07
Infant Gaze Aversion	−.13	−.12	.05	.00

*p < .05. **p < .01.

Maternal Gaze, Affect, and Adaptation, similar to the loadings at 3 months. The fourth factor loaded highly only on Infant Gaze Aversion. Weighted factor scores for each participant at 3 and 9 months were computed by summing the play measures with a loading of .50 or above on each factor according to their relative weight.

Table 3 presents cross-age correlations among the four factors at 3 and at 9 months. As expected, Maternal Responsiveness and Infant Involvement were independent dimensions at both 3 and 9 months and were relatively stable at these two ages. Significant cross-age correlations were found between the maternal and infant measures. Maternal Responsiveness at 3 months correlated with Infant Involvement at 9 months, and Infant Initiation and Infant Involvement at 3 months each correlated with Maternal Attentiveness at 9 months. These findings suggest a possible dialectic sequential relationship between the development of relatedness and self-definition.

Finally, we examined the contribution of measures of relatedness and self-definition at 3 and 9 months to the prediction of cognitive and socioemotional development at 2 years. The four factors at 3 and 9 months were entered into hierarchical multiple regressions as predictors of intelligence (Verbal and Visual IQ on the Stanford-Binet) and socioemotional adaptation (Externalizing and Internalizing symptoms on the Achenbach). Because of the assumed importance of Dyadic Reciprocity at 9 months in the emergence of intersubjectivity and affective sharing, this measure was entered as a predictor of the relat-

Table 4

Hierarchical Regression of Play Factors at 3 and 9 Months in Relation to Cognitive and Socioemotional Functioning at 2 Years

Predictor factor	Verbal IQ	Visual IQ	Externalizing symptoms	Internalizing symptoms
At 3 months				
Maternal Responsiveness	.01	.05	.13	.21
Maternal Attentiveness	.30	.28	.00	−.39*
Infant Involvement	.47*	.48*	−.20	.00
Infant Initiation	.24	.20	.32	.11
At 9 months				
Dyadic Reciprocity	.49*	.18	−.45*	−.47*
Infant Involvement	.09	.39*	.08	.09
Maternal Attentiveness	.40	.29	.10	−.30
Infant Gaze Aversion	.08	.07	−.14	−.21
Total R^2	.49*	.38+	.29	.48*

Note. The coefficients in the table are standardized betas (dfs = 8, 24).
+$p < .10$.   *$p < .05$.

edness dimension at 9 months instead of the global construct of Maternal Responsiveness.[2] Standardized beta coefficients of the 3- and 9-month predictors are presented in Table 4.

As indicated in Table 4, Verbal and Visual IQ were related to infant positive engagement in the interaction at 3 months. Visual IQ was also related to Infant Involvement at 9 months. In contrast, externalizing and internalizing symptoms, indices of socioemotional adaptation, were related to the degree of dyadic reciprocity at 9 months. Thus,

---

[2]At 9 months, the mother–infant exchange is characterized by the emergence of intersubjectivity, affect sharing, and the ability to engage in a truly reciprocal exchange. In contrast, play at 3 months is characterized by active maternal involvement, which diminishes at 9 months. We therefore examined two regression models, once using the entire composite of Maternal Responsiveness as the predictor and again with Dyadic Reciprocity as representative of the relatedness dimension at 9 months. Beta coefficients of the hierarchical regression equation predicting Externalizing and Internalizing symptoms from Maternal Responsiveness at 9 months were .33 and .35, respectively ($p < .10$).

measures of infant attention and initiation predicted cognitive development, whereas the level of dyadic reciprocity at 9 months predicted diminished externalizing and internalizing symptoms.

The salience of infant attention at 3 months and of dyadic reciprocity at 9 months in the prediction of developmental outcomes is consistent with theory and research on the early development of the self. During the first 6 months, the developmental tasks of self-regulation, attention organization, and state control are central to the early consolidation of the self (Cassidy, 1994; Sander, 1975; Sroufe, 1990). At 9 months, a major leap in affective development (Emde, 1984) introduces a stage of affective sharing (Stern, 1985) and infant-initiated activity (Hoffmann, 1994). When coordinated with maternal support, these emerging capacities serve as the foundation for the "self-in-relationship," the development of positive interpersonal relatedness and adaptive socioemotional adaptive capacity.

These findings suggest that infant initiative and alert social behavior and mother–child reciprocal exchange are independent developmental processes during infancy and are related to different types of developmental outcomes in toddlerhood. Factors of infant and mother play patterns were orthogonal at each age and were relatively stable between 3 and 9 months of age. Thus, it appears that mother and infant play patterns represent two distinct lines of infant development that evolve from the early matrix of mother–infant interaction. One developmental line defines the individual capacities of the infant as separate, autonomous, and alert and appears to lead to the development of mastery, verbal capacity, and cognitive skills. The other developmental line defining the quality of relatedness (e.g., maternal availability and reciprocity) contributes to socioemotional development.

The relationship between the two developmental lines of relatedness and self-definition may be interactive, at least in the early months of life. The quality of mother–infant relatedness at 3 months (Maternal Responsiveness) appears to lead to the emergence of self-definition as measured by the infant's alertness, focused interest, and initiatory play at 9 months. At the same time, early patterns of infant alert involvement were related to maternal attention, positive affect, and sensitive adaptation at 9 months (Maternal Attentiveness). These results are consistent with the transactional perspectives on development (e.g., Sameroff & Fiese, 1991), which suggest that mother and infant reciprocally shape each other's style over the course of early interactions. Not only does the level of maternal responsiveness affect the degree of infant's participation at play, but also a more active, socially involved infant is more adept at attracting and maintaining the mother's attention and joy in the shared activity.

The relationship found between infant alertness at 3 months and cognitive abilities at 2 years is consistent with reports of the relation between early infant attention in nonsocial settings and intelligence in toddlerhood and early childhood (Bornstein & Sigman, 1986; McCall & Carriger, 1993). Infant alertness within a social context possibly reflects both an inborn capacity for focused attention, which indexes the efficiency of the early information-processing system and later intelligence, and the maternal ability to direct infant curiosity and regulate the amplitude and pace of the infant's stimulus intake. At 9 months, early social alertness is integrated with initiation and is related to visual rather than verbal IQ. The child's involvement in interpersonal and toy-directed interactions at 9 months possibly assist the emergence of exploratory visual–tactile skills such as visual perception, cross-modal integration, and manipulative competence.

It is noteworthy that Maternal Adaptation, as indicated in Table 1, was the only play measure that had moderate loadings on three of the four factors identified at 3 months. This finding is consistent with previous emphasis on the centrality of the maternal regulatory function in early infancy (Sander, 1984, 1987). Adequate maternal regulation in the early months has been described as essential to the development of relatedness (Emde, 1988) and emotional regulation (Malatesta, 1988), as well as the development of verbal abilities (Akhtar, Dunham, & Dunham, 1991). Furthermore, the data suggest that Maternal Adaptation is an important dimension of social behavior across the first year and is not reduced between 3 and 9 months. Maternal regulation may be particularly important in the face-to-face exchange in order to maintain a balance among the biological, cognitive, affective, and interactional components in this intense social context. Additionally, consistent maternal regulation during play may be necessary to monitor the levels of arousal and excitement in this brief, highly stimulating interaction.

Maternal Responsiveness, particularly Dyadic Reciprocity at 9 months, expresses the development of a relatedness line. These patterns of interaction define a factor that accounts for the largest percentage of the variance at both 3 and 9 months. The components of that factor, however, have different developmental trajectories. Maternal imitation and elaboration decrease during the first year, whereas reciprocity increases. The give-and-take exchange (reciprocity) becomes a central dimension of social interaction at 9 months, consistent with theoretical formulations of Stern (1985) and Emde (1984). At both 3 and 9 months, Dyadic Reciprocity is part of the Maternal Responsiveness factor, findings that are consistent with previous research linking mother–child mutuality to maternal acknowledgment and positive responsivity. It appears that reciprocity is associated not with a maternal general attitude as expressed in her positive affect or continuous visual attention (Maternal Attentiveness), but is specifically related to the mother's active play patterns of acknowledgment, imitation, and elaboration. Infants identify and imitate mothers' play patterns and respond with the same imitating behavior that initiates a cycle of reciprocal interchange. As infants master the rules of emotional dialogue, play begins to revolve around two infant-originated measures: reciprocity and initiation. These two measures, possibly representing the two trends in personality development of relatedness and self-definition, are integrated into two separate factors at 9 months: Maternal Responsiveness and Infant Involvement, respectively.

The level of Dyadic Reciprocity, as well as the general factor of Maternal Responsiveness, at 9 months was significantly related to later socioemotional symptomatology. These findings are consistent with previous studies that demonstrate relations between attachment security and early mother–infant interaction, and between attachment security and socioemotional adaptation in early childhood (e.g., Sroufe, 1983). The successful mastery of give-and-take play between mother and infant was related to the lack of externalizing and internalizing symptoms at 2 years, and the degree of Maternal Attentiveness at 3 months was related to lower internalizing symptoms. As argued by Achenbach and Edelbrook (1984), the presence or absence of discrete age-related symptoms affords a useful path for studying the development of socioemotional disturbances. The relationship found between aspects of the early social system and the emergence of disruptive socioemotional symptoms underscores early reciprocity as a central predictor of adaptive social development. Generally, the results indicate the importance of differentiating between interactive patterns associated with relatedness and interactive patterns associated with the development of the infant's autonomous self. These two dimensions appear to have differential association with development in the toddler years and beyond.

Infant play activity in the first months of life appears to define the development of intelligence and self-assertion or self-definition. The mother's capacity to establish mutual reciprocity, in contrast, is central to the development of socioemotional adaptation. As discussed by Blatt and Blass (1990, 1996), these two dimensions of relatedness and self-definition enter into a dialectic process that can be described by an extension of Eric Erikson's (1950, 1982) developmental model. A relatedness developmental line that includes phases of trust, cooperation, and intimacy interacts with a self-definitional line that includes phases of autonomy, initiative, and identity. This dialectic interaction ultimately leads to the development of a "self-in-relation" (Miller, 1976, 1984; Surrey, 1991) or "ensembled individualism" (Sampson, 1988) in which themes of self and relatedness are coordinated and integrated in mature expressions of both intimacy and generativity.

In summary, mother and infant play patterns in the first year of life appear to define precursors of two fundamental developmental processes—relatedness and self-definition. These findings are consistent with theoretical formulations and empirical investigations indicating that these two fundamental dimensions evolve as a complex, dialectic, developmental process throughout the life cycle. The identification of these two dimensions may prove useful in the understanding of personality formation and a wide range of psychopathology throughout the life course.

Appendix
Mother, Infant, and Dyadic Play Patterns and Characteristics

Mother Play Codes

1. **Acknowledging:** The mother clearly demonstrates, by verbal response, facial expression, movement, or vocalization, her awareness of the infant's actions.
2. **Imitating:** The mother imitates the baby's vocalizations, movements, expressions, or gaze direction. Imitations can be in the same modality (i.e., vocal imitation of infant vocalizing) or in a different modality (i.e., facial imitation of child vocalization).
3. **Elaborating:** The mother adds variation or enlarges the imitated act in the same or in different modality.
4. **Gaze:** The mother looks at the child or object of joint attention.
5. **Affect:** The mother displays warm and relaxed emotions by her voice, handling of the infant, vocalizations, or facial expressions. Withdrawn, anxious, or angry emotions score low.
6. **Adaptation–Regulation:** Mother and infant adjust the amount of stimulation in accordance with the partner's messages (e.g., lower the intensity of voice when the partner averts his or her gaze).

Infant Play Codes

7. **Gaze Aversion:** The infant looks away from the mother or object of joint attention.
8. **Alert:** The infant is enthusiastic, actively attentive, and interested in play. This score estimates the highest level of infant alertness during play. It does not represent, as do the other measures, an average of the entire interaction.
9. **Fatigue:** The infant is tired and displays inattention, drowsy expression, and disengagement. Both the duration and the degree of fatigue are considered.
10. **Fussy:** The infant is fussy during the interaction. Both the proportion of time the infant is fussy and the intensity, loudness, and soothability of fussiness are considered.
11. **Initiation:** Play consists of infant-originated activities, and the infant frequently initiates play.

Dyadic Play

12. Dyadic Reciprocity: Mother and infant are engaged in a give-and-take interaction. Each partner participates in play, enables the other to complete his or her part, and responds to the partner's play.

References

Achenbach, T. M. (1992). *The Child Behavior Checklist (CBCL) 2–3 years.* Burlington, VT: University of Vermont Press.

Achenbach, T. M., & Edelbrook, C. S. (1984). Psychopathology of childhood. *Annual Review of Psychology, 35,* 227–256.

Adler, A. (1951). (P. Radin, Trans.). *The practice and theory of individual psychology.* New York: Humanities Press.

Ainsworth, M. D. S. (1969). Object relations, dependency, and attachment: A theoretical review of the mother–infant relationship. *Child Development, 40,* 969–1025.

Ainsworth, M. D. S., Blehar, M. C., Waters, E., & Wall, S. (1978). *Pattern of attachment.* Hillsdale, NJ: Erlbaum.

Akhtar, N., Dunham, F., & Dunham, P. J. (1991). Directive interaction and early vocabulary development: The role of joint attentional focus. *Journal of Child Language, 18,* 41–49.

Angyal, A. (1941). *Foundations for a science of personality.* New York: Viking Press.

Angyal, A. (1951). E. Hanfmann & R. M. Jones (Eds.). *Neurosis and treatment: A holistic theory.* New York: Wiley.

Bakan, D. (1966). *The duality of human existence: An essay on psychology and religion.* Chicago: Rand McNally.

Balint, M. (1959). *Thrills and repression.* London: Hogarth Press.

Behrends, R. S., & Blatt, S. J. (1985). Internalization and psychological development throughout the life cycle. *Psychoanalytic Study of the Child, 40,* 11–39.

Belsky, J., Goode, M. K., & Most, R. K. (1980). Maternal stimulation and infant exploratory competence: Cross-sectional, correlational, and experimental analyses. *Child Development, 51,* 1168–1178.

Belsky, J., Rovine, M., & Taylor, D. C. (1984). The Pennsylvania Infant and Family Development Project III: The origins of individual differences in mother–infant attachment: Maternal and infant contributions. *Child Development, 48,* 182–194.

Beutler, L. E., Johnson, D. T., Morris, K., & Neville, W., Jr. (1977). Effect of time-specific sets and patient's personality style on state and trait anxiety. *Psychological Reports, 40,* 1003–1010.

Blatt, S. J. (1974). Levels of object representation in anaclitic and introjective depression. *Psychoanalytic Study of the Child, 24,* 107–157.

Blatt, S. J. (1990). Interpersonal relatedness and self-definition: Two personality configurations and their implications for psychopathology and psychotherapy. In J. L. Singer (Ed.), *Repression and dissociation: Implications for personality theory, psychopathology and health* (pp. 299–335). Chicago: University of Chicago Press.

Blatt, S. J. (1991). A cognitive morphology of psychopathology. *Journal of Nervous and Mental Disease, 179*, 449–458.

Blatt, S. J. (1995). Representational structures in psychopathology. In D. Cicchetti & S. Toth (Eds.), *Rochester Symposium on Developmental Psychopathology: Vol. VI. Emotion, cognition, and representation* (pp. 1–33). Rochester, NY: University of Rochester Press.

Blatt, S. J., & Blass, R. (1990). Attachment and separateness: A dialectic model of the products and processes of psychological development. *Psychoanalytic Study of the Child, 45*, 107–127.

Blatt, S. J., & Blass, R. B. (1992). Relatedness and self-definition. Two primary dimensions in personality development, psychopathology, and psychotherapy. In J. W. Barron, M. N. Eagle, & D. L. Wolitsky (Eds.), *The interface of psychoanalysis and psychology* (pp. 399–428). Washington, DC: American Psychological Association.

Blatt, S. J., & Blass, R. (1996). Relatedness and self-definition: A dialectic model of personality development. In G. G. Noam & K. W. Fischer (Eds.), *Development and vulnerabilities in close relationships* (pp. 309–338). Hillsdale, NJ: Erlbaum.

Blatt, S. J., Cornell, C. E., & Eshkol, E. (1993). Personality style and differential vulnerability and clinical course in immunological and cardiovascular disease. *Clinical Psychology Review, 13*, 421–450.

Blatt, S. J., Quinlan, D. M., Chevron, E. S., McDonald, C., & Zuroff, D. (1982). Dependency and self-criticism: Psychological dimensions of depression. *Journal of Consulting and Clinical Psychology, 50*, 113–124.

Blatt, S. J., & Shichman, S. (1983). Two primary configurations of psychopathology. *Psychoanalysis and Contemporary Thought, 6*, 187–254.

Blatt, S. J., & Wild, C. M. (1976). *Schizophrenia: A developmental analysis.* New York: Academic Press.

Blatt, S. J., Wild, C. M., & Ritzler, B. A. (1975). Disturbances in object representation in schizophrenia. *Psychoanalysis and Contemporary Science, 4*, 235–288.

Blatt, S. J., & Zuroff, D. (1992). Interpersonal relatedness and self-definition: Two prototypes for depression. *Clinical Psychology Review, 12*, 527–562.

Block, J. (1971). *Lives through time.* Berkeley, CA: Bancroft Books.

Bornstein, M. H., & Sigman, M. D. (1986). Continuity in mental development from infancy. *Child Development, 57*, 251–274.

Bornstein, M. H., & Tamis-LeMonda, C. S. (1990). Activities and interactions of mothers and their firstborn infants in the first six months of life: Covariation, stability, continuity, correspondence and prediction. *Child Development, 61*, 1206–1217.

Bowlby, J. (1969). *Attachment and loss: Vol. 1. Attachment.* New York: Basic Books.

Bowlby, J. (1973). *Attachment and loss: Vol. 2. Separation, anxiety, and anger.* New York: Basic Books.

Bretherton, I. (1987). Security, communication and internal working models. In J. D. Osofsky (Ed.), *Handbook of infant development* (pp. 1061–1100). New York: Wiley.

Buss, D. M. (1987). Selection, evocation, and manipulation. *Journal of Personality and Social Psychology, 53,* 1214–1221.

Byrne, E., Barry, J., & Nelson, D. (1963). Relation of the revised repression–sensitization scale to measure of self-description. *Psychological Reports, 13,* 323–334.

Cassidy, J. (1994). Emotion regulation: Influences of attachment relationships. *Monographs of the Society for Research in Child Development, 59*(2–3) 228–250.

Chodorow, N. (1978). *The reproduction of mothering: Psychoanalysis and the sociology of gender.* Berkeley, CA: University of California Press.

Clark, G. N., & Seifer, R. (1983). Facilitating mother–infant communication: A treatment model for high–risk and developmentally delayed infants. *Infant Mental Health Journal, 4,* 67–82.

Cohn, J. F., & Tronick, E. Z. (1987). Mother–infant face-to-face interaction: The sequence of dyadic states at 3, 6, and 9 months. *Developmental Psychology, 23,* 68–77.

Cohn, J. F., & Tronick, E. Z. (1988). Mother–infant face-to-face interaction: Influence is bidirectional and unrelated to periodic cycles in either partner's behavior. *Developmental Psychology, 24,* 386–392.

Connell, J. P. (1990). Context, self, and action: A motivational analysis of self-system processes across the life span. In D. Ciccetti & M. Beeghly (Eds.), *The self in transition: From infancy to childhood* (pp. 61–72). Chicago: University of Chicago Press.

Davis, P. J., & Schwartz, G. (1987). Repression and the inaccessibility of affective memories. *Journal of Personality and Social Psychology, 52,* 155–162.

Emde, R. N. (1984). The affective self: Continuities and transformations from infancy. In J. D. Call (Ed.), *Frontiers of infant psychiatry* (pp. 38–54). New York: Basic Books.

Emde, R. N. (1988). Development terminable and interminable. *Journal of the American Psychoanalytic Association, 69,* 23–40.

Emde, R. N. (1994). Individuality, context, and the search for meaning. *Child Development, 65,* 719–737.

Epstein, S., & Fenz, W. (1967). The detection of areas of emotional stress through variations in perceptual threshold and physiological arousal. *Journal of Experimental Research in Personality, 2,* 191–199.

Erikson, E. H. (1950). *Childhood and society.* New York: Norton.

Erikson, E. H. (1982). *The life cycle completed.* New York: Norton.

Eysenck, H. (1960a). *Behavior therapy and the neuroses.* Oxford, England: Pergamon Press.

Eysenck, H. (1960b). *The structure of human personality* (rev. ed.). London: Methuen.

Feldstein, S., Jaffe, J., Beebe, B., Crown, C., Jasnow, M., Fox, H., & Gordon, S. (1994). Coordinated interpersonal timing in adult–infant vocal interactions: A cross-site replication. Infant Behavior and Development, 16, 455–470.

Field, T. (1994). The effects of mother's physical and emotional unavailability on emotion regulation. *Monographs of the Society for Research in Child Development, 59*(2–3), 208–228.

Field, T., Goldstein, S., Vega-Lahr, N., & Porter, K. (1986). Changes in imitative behavior during early infancy. *Infant Behavior and Development, 9*, 415–421.

Findji, A. (1993). Attentional abilities and maternal scaffolding in the first year of life. *International Journal of Psychology, 28*, 681–692.

Fogel, A. (1993). *Developing through relationships: Communication, self, and culture.* Chicago: University of Chicago Press.

Fogel, A., & Thelen, E. (1987). Development of early expressive and communicative action: Reinterpreting the evidence from a dynamic system perspective. *Developmental Psychology, 23*, 747–761.

Franz, C. E., & White, K. M. (1985). Individuation and attachment in personality development: Extending Erikson's theory. *Journal of Personality, 53*, 224–256.

Freud, S. (1957). Civilization and its discontents. In J. Strachey (Ed. and Trans.), *The standard edition of the complete psychological works of Sigmund Freud* (Vol. 21, pp. 64–145). London: Hogarth Press. (Original work published 1930)

Freud, S. (1957). On narcissism: An introduction. In J. Strachey (Ed. and Trans.), *The standard edition of the complete psychological works of Sigmund Freud* (Vol. 14, pp. 73–102). London: Hogarth Press. (Original work published 1914)

Freud, S. (1959). Inhibitions, symptoms and anxiety. In J. Strachey (Ed. and Trans.), *The standard edition of the complete psychological works of Sigmund Freud* (Vol. 20, pp. 87–174). London: Hogarth Press. (Original work published 1926)

Friedman, H. S., & Booth-Kewley, S. (1987). The disease-prone personality: A meta-analytic view of the construct. *American Psychologist, 42*, 539–555.

Gable, S., & Isabella, R. A. (1992). Maternal contribution to infant regulation of arousal. *Infant Behavior and Development, 15*, 95–107.

Gardner, R. W., Holzman, P. S., Klein, G. S., Lipton, H. B., & Spence, D. (1959). Cognitive control: A study of individual consistencies in cognitive behavior. *Psychological Issues, 1.*

Gardner, R. W., Jackson, D. N., & Messick, S. J. (1960). Personality organization in cognitive controls and intellectual abilities. *Psychological Issues, 2.*

Gilligan, C. (1982). *In a different voice: Psychological theory and women's development.* Cambridge, MA: Harvard University Press.

Graziano, W. G., Brothen, T., & Berscheid, E. (1980). Attention, attraction, and individual differences in reaction to criticism. *Journal of Personality and Social Psychology, 38*, 193–202.

Hamilton, V. (1983). Information-processing aspects of denial: Some tentative formulations. In S. Breznitz (Ed.), *The denial of stress* (pp. 167–195). Madison, CT: International Universities Press.

Harlap, S., Davis, A. M., Grower, M. B., & Prywes, B. (1977). The Jerusalem perinatal study: The first decade (1964–1977). *Israel Medical Journal, 13*, 1073–1091.

Hoffmann, J. M. (1994). The role of initiative in early emotional development: Organization of the second semester. *Psychiatrie de l'Enfant, 37*, 179–213.

Horney, K. (1945). *Our inner conflicts.* New York: Norton.

Horney, K. (1950). *Neurosis and human growth*. New York: Norton.

Isabella, R. A. (1993). Origins of attachment: Maternal interactive behavior across the first year. *Child Development, 64*, 605–621.

Isabella, R. A., & Belsky, J. (1991). Interactional synchrony and the origins of infant–mother attachment: A replication study. *Child Development, 62*, 373–384.

Jasnow, M., & Feldstein, S. (1986). Adult–like characteristics of mother–infant vocal interaction. *Child Development, 57*, 754–761.

Jung, C. G. (1923). *Psychological types*. London: Routledge & Kegan Paul.

Kaye, K., & Fogel, A. (1980). The temporal structure of face-to-face communication between mothers and infants. *Developmental Psychology, 16*, 454–464.

Kobasa, S. C., Maddi, S. R., & Kahn, S. (1982). Hardiness and health: A prospective study. *Journal of Personality and Social Psychology, 42*, 168–177.

Lamb, M. E., Morrison, D. C., & Malkin, C. M. (1987). The development of infant social expectation in a face-to-face interaction: A longitudinal study. *Merrill-Palmer Quarterly, 33*, 241–254.

Lester, B. M., Hoffman, J., & Brazelton, T. B. (1985). The rhythmic structure of mother–infant interaction in term and preterm infants. *Child Development, 56*, 15–27.

Loewald, H. W. (1962). Internalization, separation, mourning, and the superego. *Psychoanalytic Quarterly, 31*, 483–504.

Luthar, S. S., & Blatt, S. J. (1995). Differential vulnerability of dependency and self-criticism among disadvantaged teenagers. *Journal of Research on Adolescence, 5*, 431–449.

Maddi, S. (1980). *Personality theories: A comparative analysis* (4th ed.). Homewood, IL: Dorsey Press.

Mahler, M. S., Pine, F., & Bergman, A. (1975). *The psychological birth of the human infant*. New York: Basic Books.

Malatesta, C. Z. (1988). The role of emotions in the development and organization of personality. *Nebraska Symposium on Motivation, 36*, 1–56.

Mayes, L. C., & Carter, A. S. (1990). Emerging social regulatory capacities as seen in the still–face situation. *Child Development, 61*, 754–763.

McAdams, D. P. (1980). A thematic coding system for the intimacy motive. *Journal of Research in Personality, 14*, 413–432.

McAdams, D. P. (1985). *Power, intimacy, and the life story: Personological inquiries into identity*. Homewood, IL: Dorsey Press.

McCall, R. B., & Carriger, M. S. (1993). A meta-analysis of infant habituation and recognition memory performance as predictors of later IQ. *Child Development, 64*, 57–79.

McCaully, M. H. (1981). Jung's theory of psychological types and the Myers-Briggs Indicator. In P. McGeynolds (Ed.), *Advances in psychological assessment* (Vol. 5, pp. 294–352). San Francisco: Jossey-Bass.

McClelland, D. C. (1986). Some reflections on the two psychologies of love. *Journal of Personality, 54*, 334–353.

McClelland, D. C., Atkinson, J. W., Clark, R. A., & Lowell, E. L. (1953). *The achievement motive*. New York: Appleton-Century-Crofts.

Meltzoff, A. N. (1985). The roots of social and cognitive development: Models of man's original nature. In T. Field & N. Fox (Eds.), *Social perception of infants* (pp. 1–30). Norwood, NJ: Ablex.

Meltzoff, A. N. (1990). Toward a developmental cognitive science: The implication of cross-modal matching and imitation for the development of representation and memory in infancy. *Annals of the New York Academy of Sciences, 608,* 1–31.

Miller, J. B. (1976). *Toward a new psychology of women.* Boston: Beacon Press.

Miller, J. B. (1984). The development of women's sense of self (Works in Progress, No. 84-01). Wellesley, MA: Wellesley College, The Stone Center.

Myers, I. B. (1962). *Manual: The Myers-Briggs Type Indicator.* Palo Alto, CA: Consulting Psychologists Press.

Piaget, J. (1970). (M. Cook, Trans.). *The construction of reality in the child.* New York: Basic Books. (Original work published 1954)

Pipp, S. (1990). Sensorimotor and representational internal working models of self, other, and relationships: Mechanisms of connection and separation. In D. Cicchetti & M. Beeghley (Eds.), *The self in transition: Infancy to childhood* (pp. 243–264). Chicago: University of Chicago Press.

Pipp, S., & Harmon, K. J. (1987). Attachment as regulation, a commentary. *Child Development, 58,* 648–652.

Rank, O. (1929). (Julia Taft, Trans.). *Truth and reality.* New York: Knopf.

Rofe, Y., & Lewin, I. (1979). Who adjusts better: Repressors or sensitizers? *Journal of Clinical Psychology, 35,* 875–879.

Rutter, D. R., & Durkin, K. (1987). Turn-taking in mother–infant interaction: An examination of vocalizations and gaze. *Developmental Psychology, 23,* 54–61.

Sameroff, A. J., & Fiese, H. B. (1991). Transactional regulation and early intervention. In S. Neisels & J. Sonkoff (Eds.), *Handbook of early intervention* (pp. 119–149). New York: Cambridge University Press.

Sampson, E. E. (1988). The debate on individuation: Indigenous psychologies of the individual and their role in personal and societal functioning. *American Psychologist, 43,* 15–22.

Sander, L. W. (1975). Infant and the caretaking environment: Investigations and conceptualization of adaptive behavior in a system of increasing complexity. In E. J. Anthony (Ed.), *Exploration in child psychiatry* (pp. 129–166). New York: Plenum.

Sander, L. W. (1984). Polarity, paradox and the organizing process in development. In J. D. Call (Ed.), *Frontiers of infant psychiatry* (pp. 333–346). New York: Basic Books.

Sander, L. W. (1987). Awareness of inner experience: A systems perspective on self-regulatory process in early development. *Child Abuse and Neglect, 11,* 339–346.

Shapiro, D. (1965). *Neurotic styles.* New York: Basic Books.

Shor, J., & Sanville, J. (1978). *Illusions in loving: A psychoanalytic approach to intimacy and autonomy.* Los Angeles: Double Helix.

Slough, N., Kleinknecht, R. A., & Thorndike, R. M. (1984). Relationship of the Repression-Sensitization scales to anxiety. *Journal of Personality Assessment, 48,* 378–379.

Smith, P. B., & Pederson, D. R. (1988). Maternal sensitivity and patterns of infant–mother attachment. *Child Development, 59,* 1097–1111.

Spiegel, H., & Spiegel, D. (1978). *Trance and treatment: Clinical uses of hypnosis.* New York: Basic Books.

Sroufe, L. A. (1983). Infant-caregiving attachment and patterns of adaptation and competence: Roots of maladaptation and competence. In M. Perlmutter (Ed.), *Minnesota Symposia in Child Development* (Vol. 16, pp. 41–81). Hillsdale, NJ: Erlbaum.

Sroufe, L. A. (1990). An organizational perspective on the self. In D. Cicchetti & M. Beeghley (Eds.), *The self in transition: Infancy to childhood* (pp. 281–307). Chicago: University of Chicago Press.

Stern, D. N. (1974). The goal and structure of mother–infant play. *Journal of the American Academy of Child Psychiatry, 13,* 402–421.

Stern, D. N. (1985). *The interpersonal world of the infant.* New York: Basic Books.

Stern, D. N., & Gibbon, J. (1978). Temporal expectancies of social behavior in mother–infant play. In E. B. Thomas (Ed.), *Origins of the infant's social responsiveness* (pp. 409–429). Hillsdale, NJ: Erlbaum.

Stewart, A. S., & Malley, J. E. (1987). Role combination in women in early adult years: Mitigating agency and communion. In F. Crosby (Ed.), *Spouse, parent, worker: On gender and multiple roles* (pp. 44–62). New Haven, CT: Yale University Press.

Sullivan, P. F., & Roberts, L. K. (1969). Relationship of manifest anxiety to repression-sensitization on the MMPI. *Journal of Consulting and Clinical Psychology, 33,* 763–764.

Surrey, J. (1991). The self-in-relation: A theory of women's development. In A. Kaplan, J. B. Miller, I. Stiver, & J. L. Surrey (Eds.), *Women's growth in connectedness* (pp. 51–61). New York: Guilford Press.

Symons, D., & Moran, G. (1987). The behavioral dynamics of mutual responsiveness in early face-to-face mother–infant interaction. *Child Development, 58,* 1488–1495.

Szumatolska, E. (1992). *Severity and type of depressive affect as related to perceptual styles: Relationship of anaclitic versus introjective depressive configuration to holistic versus analytic similarity judgment.* Unpublished doctoral dissertation, New School for Social Research, New York, NY.

Tamis-LeMonda, C. S., & Bornstein, M. H. (1989). Habituation and maternal encouragement of attention in infancy as predictors of toddler language, play, and representational competence. *Child Development, 60,* 738–751.

Tempone, V. J., & Lamb, W. (1967). Repression-sensitization and its relation to measures of adjustment and conflict. *Journal of Consulting Psychology, 31,* 131–136.

Thelen, E., & Smith, L. (1994). *A dynamic systems approach to the development of cognition and action.* Cambridge, MA: MIT Press.

Thorndike, R. L., Hagen, E. P., & Sattler, G. M. (1986). *The Stanford-Binet Intelligence Scale* (4th ed.). Chicago: Riverside.

van den Boom, D. C., & Hoeksma, J. B. (1994). The effect of infant irritability on mother–infant interactions: A growth-curve analysis. *Developmental Psychology, 30,* 581–590.

Weinberg, K. M., & Tronick, E. Z. (1994). Beyond the face: An empirical study of infant affective configurations of the facial, vocal, gestural, and regulatory behaviors. *Child Development, 65,* 1503–1515.

Weinberger, D. A., Schwartz, G. E., & Davidson, J. R. (1979). Low-anxious, high-anxious, and repressive coping styles: Psychometric patterns and behavioral and physiological responses to stress. *Journal of Abnormal Psychology, 88,* 369–380.

White, M. D., & Wilkins, W. (1973). Bogus physiological feedback and response thresholds of repressors and sensitizers. *Journal of Research in Personality, 7,* 78–87.

Wiggins, J. S. (1991). Agency and communion as conceptual coordinates for the understanding and measurement of interpersonal behavior. In W. W. Grove & D. Cicchetti (Eds.), *Thinking clearly about psychology: Vol. 2. Personality and psychotherapy* (pp. 89–113). Minneapolis: University of Minnesota Press.

Winter, D. (1973). *The power motive.* New York: Free Press.

Witkin, A. H. (1965). Psychological differentiation and forms of pathology. *Journal of Abnormal Psychology, 70,* 317–336.

Witkin, A. H., Dyk, R. B., Faterson, H. I., Goodenough, D. R., & Karp, S. A. (1962). *Psychological differentiation.* New York: Wiley.

Zanna, M. P., & Aziza, C. (1976). On the interaction of repression–sensitization and attention in resolving cognitive dissonance. *Journal of Personality, 44,* 577–593.

2

Bridging the Gap Between Psychodynamic and Scientific Psychology:
The Adelphi Early Memory Index

Rachel Karliner, Ellen Katz Westrich, Jonathan Shedler, and Martin Mayman

What I'm about to relate is a mixture of what I remember and what I've been told happened; something I suppose, like one's earliest memories—life as martini, one part fact to three parts hearsay and legend. Most, even that to which I'd swear, is probably filtered through the blown circuits of confusion and madness and is, I suppose, artful forgery, rigged document, a knocked-off passport of the soul.

—Stanley Elkin
"Out of One's Tree: My Bout
With Temporary Insanity"

The authors thank Jonathan Jackson, Mort Kissen, and Joel Weinberger of the Derner Institute of Advanced Psychological Studies, Adelphi University, for providing the expert clinical judgments used in this study.

In recent years, philosophers of science have increasingly emphasized the role of interpretation in scientific inquiry (e.g., Bernstein,
1983; Rorty, 1993; Schwartz, 1995; Taylor, 1985). There is a general
recognition that data are inseparable from the context of observation
and that observer and observation are intertwined. Perhaps in a parallel vein, contemporary psychoanalytic thinkers have increasingly
emphasized the subjectivity of the clinician in psychological inference
(e.g., Aron, 1992; Benjamin, 1988; Hoffman, 1991, 1992; Mitchell, 1993;
Schafer, 1983). The emotional reactions and contributions of the clinician, far from "contaminating" clinical data, are more often understood to be a vital part of that data. Oddly, academic psychology has
remained largely isolated from these intellectual trends. Most empirical research in psychology still rests on the implicit assumption that
truth will be found through observation of "brute data" requiring no
interpretation (Taylor, 1985, p. 19).

Consider the assessment of mental health. Most researchers assess
mental health using one or another "objective" self-report scale,
avoiding methods that make use of clinical judgment or inference.
Studies with findings resting on self-report measures of psychological
health or distress (e.g., measures of anxiety, depression, neuroticism,
and self-esteem) number in the thousands. On the face of it, scores on
these "objective" self-report scales require no interpretation. They
appear, and are treated, as straightforward reflections of the respondents' psychological states.

Both philosophers of science and psychodynamic clinicians might
disagree. In fact, these self-report scales define, prestructure, and con-
strain the domain of information to be examined. Moreover, studies
based on such scales are laden with pretheoretical assumptions (Kuhn,
1962). One such assumption is that people's conscious beliefs about
themselves provide a sufficient basis for developing and testing psychological theory. This assumption is explicitly at odds with the most
basic premise of psychodynamic psychology, which is that people
have limited access to their own mental processes and that, indeed,
much of inner life is actively excluded from awareness. From a psychodynamic perspective, a person's conscious beliefs must always be
open to inquiry and interpretation. Statements to the effect that a person regards himself or herself as psychologically healthy may reflect
genuine psychological health, or they may reflect the operation of
unconscious defensive processes designed to guard against awareness
of vulnerability and pain. For the contemporary psychodynamic

thinker, meaningful conclusions about psychological health or distress necessarily rest on inference and interpretation.

Evidence for the Value of Clinical Judgment in Research

Research on "illusory mental health" illustrates the limitations of self-report mental health scales taken at face value (Shedler, Mayman, & Manis, 1993). Shedler et al. assessed mental health using standard self-report measures (e.g., the Beck Depression Inventory [BDI; Beck, Ward, Mendelson, Mock, & Erlbaugh, 1961] and the Eysenck Neuroticism scale [Eysenck & Eysenck, 1975]) and also had their research participants evaluated by experienced psychodynamically oriented clinicians. When participants scored in the healthy range on the self-report scales and were judged healthy by the clinicians, they were classified as having *genuine mental health*. When participants reported psychological health but were judged distressed by the clinicians, they were classified as having *illusory mental health*. Those who both reported distress and were judged distressed were termed *manifestly distressed* and provided a third comparison group. The clinicians based their evaluations solely on inferences they drew from participants' accounts of their earliest childhood memories. The Early Memory Test (EMT; Mayman, 1963, 1968) has a long history among psychodynamic clinicians but remains largely unknown among academic researchers.

Shedler et al. (1993) found that the participants identified as having illusory mental health were distinctly different from both genuinely healthy and manifestly distressed comparison respondents. They were highly physiologically reactive to laboratory stressors, relative to both genuinely healthy and manifestly distressed respondents, showing a pattern of heart rate and blood pressure reactivity implicated in the etiology of coronary heart disease. Physiological differences between participants with illusory mental health and comparison participants were not merely statistically significant, but medically significant: Indeed, the level of physiological reactivity for those with illusory mental health was approximately twice that of genuinely healthy respondents. Those with illusory mental health also showed more evidence of psychological defense in their verbal responses to psychologically threatening stimulus phrases than either genuinely healthy or manifestly distressed participants. More often than other participants, they forgot what they were going to say, attempted to change the subject, misunderstood the stimulus phrase, were unable to think of a response, and so on.

It was the *combined* use of self-report measures and subjective, psychodynamically informed clinical judgment that allowed Shedler and his associates (1993) to identify defensive respondents and predict both physiological reactions and verbal manifestations of defense. Without incorporating clinical inference, none of these findings would or could have emerged.

Psychoanalytic Conceptions of Psychological Health

If psychodynamic psychologists do not rely on self-report, on what basis, then, do they infer psychological health? The answer is not as straightforward as one might think, because there is not one psychoanalytic model or perspective, but many. Four broad perspectives appear to dominate the psychoanalytic landscape at the moment, although there are multiple variants and blends of each: classical psychoanalysis, object relations, ego psychology, and self psychology (cf. Pine, 1990). Each leads one to consider psychological health from a different vantage point.

Classical psychoanalysis focuses on wishes and fears and on what happens when these wishes and fears come inevitably into conflict. Do compromise formations allow genuine pleasures and gratifications? Do they permit flexibility and creativity in adapting to the exigencies of life? Do they tax energies to the limits—allow the emotional resources to live richly and fully? Object relational perspectives direct attention to one's internal experience of self and others. Is the inner world populated with figures that are benevolent or malevolent? Can one perceive self and others in their full complexity, integrating good and bad, or does one oscillate between perceptions that are simplistic and one-dimensional? Are relationships rich and textured, or dominated by the affect of the moment? Ego psychology draws attention to the cognitive and emotional strengths and resources at one's disposal. Finally, self psychology focuses on the capacity to regulate and maintain self-esteem, to soothe oneself in times of distress, and to recognize the events and experiences in one's life as having coherence and continuity. It poses the question of whether one can do these things for oneself or must rely on others to perform these functions.

This listing of issues is necessarily abridged and oversimplified, and analysts of one or another camp might argue with our emphases in describing the various perspectives. Yet we think most would agree that all these concepts describe aspects of psychological health. Moreover, they are things that clinicians do not always ask their patients to tell them directly. Rather, they are elements of an individual's psychology that clinicians come to understand through their relationships with their patients or that they infer from their patients' narratives (or, in the case of the EMT, from material they can treat and interpret like a clinical narrative). Unfortunately, they are precisely the things that most mental health researchers *do not* consider. (No wonder psychotherapy studies keep finding that all forms of therapy are equivalent [Lambert, Shapiro, & Bergin, 1986]. The treatment outcome measures, which generally depend on self-report, do not even measure the things that psychodynamic clinicians are trying to change.)

Converging Evidence From the Literature on Attachment

While a great many academic researchers continue to eschew clinical judgment in favor of self-report, researchers in the area of attachment have increasingly recognized the limitations of self-report scales. Evidence from the developmental psychology literature on attachment style makes a compelling case that self-report measures of mental health do not tell the whole story. Several recent studies on attachment classification and psychopathology show that many people underreport symptomatology and overreport mental health (Allen, Hauser, & Borman-Spurrell, 1996; Cassidy & Kobak, 1988; Dozier, 1990; Dozier & Lee, 1995; Kobak & Sceery, 1988; Pianta, Egeland, & Adam, 1996; Toth & Cicchetti, 1996). Self-reports of mental health are often contradicted by peer evaluations (e.g., Kobak & Sceery, 1988), by observer ratings and by clinicians' assessments (e.g., Dozier & Lee, 1995), suggesting the operation of psychological defensive processes (Cassidy & Kobak, 1988).

Adult attachment classification is assessed via the Adult Attachment Interview (AAI; see, e.g., Main, 1991; Main, Kaplan, & Cassidy, 1985), a semiclinical interview designed to elicit attachment-related memories, thoughts, and feelings. The AAI yields four categories: (a) secure–autonomous, (b) dismissing of attachment, (c) preoccupied by past attachments, and (d) unresolved with respect to past trauma. These categories parallel the four attachment categories for infants derived from the Strange Situation test: secure, insecure–avoidant, insecure–ambivalent, and insecure–disorganized/disoriented (Ainsworth, Blehar, Waters, & Wall, 1978). Several studies indicate that parents who were judged secure on the AAI tend to have secure children, dismissing parents tend to have insecure–avoidant children, preoccupied parents tend to have insecure–ambivalent children, and unresolved parents tend to have insecure–disorganized/disoriented children (see, e.g., Main, 1991; Main et al., 1985).

For the present purposes, it is important to note that the AAI evaluates participants' responses not on the basis of their content per se but according to their coherence, cohesiveness, and plausibility (Main, 1991), as evaluated by the assessors. Thus, individuals are judged secure if they readily recall attachment-related experiences; can discuss attachment memories with a balanced, integrated acknowledgment of good and bad feelings; and appear to recognize the value of attachment relationships and their influence on personality. In contrast, individuals are judged dismissing if they tend to minimize the value and influence of attachment relationships, cannot recall attachment-related experiences, and give descriptions of attachment relationships that contain inner contradictions and inconsistencies (Main, 1991; Main et al., 1985).

In studies investigating the relation between adult attachment classification and psychopathology, dismissing individuals tend to present a healthy self-report profile. For example, on the Minnesota Multiphasic Personality Inventory-2, first-time mothers classified as dismissing reported fewer somatic complaints and less general dissatisfaction; they suppressed anxiety and emotion while describing themselves as strong, emotionally healthy, and independent of others (Pianta et al., 1996). In a study of college students, dismissing respondents acknowledged little psychological distress (Kobak & Sceery, 1988). In the context of treatment, participants with serious psychopathological disorders who were also classified as dismissing tended to seek treatment less, reject treatment more, deny psychological vulnerability, and self-disclose less (Dozier, 1990; Dozier, Cue, & Barnett, 1994). On the Brief Symptom Inventory, they tended to report fewer psychiatric symptoms (Dozier & Lee, 1995).

Despite their tendency to underreport distress and overreport health, when dismissing individuals (whether from a normal or clinical sample) are evaluated by others, they are consistently seen as exhibiting greater pathology than secure individuals, and often more pathology than preoccupied individuals. Dismissing individuals with serious psychopathological disorders have been judged to have looser thinking than preoccupied individuals and to be more psychotic than preoccupied or secure individuals (Dozier & Lee, 1995). Furthermore, despite these individuals' self-presentation as self-sufficient, sensitive clinicians notice and become concerned with their psychological vulnerability and distress (Dozier et al., 1994). Similarly, dismissing college students, although they disavow psychological distress, are judged by their peers to have less ego resiliency than secure individuals and more hostility than secure or preoccupied individuals (Kobak & Sceery, 1988).

Similar discrepancies emerge between the seeming self-reliance of children classified as insecure–avoidant during the first year of life and later assessments of behavior. Avoidant children have been assessed as less socially competent; having less ego resiliency, self-esteem, and empathy; and more hostile than secure children (Elicker, Englund, & Sroufe, 1992). They have been recognized as more resistant to seeking help in problem solving, more distant and detached in social interaction, more likely to present behavioral problems in preschool, and having less confidence (Bretherton, 1985). Again, despite avoidant children's seeming self-reliance, sensitive teachers often recognize their vulnerability (Erickson, Sroufe, & Egeland, 1985).

Similarities Between Dismissing Attachment Strategies and Illusory Mental Health

There are clear similarities between individuals classified as dismissing on the AAI and those classified as having illusory mental health according to the Shedler et al. (1993) procedures. Both groups tend to minimize acknowledgment of negative affect and psychological distress but are judged by clinical observers to be distressed. Furthermore, there are physiological data indicating that those with dismissing attachment styles are not simply unaffected by attachment-related thoughts and feelings as they might overtly appear: During the AAI, dismissing respondents showed heightened levels of galvanic skin response (GSR) in comparison to secure and preoccupied respondents (Dozier & Kobak, 1992). This finding is consistent with earlier work showing insecure–avoidant infants to have accelerated heart rates during Strange Situation reunion episodes (Sroufe & Waters, 1977). Although the avoidant infants *appeared* unperturbed by separation from a parent and lacking in distress upon reunion, their accelerated heart rates revealed their underlying distress. These data are consistent with the findings reported by Shedler et al. (1993) indicating that individuals with illusory mental health manifest distress via physiological pathways. The heightened physiological responses of both illusorily healthy and dismissing respondents may indicate their expenditure of a great deal of effort—physiological as well as emotional—to avoid conscious awareness of emotionally disturbing thought or affect (cf. Dozier & Kobak, 1992).

The growing body of evidence pointing to the avoidant child's and the dismissing adult's tendency to minimize acknowledgment of distress underscores the notion that a sizable group of people tend to underreport psychological distress and overreport health. These individuals may be confused with secure individuals, who also generally report few psychological symptoms and relatively little distress (Kobak & Sceery, 1988). It remains to be seen whether dismissing individuals are identical to those who exhibit illusory mental health. Future research may shed light on this question. For our purposes, however, the relevant point remains: In any research involving assessment of psychopathology, whether it be attachment related or not, psychodynamically informed clinical judgment can play a crucial role in distinguishing respondents who are truly healthy from those who simply appear to be healthy.

Clinicians and Researchers Do Not Talk to One Another

The research summarized above illustrates how researchers can miss psychological phenomena of the utmost importance when they exclude clinical inference from their research design. It also demonstrates that psychodynamically informed clinical judgment can be incorporated into empirical mental health research without compromising either the clinician's interpretive methods or the rigor of the research design. Unfortunately, psychodynamic and scientific psychology have remained largely separated and isolated from each other. Areas of convergence, such as research on attachment style and research on illusory mental health, are rare indeed.

This separation is apparent from even the most cursory inspection of the bibliographies of current research and clinical writings: hardly a cross-citation can be found. The lack of discourse impoverishes both disciplines. Empirical researchers do not benefit from the insights of decades of clinical observation, and psychodynamic psychologists cut themselves off from the corrective feedback that rigorous research could provide.

Bridging the Gap Between Scientific and Psychodynamic Psychology

Our goal in this chapter is to build a bridge between psychodynamic and empirical perspectives by providing a systematic procedure for incorporating psychodynamic clinical judgment into empirical mental health research. We use the EMT as a means of building this bridge, both because early memories provide a personal narrative from each respondent—a self-reflexive text that provides a rich source of clinical data—and because the EMT has previously demonstrated its validity and utility in the illusory mental health research paradigm (Shedler et al., 1993).

It is one thing to make a theoretical case for incorporating clinical judgment into research, however, and another to provide a practical means of doing so. The major findings reported by Shedler et al. (1993) rested on the subjective judgments of individual, highly experienced clinicians. Shedler et al. provided no systematic scoring system for the EMT and did not attempt to articulate the process through which the clinicians arrived at their inferences.

The Adelphi Early Memory Index

To address these limitations, we developed the Adelphi Early Memory Index (AEMI) as a way of providing researchers with a systematic procedure for interpreting the EMT. The AEMI is unconcerned with whether the memories reported by subjects represent factual accounts of their childhood experiences. Rather, like the AAI, the AEMI is concerned with how individuals construct, organize, and present their experience, both consciously and unconsciously. In essence, early memories provide information about the psychological "lenses" through which individuals experience themselves and their world.

Clinical experience indicates that the EMT provides a viable means of making inferences about unconscious material (see, e.g., Acklin, Bibb, Boyer, & Jain, 1991; Krohn & Mayman, 1974; Mayman, 1968; Ryan & Bell, 1984). It has also proven of value in empirical research contexts, providing a source of data independent of that provided by standard mental health measures (Shedler et al., 1993). The AEMI offers the first systematic, empirically derived interpretive system for assessing global psychological health and distress using the EMT. To develop the measure, we took the following steps: We (a) studied the inference processes of psychodynamic clinicians and identified key elements of the clinical judgment process, (b) generated variables to score the EMT that we believed reflected aspects of the clinical judgment process, and (c) validated this scoring system against external criteria, including experienced clinicians' judgments of EMT protocols and physiological indices of anxiety and distress. Scoring the AEMI does not require extensive clinical training. However, it makes accessible to nonpsychodynamically and nonclinically trained investigators the techniques inherent in the process of psychodynamic clinical judgment.

Early Memories and the EMT

Before we outline the development of the AEMI, let us take a moment to describe early memories and their clinical use via the EMT. Beginning with Freud's (1899/1950) concept of the screen memory, earliest childhood memories have been the focus of much interest and attention on the part of psychodynamically oriented clinicians. Historically, most authors have agreed that early memories represent a blend of fact, fantasies, and aspects of one's current psychological state (Mayman, 1968). In other words, memories are not necessarily a recollection of objective historical truths but rather can be reflective of, and shaped by, one's current needs, desires, and struggles, which create the illusion of "facts that were" (Rosenheim & Mane, 1984). Indeed, early memories may be thought of as a unique blueprint of one's internal experience; that is, the manner in which one reconstructs one's early experience is based on enduring intrapsychic forces that articulate the psychological state as much, if not more, than one's external experiences (Barrett, 1980; Mayman, 1968; Mosak, 1958).

On the basis of these ideas, Mayman (1963, 1968) developed the EMT as a means of studying the self. The procedure simply involved asking patients to recount a number of earliest memories of the self and of caregivers, as a natural extension of a clinical assessment interview. The EMT goes on to ask for the patient's description of the relationships in the memories, the patient's impression of self and others, and the overall mood or feeling tone of the memories. Through his clinical use of early memories, Mayman came to understand them as reflecting aspects of a person's earliest relationships as he or she may have experienced them at the time the identity was in the process of consolidation (Mayman & Faris, 1960). Important elements of these relationships with significant others are often replayed in new, present-day relationships. These "relationship paradigms" become a rich source of information for the clinician about how a person currently experiences self in relation to others. As such, clinicians may use the EMT as a tool for assessing patients' ongoing object relations without having to rely on their conscious reports of current relationships, providing insights that might otherwise elude both clinician and patient.

These ideas have been borne out through a great deal of empirical research demonstrating the efficacy of the EMT as a projective tool for use in both clinical and empirical work (Bruhn, 1984, 1985; Langs, 1965a, 1965b; Last & Bruhn, 1983, 1985; Nigg, Lohr, Westen, Gold, & Silk, 1992; Nigg et al., 1991; Ryan & Bell, 1984). Several researchers have developed scoring systems for the EMT, attempting to systematize an otherwise subjective process of interpretation. However, when we began our research, no system existed that assessed global psychological health or distress using early memories.

Development of the AEMI

Step 1: Establishing the Reliability of Clinical Judgment

As we outlined above, our intent was to develop a measure that reproduces objectively a psychodynamically oriented clinician's subjective clinical inferences, drawn from the EMT, regarding a patient's psychological health or distress. Before proceeding with a research program aimed at modeling the clinical judgment process, however, it seemed advisable to demonstrate that there is indeed something to model—in other words, to demonstrate that the judgments of experienced clinical psychologists are reliable. Given the doubts so many psychologists have regarding the subjective nature of clinical inference, we believed it was necessary to show that these judgments will survive tests of clinical consensus and congruence (Bruner, 1993). To this end, we recruited a panel of four senior clinical psychologists. We asked them to assess psychological health or distress in a large nonclinical sample using the EMT-S[1] as a basis for their evaluations. One (the fourth author) was the developer of the EMT procedure. All were psychodynamic in orientation, and three were graduates of postdoctoral training programs in psychoanalysis. The most junior clinician had more than 15 years of clinical practice experience, and the most senior had more than 50.

The clinicians' job was to evaluate the EMTs of 115 participants, 51 men and 64 women, who were graduate and professional students enrolled either in law school or a doctoral program in clinical psychology. Each clinician evaluated the full set of EMT protocols from this sample (which we called the AEMI Development Sample), rating each participant's mental health on a 5-point scale (-2 = distressed, -1 = probably distressed, 0 = unsure, $+1$ = probably healthy, $+2$ = healthy). The clini-cians received no special instructions regarding the

---

[1]The EMT may be administered verbally or in writing. For research purposes, we currently use a short form of the EMT (EMT-S) that asks respondents for written accounts of five early childhood memories. The test begins with the following instructions, printed on a separate cover page:

> In the next few pages, we will ask you to remember some of your earliest memories, and to tell us about these memories in writing. These memories are very important to us. Please do not rush, but take the time to describe your memories in detail.
>
> We will ask you to recall a total of five memories. Before you turn the page, take a moment to relax. Let your thoughts go back to your childhood, think back as far as you can, and try to recall your very *earliest* childhood memory. Try to remember a specific incident or event, not just a fragmentary impression.
>
> When you have recalled this earliest memory, turn ahead to the next page where there will be space to write about it.

On subsequent pages, the test goes on to ask for an account of the respondent's next earliest memory, earliest memory of mother, earliest memory of father, and a memory of a " low point" in the individual's life. For each memory, follow-up questions ask for the participant's impressions of himself or herself and others in the memory, the mood or feeling tone that goes along with the memory, and the approximate age at which the memory took place.

interpretation of the EMT but were simply asked to make their best clinical inference about the psychological status of each respondent. The clinicians worked independently and had access to no other data. The purpose was to see if clinicians, working independently, and using their own interpretive frameworks, could arrive at some consensus in their judgments of mental health.

We averaged the mental health ratings provided by the four clinical psychologists to obtain a composite mental health score for each respondent. Composite or aggregate ratings are generally more reliable than the ratings of individual judges because the idiosyncrasies of individual judges tend to cancel out, and the composite rating comes to reflect the core consensual wisdom of the group (the principle of aggregation; see, e.g., Horowitz, Inouye, & Siegelman, 1979; Rushton, Brainerd, & Preisley, 1983). The alpha reliability for the composite mental health rating was .79, easily exceeding the reliability levels often reported in personality research, and indicating that, indeed, there was something important about which the clinicians agreed.

It is also interesting that the clinicians had little trouble in discriminating levels of mental health even within this sample of high-functioning graduate and professional students (most of whom had self-reported as unambiguously healthy on the BDI). The composite mental health ratings spanned nearly the full range of possible scores, ranging from –2.0 to 1.75 ($M = 0.33$, $SD = 0.94$). Given the high level of agreement among the panel of clinicians, we concluded that there was sufficient justification for proceeding with research aimed at modeling the clinical judgment process.

Step 2: Generation of Items for the AEMI

Our intent in developing the AEMI was to create a systematic procedure for scoring EMT protocols. We wished to enable other investigators to reproduce the process implicit in the interpretive mental health judgments provided by our panel of clinicians. To accomplish this, we attempted to create a set of items or variables that could be scored readily and that might tap the dimensions to which the clinicians had responded. Because we were uncertain about exactly what features of the early memories were the most important determinants of the clinical judgments, we began by generating a large pool of variables for further study.

We based ideas for initial variables or items on our clinical experience with the EMT and also on hypotheses derived from psychoanalytic theory. Furthermore, we generated items based on a comprehensive review of previous literature on the EMT. To facilitate subsequent psychometric work, we wrote all items in such a way that they could be rated on 5-point unipolar scales (1 = not applicable, 3 = somewhat applicable, 5 = highly applicable). Additionally, we decided that raters should score the full set of memories provided by a given respondent, not individual memories considered in isolation. This would allow the raters' judgments to parallel more closely those of the original clinicians. It also lessened the burden on raters, reducing the time needed to score the EMT protocols.

Step 3: Iterative Revision of the Initial Variable Set

The initial item generation phase produced 34 variables that served as a basis for subsequent research. We revised and refined this initial item set using an iterative procedure. Four raters (graduate students in clinical psychology) used the first generation of the AEMI to score the 115 EMT protocols from the AEMI Development Sample (see Step 1, above). After computing interrater reliability coefficients for each item, we retained items with Spearman-Browne corrected reliabilities of approximately .60 or above. We dropped or rewrote items that did not meet this criterion. Additionally, we solicited feedback from the raters regarding possible ambiguities, redundancies, omissions, and so on, and we revised, combined, dropped, and added items based on this information as well. This revision process yielded a refined, "second generation" of the AEMI, which we used to repeat the entire process: Two new raters (the first and second authors) scored the EMT protocols from the AEMI Development Sample. Again, we computed interrater reliabilities, revised, dropped, and added items. After three such iterative cycles, we arrived at a set of 18 variables that were clearly worded, easily scored, and adequately reliable.

Step 4: Discerning the Factors Underlying Clinical Judgment

To understand better the constructs embedded in the 18 variables of the AEMI, we conducted a factor analysis, which yielded three clear, conceptually interpretable factors (the items and factor loadings are reproduced in Exhibit 1). We interpreted the first factor as a general affectively toned object representation factor that reflected the affect tone of the memories and reflected whether the self, others, and memory outcomes were depicted in a generally positive or negative light. We interpreted the second factor as a narrative style or narrative quality factor. The third factor reflects the presence or absence of traumatic experiences in the memories (e.g., physical or sexual abuse). Interestingly, these factors reflected much of the previous theoretical and empirical work on the EMT, which indicated that affect tone, object representations, narrative structure, and trauma were significant indicators of psychological health or distress. Although in the literature, affect tone and object representation have often been treated separately, the AEMI items that tapped these constructs loaded on the same factor, indicating that they are interrelated (cf. Nigg et al., 1992).

At this point in our research, we had succeeded in identifying three clear and conceptually straightforward factors on the AEMI. Whether these factors could be used to reproduce the judgments of our panel of clinicians remained an open question and became the focus of Step 5.

Step 5: Validating the AEMI Against the Judgments of Clinicians

All the work described above—generating a variable set for scoring the EMT, checking item reliabilities, refining the item set through an iterative revision process—represented but a step toward a greater goal: creating a scoring system that would allow raters to reproduce the kind of interpretive judgments provided by a panel of experienced clinicians. Our intent in Step 5 was to use the factors described above, singly or in combination, to predict the composite clinical judgment obtained by our panel of clinicians.

Factor I—Affect/Object Representation—correlated most highly with the composite clinical judgments of mental health ($r = .80$, $p < .001$). Given the reliability of the composite clinical judgment ($\alpha = .79$), this correlation approaches the theoretical limit for the maximum possible correlation, indicating that Factor I accounts for nearly all of the systematic or explainable variance in the composite clinical judgments. In other words, the elements to which the panel of clinicians were responding in their global mental health assessments were

Factors I, II, and II of the Adelphi Early Memory Index: The Items and Their Factor Loadings

Factor I

Predominant affect tone is positive (e.g., memories convey happiness, contentment, well-being, excitement, etc.).	.92
Predominant affect tone is negative (e.g., memories convey sadness, anger, frustration, fear, hurt, etc.).	.92
The memories have predominantly positive outcomes (e.g., subject ultimately succeeds, experiences gratification, etc.).	.88
The memories have predominantly negative outcomes (e.g., subject ultimately fails, experiences pain, frustration, etc.).	−.87
Others are depicted as benevolent; they are seen as sources of gratification, pleasure, comfort, security, etc.	.84
Subject comes across as confident, self-assured.	.84
Subject comes across as ignored, deprived, not cared for.	−.79
Others are depicted as malevolent; they are seen as sources of frustration, pain, punishment, injury, etc.	−.72
Caregivers are portrayed as abandoning or under-protective.	−.72

Factor II

The memories seem "real," full-bodied, palpable, easy to imagine; one gets a sense of being there; one can empathize with subject's feelings.	.90

continues

Exhibit 1

The memories are lacking in evocative detail; descriptions seem thin, two-dimensional, clichéd, or otherwise lacking in supportive detail; one cannot really get a sense of what it was like to be there; one cannot readily empathize with subject's feelings.	−.90
Emotions reported by subject are congruent with the content of the memory, i.e., details of the memory are consistent with the reported emotions.	.89
Emotions reported by subject are incongruent with the content of the memory, i.e., supporting details are lacking, or details of the memory are inconsistent with the reported emotions.	−.86
The narrative lacks inner narrative coherence; there are pieces that do not seem to "fit"; there is a sense that things have been omitted or distorted.	−.84

Factor III

Subject experiences others as deliberately inflicting physical injury on him or her.	.86
There is at least one memory of an extremely traumatic event falling outside the realm of normal childhood experience (e.g., of physical or sexual abuse, violence between parents, a parent drunk and out of control, etc.).	.76
Subject perceives others as deliberately inflicting injury on others (e.g., domestic violence, schoolyard fights).	.66
Subject experiences injury or illness.	.60

Exhibit 1 (continued)

mainly tapped by the AEMI items having to do with the self and object representations depicted in the early memories and with the affect tone of the memories.

The correlations of Factors II and III with the composite clinical judgment were smaller but also statistically significant (rs = .20 and .31, respectively). In a stepwise regression of the composite clinical judgments on all three factors together, Factors II and III did not account for additional variance after the first factor entered the regression equation. We thus retained the nine variables that constituted Factor I as the final version of the AEMI. (The AEMI is reproduced in Exhibit 2.) These variables were conceptually clear and could be scored reliably. Most important, they could be averaged to form a psychological health or distress score that, for all intents and purposes, duplicated the judgments of the clinicians on our panel.

Step 6: Validating the AEMI Against External Criteria: Predicting Illusory Mental Health

The final step in our research program was to validate the AEMI against external criteria. To do so, we reanalyzed the early memories collected in the Shedler et al. (1993) studies, in which Mayman's clinical judgments were used to differentiate between genuine and illusory mental health. As we described earlier, participants with illusory mental health responded differently to laboratory stressors than did genuinely healthy or manifestly distressed participants, exhibiting high levels of coronary reactivity and more verbal manifestations of psychological defense than did participants in either comparison group. Our goal was to determine whether the AEMI could stand in for the clinicians' judgments for purposes of assessing illusory mental health. Could we replicate the original Shedler et al. findings using the AEMI scoring system instead of the clinician?

Two coders (the first and second authors) used the nine-variable AEMI scoring system to rescore the EMT protocols of the 58 participants from the original Shedler et al. (1993) sample. These coders worked independently and were blind to the participants' original classification. We averaged the scores provided by the two raters for each AEMI variable, then averaged the nine AEMI variables (after reversing the negatively coded items) to create the AEMI psychological health or distress index described above. Participants with low scores on the Eysenck Neuroticism scale (below the median) and high

The Adelphi Early Memory Index (AEMI)

1 = not applicable   3 = somewhat applicable
5 = highly applicable

1. Predominant affect tone is positive (e.g., memories convey happiness, contentment, well-being, excitement, etc.).

2. Predominant affect tone is negative (e.g., memories convey sadness, anger, frustration, fear, hurt, etc.).

3. Others are depicted as benevolent; they are seen as sources of gratification, pleasure, comfort, security, etc.

4. Others are depicted as malevolent; they are seen as sources of frustration, pain, punishment, injury, etc.

5. The memories have predominantly positive outcomes (e.g., subject ultimately succeeds, experiences gratification, etc.).

6. The memories have predominantly negative outcomes (e.g., subject ultimately fails, experiences pain, frustration, etc.).

7. Caregivers are portrayed as abandoning or underprotective.

8. Subject comes across as confident, self-assured.

9. Subject comes across as ignored, deprived, not cared for.

Scoring instructions:
Rate each item on a 5-point rating scale (1 = not applicable, 3 = somewhat applicable, 5 = highly applicable). Sum the scores for all items, after reversing scores for Items 2, 4, 6, 7, and 9.

Exhibit 2

scores on the AEMI (above the median) were classified as having genuine mental health ($n = 23$). Participants with low scores on the Eysenck Neuroticism scale (below the median) and low scores on the AEMI (below the median) were classified as having illusory mental health ($n = 14$). Participants with high Neuroticism scores and low AEMI scores were labeled "manifestly distressed" and provided a third comparison group ($n = 12$). This classification procedure paralleled that of Shedler et al.

All findings originally reported by Shedler et al. (1993) were replicated using the AEMI in place of the expert clinical judge. The participants identified as having illusory mental health showed significantly greater coronary reactivity than either genuinely healthy or manifestly distressed participants. Similarly, participants with illusory mental health showed significantly more verbal manifestations of defense than either genuinely healthy or manifestly distressed participants (see Shedler, Karliner, Westrich, & Mayman, 1995 for a detailed description of the methods and findings). These data demonstrate that psychological health or distress scores based on the AEMI can stand in for the experienced clinician without compromising the findings in any way.

Conclusions and Discussion

Our intent in developing the AEMI was to begin to bridge the widening gulf between psychodynamic psychologists and empirical researchers. This gulf has developed over many years and has complex historical origins. One factor that perpetuates it, however, is the divergence in perspective between psychodynamic clinicians, who take seriously the concept of unconscious processes and unconscious defenses and who are committed to interpretive clinical judgment, and empirical researchers, who wish to study variables that are observable, measurable, and reproducible. Our work has focused on modeling aspects of the clinical judgment process and making aspects of that process accessible to nonclinicians. To summarize our findings, we demonstrated that (a) experienced clinical judges can make reliable assessments of psychological health or distress using the EMT; (b) the AEMI psychological health or distress scores can account for virtually all of the systematic variance in the clinicians' judgments; and (c) these scores can be used in combination with standard self-report scales to differentiate between genuine mental health and the façade or illusion of mental health created by psychological defenses.

What is the significance of these results? The AEMI is an empirically derived, quantifiable scoring system that models a key feature of psychodynamic clinical judgment. Although additional research will no doubt contribute to a nomological net surrounding the AEMI, the present findings provide strong evidence that it can be a useful tool in mental health research. Thus, it provides a means of incorporating a key aspect of clinical judgment in empirical research. Moreover, findings on illusory mental health make clear that there is an important role for such data in mental health research. Indeed, the failure to make use of clinical data may obscure psychological phenomena of the utmost importance.

From a more philosophical perspective, we believe that the AEMI represents a step toward bridging the gap between psychodynamic and scientific psychology. Because the AEMI's development was based on the interpretive judgments of psychodynamic clinicians, researchers now have a tool at their disposal that will allow them to take account of unconscious processes. Furthermore, in using the AEMI, even nonpsychodynamically trained researchers may take advantage of the interpretive process that occurred during the development of the measure; thus, they will benefit not only from the insights of experienced clinicians but also from the subtleties of this inferential aspect of the process of psychoanalytic inquiry. Conversely, the AEMI lends credence to the idea that when clinicians use their subjective experience of patients or projective material in order to make clinical inferences, they are not simply involved in an act of fortune-telling (as has occasionally been implied by academic psychologists; cf. Myers, 1983). Rather, they are engaging in a systematic, albeit unique, process, verifiable through "tests of congruence and verisimilitude" (Bruner, 1993, p. 16) with the judgments of other, equally unique, individual clinicians.

Unanswered Questions and Suggestions for Future Research

There are sufficient data to merit the use of the EMT and the AEMI as research tools. Nevertheless, many questions remain unanswered. One question concerns the scope of application of the AEMI. The research described here has to do with the ability of the AEMI to discriminate between levels of psychological health in samples of "healthy," high-functioning participants and to predict responses associated with illusory mental health. However, the utility of the AEMI within clinical populations remains unknown. Similarly, we do not know whether the AEMI can discriminate between clinical and nonclinical populations. Whether it can be used in these contexts, or whether "floor effects" or other difficulties will diminish its utility, remains a question for future research. Indeed, it is possible that (the presently unused) AEMI Factors II and III may be more relevant within clinical samples and would correlate more highly with clinicians' judgments within these samples.

Another issue is whether the AEMI can be applied to materials other than the EMT. In principle, the nine variables making up the AEMI could be used to score other types of narrative material, such as accounts of recent life experiences, dreams, Thematic Apperception Test stories, and so on. We believe there is indeed something unique about one's earliest memories—that they are to a large extent constructed retrospectively and that they crystallize around issues central to one's (not necessarily conscious) self-concept (cf. Mayman, 1968). As such, we believe that they are particularly salient to one's level of psychological health or distress. It remains to be seen whether the AEMI will provide relevant information when used to score other projective material.

Finally, relatively little is known about the stability or malleability of AEMI scores over time. Adler theorized that the content of early memories changes as soon as one resolves particular conflicts or issues in one's life. We tend more toward the notion (consistent with Ryan & Bell's, 1984 findings) that the main themes of early memories remain constant over time; rather, it is the way one tells the memory, and the manner in which one depicts oneself and others, that might change as one's psychological state worsens or improves. If this is the case, researchers might use the AEMI to assess changes in global mental health over time. The AEMI might even be useful as an outcome measure to gauge the success of psychotherapy—as distinguished from those measures that rely on symptomatology checklists or self-report measures. Indeed, these and more questions await answers. Implicit in each answer will be a combination of empirical methodology and clinical wisdom, narrowing the gap between psychodynamic and "scientific" psychology.

References

Acklin, M. W., Bibb, J. L., Boyer, P., & Jain, V. (1991). Early memories as expressions of relationship paradigms: A preliminary investigation. *Journal of Personality Assessment, 57,* 177–192.

Ainsworth, M. D. S., Blehar, M. C., Waters, E., & Wall, S. (1978). *Patterns of attachment: A psychological study of the Strange Situation.* Hillsdale, NJ: Erlbaum.

Allen, J. P., Hauser, S. T., & Borman-Spurrell, E. (1996). Attachment insecurity and related sequelae of severe adolescent psychopathology: An eleven-year follow-up study. *Journal of Consulting and Clinical Psychology, 64,* 254–263.

Aron, L. (1992). Interpretation as expression of the analyst's subjectivity. *Psychoanalytic Dialogues, 2,* 475–508.

Barrett, D. (1980). The first memory as a predictor of personality traits. *Journal of Individual Psychology, 36,* 136–149.

Beck, A. T., Ward, C. H., Mendelson, M., Mock, J., & Erlbaugh, J. (1961). An inventory for measuring depression. *Archives of General Psychiatry, 4,* 561–571.

Benjamin, J. (1988). *The bonds of love: Psychoanalysis, feminism and the problem of domination.* New York: Pantheon Books.

Bernstein, R. (1983). *Beyond objectivism and relativism: Science, hermeneutics, and praxis.* Philadelphia: University of Pennsylvania Press.

Bretherton, I. (1985). Attachment theory: Retrospect and prospect. *Monographs of the Society for Research in Child Development, 50*(1–2), 3–35.

Bruhn, A. R. (1984). Use of early memories as a projective technique. In P. McReynolds & C. J. Chelume (Eds.), *Advances in psychological assessment* (Vol. 6, pp. 109–150). San Francisco: Jossey-Bass.

Bruhn, A. R. (1985). Use of early memories as a projective technique—the cognitive perceptual method. *Journal of Personality Assessment, 49,* 587–597.

Bruner, J. (1993). Loyal opposition and the clarity of dissent: Commentary on Donald Spence's "The hermeneutic turn." *Psychoanalytic Dialogues, 3,* 11–19.

Cassidy, J., & Kobak, R. R. (1988). Avoidance and its relation to other defensive processes. In J. Belsky & T. Nezworski (Eds.), *Clinical implications of attachment* (pp. 300–323). Hillsdale, NJ: Erlbaum.

Dozier, M. (1990). Attachment organization and treatment use for adults with serious psychopathological disorders. *Development and Psychopathology, 2,* 47–60.

Dozier, M., Cue, K., & Barnett, L. (1994). Clinicians as caregivers: Role of attachment organization in treatment. *Journal of Consulting and Clinical Psychology, 62,* 793–800.

Dozier, M., & Kobak, R. R. (1992). Psychophysiology in attachment interviews: Converging evidence for deactivating strategies. *Child Development, 63,* 1473–1480.

Dozier, M., & Lee, S. W. (1995). Discrepancies between self- and other-report of psychiatric symptomatology: Effects of dismissing attachment strategies. *Journal of Consulting and Clinical Psychology, 7,* 217–226.

Elicker, J., Englund, M., & Sroufe, L. A. (1992). Predicting peer competence and peer relationships in childhood from early parent–child relationships. In R. D. Parke & G. W. Ladd (Eds.), *Family-peer relationships: Modes of linkage* (pp. 77–106). Hillsdale, NJ: Erlbaum.

Elkin, S. (1993, January). Out of one's tree: My bout with temporary insanity. *Harper's Magazine*, pp. 69–77.

Erickson, M. F., Sroufe, L. A., & Egeland, G. (1985). The relationship between quality of attachment and behavior problems in preschool in a high-risk sample. *Monographs of the Society for Research in Child Development, 50,* 147–167.

Eysenck, H. J., & Eysenck, S. B. G. (1975). *Eysenck Personality Questionnaire manual.* San Diego, CA: Educational & Industrial Testing Service.

Freud, S. (1950). Screen memories. In J. Strachey (Ed. and Trans.), *The standard edition of the complete psychological works of Sigmund Freud* (Vol. 3, pp. 303–322). London: Hogarth Press. (Original work published 1899)

Hoffman, I. Z. (1991). Discussion: Toward a social-constructivist view of the psychoanalytic situation. *Psychoanalytic Dialogues, 1,* 74–105.

Hoffman, I. Z. (1992). Some practical implications of a social-constructivist view of the psychoanalytic situation. *Psychoanalytic Dialogues, 2,* 287–304.

Horowitz, L., Inouye, D., & Siegelman, E. (1979). On averaging judges' ratings to increase their correlation with an external criterion. *Journal of Consulting and Clinical Psychology, 47,* 453–458.

Kobak, R. R., & Sceery, A. (1988). Attachment in late adolescence: Working models, affect regulation, and representations of self and others. *Child Development, 59,* 135–146.

Krohn, A., & Mayman, M. (1974). Object representation in dreams and projective tests. *Bulletin of the Menninger Clinic, 38,* 445–467.

Kuhn, T. S. (1962). *The structure of scientific revolutions.* Chicago: University of Chicago Press.

Lambert, M., Shapiro, D., & Bergin, A. (1986). The effectiveness of psychotherapy. In S. L. Garfield & A. E. Bergin (Eds.), *Handbook of psychotherapy and behavior change* (pp. 137–211). New York: Wiley.

Langs, R. J. (1965a). First memories and characterological diagnosis. *Journal of Nervous and Mental Disease, 141,* 318–320.

Langs, R. J. (1965b). Earliest memories and personality: A predictive study. *Archives of General Psychiatry, 12,* 379–390.

Last, J. M., & Bruhn, A. R. (1983). The psychodiagnostic value of children's earliest memories. *Journal of Personality Assessment, 47,* 597–603.

Last, J. M., & Bruhn, A. R. (1985). Distinguishing childhood diagnostic types with early memories. *Journal of Personality Assessment, 49,* 187–192.

Main, M. (1991). Metacognitive knowledge, metacognitive monitoring, and singular (coherent) vs. multiple (incoherent) model of attachment: Findings and directions for future research. In C. M. Parkes, J. Stevenson-Hinde, & P. Harris (Eds.), *Attachment across the life cycle* (pp. 127–159). London: Routledge.

Main, M., Kaplan, N., & Cassidy, J. (1985). Security in infancy, childhood and adulthood: A move to the level of representation. *Monographs of the Society for Research in Child Development, 50*(1–2), 66–104.

Mayman, M. (1963). Psychoanalytic study of the self-organization with psychological tests. In *Proceedings of the Academic Assembly on Clinical Psychology* (pp. 97–117). Montreal, Quebec, Canada: McGill University Press.

Mayman, M. (1968). Early memories and character structure. *Journal of Projective Techniques and Personality Assessment, 32*, 303–316.

Mayman, M., & Faris, M. (1960). Early memories as expressions of relationship paradigms. *American Journal of Orthopsychiatry, 30*, 507–529.

Mitchell, S. A. (1993). *Hope and dread in psychoanalysis*. New York: Basic Books.

Mosak, H. H. (1958). Early recollections as a projective technique. *Journal of Projective Techniques, 22*, 302–311.

Myers, D. G. (1983). *Social psychology*. New York: McGraw-Hill.

Nigg, J., Lohr, N., Westen, D., Gold, L., & Silk, K. R. (1992). Malevolent object representations in borderline personality disorder. *Journal of Abnormal Psychology, 101*, 61–17.

Nigg, J., Silk, K. R., Westen, D., Gold, L., Goodrich, S., & Ogata, S. (1991). Object representations in the early memories of sexually abused borderline patients. *American Journal of Psychiatry, 148*, 864–869.

Pianta, R. C., Egeland, B., & Adam, E. K. (1996). Adult attachment classification and self-reported psychiatric symptomatology as assessed by the Minnesota Multiphasic Personality Inventory-2. *Journal of Consulting and Clinical Psychology, 64*, 273–281.

Pine, F. (1990). *Id, ego, object and self: A synthesis for clinical work*. New York: Basic Books.

Rorty, R. (1993). Centers of moral gravity: Commentary on Donald Spence's "The hermeneutic turn." *Psychoanalytic Dialogues, 3*, 21–28.

Rosenheim, H., & Mane, R. (1984). Inferences of personality characteristics from earliest memories. *Israeli Journal of Psychiatry and Related Science, 21*, 93–101.

Rushton, J. P., Brainerd, C. J., & Preisley, M. (1983). Behavioral development and construct validity: The principle of aggregation. *Psychological Bulletin, 94*, 18–38.

Ryan, E. R., & Bell, M. D. (1984). Changes in object relations from psychosis to recovery. *Journal of Abnormal Psychology, 93*, 209–215.

Schafer, R. (1983). *The analytic attitude*. New York: Basic Books.

Schwartz, J. (1995). What does the physicist know? Thraldom and insecurity in the relationship of psychoanalysis to physics. *Psychoanalytic Dialogues, 5*, 45–62.

Shedler, J., Karliner, R., Westrich, E., & Mayman, M. (1995). *Cloning the clinician: The Adelphi Early Memory Index and the assessment of illusory mental health*. Manuscript submitted for publication.

Shedler, J., Mayman, M., & Manis, M. (1993). The illusion of mental health. *American Psychologist, 48*, 1117–1131.

Sroufe, L. A., & Waters, E. (1977). Heart rate as a convergent measure in clinical and developmental research. *Merrill-Palmer Quarterly, 23*, 3–27.

Taylor, C. (1985). *Philosophy and the human sciences: Philosophical papers 2*. Cambridge, England: Cambridge University Press.

Toth, S. L., & Cicchetti, D. (1996). Patterns of relatedness, depressive symptomatology and perceived competence in maltreated children. *Journal of Consulting and Clinical Psychology, 64*, 32–41.

3

Psychoanalytic Theory and Creativity:
Cognition and Affect Revisited

Sandra W. Russ

The psychoanalytic conceptualization of creativity is rich and complex and encompasses the complexity of the creative process. Some of the basic tenets of this conceptualization have been tested and supported. Recent theories and research in other areas of psychology, such as cognitive psychology and social psychology, have advanced the understanding of the creative process and some of the findings are consistent with predictions from psychoanalytic theory. For example, the finding that positive affect facilitates creative problem solving supports the psychoanalytic view of a significant relationship between primary process and creative thinking. Applying such recent developments to theory can develop new concepts and generate new hypotheses. New conceptualizations then shed more light on how individual processes might actually work.

This chapter will review basic principles of psychoanalytic theory and creativity, research evidence for those principles, mood-induction research, new conceptualizations of affect and creativity, the role of children's play in facilitating creativity, future research directions, and implications for treatment.

Basic Concepts

The key concept in the area of psychoanalytic theory and creativity is primary process thinking. Although other facets of psychoanalytic theory pertain to creativity, primary process thinking is the key characteristic within the individual that enables creative thinking to occur. Therefore, this chapter focuses on aspects of primary process thinking.

Primary Process Thinking

S. Freud (1915/1958) first conceptualized primary process thought as an early, primitive system of thought that was drive laden and not subject to rules of logic or oriented to reality. A good example of primary process thinking is the kind of thinking that occurs in dreams. Dreams are illogical, are not oriented to rules of time and space, and frequently include affect-laden content and images. Dudek (1980) saw primary process as the surfacing of unconscious instinctual energy in the form of images or ideas. Holt (1977) categorized the drive-laden content in primary process thinking as oral, aggressive, and libidinal. As Holt developed a system to measure primary process thinking, he defined content properties and formal properties. Content properties include affect-laden oral, aggressive, and libidinal content. Formal properties include qualities of illogical thinking, condensation (fusion of two ideas or images), and loose associations. Formal expressions and content expressions of primary process may or may not go together. These definitions of primary process thinking imply a cognitive component and an affective component.

Access to primary process thought has been hypothesized to relate to creative thinking because associations are fluid and primitive images and ideas can be accessed and used. According to classic psychoanalytic theory, primary process thinking is characterized by "mobility of cathexis," that is, the energy behind the ideas and images is easily displaced (Arlow & Brenner, 1964). Therefore, there is a free flow of energy not bound by specific ideas or objects. In this mode of thinking, ideas are easily interchangeable and attention is widely and flexibly distributed. Consequently, access to primary process thinking should facilitate a fluidity of thought and flexibility of search among all ideas and associations. Martindale (1989) stated that "because primary process cognition is associative, it makes the discovery of new combinations of mental elements more likely" (p. 216).

There is much similarity between characteristics of primary process thinking and characteristics of two of the most important cognitive processes involved in creative thinking. According to Guilford (1968), divergent thinking and transformation abilities are the major cognitive processes that are unique to the creative process. Divergent thinking refers to the ability to generate a variety of associations to a word or solutions to a problem, and it flows in a number of directions. A typical item on a divergent thinking test would be, "How many uses for a brick can you think of?" A high scorer on this test would generate a high number of different, acceptable uses for the object. Individuals who can use primary process and the fluidity of thought and breadth of associations inherent in it should be highly divergent thinkers. They should also score high on Guilford's second important cognitive process, transformation abilities. These involve the ability to transform or revise what one knows into new patterns or configurations and to be flexible and break out of an old set. Again, the broad associations and flexible-thinking characteristic of primary process should facilitate transformation abilities. Although there are cognitive processes involved in creative thinking other than divergent production and transformation abilities, the role of primary process thinking has been thought to be most important in these two categories. Most of the research that has investigated the relationship between primary process and creativity has focused on these two cognitive processes.

Regression in the Service of the Ego

Kris's (1952) concept of "regression in the service of the ego" stressed the importance of being in control of primary process thinking. Kris postulated that creative individuals could regress, in a controlled fashion, and tap into primary process thinking. The individual could go back and forth between early, primary process thought and more mature, rational, secondary process thinking. Regression was an important concept because the individual would, at will, go back to an earlier, primitive mode of thought and use it adaptively for creative purposes. The creative individual could be distinguished from the individual with a thought disorder in that the creative individual was in charge of this regressive process and could logically evaluate the loose, primitive associations and images. Russ (1993) presented creative individuals' descriptions of the creative process that describe getting in touch with primary process thinking. One good example is a description of the free flow of associations in a monologue by the comedian Robin Williams. In commenting about the process, he said, "And sometimes there are times when you're just on it—when you say the muse is with you and it's just flowing and that's when you know that the well is open again and you just put in the pipe and you stand back and say 'yes'—you're in control but you're not—the characters are coming through you" (Culbane, 1988, pp. 5–14).

Several features of the conceptualization of primary process thinking according to classic psychoanalytic theory have limited the influence of primary process theory on current creativity research. First, as Urist (1980) pointed out, primary process thinking is based on the energy model. Most contemporary approaches have moved away from this model of instinctual energy. A second feature, regression, has also been difficult to operationalize and test. However, recent conceptualizations of primary process have moved away from both the energy model and the concept of regression. Holt (1967) proposed a structural model for primary process thought, with primary process as a group of structures having its own course of development. Noy (1969) also viewed primary process as developing its own structure. Rothenberg (1994) identified dimensions of the ego involving regression that are used to "unearth" and transform primary process material. His conceptualization grew out of his intensive interviews with novelists, poets, and playwrights during a time when they were creatively active. He carried out a similar study with Nobel prize laureates in science and literature. He proposed three ego processes important in creativity that are logic-transcending operations: (a) homospatial processes, superimposing visual images; (b) Janusian processes, simultaneous conceiving of opposites; and (c) articulation, joining and separating elements in a constant reworking process. In an empirical study of creative writers, superimposed images that were presented externally resulted in more creative metaphor production than side-by-side images. In another study, Nobel laureates produced more opposite responses to a word-association test than did other populations when intelligence was considered. Arieti (1976) and Suler (1980) also suggested that the concept of regression to an earlier mode of thought may not be necessary. They both proposed that primary process may be a separate entity that develops simultaneously with secondary process thought. Fischer and Pipp (1984) thought of primary process as a separate mode of thought that followed its own systematic developmental line. The implications of these different conceptualizations is that the mechanism for access to primary process may not be regression, but an entirely different kind of mechanism.

One of the overlooked features of primary process thinking is affect, an important aspect linking primary process to creativity and to contemporary theory and research in the creativity area.

Primary Process and Affect

Primary process thinking contains both cognitive and affective elements. The latter could play as important a role in creative thinking as the cognitive elements. Theoretically, affect is a major component of primary process thinking. The concepts of drive-laden and instinctual energy bring us into the realm of affect. Rapaport (1951) used the phrase "affect-charge" in discussing primary process thought. Primary process content, in Holt's (1967) conceptualization, contains categories of oral, libidinal, and aggressive affect. S. Freud (1895/1966), in "The Project for a Scientific Psychology," stated that primary process thought is frequently accompanied by affect.

Primary process thinking has usually been regarded as a blend of cognitive and affective processes (Martindale, 1981; Zimiles, 1981). A deeper and more refined understanding of the affective processes involved is needed in order to theorize and measure more effectively. Russ (1987) proposed that primary process is a subtype of affective content in cognition. Primary process content is material around which the child had experienced early intense feeling states (e.g., oral, anal, aggressive). Learning to regulate these intense emotions and affect-laden thoughts and images is a major developmental task. Children differ widely as to whether this content is thought about, how it is expressed in fantasy and play, and how it is integrated into fantasy and imagination. Pine and Holt (1960) suggested that primary process becomes a kind of cognitive style that reflects how affective material is dealt with. Russ (1987) proposed that current primary process expressions may reflect either current affect or a kind of "affective residue" in cognition left over from earlier developmental stages.

How primary process material is dealt with by the child might affect the kinds and amounts of memories that are encoded. Recent work in the area of memory and cognition suggests that affect influences the memory process.

Primary Process, Affect, and Creativity

Why should primary process and affect be important in the creative process? Russ (1993) developed a model of affect and creativity, based on theory and the research literature (see Figure 1). One major assumption of the model is that specific affective processes facilitate creative cognitive abilities. These affective processes are also related to global personality traits related to creativity. For purposes of the present discussion, the two affective processes of major interest are access to affect-laden thoughts, which includes primary process thinking, and openness to affect states. Access to affect-laden thoughts is the ability to call up thoughts with emotion-laden content. Primary process thinking and affective fantasy in daydreams and in play are examples of this category. Openness to affect states is the ability to experience the emotion itself. Comfort with intense emotion, the ability to experience and tolerate anxiety, and passionate involvement in a task or issue are examples of openness to affect states. A third affect category, cognitive integration of affective material, is also important. Although this category is probably more cognitive than affective, it does reflect both cognitive and affective elements. These affect categories have been found to be related to the cognitive processes of divergent thinking and transformation abilities (Dudek & Verreault, 1989; Russ, 1982; Russ & Grossman-McKee, 1990). In some studies, these processes have been found to facilitate creativity (Isen, Daubman, & Nowicki, 1987). I review this research later in this chapter.

According to psychoanalytic theory, the affective components of primary process are linked to creativity. S. Freud's (1926/1959) formulation that repression of "dangerous" drive-laden material leads to a more general intellectual restriction predicts that individuals with less access to affect-laden cognitions would have fewer associations in general. Mobility of energy and flexibility of thought in the affective realm should generalize to more neutral, non-affect-laden thoughts and ideas. Before moving to more recent conceptualizations of affect and creativity, I review the research literature. Relevant research literature includes research with primary process and mood-induction research.

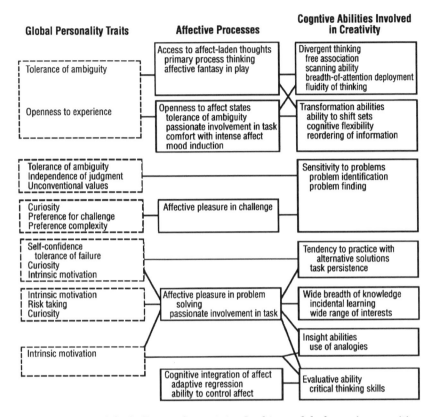

Figure 1. A model of affect and creativity. In this model, the major cognitive abilities that emerge as unique to and important in the creative process are linked to related specific affective processes and to global personality traits. In some cases, the personality traits are behavioral reflections of the underlying affective process. One assumption of this model is that these specific affective processes and personality traits facilitate creative cognitive abilities. From *Affect and Creativity: The Role of Affect and Play in the Creative Process* (p. 10), by S. Russ, 1993, Hillsdale, NJ: Erlbaum. Copyright 1993 by Lawrence Erlbaum Associates, Inc. Reprinted with permission.

Research Evidence

Primary Process Thinking Research

Most of the research investigating primary process thinking and creativity has used Holt's Scoring System for Primary Process Responses on the Rorschach (Holt, 1977; Holt & Havel, 1960). Research studies did not attempt to separate the cognitive dimension from the affective dimension of primary process thinking. Most of the research in the area was reviewed by Holt (1977), Suler (1980), and Russ (1993).

Holt made a major contribution to the field by operationalizing the construct of primary process thinking and developing a scoring system for the Rorschach that could achieve good interrater reliability and convincing validity data. As described by Russ (1993), the Holt system scores the responses that contain primary process content (aggressive and libidinal content that actually encompasses a broad range of affective content). The system measures the percentage of primary process content in the Rorschach protocol and the effectiveness of the control of that content. A controlled response would express primary process content in a way that fits the form of the blot and is appropriately qualified. For example, two talking bugs can be made into a more appropriate response by making them cartoon figures. It also measures formal characteristics of thought such as condensation and illogical associations. The scale was developed by Holt for use with adults. When used with children, the scale largely measures primary process content and adaptiveness of that. Scorings of formal characteristics are a very small percentage in children's protocols (Dudek, 1975; Russ, 1982). Major scores in Holt's Scoring System include the percentage of primary process (%PP) responses in the entire protocol; the Defense Demand (DD) score, which measures the intensity of the content; the Defense Effectiveness (DE) score, which measures the control and cognitive integration of primary process responses; and the Adaptive Regression (AR) score, which measures both the intensity of the primary process content and the integration of the content. The Holt System measures both access to affect-laden material and the cognitive integration of that material. Scores on Holt's system show whether an individual can allow affect-laden content to surface and be expressed. Scores also indicate how well controlled and well integrated that content is in cognition.

In adults, the AR score on the Rorschach has been significantly positively related to a number of measures of creativity (Cohen, 1961; Pine & Holt, 1960) and to problem-solving efficiency (Blatt, Allison, & Feirstein, 1969). The AR score was related to divergent thinking in the Pine and Holt (1960) study and to the ability to make remote associations (Murray & Russ, 1981). Gamble and Kellner (1968) found that creative individuals had greater access to primary process. In a study by Dudek (1968), there was more primitive primary process content (Level I in Holt's system) in artists than in nonartists and more primitive primary process in good artists than in poor artists. In another study by Dudek (1984), top-ranked creative architects produced more libidinal primary process content than lower ranked architects.

In children, age, gender, and specific measures and scores emerge as important factors. Dudek (1975), one of the first to study children in this context, found no relationship between primary process thinking on the Rorschach and divergent thinking on the Torrance tests in fourth graders. However, primary process expression on a drawing task was related to divergent thinking. Dudek concluded that the relationship between primary process and creativity is ambiguous in childhood and that children have not yet learned to use primary process adaptively. In a recent study by Dudek and Verreault (1989), creative children (fifth and sixth graders) gave significantly more total primary process ideation than did noncreative children, as measured by Holt's system as applied to the Torrance Tests of Creative Thinking. More creative children also demonstrated more effective use of regression in the service of the ego than did noncreative children when popular responses were used to determine defense effectiveness.

Rogolsky (1968) found no relationship between the AR score and artistic creativity in third-grade children. However, a new adaptive regression score that combined amount of primary process with control measures for the entire Rorschach protocol (including populars) did significantly relate to artistic creativity for third-grade boys but not for girls.

Russ's (1980, 1981, 1982, 1988) research studies investigating primary process on the Rorschach, achievement, and creativity in children obtained positive results. (A full review of Russ's research can be found in Russ, 1993.) However, gender differences repeatedly occurred, and different scores within Holt's system predicted creativity in different studies. In all studies, each child was individually administered the Rorschach according to Exner's (1974) system. Holt's (1970) scoring manual for primary process was followed exactly, except for two minor adaptations for use with a child population. There was no affect inquiry because of the difficulty many children have tolerating a long inquiry. However, affective expressions, verbal and nonverbal, were noted by the examiner and considered in the scoring. Also, the percept of spider was scored as an aggressive percept and given a low intensity rating, except for the common spider on Card X, which was not scored. Typical aggressive content in children's protocols were fighting animals, monsters, exploding volcanoes, blood, and scary insects. Typical oral content was people eating, food, and mouths. In Russ's studies, the mean percentage of primary process content in the entire Rorschach protocol was about 50% for these child populations.

In the first study, Russ (1980) found a significant positive relationship between the AR score and reading achievement in second-grade children, $r(37) = .54$, $p < .001$. This relationship remained significant ($r = .45$) after IQ was partialed out. The relationship also remained significant when productivity and general perceptual accuracy ($F+ \%$) were partialed out. In a third-grade follow-up with these children, the size of the relationship between third-grade AR scores and reading achievement remained consistent, $r(39) = .52$, $p < .001$ (Russ, 1981). Although reading achievement does not specifically speak to creativity, the underlying rationale for using this criterion was that children who had access to primary process thinking and integrated it well would be flexible problem solvers and be open to ideas. Thus, they should be better learners than children with less access to primary process content.

Russ's next series of studies specifically investigated the relationship between primary process thinking and creativity. In the first of these, Russ (1982) focused on the relationship between primary process thinking and transformation abilities in third-grade children, using two independent samples of third-grade children and Holt's scoring system for the Rorschach as the primary process measure. For a measure of flexibility of thinking for young children, Russ adapted the Luchins's Water-Jar Test (Luchins & Luchins, 1959). The task requires the child to break out of an old set in solving a problem and to discover a new, more adaptive approach. The child must see new relationships in old patterns and be able to shift sets.

The results found that, for boys, the AR score was significantly related to flexibility of shifting sets in both samples of children. That is, the ability to express well-controlled primary process content on the Rorschach was related to the ability to shift problem-solving strategies. This result was replicated with a second sample of children, suggesting the stability and robustness of this relationship. When samples were combined, the size of the correlation was .39 ($df = 34$), $p < .01$. This relationship was independent of IQ. For girls in both samples, AR was not related to the Luchins's task. In the second sample, the pure percentage of primary process predicted flexibility of shifting sets, $r(17) = .43, p < .05$, for girls.

The next study investigated the relationship between divergent thinking and primary process in a fifth-grade follow-up study of 53 children who remained from the third-grade samples (Russ, 1988). The results were significant for boys but not for girls. AR and percentage of primary process were significantly related to the Alternate Uses Test for boys, $r(27) = .34, p < .05$, and $r(27) = .33, p < .05$, respectively. Primary process scores did not predict divergent thinking for girls.

Russ and Grossman-McKee's (1990) study of second-grade children obtained the same pattern of gender differences. For boys, percentage of primary process on the Rorschach predicted divergent thinking on the Alternate Uses Test, $r(20) = .72, p < .001$. This relationship was independent of intelligence. There was no significant relationship for girls. AR did not predict divergent thinking for either gender. It may be that in children this young, the frequency of primary process expression rather than the integration of primary process is the more important aspect of primary process in creativity. This point was also made by Dudek and Verreault (1989).

In summary, all of Russ's studies with the Rorschach found gender differences in the magnitude of the correlations between primary process and creativity. For boys, primary process was significantly related to divergent thinking and to transformation abilities. Usually, the integration of primary process material (AR) was the best predictor, but percentage of primary process content was also a significant predictor in several studies. For girls, in most studies, there was no significant relationship between any primary process scores and creativity. In one study (Russ, 1982), percentage of primary process did predict flexibility on the Luchin's Water-Jar Test.

The gender differences in the relationship between primary process thinking and cognitive processes thought to be important in creativity that occurred in the third-grade, fifth-grade follow-up, and second-grade studies are consistent with other studies of adults and children. With children, Rogolsky's new AR score predicted artistic creativity for boys, not for girls. With adults, Holt (1977) stated that, in general, in studies that relate AR with creativity criteria, "negative findings from well-executed studies came entirely from samples of females" (p. 413). With adults, the relationship between AR and divergent thinking (Pine & Holt, 1960) and between AR and associational fluency (Murray & Russ, 1981) occurred for males, but not for females. Suler's (1980) thorough review of the literature also concluded that gender is an important moderator variable. Positive results occasionally occur with female samples when the pure amount of primary process is the predictor. Pine and Holt (1960) concluded from their results with adult samples that the amount of primary process expressed was the better predictor of creativity in female participants, whereas integration of primary process (AR) was the better predictor for males. This is consistent with Russ's (1982) study with third-grade children, in which percentage of primary process content did predict flexibility for shifting sets in the second sample of girls. On the other hand, percentage of primary process content has also significantly predicted divergent thinking for second- and fifth-grade boys.

A related finding is that in both samples in the Russ (1982) third-grade study, boys had a significantly greater percentage of primary process content than girls. This was specifically true for aggressive percepts. In the fifth-grade study, there was a trend ($p < .07$) for boys to have a greater percentage of primary process responses. Kleinman and Russ (1988) also found that fourth- and fifth-grade boys expressed significantly more primary process content on the Rorschach than did girls. These results are consistent with other studies in the child literature. Boys have consistently shown more aggression in their behavior and play (Maccoby & Jacklin, 1974). Girls recall fewer details of aggressive modeling (Bandura, 1965) and require longer tachistoscopic exposures than do boys for the aggressive scenes (Kagan & Moss, 1962). Russ (1980) speculated that there may be more cultural taboos against expression of primary process material for girls than for boys.

In summary, a substantial body of research suggests that access to affect-laden primary process thinking is related to cognitive processes important to creativity for males. Specifically, primary process thinking relates to divergent thinking and to transformation abilities in males. The results are consistent with different samples and researchers. For females, the results are mixed. A few studies find that pure access to primary process is related to creativity. One possible explanation of the gender differences may be that females do not have as much access to primary process thinking as do males. Cultural taboos against the expression of primary process content for girls, especially aggressive content, could lead to a restriction of primary process thought. This restriction could affect the development of the relationship between primary process and creativity in girls. Another possibility is that the major measure of primary process thinking, Holt's system for the Rorschach, may not be a valid and appropriate measure for females. Girls give fewer primary process responses than do boys. Inhibitions in the test-taking process may be a factor for girls (Kogan, 1974). Another type of situation, such as play, might be a more natural form of expression for girls.

Mood-Induction Research

A second line of investigation relevant to psychoanalytic theory and creativity is mood-induction research. The mood-induction paradigm provides a way of altering affect states so that the effect on cognitive processes of both adults and children can be observed. The mood-induction procedure developed by Mischel, Ebbesen, and Zeiss (1972) has the experimenter ask children to think affectively valenced thoughts such as "Think about something that is fun." Children recall and think about an experience associated with a particular emotion. Affect can be induced also by giving gifts or showing films.

A growing body of research has found that induced affect facilitates creative thinking. Alice Isen has carried out a series of important, carefully controlled studies in the mood-induction area. In a study by Isen and Daubman (1984), adults in a positive affect mood-induction condition categorized stimuli more inclusively than did controls. Isen (1985) found that positive affect resulted in more divergent associations to neutral words than in controls. Isen et al. (1987) found that induced positive affect (induced by a comedy film) resulted in more creative problem solving than did control conditions. The problem-solving task in one study was the Duncker (1945) candle task, a measure of functional fixedness. To solve the problem, one must break a set and consider alternative solutions to the problem. This problem seems quite similar to Luchins's Water-Jar Test used in Russ's (1982) study. In Russ's study, in two separate samples of boys, access to primary process material was related to the ability to break the set. Positive results for girls occurred in one of Russ's samples. Both the Duncker candle task and the Luchins's Water-Jar Test are measures of Guilford's transformation ability. Isen et al. (1987) reported no gender differences.

Isen et al. (1987) also found that positive affect improved performance on the Remote Associates Test, a measure of creativity that calls for diverse associations and seeing the relatedness of ideas. Isen concluded that the underlying mechanism for these results is that positive affect cues positive memories and a large amount of cognitive material. This process results in defocused attention and a more complex cognitive context. This, in turn, results in a greater range of associations and interpretations. There is an increasing awareness of different aspects of stimuli and more ways of relating and combining information.

Isen et al. (1987) induced a negative affect state, using a film, and found no effect on problem solving. They cautioned against overinterpreting the lack of results with the negative affect condition. The film was an extremely negative one of the Holocaust that may have aroused very strong negative affect.

Jausovec (1989) found that induced positive affect facilitated analogical transfer in ill-defined problems, a cognitive task. Analogical transfer is thought to be important in creative thinking (Sternberg, 1988), and ill-defined problems are those with a number of different possible solutions. Another finding by Jausovec was that positive affect impaired performance on a logical problem-solving task. He concluded from these studies that affect influences the way in which material is processed. Positive affect facilitates the uses of analogy in insight, perhaps by creating a more complex cognitive context. More associations are available that increase the likelihood that a "pointer" in memory will trigger the analogy. Positive affect interferes with logical problem solving because the increased complexity of the cognitive context brought about by the affect state increases the amount of information in the system. Jausovec found no effect of negative affect on problem solving. However, as Isen did, Jausovec used a very negative Holocaust film.

The one published study in the child area also found that induced positive affect in eighth-grade children facilitated problem solving on the Duncker Candle Task, generating examples of categories of a word and generating unusual uses of words (Greene & Noice, 1988).

These mood-induction studies are important because one can infer causation from the results. Induced positive affect facilitates creative problem solving. The primary process and creativity research is all correlational, although psychoanalytic theory predicts that access to primary process facilitates creativity. Although primary process thinking is not the same as an induced mood state, there are similarities in these affective processes. One can speculate that similar underlying mechanisms that facilitate creativity are operating in both processes.

New Conceptualizations of Affect and Creativity

The findings of the primary process research and the mood-induction research are consistent with Bower's (1981) conceptualization of affect and memory processes (Russ, 1993). The work on mood and memory suggests that the search process for associations is broadened by the involvement of emotion. This broadened search process facilitates creative cognitive processes such as divergent thinking and transformation abilities. The role of primary process thinking in creativity is better understood if it is conceptualized as mood-relevant cognition (Russ, 1993). When stirred, it triggers a broad associative network. Bower's (1981) classic article, "Mood and Memory," reviewed a series of studies and presented a theoretical framework of affect and memory processes. Bower induced happy and sad moods in adults by hypnotic suggestion. Participants demonstrated a greater percentage of recall of those experiences that were affectively congruent with the mood during recall. Individuals in an induced pleasant mood state recalled a greater percentage of recent pleasant life experiences than of unpleasant life experiences. The opposite effect occurred for the unpleasant mood states. The same effect held for childhood memories. Emotions also influenced free associations and imaginative fantasies. These results reflected two basic phenomena:

1. *Mood congruity effect*: People attend to and learn more about events that match their emotional state.
2. *Mood state dependent retention*: If, during recall, the original emotional state when the material was originally learned is reinstated, then recall is better.

Bower's associative network theory was developed to explain these phenomena. Each emotion is a memory unit and has a special node or unit in memory. The activation of the emotion unit aids the retrieval of events associated with it. It primes emotional themata for use in free association, fantasies, and perceptual categorization. Each emotion node includes autonomic reactions, expressive behavior, descriptions, and verbal labels. When activated, it spreads activation through memory structures. Therefore, if material was learned in a specific affect state, search cues are activated in memory when that affect state occurs. This effect is most evident in the free-recall condition.

In the encoding process itself, emotion should affect the salience of mood-congruent material for selective attention and learning. The associative links would be stronger for mood-congruent events. The emotional response is part of the associative network. Bower's (1981) theory is applicable to the area of creativity because the search process is broadened by the involvement of emotion. A broad search process would aid divergent thinking and transformation abilities.

Since 1981, a number of studies have empirically supported Bower's theory and empirical results. Rholes, Riskind, and Lane (1987) have reviewed these studies. For example, Clark and Teasdale (1982) demonstrated that, in naturally occurring depression, there was an increase in access to memories of affectively consistent life experiences. Rholes et al. (1987) expanded Bower's theory and discussed mood-related cognitions. Affect states activate a set of relevant cognitions that stir other memories and stir mood-related cognitions. A cognitive priming process occurs. Both positive and negative affect states show activation of mood-relevant cognition. Natale and Hanlas (1982) found that induced depression caused a decrease in recall of pleasant life experiences and tended to cause the recall of more unpleasant life experiences. However, as Rholes et al. (1987) concluded, positive mood induction has stronger effects on memory than does negative mood induction. They speculated that it may be harder in general to gain access to negative content.

Although Bower and Mayer (1989) more recently concluded that mood-dependent memory was an "unreliable chance event" (p. 145), researchers have continued to study the phenomenon. Eich (1995) summarized current thinking in the field as supporting the existence of mood-dependent memory under certain conditions, stressing the importance of the effectiveness of the mood manipulation. Moreover, mood state affects internal events and self-generated thoughts more than do externally generated stimuli. Finally, mood influences memory more in free recall than in situations in which external cues are provided. Riskind (1989) identified another condition, personal relevance of the material. Mood has more of an impact on memory for personal material than for impersonal material. According to Riskind, mood primes cognitive schemas and ideational themes.

Primary process thinking might be conceptualized as mood-relevant cognition, occurring when emotion nodes are activated. Perhaps emotion and cognition are fused in many primary process thoughts. If, as Russ (1987) proposed, primary process is a subtype of affect in cognition that consists of content around which the child had experienced early intense feeling states (e.g., oral, anal, aggressive), then current primary process expressions could reflect these early encodings of fused affect and cognition. The primary process content was stored when emotion was present. Access to this primary process material would activate emotion nodes and associations, thus broadening the search process.

It is also possible that some cognitive and affective components of primary process are separate dimensions. This conceptualization would be consistent with the view of Zajonc (1980, 1990) that affect and cognition can at times be two separate processes. Affective reactions can occur without prior involvement of cognitive processes. Cognition and affect are two interacting but independent functions. Furthermore, some stimuli pull for affective responses without cognitive involvement.

Zajonc's (1980, 1990) hypothesis is consistent with recent work by LeDoux (1989). In research with rats, LeDoux found that the amygdala triggers an emotional reaction before the thinking brain has fully processed the nerve signals. The amygdala can receive input from the senses before going through the cortex. LeDoux referred to the existence of emotional memories. His work has discovered neural pathways that do not pass through the cortex. Thus, the emotional system can act independently of the cognitive system. LeDoux suggested that these precognitive emotions are functional in infants during the early formative years. Behavior is affected, but there is no conscious memory of the events.

Primary process thinking could involve pure cognitive components. For example, Martindale (1989) theorized that creative individuals engage more than do noncreative individuals in states of defocused attention, during which a large number of nodes (neurons or groups of neurons) are activated simultaneously. Defocused attention is more likely to occur during low cortical arousal, and there is evidence that primary process thinking involves defocused attention and low cortical arousal (Martindale, 1981).

Primary process could be a mode of thinking that is dominant in processing stimuli that are unconscious or below the level of awareness. In a review of the literature on subliminal perception, Masling (1992) concluded that the spread of associations is greater when stimuli do not quite reach awareness. A study by Spence and Holland (1962) found that subliminal presentation of a word resulted in greater recall of associated words than did no presentation or above-threshold presentation of the word. They speculated that a different pattern of cognitive activity with different associative processes operated in reduction of awareness situations. Masling (1992) hypothesized that a "subliminal message stimulates a broad band of association pathways, allowing a spread of activation over a wide area of association traces" (p. 273). This broad band would be facilitative in tasks requiring divergent thinking and transformation abilities.

In summary, Bower's (1981) associative network theory and Martindale's (1989) defocused attention framework might explain different aspects of primary process thinking. Bower's theory speaks to the importance of affect and affect-laden fantasy in facilitating creativity. Individuals who are open to affect states and to affect-laden cognition would have access to more cues that activate other nodes in the search process than individuals who are closed off to those states. Isen et al. (1987) explained their findings that positive affect induction facilitated creativity by citing Bower's theory. In essence, individuals who are more open to affect would activate more emotion nodes and emotion-relevant associations than would individuals who are less open. This aids the divergent thinking process by increasing the number of associations available. It would also aid the ability to shift sets, see new solutions to problems, and develop new insights. The creative process would also be facilitated because more emotionally salient material would get coded and stored when individuals were emotionally aroused. For individuals open to affect, more would "get in," thus providing the individual with a richer network of affect-relevant associations. There is evidence that creative individuals are more sensitive and open to experience (McCrae & Costa, 1987) than noncreative people. This storing of affective content would be especially important for artistic creativity, wherein one is often dealing with affect and the transformation of affect content into universal symbols. Richards (1990) has concluded that mild positive mood elevation may carry advantages for creativity. Kaufmann and Vosburg (1995) found that a self-report measure of hypomania was significantly related to divergent thinking and number of creative accomplishments.

The physiological state that accompanies primary process thinking may also facilitate creativity. Martindale's (1981, 1989) view of low cortical arousal and defocused attention hypothesizes the existence of a different cognitive process that also aids creativity. It is possible that individuals who are comfortable with affect and primary process thinking let these low cortical arousal states occur because they are comfortable with the results. This is what Kris (1952) was saying with his concept of "regression in the service of ego." Individuals who can gain controlled access to primary process are more likely to let this state occur.

Finally, primary process also involves the preverbal origins of this thinking and visual imagery. Recently, work by Marcus Raichle with the position emission tomography scanner showed that the visual processing area is involved in some memory tasks (Begley, 1991). Raichle found that a number of different areas of the brain are involved in memory tasks. One might speculate that access to primary process preverbal images somehow aids search strategies in creative thinking. As presented by Penrose (1989), Einstein spoke of the importance of images in his thinking process:

> The words or the language, as they are written or spoken, do not seem to play any role in any mechanism of thought. The psychical entities which seem to serve as elements of thought are certain signs and more or less clear images which can be "voluntarily" reproduced and combined. The above mentioned elements are, in my case, of visual and some muscular type. Conventional words or other signs have to be sought for laboriously only in a second stage, when the mentioned associative play is sufficiently established and can be reproduced at will. (p. 423)

Play and Creativity

Another important body of research in the area of creativity is that of play and creativity. Play is important because it is a context in which so many creative processes are expressed and developed. Many of the cognitive, affective, and personality processes important to creativity occur in play. As Waelder (1933) has said, play is a "leave of absence from reality" (p. 222). Play is a place to let primary process thinking occur and could be important in its development. Russ (in press) has recently reviewed the play and creativity area. The following discussion is drawn from that review.

The type of play most important to the area of creativity is *pretend play*. Pretend play is play that involves pretending, the use of fantasy and make-believe, and the use of symbolism. Fein (1987) stated that pretend play is a symbolic behavior in which "one thing is playfully treated as if it were something else" (p. 282). Fein also stated that pretense is charged with feelings and emotional intensity; affect is inter-twined with pretend play. Fein viewed such play as a natural form of creativity.

Slade and Wolf (1994) stressed the importance of studying the role of play in both the development of cognitive structure and the mastering of emotions. Historically, these two questions have been studied separately, usually by different theoretical and research traditions. As Rubin, Fein, and Vandenberg (1983) have pointed out, most of the measures of children's play have assessed cognitive processes, not affective processes. Thus, they refer to the "cognification" of play. Slade and Wolf (1994) posited that the cognitive and affective functions of play are intertwined: "Just as the development of cognitive structures may play an important role in the resolution of emotional conflict, so emotional consolidation may provide an impetus to cognitive advances and integration" (p. xv). They imply a working together of emotional functioning and cognitive structure. This working together could be especially important in creativity—access to emotions might alter developing cognitive structure and vice versa.

Fein (1987) studied 15 "master players" and categorized her observations. She concluded that good pretend play consisted of (a) cognitive characteristics such as object substitutions and the manipulation of object representations and (b) the affective characteristic of what she called *affective relations*. Affective relations are symbolic units that represent affective relationships such as *fear of, love of,* and *anger at.* Fein proposed an affective symbol system that represents real or imagined experience at a general level. She stated that these affective units constitute affect-binding representational templates that store salient information about affect-laden events. The units are "manipulated, interpreted, coordinated and elaborated in a way that makes affective sense to the players" (Fein, 1987, p. 292). These affective units are a key part of pretend play. In fact, Fein viewed pretend play as symbolic behavior organized around emotional and motivational issues. Fein implied that this affective symbol system is especially important for creative thinking. She stated that divergent thinking abilities such as daydreams, pretend play, or drawing can activate the affective symbol system. One of Fein's major conclusions is that creative processes cannot be studied independently of an affective symbol system, a system probably facilitated through pretend play.

Fein's (1987) conceptualization is consistent with the concepts of Bower's (1981) associative network theory and the psychoanalytic concept of pri-mary process and creativity. Primary process content could be stored in these affective symbol systems. This affective symbol system could translate into memory systems that operate according to Bower's associative network theory. Children who are more expressive of and open to affective content would develop a richer, more complete and more complex store of affect symbols. This richer store of affect symbols would facilitate divergent thinking and transformation abilities because it provides a broader range of associations and a more flexible manipulation of images and ideas.

Fein also suggested that pretend play facilitates the development of an affective symbol system and, in turn, creativity. Vygotsky (1930/1967) also thought that play facilitated creativity. In a recent translation and integration of Vygotsky's work, Smolucha (1992) stated that Vygotsky viewed creativity as a developmental process facilitated through play. Vygotsky (1930/1967) stated, "The child's play activity is not simply a recollection of past experience but a creative reworking that combines impressions and constructs from them new realities addressing the needs of the child" (p. 7). Through play, children develop combinatory imagination, that is, the ability to combine elements of experience into new situations and new behaviors. Combinatory imagination is part of artistic and scientific creativity. By adolescence, play evolves into fantasy and imagination, which combines with conceptual thinking. Imagination has two parts in the adolescent: objective imagination and subjective imagination. Subjective imagination includes emotion and serves the emotional life. Impulse and thinking are combined in the activity of creative thinking.

Research Evidence

A growing body of research has found a relationship between play and creativity. Most of the research has been correlational in nature. J. L. Singer and Singer (1976), in a review of the literature, concluded that the capacity for imaginative play is positively related to divergent thinking. D. L. Singer and Rummo (1973) found a relationship between play and divergent thinking in kindergarten children. Play was found to facilitate divergent thinking in preschool children by Dansky and Silverman (1973) and by Dansky (1980). Dansky and Silverman found that children who played with objects during a play period gave significantly more uses for those objects than did control children. In a later study, Dansky (1980) found that make-believe play was the mediator of the relationship between play and divergent thinking. Free play facilitated divergent thinking, but only for children who engaged in make-believe play. Also, in this second study, play had a generalized effect in that the objects in the play period were different from those in the test period. These two experimental studies are important because they show a direct effect of play on divergent thinking.

Dansky's (1980) theoretical rationale for hypothesizing that play would facilitate divergent thinking was that the process of free combination of objects and ideas involved in play is similar to the elements involved in creative thinking. Dansky speculated that the free symbolic transformations inherent in pretend play helped create a temporary cognitive set toward the loosening of old associations. These ideas are consistent with the work of Sutton-Smith (1966), who stressed the role of play in the development of flexibility in problem solving. Play provides the opportunity to explore new combinations of ideas to develop new associations for old objects. The object transformations that occur in play help develop the capacity to see old objects in new ways. Kogan (1983) also suggested that children's play behavior involves a search for alternate modes of relating to the object, a process similar to searching for alternate uses for objects in divergent thinking tasks.

Until recently, the research on play and creativity has focused on cognitive variables as the explanatory mechanisms underlying the relationship. The various theoretical explanations of affect in play and creativity are just beginning to be tested.

Lieberman's (1977) work supports a relationship between affect and divergent thinking. She focused on the variable of playfulness, which included the affective components of spontaneity and joy. She found that playful kindergarten children did better on divergent thinking tasks than nonplayful children. D. L. Singer and Singer (1990) reported that positive affect was related to imaginative play. J. L. Singer and Singer (1981) also found that preschoolers who were rated as high-imagination players had significantly more themes of danger and power than did children with low imagination.

I was especially interested in investigating affective dimensions of play and creativity in my research program. In order to do so, I developed the Affect in Play Scale (APS). The APS was developed, then, to meet the need for a standardized measure of affect in pretend play.

Play sessions are individually administered 5-min standardized puppet-play sessions. The play task uses two neutral-looking puppets, one boy and one girl, with three small blocks laid out on a table. The instructions are standardized and direct the children to play with the puppets any way they like for 5 min in a free-play period. The play task and instructions are unstructured enough that individual differences in the use of affect in pretend play can emerge. The APS is appropriate for children from 6 to 10 years of age. The play session is videotaped so that coding can occur later.

The APS measures the amount and types of affective expression in children's pretend play. It also measures cognitive dimensions of the play, such as quality of fantasy and imagination. Conceptually, the APS taps three dimensions of affect in fantasy: (a) affect states—actual emotional experiencing through expression of feeling states; (b) affect-laden thoughts—affective content themes that include emotional content themes and primary process themes; and (c) cognitive integration of affect.

These three categories of affect are three of the five affective dimensions I proposed to be important in the creative process (Russ, 1993). This conceptualization of affect and creativity guided the development of the scale. In addition, both Holt's (1977) Scoring System for Primary Process on the Rorschach and J. L. Singer's (1973) play scales were used as models. Details of the instructions and scoring system for the APS can be found in Russ (1993).

There are eight major scores for the APS:

1. Total frequency of units of affective expression. A unit is defined as one scorable expression by an individual puppet. A unit can be the expression of an affect state, an affect theme, or a combination of the two.
2. Variety of affect categories. There are 11 possible affect categories, the last 6 of which are primary process categories. The categories are Happiness/Pleasure; Anxiety/Fear; Sadness/Hurt; Frustration/Displeasure; Nurturance/Affection; Aggression; Oral; Oral Aggression; Anal; Sexual; and Competition. The categories can also be divided into positive and negative affect groups.
3. Mean intensity of affective expression for each affective unit (1–5 rating).
4. Mean Intensity × Frequency of Affect.

5. Comfort in play score (1–5 global rating). This score captures the child's enjoyment of and involvement in the play.
6. Global quality of fantasy (1–5 global rating).
7. Mean quality of fantasy, based on subscores of organization, elaboration, imagination, and repetition.
8. Affective integration score. This score captures the cognitive integration of affective material. The most useful combination of scores has been the Mean Quality of Fantasy × Frequency of Affect score.

Once the APS was constructed, pilot studies were carried out to ensure that the task was appropriate for young children and would result in adequate individual differences among normal school populations (Russ, Grossman-McKee, & Rutkin, 1984). By 1984, the basics of the task and scoring system were in place. Recent studies have resulted in refinement of the scoring criteria and a shortening of the play period from 10 min to 5 min. Children who express a high frequency of affect in their play typically have the puppets playing competitive games, fighting with each other, having fun together, eating (oral content), and expressing affection.

Affect in Play Scale and Creativity

To date, my colleagues and I have carried out nine validity studies with the APS. In each study, we obtained interrater reliabilities on 15 or 20 respondents. Interrater reliabilities have been good, usually in the .80s and .90s, using a variety of different raters. We also obtained split-half reliability for frequency of affective expression comparing the second and fourth minutes with the third and fifth minutes. We found a split-half reliability of .85, which is very adequate (Russ, 1993; Russ & Peterson, 1990).

Two types of validating criteria have been used. One body of studies investigated affect in play and creativity. A second line of studies, not reviewed in this chapter, investigated play and coping/adjustment.

The first study in the affect and creativity area (Russ & Grossman-McKee, 1990) investigated the relationships among the APS, divergent thinking, and primary process thinking on the Rorschach in 60 first- and second-grade children. As predicted, affective expression in play was significantly positively related to divergent thinking, as measured by the Alternate Uses Test. All major scores on the APS were significantly correlated with divergent thinking, with correlations ranging from .23 (df = 58, p < .05) between comfort and divergent thinking to .42 (df = 58, p < .001) between frequency of affective expression and divergent thinking. All correlations remained significant when IQ was partialed out, because IQ had such low correlations with the APS. The lack of relationship between intelligence and any of the play scores is consistent with the theoretical model for the development of the scale and is similar to the results of J. L. Singer (1973). Also, there were no gender differences in the pattern of correlations between the APS and divergent thinking. This study also found a relationship between the amount of primary process thinking on the Rorschach and the APS scores. Children who had more primary process responses on the Rorschach had more primary process in their play, more affect in their play, and higher fantasy scores than did children with less primary process on the Rorschach. This is an important finding because it shows consistency in the construct of affective expression across two different types of situations.

The finding of a relationship between affect in play and divergent thinking (Russ & Grossman-McKee, 1990) was replicated by Russ and Peterson (1990; Russ, 1993), who used a larger sample of 121 first- and second-grade children. Once again, all the APS scores were significantly positively related to the Alternate Uses Test, independent of intelligence. Again, there were no gender differences in the correlations. Thus, with this replication, we can have more confidence in the robustness of the finding of a relationship between affect in pretend play and creativity in young children.

An important question about the APS is whether it is indeed measuring two separate dimensions of play (an affective dimension and a cognitive dimension) or is measuring one dimension (an affect in fantasy dimension). The results of two separate factor analyses with the scale suggest two separate dimensions. In the Russ and Peterson (1990) study, a factor analysis of the total sample was carried out using the principal-components analysis with oblique rotation. An oblique solution yielded two separate factors as the best solution. The first and dominant dimension appears to be cognitive. Imagination, organization, quality of fantasy, and comfort loaded on this first dimension. The second factor appears to be affective. Frequency of affective expression, variety of affect categories, and intensity of affect loaded on this second factor. The factors, although separate, shared a significant amount of variance (r = .76), suggesting that they overlap. A recent study by D'Angelo (1995) found two identical factors, one cognitive and one affective, with a sample of 95 first-, second-, and third-grade children. Future studies with the APS should use factor scores on the cognitive and affective factors as predictors of creativity.

Another interesting finding by D'Angelo (1995) was a significant relationship between the APS and J. L. Singer's (1973) imaginative play predisposition interview. Good players in the APS reported that they prefer activities that require using imagination.

A recent study (Russ, Robins, & Christiano, 1995) followed up the first and second graders in the Russ and Peterson (1990) study who were then fifth and sixth graders. This was a longitudinal study that explored the ability of the APS to predict creativity over a 4-year period (5 years in some cases, because the study took 2 years to complete). Thirty-one children agreed to participate in the follow-up. The major finding was that quality of fantasy ($r = .34$, $p < .05$) and imagination ($r = .42$, $p < .01$) on the APS predicted divergent thinking over a 4-year period. The correlation between variety of affect and divergent thinking was .25 but did not reach significance, possibly because of the small sample size. My colleagues and I also administered an adapted version of the play task to the older children with instructions "to put on a play with the puppets." We then scored the task on the basis of scoring criteria for the APS. Raters did not know the earlier scores. We found good stability in the dimensions being measured by the APS. For example, the size of the correlation between the two frequency of affect scores was .33 ($p < .05$); between the two variety of affect scores, it was .38 ($p < .05$); and between the two frequency of positive affect scores, it was .51 ($p < .01$). These correlations were for two scores separated by 5 years. In general, the size of the correlations is excellent for a period of 4 and 5 years and supports enduring, stable constructs of affective expression in fantasy that are predictive of creative thinking over time. These findings also suggest an enduring quality to the affective and cognitive dimensions of the APS over a 5-year period.

Future Research Directions

One important question in research in affect and creativity is whether the relationship between affect and cognitive creative processes is supported only for primary process affect categories, as psychoanalytic theory would suggest, or is true for all affect categories. Psychoanalytic theory had stressed that it is the access to "dangerous," taboo-laden primary process material, around which the individual has experienced conflict, that facilitates creative thinking. Repression of this uncomfortable content inhibits the creative process. This question was specifically addressed in two studies. Russ and Grossman-McKee (1990) found that primary process affect in play was significantly related to divergent thinking, whereas non–primary process thinking was not. The difference in the size of the correlations was significant. However, Russ and Peterson (1990) found that both primary process content and non–primary process content were significantly related to divergent thinking. In addition, the mood-induction research findings that positive affect facilitates creativity suggests that affect categories other than primary process content also facilitate creativity. The complex question of the differential effects of different types of affect and different amounts of affect intensity on creativity is an important area for future research.

The effect of negative affect on creativity needs to be systematically investigated. Most of the mood-induction research found no effect. Much of the Rorschach and the play research has found relationships between negative affect and creativity. In Russ's research with play, for example, many of the play themes for boys were in the aggressive affect category. Perhaps what will emerge in future research is a curvilinear relationship between negative affect and creativity (Russ, 1993). Negative affect may facilitate creativity when it is of low to moderate levels. Negative affect in play could be a very mild amount of negative affect that cues memories and associations. In play, most children are in charge of the amount of negative affect and the pace of its expression. In more intense mood induction, where a Holocaust film is shown, the intense affect could interfere with creative thinking. This finding would be consistent with research on anxiety and problem solving and research by Easterbrook (1959) that found that negative affect resulted in constriction of thinking and a decrease in cue utilization. This type of curvilinear relationship has been found by Toplyn and Maguire (1991) for creativity under different levels of noise conditions for highly original respondents.

Another important question for future research is the differential effects of affect-laden fantasy as opposed to affect states on creativity. It is possible that these two hypothesized dimensions of affect are so intertwined that they are actually one dimension. Riskind (1989) has made the important point that, in the mood and memory research, mood might be better conceptualized as a cognitive state rather than a subjective mood state. A mood is characterized by cognitive sets, schemas, and themes. In the APS, although affect states and affect-laden fantasy are conceptualized as different processes, the total frequency of affect score is composed of both types of affective processes. Although it would be a complex coding procedure to score the affect–fantasy dimension separately from the affect state dimension in one affect unit expression, if reliable measurement could be achieved, it would be useful to tease out separate effects and investigate this question. Currently, mood-induction studies may be best at investigating affect states, whereas studies that manipulate instructions for the Rorschach, Thematic Apperception Test, and pretend play may be better for investigating the effect of affect-laden cognition and primary process on creative processes.

Gender differences should continue to be investigated. Much of the research has supported the relationship between primary process thinking and creativity for males, but not for females. However, in play situations, there were no gender differences in the correlations between primary process expression and creativity measures or for the broader affective measures and creativity. The APS has proved to be a valid instrument for both boys and girls. On the APS, boys give significantly more aggressive responses than girls. However, there is a wide range of possible affect scores categories. Obviously, there are more opportunities for different types of affective expression than on the Rorschach. There are no gender differences on the APS in the total amount of affect expressed. Thus, the play scores may reflect the girls' true ability for access to and expression of affect material and primary process material. Nevertheless, the question of whether girls are at a disadvantage because they express less aggression in play and in fantasy needs to be addressed. Does access to aggressive percepts and ideas have a unique relationship to creative thinking?

The role of affect in specific cognitive processes important in creativity needs to be investigated. Different types of affective processes could facilitate different types of creative cognitive processes in various ways. Positive and negative affect could differentially influence divergent thinking and transformation abilities. All types of cognitive abilities important in creative thinking should be investigated. For example, Rothenberg (1994) stated that the three ego processes he identified as important in creativity produce transformations of affect and experience that can induce mental tension. One might speculate that individuals who can tolerate superimposed imagery and the simultaneous consideration of opposites can tolerate uncomfortable affect or might actually enjoy the tension that develops. Runco (1994) has postulated that creative individuals can tolerate the necessary tension involved in the creative process. One would expect that if studies similar to Rothenberg's with creative adults were carried out with children using age-appropriate tasks, similar results would be found. Children who were comfortable with feelings and could tolerate tension should be more likely to engage in homospatial and Janusian thought.

Longitudinal studies are needed to investigate the development of cognitive and affective processes important in creativity. Are there different stages of development for different kinds of cognitive creative processes? What is normal development for the different affective processes? Are the correlations between affect measures and creativity tasks stable over time, or are different types of affective processes better predictors of creativity in adulthood than in childhood? Only carefully designed longitudinal studies will answer these questions.

Finally, the mechanisms that underlie the relationships among primary process, affect, and creativity need to be explored. For example, the reason that positive affect induction facilitates divergent thinking needs to be investigated. Can it be shown that positive affect does increase the number of mood-relevant memories? Will an increase in mood-relevant memories facilitate divergent thinking? Which types of divergent thinking tasks are most affected? Very specific questions about specific tasks and processes need to be addressed in order to increase understanding of the creative process and how to facilitate the creative process in children and in adults.

Implications for Psychoanalytic Treatment

Theory and research both suggest that access in a controlled fashion to affect-laden fantasy and affect states is an adaptive resource for the child and adult. The ability to think about and express emotion should facilitate creative problem solving.

Psychotherapy for adults should result in increased access to affect-laden material. As the individual gains access to taboo-laden primary process material and to repressed feeling states, then thinking should become freed-up. As these memories and affect states are stirred, the associative network should be more available. Although the main goal of psychotherapy, in most cases, is not to foster creativity, enhanced creativity should be a by-product of successful psychotherapy.

Psychotherapy can also help individuals work through conflicts that are blocking creative work (Gedo, 1990). Fear of risk taking or fear of success are examples of conflicts that might interfere with creativity. Some individuals might be concerned that if conflicts are resolved, then the "grist-for-the-mill" for their creative work would be removed. Thus, they might avoid psychotherapy. I would speculate that the affective and cognitive processes important for creativity would not be negatively interfered with. The content that was grist-for-the-mill, such as fear of separation and loss or sexual images, would change. Other issues would replace them as content in the creative work. Therapy can also be an integral part of the creative development of the individual. Middlebrook (1991) described how poet Anne Sexton used psychotherapy to develop her creativity. As Middlebrook pointed out, the therapist was internalized as part of her creative mind.

Play is especially helpful to children in that affective and cognitive processes important in creativity are partially developed in play. The therapist can focus on play in two ways. First, the therapist can use play as a therapeutic tool in therapy. Traditionally, much change occurs in therapy through the process of play (A. Freud, 1965). Erikson (1963) stated that children use play to gain mastery over traumatic events and everyday conflicts. Play is a major tool of conflict resolution. Therapists use play to help children "work through" conflicts and, to use Waelder's (1933) term, *digest events*. Second, the therapist can help the child become a better player, so that, after therapy, the child can continue to use play to express emotions and affect-laden fantasy. The child would continue, through play, to evolve a complex affective symbol system, to use Fein's (1987) terms. The therapist would be helping the child develop an internal resource to carry with him or her into adulthood. Helping children to learn to use play to develop their emotional world could be the greatest gift the therapist has to offer. The cognitive and affective processes that children develop through play could help them become more creative adults.

References

Arieti, S. (1976). *Creativity: The magic synthesis.* New York: Basic Books.

Arlow, J., & Brenner, C. (1964). *Psychoanalytic concepts and structural theory.* Madison, CT: International Universities Press.

Bandura, A. (1965). Influence of models' reinforcement contingencies in the acquisition of imitative responses. *Journal of Personality and Social Psychology, 1*, 589–595.

Begley, S. (1991, November). Thinking looks like this. *Newsweek*, p. 67.

Blatt, S., Allison, O., & Feirstein, A. (1969). The capacity to cope with cognitive complexity. *Journal of Personality, 37*, 269–288.

Bower, G. H. (1981). Mood and memory. *American Psychologist, 36*, 129–148.

Bower, G. H., & Mayer, J. (1989). In search of mood dependent retrieval. *Journal of Social Behavior and Personality, 4*, 133–168.

Clark, D., & Teasdale, J. (1982). Diurnal variation in clinical depression and accessibility of memories of positive and negative experiences. *Journal of Abnormal Psychology, 91*, 87–95.

Cohen, I. (1961). Adaptive regression, dogmatism, and creativity. *Dissertation Abstracts International, 21*, 3522–3523.

Culbane, J. (1988, January 10). Throw away the script. *The Cleveland Plain Dealer*, pp. 1–5.

D'Angelo, L. (1995). *Child's play: The relationship between the use of play and adjustment styles.* Unpublished dissertation, Case Western Reserve University, Cleveland, OH.

Dansky, J. (1980). Make-believe: A mediator of the relationship between play and associative fluency. *Child Development, 51*, 576–579.

Dansky, J., & Silverman, F. (1973). Effects of play on associative fluency in preschool-aged children. *Developmental Psychology, 9*, 38–43.

Dudek, S. (1968). Regression and creativity. *Journal of Nervous and Mental Disease, 147*, 535–546.

Dudek, S. (1975). Regression in the service of the ego in young children. *Journal of Personality Assessment, 39*, 369–376.

Dudek, S. (1980). Primary process ideation. In R. H. Woody (Ed.), *Encyclopedia of clinical assessment* (Vol. 1, pp. 520–539). San Francisco: Jossey-Bass.

Dudek, S. (1984). The architect as person: A Rorschach image. *Journal of Personality Assessment, 48*, 597–605.

Dudek, S., & Verreault, R. (1989). The creative thinking and ego functioning of children. *Creativity Research Journal, 2*, 64–86.

Duncker, K. (1945). On problem solving. *Psychological Monographs, 58*(5, Whole No. 270).

Easterbrook, J. A. (1959). The effect of emotion on cue utilization and the organization of behavior. *Psychological Review, 66*, 183–201.

Eich, F. (1995). Searching for mood dependent memory. *Psychological Science, 6*, 67–75.

Erikson, E. H. (1963). *Childhood and society.* New York: Norton.

Exner, J. (1974). *The Rorschach: A comprehensive system.* New York: Wiley.

Fein, G. (1987). Pretend play: Creativity and consciousness. In P. Gorlitz & J. Wohlwill (Eds.), *Curiosity, imagination, and play* (pp. 281–304). Hillsdale, NJ: Erlbaum.

Fischer, K., & Pipp, S. (1984). The unconscious and psychopathology. In K. S. Bowers & D. Meichenbaum (Eds.), *The unconscious reconsidered* (pp. 88–148). New York: Wiley.

Freud, A. (1965). *Normality and pathology in childhood: Assessment of development.* Madison, CT: International Universities Press.

Freud, S. (1958). The unconscious. In J. Strachey (Ed. and Trans.), *The standard edition of the complete psychological works of Sigmund Freud* (Vol. 14, pp. 159–215). London: Hogarth Press. (Original work published 1915)

Freud, S. (1959). Inhibition, symptoms, and anxiety. In J. Strachey (Ed. and Trans.), *The standard edition of the complete psychological works of Sigmund Freud* (Vol. 20, pp. 87–172). London: Hogarth Press. (Original work published 1926)

Freud, S. (1966). Project for a scientific psychology. In J. Strachey (Ed. and Trans.), *The standard edition of the complete psychological works of Sigmund Freud* (Vol. 1, pp. 283–413). London: Hogarth Press. (Original work published 1895)

Gamble, K., & Kellner, H. (1968). Creative functioning and cognitive regression. *Journal of Personality and Social Psychology, 9,* 266–271.

Gedo, J. (1990). More on creativity and its vicissitudes. In M. Runco & R. Albert (Eds.), *Theories of creativity* (pp. 35–45). Thousand Oaks, CA: Sage.

Greene, T., & Noice, H. (1988). Influence of positive affect upon creative thinking and problem solving in children. *Psychological Reports, 63,* 895–898.

Guilford, J. P. (1968). *Intelligence, creativity and their educational implications.* San Diego, CA: Knapp.

Holt, R. (1967). The development of the primary process: A structural view. In R. Holt (Ed.), *Motivation and thought* (pp. 344–384). Madison, CT: International Universities Press.

Holt, R. (1970). *Manual for the scoring of primary process manifestations in Rorschach responses* (10th ed.). New York: Research Center for Mental Health, New York University.

Holt, R. R. (1977). A method for assessing primary process manifestations and their control in Rorschach responses. In M. Rickers-Ovsiankina (Ed.), *Rorschach psychology* (pp. 375–420). New York: Kreiger.

Holt, R. R., & Havel, J. (1960). A method for assessing primary and secondary process in the Rorschach. In M. Rickers-Ovsiankina (Ed.), *Rorschach psychology* (pp. 283–315). New York: Wiley.

Isen, A. (1985). The asymmetry of happiness and sadness in effects on memory in normal college students. *Journal of Experimental Psychology: General, 114,* 388–391.

Isen, A., & Daubman, K. (1984). The influence of affect in categorization. *Journal of Personality and Social Psychology, 47,* 1206–1217.

Isen, A., & Daubman, K., & Nowicki G. (1987). Positive affect facilitates creative problem solving. *Journal of Personality and Social Psychology, 52,* 1122–1131.

Jausovec, N. (1989). Affect in analogical transfer. *Creativity Research Journal, 2,* 255–266.

Kagan, J., & Moss, H. A. (1962). *Birth to maturity: A study in psychological development.* New York: Wiley.

Kaufmann, G., & Vosburg, S. (1995, August). *Mood and creativity: A swing or a level thing?* Paper presented at the 103rd Annual Convention of the American Psychological Association, New York.

Kleinman, M., & Russ, S. (1988). Primary process thinking and anxiety in children. *Journal of Personality Assessment, 52,* 538–548.

Kogan, N. (1974). Creativity and sex differences. *Journal of Creative Behavior, 8,* 1–14.

Kogan, N. (1983). Stylistic variation in childhood and adolescence: Creativity, metaphor, and cognitive styles. In P. Mussen (Ed.), *Handbook of child psychology* (Vol. 3, pp. 631–706). New York: Wiley.

Kris, E. (1952). *Psychoanalytic exploration in art.* Madison, CT: International Universities Press.

LeDoux, J. E. (1989). Cognitive–emotional interactions in the brain. *Cognition and Emotion, 3,* 267–289.

Lieberman, J. N. (1977). *Playfulness: Its relationship to imagination and creativity.* New York: Academic Press.

Luchins, A., & Luchins, E. (1959). *Rigidity of behavior.* Eugene, OR: University of Oregon Books.

Maccoby, E., & Jacklin, C. (1974). *The psychology of sex differences.* Stanford, CA: Stanford University Press.

Martindale, C. (1981). *Cognition and consciousness.* Homewood, IL: Dorsey Press.

Martindale, C. (1989). Personality, situation, and creativity. In J. Glover, R. Ronning, & C. R. Reynolds (Eds.), *Handbook of creativity* (pp. 211–232). New York: Plenum.

Masling, J. (1992). What does it all mean? In R. Bornstein & T. Pittman (Eds.), *Perception without awareness* (pp. 259–276). New York: Guilford Press.

McCrae, R. R., & Costa, P. T., Jr. (1987). Validation of the five-factor model across instruments and observers. *Journal of Personality and Social Psychology, 52,* 81–90.

Middlebrook, D. W. (1991). *Anne Sexton.* Boston: Houghton Mifflin.

Mischel, W., Ebbesen, E., & Zeiss, A. (1972). Cognitive and attentional mechanisms in delay of gratification. *Journal of Personality and Social Psychology, 50,* 204–218.

Murray, J., & Russ, S. (1981). Adaptive regression and types of cognitive flexibility. *Journal of Personality Assessment, 45,* 59–65.

Natale, M., & Hanlas, M. (1982). Effect of temporary mood states on selective memory about the self. *Journal of Personality and Social Psychology, 42,* 922–934.

Noy, P. (1969). A revision of the psychoanalytic theory of the primary process. *International Journal of Psycho-Analysis, 50,* 155–178.

Penrose, R. (1989). *The emperor's new mind.* Oxford, England: Oxford University Press.

Pine, R., & Holt, R. (1960). Creativity and primary process: A study of adaptive regression. *Journal of Abnormal and Social Psychology, 61,* 370–379.

Rapaport, D. (1951). *Organization and pathology of thought.* New York: Columbia University Press.

Rholes, W., Riskind J., & Lane, J. (1987). Emotional states and memory biases: Effects of cognitive priming and mood. *Journal of Personlaity and Social Psychology, 52,* 91–99.

Richards, R. (1990). Everyday creativity, eminent creativity, and health: Afterview for CRT issues on creativity and health. *Creativity Research Journal, 3,* 300–326.

Riskind, J. (1989). The mediating mechanisms in mood and memory: A cognitive–priming formulation [Special issue]. *Journal of Social Behavior and Personality, 4,* 173–184.

Rogolsky, M. M. (1968). Artistic creativity and adaptive regression in third grade children. *Journal of Projective Techniques and Personality Assessment, 32,* 53–62.

Rothenberg, A. (1994). Studies in the creative process: An empirical approach. In J. Masling & R. Bornstein (Eds.), *Empirical perspectives on object relations theory* (pp. 195–245). Washington, DC: American Psychological Association.

Rubin, K., Fein, G., & Vandenberg, B. (1983). Play. In P. Mussen (Ed.), *Handbook of child psychology* (Vol. 4, pp. 693–774). New York: Wiley.

Runco, M. A. (1994). Creativity ands its discontents. In M. Shaw & M. A. Runco (Eds.), *Creativity and affect* (pp. 102–123). Norwood, NJ: Ablex.

Russ, S. (1980). Primary process integration on the Rorschach and achievement in children. *Journal of Personality Assessment, 44,* 338–344.

Russ, S. (1981). Primary process on the Rorschach and achievement in children: A follow-up study. *Journal of Personality Assessment, 46,* 473–477.

Russ, S. (1982). Sex differences in primary process thinking and flexibility in problem solving in children. *Journal of Personality Assessment, 45,* 569–577.

Russ, S. (1987). Assessment of cognitive affective interaction in children: Creativity, fantasy, and play research. In J. Butcher & C. Spielberger (Eds.), *Advances in personality assessment* (Vol. 6, pp. 141–155). Hillsdale, NJ: Erlbaum.

Russ, S. (1988). Primary process thinking on the Rorschach, divergent thinking, and coping in children. *Journal of Personality Assessment, 52,* 539–548.

Russ, S. (1993). *Affect and creativity: The role of affect and play in the creative process.* Hillsdale, NJ: Erlbaum.

Russ, S. (in press). Creativity and play. In M. Runco (Ed.), *Creativity research handbook.* Cresskill, NJ: Hampton Press.

Russ, S., & Grossman-McKee, A. (1990). Affective expression in children's fantasy play, primary process thinking on the Rorschach, and divergent thinking. *Journal of Personality Assessment, 54,* 756–771.

Russ, S., Grossman-McKee, A., & Rutkin, Z. (1984). [Affect in Play Scale: Pilot project]. Unpublished raw data.

Russ, S., & Peterson, N. (1990). *The Affect in Play Scale: Predicting creativity and coping in children.* Unpublished manuscript.

Russ, S., Robins, D., & Christiano, B. (1995, March). *The Affect in Play Scale: Longitudinal prediction.* Paper presented at the annual meeting of the Society for Personality Assessment, Atlanta, GA.

Singer, D. L., & Rummo, J. (1973). Ideational creativity and behavioral style in kindergarten age children. *Developmental Psychology, 8,* 154–161.

Singer, D. L., & Singer, J. (1990). *The house of make-believe.* Cambridge, MA: Harvard University Press.

Singer, J. L. (1973). *Child's world of make-believe.* New York: Academic Press.

Singer, J. L., & Singer, D. L. (1976). Imaginative play and pretending in early childhood: Some experimental approaches. In A. Davids (Ed.), *Child personality and psychopathology* (Vol. 3, pp. 69–112). New York: Wiley.

Singer, J. L., & Singer, D. L. (1981). *Television, imagination, and aggression.* Hillsdale, NJ: Erlbaum.

Slade, A., & Wolf, D. (1994). *Children at play.* New York: Oxford University Press.

Smolucha, F. (1992). A reconstruction of Vygotsky's theory of creativity. *Creativity Research Journal, 5,* 49–67.

Spence, D., & Holland, B. (1962). The restricting effects of awareness: A paradox and explanation. *Journal of Abnormal and Social Psychology, 64,* 163–174.

Sternberg, R. (1988). A three-facet model of creativity. In R. Sternberg (Ed.), *The nature of creativity* (pp. 125–147). Cambridge, England: Cambridge University Press.

Suler, J. (1980). Primary process thinking and creativity. *Psychological Bulletin, 88,* 144–165.

Sutton-Smith, B. (1966). Piaget on play: A critique. *Psychological Review, 73,* 104–110.

Toplyn, G., & Maguire, W. (1991). The differential effect of noise on creative task performance. *Creativity Research Journal, 4,* 337–346.

Urist, J. (1980). The continuum between primary and secondary process thinking: Toward a concept of borderline thought. In J. Kwawer, H. Lerner, P. Lerner & A. Sugarman (Eds.), *Borderline phenomena and the Rorschach test* (pp. 133–154). Madison, CT: International Universities Press.

Vygotsky, L. S. (1967). Voabraszeniye I tvorchestvo v destrom vosraste [Imagination and creativity in childhood]. Moscow: Prosvescheniye. (Original work published 1930)

Waelder, R. (1933). Psychoanalytic theory of play. *Psychoanalytic Quarterly, 2,* 208–224.

Zajonc, R. (1980). Feeling and thinking: Preferences need no inferences. *American Psychologist, 35,* 151–175.

Zajonc, R. (1990, August). *Emotions and brain temperature.* Paper presented at the 98th Annual Convention of the American Psychological Association, Boston.

Zimiles, H. (1981). Cognitive–affective interaction: A concept that exceeds the researcher's grasp. In E. Shapiro & E. Weber (Eds.), *Cognitive and affective growth* (pp. 49–63). Hillsdale, NJ: Erlbaum.

4

Attachment Research and Psychoanalytic Theory

Morris N. Eagle

In a previous discussion of object relations (Eagle, 1982), I argued that an important impetus to the development and growth of psychoanalytic theories is research (and theorizing) in areas that are not expressly psychoanalytic but that are relevant to psychoanalytic theory. Ironically, such research is often more vital to psychoanalytic theory than are attempts at direct experimental testing of psychoanalytic hypotheses and concepts. As examples of the latter, consider Sears' (1944) program of research on psychoanalytic propositions and many years of (in my view, not very useful) attempts to demonstrate experimentally the existence of repression (see Holmes, 1990).

Contrast the relatively minor influence that these research programs have had with the strong impact of research in such areas as infant development, infant–mother interaction, infant–mother attachment, and even cognitive psychology (see, e.g., Erdelyi, 1985 and Wakefield,

1992). With regard to the latter, the ascendancy in contemporary psychoanalytic theorizing of the concept of representations, for example (and related concepts such as *internal working models* [Bowbly, 1973] and *interactional structures* [Beebe & Lachmann, 1988]), cannot be properly understood without reference to the prevailing zeitgeist.

Kitcher (1992) has made a convincing case that Freudian theory is essentially interdisciplinary, borrowing from the neurology, physics, psychology, and other fields of the day. Hence, it would be especially susceptible to zeitgeist influences. I think that contemporary psychoanalytic theories continue to be interdisciplinary in the sense that their content is shaped to a significant degree by surrounding disciplines. To the extent that at their most general, psychoanalytic theories are theories of personality functioning and of human nature, it is not surprising that they should be interdisciplinary.[1]

I believe that one of the criteria that is and should be implicitly used in the "selection" of material to strongly influence psychoanalytic theories is *ecological validity*—that is, the degree to which the phenomena being studied and the research findings being generated bear on real-life clinical issues. For example, as Rapaport (1942) pointed out at the time, the many laboratory studies on so-called repression—which dealt primarily with memory for pleasant and unpleasant words—were, for good and understandable reasons, of little or no interest to psychoanalytic clinicians and theorists. Memory for pleasant and unpleasant words bore only the most general and remotest connection to the kinds of intense and vital phenomena and processes in which psychoanalytic clinicians and theorists are interested. In short, these studies lacked ecological validity. Furthermore, most of the findings reported could be explained by more parsimonious concepts than repression (see Erwin, 1996; Holmes, 1990).

Attachment Theory:
Origins in Real Events Versus Fantasy

In contrast to the studies just described, research (and theory) on attachment represents the quintessential case of empirical and theo-

---

[1]In arguing that psychoanalytic theories are strongly influenced by surrounding disciplines, I am not suggesting that the influence is not bidirec-

retical work that has appropriately influenced psychoanalytic theory. This is so for a number of reasons. First, Bowlby, the father of attachment theory, was trained as a psychoanalyst and thought of himself as an analyst throughout his life. Indeed, he viewed attachment theory as constituting a reaction against, and a corrective to, particular aspects of Freudian and Kleinian theory (Bowlby, 1969) As for Bowlby's reaction to Freudian theory, a central claim of attachment theory is that infant–mother attachment is based on a primary and autonomous instinctual system rather than representing a secondary derivative of the hunger drive or oral gratification, as Freudian theory suggests. This claim parallels Fairbairn's (1952) insistence that "libido is object-seeking rather than pleasure-seeking" (p. 137), and in this sense, attachment theory can be viewed as an object relational variant of psychoanalytic theory. In reaction to certain aspects of Kleinian theory, Bowlby (1969) wanted to demonstrate that actual events (e.g., loss, separation, and threats of separation) greatly affect the development of the child and the later personality functioning of the adult. As Bowlby (1988b) wrote, "It was regarded as almost outside the proper interest of an analyst to give systematic attention to a person's real experiences" (p. 43). He characterized the standard psychoanalytic view in the following way: "Anyone who places emphasis on what a child's *real experiences* may have been . . . was regarded as pitifully naive. Almost by definition, it was assumed that anyone interested in the external world could not be interested in the internal world, indeed was almost certainly running away from it" (pp. 43–44). Bowlby's own analyst, Riviere (1927)—who was a Kleinian—wrote, "Every day we see how little . . . phantasies tally with what the parents really were and really did and had" (p. 374). She added: "Psychoanalysis is . . . not concerned with the real world, nor with the child's or the adult's adaptation to the real world, nor with sickness or health, nor virtue or vice. It is concerned simply and solely with the imaginings of the childish mind, the fantasied pleasures and the dreaded retributions" (pp. 376–377). In reaction against this view, Bowlby focused on actual events in the life of the child, and one of the early empirical sources for the development of attach-

---

tional. There is little doubt that psychoanalytic ideas have also influenced research and theory in other disciplines. This is most evident in the discipline of psychology (see Barron, Eagle, & Wolitzky, 1992).

ment theory was the observation of children who were separated from their caregivers.[2]

Central Tenets of Attachment Theory

Attachment as an Autonomous Instinctual System

In the remaining pages of this chapter, I will very briefly summarize the central tenets of attachment theory and will present a selective sampling of attachment research findings and issues that are especially relevant to psychoanalytic theory. As already noted, a core aspect of Bowlby's attachment theory is his claim that the infant's attachment to the caregiver is neither secondary to nor derived from satisfaction of hunger and oral needs, but rather is based on an autonomous behavioral system. Citing Sroufe (1986), West and Sheldon-Keller (1994) wrote, "There is a sense in which Bowlby's (1969, 1973, 1980) entire trilogy on attachment is a corrective reproach to the view that relatedness is secondary to the satisfaction of basic drives such as orality" (p. 7).

Borrowing from ethology and control theory, Bowlby (1969, 1973, 1980) argued for the existence of an instinctually based (in the sense of being "environmentally stable" [Hinde, 1959]) behavioral system whose "set-goals" are to maintain the infant's proximity to the caregiver and to restore proximity when it has been disrupted. According to Bowlby (1969), this behavioral system has been selected in the course of evolution because of its adaptive (survival) value, namely, protection from predators. The behaviors that mediate attachment include crying and calling, babbling and smiling (social signaling behaviors), clinging, sucking, and locomotion used in approaching and following the caregiver.

Attachment, Secure Base, and Exploratory Behavior

The conditions that trigger and intensify the child's attachment behavior include alarm and danger, hunger, separation, and illness, whereas the conditions that reduce the intensity of attachment behavior include the caregiver's availability as a safe or secure base

---

[2]Karen (1994) noted that Bowlby wrote in the margin of his copy of the journal in which Riviere's remarks appeared, "Role of Environment = Zero."

combined with the opportunities for play and exploratory behavior. In general, attachment and exploratory behaviors are inversely related. That is, intense attachment behaviors (and the conditions that trigger them) tend to preclude exploratory behavior, and exploratory behavior is more likely to occur when intense attachment behaviors are not triggered.

The function of the caregiver as a secure base is most clearly seen in the relationship between exploratory and attachment behaviors. All one need do to get a clear impression of the caregiver's function as a safe base is observe children in a playground. Most children will play contentedly as long as the caregiver is available and in their sight. One might also see the child return to the mother (or other caregiver) periodically, a behavior that Mahler (1968) has referred to as *emotional refueling*. The hitherto silent function of the secure base in facilitating play and exploratory behavior is clearly illustrated when the child looks and suddenly finds the caregiver gone. The child's play and exploratory behavior are likely to come to an abrupt halt, to be replaced with intense attachment behavior (e.g., seeking, crying, protest). There is evidence that in a wide range of species (e.g., chicks, dogs, monkeys, and children), the availability of a secure base facilitates exploratory behavior (Rajecki, Lamb, & Obmascher, 1978). Even a symbolic representation of the secure base, such as the mother's photograph (Passman & Erck, 1977), as well as the availability of a blanket in blanket-attached toddlers (Passman & Weisberg, 1975), increases the range of exploratory behavior.

Internalization of a Secure Base and Felt Security

As one gets older, the secure base becomes increasingly internalized in the form of representations and cognitive–affective links. In other words, representations of and feelings (of connection) toward the attachment figure, rather than his or her actual presence, can serve as a secure base. One is reminded of Winnicott's (1965) idea that the introjection of an ego-supportive environment facilitates the capacity to be alone without feeling isolated and abandoned.

There has been some controversy in the attachment literature as to whether physical proximity to the caregiver or *felt security* should be emphasized as the set-goal of the attachment behavioral system (e.g., Sroufe & Waters, 1977, p. 1185). This is probably an unnecessary controversy because, as pointed out by Ainsworth and Bowlby (1991), actual closeness to the attachment figure is frequently the means by which the child is able to feel secure. Also, the controversy seems to reflect a possible conflation between the distal (i.e., evolutionary) function of the attachment system, which is to contribute to survival through the protection from predators that physical proximity to the caregiver provides, and the proximal personal motive of wanting to feel secure. The latter, which would be primarily interesting to psychologists, can be achieved through physical proximity to the caregiver or through other means, including symbolic and representational means. There is little doubt that with increasing age, the experience of felt security comes to depend more and more on internal representations.

Internal Working Models

According to Bowlby (1969, 1973), in the course of experience with the caregiver, the child constructs (a) a working model of the attachment figure, a central feature of which concerns the latter's expected availability, and (b) a complementary working model of the self, a key feature of which is a representation of how acceptable or unacceptable one is in the eyes of the attachment figure. For example, a child rejected by the attachment figure is likely to develop a complementary working model of the self as unlovable and unworthy of acceptance and love. Thus, although not explicitly noted by Bowlby, internal working models include representations of prototypic interactions with the attachment figure. In this regard, the concept of internal working model is similar to other concepts such as Stern's (1985) *representations of interactions generalized* and Beebe and Lachmann's (1988) interactional structures. Also, as Bowlby (1973) noted, the concept of working models "is no more than a way of describing, in terms compatible with systems theory, ideas traditionally described in such terms as 'introjection of an object' (good or bad) and 'self-image'" (p. 204).[3]

---

[3]I do not believe that this is entirely accurate. Whereas the concept of internal working model suggests an integrated cognitive structure that helps one order and predict the world and one's place in it, Fairbairn's (1952) concept of an internal object suggests a non–fully assimilated or integrated internalization that is often experienced as a foreign body (i.e., an archaic introject) existing within the structure of the personality, serving to divide or "split" the personality. An example of an internalized object is an "internal saboteur," which functions as a hostile and divisive force within the personality structure.

According to Bowlby (1973), internal working models are "built up slowly during the years of immaturity-infancy, childhood, and adolescence—and . . . whatever expectations are developed during these years tend to persist relatively unchanged throughout the rest of life" (p. 202). (As we shall see, the question of the stability of attachment patterns over time is far from definitively answered and is a subject of much research.) Finally, Bowlby (1973) proposed the idea that some individuals operate with multiple working models—one of which developed early, is constructed on primitive lines, and is largely unconscious, whereas the others are developed later, are fairly sophisticated, are radically incompatible with the primitive unconscious working model, and are relatively accessible to conscious awareness. As Bowlby (1973) noted, the primitive unconscious working model is most closely related to the psychoanalytic concept of transference.

Before turning to a discussion of attachment research, I wish to comment on several issues not covered under the previous headings. Although concepts such as attachment patterns and internal working models seem to refer only or primarily to behavior and cognitive structures, it is nevertheless true that intense feelings and affects are part and parcel of the attachment system. For example, feeling rejected by the attachment figure can undoubtedly be experienced as extraordinarily distressing and painful and can induce such emotions as rage and despair. Conversely, feeling accepted by and experiencing the availability of the attachment figure and the concomitant feelings of safety and security can be experienced as enormously pleasurable and conducive to feelings of well-being. It is likely that feelings and affects surrounding the attachment figure and one's relation to that figure can be as intense, driven, and peremptory as the sexual and aggressive impulses emphasized by Freud. It is also likely that ideas, wishes, and feelings linked to the attachment system can be as embedded in conflict, anxiety, and defense as sexual and aggressive ideas, wishes, and feelings. The affective aspects of the attachment system have not been as much pursued as have the cognitive aspects.

Finally, I want to note that attachment behavior is as universal and as trans-species as sexual and aggressive behavior. As ethologists have shown and as Bowlby (1969) has pointed out, the young across a wide range of species try to maintain proximity to and become attached to the mother. The trans-species nature of attachment behavior suggests that it is a biologically rooted and essential aspect of human nature.

Attachment Research

There is a huge and burgeoning attachment research literature that cannot be fully covered in this chapter. I will selectively review those findings that are especially basic and those that are especially relevant to psychoanalytic theory.

Different Patterns of Attachment: The Strange Situation

The availability of a meaningful (i.e., ecologically valid) and reliable measuring instrument can greatly facilitate research in a particular area. Thus it was with Ainsworth, Blehar, Waters, and Wall's (1978) development of the Strange Situation. As Karen (1994) observed, the Strange Situation is "a laboratory assessment that . . . would come to be more widely used than any other in the history of developmental psychology" (p. 151). The Strange Situation is rather simple, involving observations of the baby with the mother; then the baby with a stranger but without the mother; then the baby alone; and finally, the baby's reunion with the mother. Ainsworth et al. (1978) reported the following three attachment patterns (described here very briefly):

1. *Securely attached*: The baby seeks the mother when distressed, is upset when the mother leaves, eagerly greets her when she returns, and is comforted by her return.
2. *Insecurely attached—avoidant*: The baby continues to engage in exploratory behavior when the mother leaves and seems to show no interest in her when she returns.
3. *Insecurely attached—ambivalent*: The baby is upset when the mother leaves, but, unlike the securely attached babies, is not comforted or soothed by the mother's return and may demand to be picked up, but may then insist on being put down.[4]

In addition to these three attachment categories, later work by Main and her colleagues (e.g., Main & Hesse, 1990; Main & Solomon, 1990) identified a fourth attachment category labeled *disorganized/disoriented*, which was characterized by, among other features, the baby's seeking proximity to the mother in strange and disoriented ways (e.g.,

---

[4]Ainsworth (1984) later divided the above three categories into a number of subgroups. However, those are not discussed in this chapter.

approaching the mother backward; staring into space; suddenly freezing in the middle of a movement).

Relation Between Attachment Category and Maternal Behavior

Given the reliable identification of attachment categories, a critical question then becomes how these attachment categories relate to the behavior of the attachment figure and the prototypic interactions between the child and the attachment figure. Ainsworth et al. (1978) developed four scales to rate the mother's way of behaving with her baby. Very briefly, Ainsworth et al. reported that mothers of securely attached babies were rated higher in sensitive responsiveness, acceptance, emotional accessibility, and pleasure in handling their infants. Mothers of the two categories of insecurely attached babies were rated relatively low in these areas, the main difference between the two categories being that mothers of avoidant children were more rejecting and mothers of ambivalent children were more inconsistent and unpredictable.

Stability of Attachment Patterns

One of the central claims of attachment researchers and theorists is that once formed, attachment patterns are relatively resistant to change—that is, they are relatively stable. The (purported) stability of attachment patterns is one of the properties that makes them important for theories of personality development in general and for psychoanalytic theory in particular. After all, fundamental and common to different psychoanalytic theories—it is virtually axiomatic—is the assumption that early experiences exert a determinative and lasting influence on adult personality. Recall Freud's (1940/1964) bold assertion that the relationship between infant and mother is "unique, without parallel, established unalterably for a whole lifetime as the first and strongest love-object and as the prototype of all later love relations —for both sexes" (p. 188).

What is the evidence regarding the stability of attachment patterns? Unfortunately, there is no simple answer to this question, but rather competing answers that are embedded in some degree of controversy. A number of studies report positive correlations between attachment status at an early age and certain behaviors at a later age. For example, the social behavior of 2- and 3-year-old children whose attachment pattern was identified by the Strange Situation when they were 18 months of age was observed in free-play interaction with a securely attached, unfamiliar playmate (Jacobson & Wille, 1986). By age 3, securely attached children were receiving the greatest number of positive responses from the playmate, suggesting that they were more attractive as an interactive partner.

Main, Kaplan, and Cassidy (1985) reported that children who were judged to be secure in the Strange Situation at 12 to 18 months of age showed, at 6 years of age, greater fluency of parent–child discourse and greater emotional openness in their reaction to a family photograph. Kaplan (1987) found that for 79% of the 6-year old children, she was able to retrodict accurately their attachment status at 12 to 18 months of age, based on how long they reacted to photographs depicting children who were undergoing separation from their parents. In general, securely attached children could speak about the pictured child's sadness and loneliness and had constructive ideas about how the child in the picture might respond. In contrast, the insecurely attached children either were at a loss as to what the pictured child could do (mainly the avoidant children) or reacted with great intensity and suggested contradictory courses of action (mainly the anxious/ambivalent children).

Sroufe (1990) summarized a series of studies showing that preschool teachers, blind to the earlier attachment classification of a group of children, judged those with an earlier secure classification to be more independent and resourceful than those with an earlier avoidant classification. Six years later, camp counselors provided congruent data. A very important finding reported is that the preschool teachers behaved differently toward secure and insecure children. I will return to these findings when I discuss the issue of the different cues elicited by secure and insecure children and adults.

Let us assume that there is clear evidence of continuity between earlier and later attachment status. The question is what accounts for that continuity. There is much controversy regarding the answers to this question. Furthermore, the debate is very relevant to issues and assumptions linked to psychoanalytic theory.

From the point of view of attachment theory, the story is that the attachment pattern and the associated underlying internal working model, once formed early in life (between 1 and 2 years of age), is relatively resistant to change for a number of related reasons. One is that the internal working model helps make the world orderly and predictable because it serves an adaptive function and is not easily relinquished or modified. A narrower version of this formulation is that insecure attachment patterns are, in part, adaptive strategies for dealing with the attachment figure. Thus, the avoidant pattern can be understood as a strategy by which the child avoids both the experience of repeated painful rejection and the caregiver's anger in response to the child's attachment demands. Given its adaptive value, it is difficult to alter.

Note that the logic there is directly analogous to the understanding of defense in classical psychoanalytic theory. Because defenses are adaptive to the extent that they succeed in forestalling anxiety and distress, they are not easily given up. The link between defense and attachment pattern was made explicit by Bowlby (1980) when he related "defensive exclusion" of ideas and feelings connected with attachment needs to the avoidant attachment style.[5] Just as is the case with repression and other defenses, in the context of psychoanalytic theory, the function of defensive exclusion is to banish painful mental contents from conscious awareness.

---

[5]It appears that not all insecure attachment patterns can be easily seen as adaptive strategies, or, at least, not simply as adaptive strategies. Thus, there is little in the description of the "disorganized/disoriented" pattern that suggests that it can be viewed as an adaptive strategy. Rather, it can be best described as the *breakdown* or *failure* of any adaptive strategy. One is reminded of the distinction in the contemporary psychoanalytic literature between dynamic intrapsychic conflict and defense, which presumably characterize neuroses, and so-called structural or self defects, which presumably characterize narcissistic and borderline personality disorders. If one accepts this distinction (and I do not entirely; see Eagle, 1984), the avoidant attachment pattern is described as if it constituted, at least in part, a motivated defensive strategy, whereas the disorganized/disoriented attachment pattern is more a description of a defect, characterized by a breakdown of any adequate defensive strategy.

To a certain extent, this characterization of the disoriented/disorganized pattern is also applicable to an extreme degree of the ambivalent/resistant attachment style as well as to its adult counterpart, an enmeshed/preoccupied attachment style. In other words, the evidence suggests that an intense enmeshed/preoccupied attachment style is partly defensive strategy and partly a failure of defense and of adequate regulation of cognition and affect. Adam, Keller, and West (1995) reported that among young adults who have been diagnosed as having a borderline personality disorder, an avoidant attachment style is a protective factor against suicide, whereas an enmeshed/preoccupied pattern is a risk factor. This suggests that the latter individuals have not been successful in the control and regulation of overwhelming dysphoric affect.

Another reason given for the presumed stability of attachment patterns, derived from Piaget's (1952) formulations, is that once formed, internal working models tend to assimilate new experiences to one's preexisting structure. Thus, if an individual's working model includes the expectation of the attachment figure's rejection and unavailability, along with a sense of oneself as unlovable and worthy of rejection, then one is more likely to *interpret* new experiences, particularly ambiguous ones, in accord with these expectations and self-concept. In a sense, there is only a very narrow opening to disconfirming experiences and gaping possibilities of confirming the preexisting internal working models. Thus, although from a more realistic and "objective" point of view, a set of events should logically *disconfirm* the preexisting internal working model, they may nevertheless be subjectively experienced as tending to *confirm* old schemas and expectations. In addition to the role of assimilation, I want to suggest an interactional factor that makes for stability and works against change.

Eliciting Cues That Confirm Working Models

Until recently, psychoanalytic theory tended to ignore the role of interactional factors in perpetuating repetitive maladaptive patterns (frequently referred to as the *repetition compulsion*) and instead focused on such exclusively intrapsychic and quasi-biological factors as the "adhesiveness of the libido" (Freud, 1937/1953, p. 241), the persistence of infantile sexual wishes and impulses and of attempts to gratify them, the failure to resolve intrapsychic conflicts, the rigidity of defenses, and, ultimately, the death instinct (Freud, 1920/1955). Little or no emphasis was given to the interactional factors that perpetuate maladaptive relationship patterns in the form of a "vicious cycle" (see Strupp & Binder, 1984; Wachtel, 1982, 1987, 1993). Furthermore, even the recent increased focus on transference and countertransference (and their reconceptualizations as interactional processes) and the general shift from a "one-person" to a "two-person" psychology (e.g., Modell, 1984) tend to be limited to the treatment situation. Psychoanalytic theories have generally ignored the kinds of behaviors that elicit just those reactions from others that perpetuate maladaptive patterns.

Some attachment research suggests that one way people perpetuate both adaptive and maladaptive relationship patterns is that they emit behavioral cues that tend to elicit from others just those reactions that will confirm preexisting internal working models, thereby keeping these models and their associated attachment styles unchanged. Let me provide a few illustrative examples. As noted earlier, Jacobson and Wille (1986) found that 3-year-old secure children received more positive responses from peers than did insecure children. How does one account for this finding? Surely, these peers did not say to themselves, "I want to play with A. She is more securely attached." There simply must be cues emitted by A that elicit positive (in the case of secure children) or negative (in the case of insecure children) reactions from peers. Furthermore, in both cases, the reactions elicited tend to confirm preexisting expectations, in the case of the secure child, triggering what one might call a benevolent cycle and, in the case of the insecure child, a vicious cycle. Jacobson and Wille's (1986) results are especially interesting, given the report by Cowen, Pederson, Barbigian, Izzo, and Frost (1973) that the number of negative sociometric nominations in third grade predicted adult psychiatric disturbance better did than a battery composed of school records, intelligence test performance, and self-report data.

Sroufe's (1990) work discussed earlier is quite relevant here. Recall that preschool teachers, blind to the attachment history of the children, not only made differential judgments of independence, resourcefulness, and so forth of secure and insecure children, but also *behaved* differently toward these children (as did camp counselors 6 years later). The behavior of the teachers toward securely attached children tended to be warm, uncontrolling, positive, and age-appropriate. Their behavior toward avoidant children tended to be high on control/negative expectations for control and anger, and their behavior toward anxious/resistant children tended to be both unduly nurturant and tolerant of rule violations, but also controlling and suggesting low expectations. As Sroufe (1990) noted, the teachers' behaviors were "quite reminiscent of what these children had experienced with their caregiver" and were "in remarkable accord with patterns of adaptation shown by the children and therefore confirmed the children's working models of self" (p. 299)—and, I would add, working models of significant other and of prototypic interactions between self and other.

Main and George (1985) observed the responses to distress in age-mates of 10 abused and 10 nonabused toddlers, both groups from disadvantaged families. Their responses were dramatically different. The nonabused children reacted to the distressed age-mates with simple interest, concern, empathy, or sadness, whereas not one abused child showed concern. Instead, the abused children reacted with disturbing behavior, such as fear, physical attacks, anger, or attacks alternating with attempts to comfort the child in distress. Surely, a child who responds to another child in distress with fear, anger, and physical attacks will elicit negative and rejecting responses not only from the distressed child, but also from any adults or other children who observe the interaction. If one assumes that abused children are very likely to be insecurely attached (and there is a good deal evidence that this is so [e.g., Cicchetti, 1989]), then one can conclude that insecurely attached children are much more likely to engage in those disturbing behaviors that will almost certainly alienate other children.

The final study I will describe, although not dealing with attachment, is quite relevant to the current discussion. Dodge, Bates, and Pettit (1990) found, as one might expect, that children who were physically harmed by their parents were more likely than nonharmed children to show aggressive behavior during adolescence. However—and this is the critical point here—only that subset of physically harmed children who habitually attributed hostile intent to others were aggressive adolescents. In other words, the relationship between being physically harmed and later aggression was virtually entirely a function of whether the physically harmed children developed a particular form of social perception in which one is likely to attribute hostile intent to others. When the social perception variable is statistically partialed out, there is no significant relationship between physical harm and later aggression. The relevance of these findings to the current discussion is as follows: When being physically harmed (which is presumably associated with insecure attachment) generates a habitual attribution of hostile intent to others, it is more likely to lead to aggressive behavior toward others, which, in turn, is likely to alienate them, encourage their rejecting behavior, and thereby confirm the harmed (insecurely attached) person's preexisting propensity to attribute hostile intent to others.

In ending this section, let me recapitulate its basic points. An important reason that internal working models and accompanying attachment styles tend to remain unchanged is that behavioral cues tend to elicit behaviors from others that confirm one's working models, thus triggering either a benevolent or a vicious cycle, depending on the nature of one's behavior and working models.

Although psychoanalytic theories and therapists attend to interactional processes, including the kind I have been describing, they tend to do this primarily in the treatment situation—generally in the context of dealing with transference and countertransference—and tend to ignore them in their general theories of personality development and of psychopathology. Instead, they invoke explanations in which early events serve to lay down certain processes or "structures" that then are assumed to have a relatively permanent effect on functioning. Some examples of this kind of account include the following:

1. Early deprivation leads to the internalization of bad objects, which from that point on exert their pathogenic influence (Fairbairn, 1952).
2. Traumatic failures in the provision of empathic mirroring result in self-defects that then account for subsequent pathology (Kohut, 1971, 1977, 1984).
3. Early psychosexual fixations lead to the enduring persistence of infantile wishes.

One common characteristic of these sorts of accounts is that they focus virtually exclusively on *origins* of behavior and have little or nothing to say about ongoing contemporary factors that *maintain* behavior. Or, to put it more accurately, they assume that the phenomena triggered by early events (e.g., internalization of bad objects, self-defects, infantile wishes) have relatively permanent structural consequences, continue to operate relatively unchanged, and therefore do not require maintaining processes over the course of time. This issue also arises in current debates in the attachment theory literature.

The Role of Situations in Attachment Style

As I have shown, a basic assumption of attachment theory is that the individual's attachment pattern is formed early in life and is then relatively resistant to change. In short, one's attachment pattern is held to be relatively stable. As I have also shown, a good deal of evidence attests to the continuity of attachment patterns over time. The question is how one accounts for this stability. One possibility not yet discussed in this chapter is that a major factor in the stability of attachment patterns is *the stability of caretaking conditions*. Thus, Lamb (1987) argued that the child's early attachment pattern predicts other characteristics of the child at a later age "only when there is continuity in caretaking conditions" (p. 823). Hence, he concluded, one can say little about the *formative* significance and influence of early parent–child interactions.

There is evidence that changes in the family and home environment (e.g., loss of job, divorce, decline in income, parental illness) can lead to changes in the attachment pattern of the child. This suggests that when certain external conditions are altered, internal representations, including those supposedly resistant to change, do in fact change. This suggests further, as Lamb (1987) argued, that the continuity of certain behavioral patterns, including attachment patterns, and of internal representations or models may be, in good part at least, a function of continuity in particular external circumstances. Linking this to the previous section, one can say that the continuity or sameness in external circumstances functions as a "silent" *maintaining* factor in the stability of certain behavioral patterns and internal structures. It is silent insofar as it is in the background and tends to be taken for granted and therefore easily overlooked. It is generally only when external circumstances change dramatically that one becomes aware of the degree to which *unchanging* external conditions function to maintain the stability of various behavior patterns.

Psychoanalytic theory shares with attachment theory the core assumption that certain early experiences (primarily infant–mother interactions) are especially formative in personality development. In other words, the assumption is that certain early experiences have a lasting and determinative effect on later personality development and functioning. This idea is particularly clear and salient in the contemporary emphasis on the role of early discrete trauma (most frequently, sexual abuse) in later adult disturbances. A particular set of early experiences, including early discrete traumas, may well exert a powerful influence on later personality development. However, as is implied in Lamb's (1987) critique and as noted by Mitchell (1988) in the context of examining certain psychoanalytic assumptions, an adequate distinction is not made between the formative effects of early and discrete events, such as a particular traumatic experience, and the cumulative effects of *continuing* experiences of a similar kind over long periods. The two classes of events tend to be conflated. Let me provide a specific example to illustrate this distinction.

Let us assume that being sexually abused at, say, age 3 is highly correlated with certain forms of adult pathology. One would be tempted to interpret such findings as indicating that early sexual abuse plays a *formative* role in determining later pathology. However, such a conclusion might not be at all warranted. For one would not know whether the adult pathology is linked to the formative influence of a discrete event (i.e., the sexual abuse) or to the cumulative effects of continuing stressful experiences, *of which the sexual abuse is a salient marker.* Thus, a parent who would sexually abuse a child *is also likely to be a particular kind of parent over an extended period of time.* Therefore, one might well not be able to distinguish between the specific effects of the sexual abuse and the cumulative, time-extended effects of a long series of negative experiences and interactions. Thus, the significant relationship may not be between a discrete and limited set of events (i.e., a certain kind of toilet-training regimen during a limited time period) and adult personality characteristics, but rather between a certain kind of long-term parenting and adult personality characteristics.

Adult Attachment

Along with Bowlby, attachment theorists and researchers believe that attachment remains a central issue throughout one's life. In the past number of years, research on the attachment status of adults has burgeoned. Work in this area has relied both on quasi-clinical interviews and self-report measures. The best known of the former is George, Kaplan, and Main's (1985) Adult Attachment Interview (AAI), which I will discuss in the next section. Research on adult romantic attachment began with the work of Hazan and Shaver (1987), who designed a relatively simple self-report measure in which respondents were asked to think about all the romantic relationships in their lives and then to endorse one of three descriptions as fitting them best. The three descriptions are adult analogues of Ainsworth's three infant attachment categories (i.e., secure; avoidant; and anxious/ambivalent). Since Hazan and Shaver's (1987) study, there has been an explosion of self-report measures of adult attachment. In a 1994 chapter, Shaver and Clark (1994) reported that they knew of at least 21 self-report adolescent and adult attachment measures. As a consequence of research on adult attachment, the original attachment categories taken from research on infants has been altered, most significantly by Bartholomew and Horowitz (1991), who developed a four-category scheme: secure, preoccupied, dismissing, and fearful. Using these categories, Bartholomew and her colleagues have reported significant relationships between attachment category and personality disorders (Bartholomew & Horowitz, 1991), dependency and counterdependency (Bartholomew & Keelan, 1993), self-esteem (Bartholomew & Horowitz, 1991), and other behaviors. There are simply too many studies on adult attachment to cover in this chapter. For an excellent survey of this literature, see Shaver and Clark (1994).

Intergenerational Transmission of Attachment Patterns

Stability of attachment patterns refers most obviously to sameness within a single individual. However, there is evidence that perhaps attachment patterns can remain stable across generations, that is, from mother to child.

In what has become a landmark study, Main and Goldwyn (1984) administered the AAI to a group of mothers. They found that mothers who were classified on the basis of their AAI narratives as autonomous–secure were likely to have securely attached infants, as measured by the Strange Situation (Ainsworth et al., 1978). Mothers whose AAI narratives fell into the insecurely attached categories (avoidant/dismissive and preoccupied/enmeshed) were more likely to have insecurely attached infants. Thus, mothers' presumed attachment status as measured by the AAI narrative predicts the infants' attachment status as measured by the Strange Situation.

For the reader unfamiliar with the AAI, it is necessary to describe it briefly and to describe how the attachment categories are determined from the AAI narrative. The AAI is a semistructured, quasi-clinical interview in which individuals are asked about their early attachment experiences. The scoring, which apparently requires special training, is not based primarily on the content of the interviewees' responses but on formal features of the narrative. For example, the coherence and plausibility of the narrative are criteria for classifying the narrator as autonomous–secure. As another example, idealization of parents coupled with a failure to provide specific instantiations serves as a criterion contributing to a classification of insecure attachment. The theoretical considerations underlying this decision are quite complex and will be discussed later. However, for the present, it is important to identify one important component of Main's rationale for her attachment classifications. Main (1985) noted that the mother's attachment classification, based on her AAI score, predicts her infant's attachment status. Furthermore, because the infant's attachment status is known to be related to the mother's behavior toward her infant, it suggests that the mother's AAI classification is lawfully related to her behavior with the infant. Whether this really means that it is specifically the mother's attachment status that predicts the infant's attachment status is a question that I will discuss later. What does seem clear, however, is that whatever they measure, the mothers' classifications on the AAI predict their infants' attachment status.

Let me now turn to a remarkable study of Fonagy, Steele, and Steele (1991), who administered the AAI to a group of pregnant women during their second trimester of pregnancy. Based on the mothers' AAI classifications, Fonagy et al. were able to predict with about 80% accuracy the attachment status at 12 months of age of the unborn infants. This study is fascinating in its own right, but it also constitutes an important replication of the predictive capacity of Main's (1985) AAI classification scheme. Similar findings were obtained by Levine, Tuber, Slade, and Ward (1991), who reported that the attachment classification of pregnant adolescents on the AAI (as well as quality of object relations, as measured by the Krohn Object Representation Scale) correlated significantly with the attachment classification of their infants at 15 months of age, as determined by the Strange Situation.

What are the intermediate processes linking the mother's classification on the AAI to her infant's attachment status, as determined by the Strange Situation? Both Main (1985) and Fonagy et al. (1991) have invoked the mother's metacognitive functioning, particularly her ability to reflect on her own internal working models of her attachment experiences. Therefore, I will return to this question when I discuss the relationship between attachment and metacognitive functioning.

Attachment Patterns and Psychopathology

Bowlby (e.g., 1977, 1988a) always seemed to believe that insecurity of attachment represented a central factor in psychopathology. Later attachment researchers and theorists tended to dampen or modulate this claim and frequently noted that with the exception of the disorganized/disoriented attachment pattern, the other patterns of insecure attachment constituted different kinds of adaptations made by the child (and later, the adult) and did not necessarily indicate psychopathology (e.g., Freedman & Gorman, 1993).

However, recent evidence suggests that the preoccupied/emmeshed attachment pattern does constitute a risk factor in psychopathology, at least in our culture. For example, Adam et al. (1995) reported that a preoccupied attachment status constituted a risk factor for suicide and suicide attempts, whereas dismissive attachment represented a protective factor in regard to suicide. West, Keller, Links, and Patrick (1993) found that borderline individuals are more likely to show a preoccupied/enmeshed attachment pattern.

A number of other studies also suggest a link between certain forms of insecure attachment and psychopathology, particularly borderline personality disorder (BPD). For example, Livesley and Schroeder (1991) reported that a panel of psychiatrists considered attachment problems, in particular the tendency toward regression triggered by separation from attachment figures, to be a typical feature of BPD. Livesley, Schroeder, and Jackson (1990) identified two orthogonal factors that accounted for 71% of the variance in a clinical sample of personality disorders. One factor, the attachment factor, included scales of separation protest, secure base, proximity seeking, feared loss, and need for affection.

Alexander et al. (1995) administered the Family Attachment Interview, which was adapted from the AAI by Bartholomew and Horowitz (1991), along with a number of other tests, to 86 women who responded to newspaper announcements and agreed to participate in a study of family relationships and long-term effects among incest survivors. They found that distress, as measured by the Symptom Check List-10 (SCL-10; Nguyen, Attkisson, & Stegner, 1983), was significantly related to attachment pattern, with fearful individuals reporting significantly more distress than secure, preoccupied, or dismissing individuals. Also, avoidant, dependent, self-defeating, and borderline personality disorders, as measured by the Millon Clinical Multiaxial Inventory–II (MCMI–II; Millon, 1987), were all significantly related to the respondents' attachment category. Of special interest, given the findings described earlier, higher scores on the MCMI–II Borderline scale were more likely among either fearful or preoccupied individuals than either secure or dismissing individuals. (The latter attachment scores were negatively correlated with BPD.) Also of special interest is the finding that the amount of distress reported on the SCL-10 was inversely related to scores on the Dismissing and Secure Attachment scales. Finally, scores on the Beck Depression Inventory were negatively related to secure attachment.

None of the four scales of the MCMI–II previously noted (Avoidant, Dependent, Self-Defeating, and Borderline) was significantly related to severity of abuse (as measured by age of onset of abuse type of abuse, degree of coercion, and relationship to the perpetrator). Neither was distress, as measured by the SCL-10. Only intrusive thoughts as measured by the Impact of Event Scale (IES; Horowitz, Wilner, & Alvarez, 1979) were significantly related to severity of abuse.

In the present context, what is especially noteworthy about these results is that attachment scores accounted for more of the variance on virtually all of the dependent variables (with the exception of intrusive thoughts) than severity of abuse. One way of interpreting these results, as the title of the Alexander et al. (1995) paper suggests, is that attachment status tends to mediate the long-term effects of abuse. Thus, despite having been abused, if one is securely attached (11% of the sample), one is not likely to manifest distress or show evidence of a personality disorder, whereas if one shows a fearful or preoccupied attachment pattern, one is more likely to demonstrate distress and show evidence of a personality disorder. Furthermore, severity of abuse predicts only likehood of intrusive thoughts (a presumably classic specific symptom associated with posttraumatic stress disorder) but does not predict general distress or evidence of personality disorder.

I am devoting a good deal of space to this study because the results strike me as especially important in that they may generally represent the role that attachment status plays in mediating the long-term effects of early (and even later) traumatic events. In other words, it appears that if for whatever reason one is securely attached despite being subjected to trauma, then one is less likely to suffer general distress and show evidence of a personality disorder. If, however, one is insecurely attached (especially if one is attached in a preoccupied or fearful way), then one is quite likely to report distress and to show evidence of a personality disorder.

The Dodge et al. (1990) study I referred to earlier reported that the effects of early physical punishment on later aggressive behavior was mediated by the degree to which the individual's social perception was characterized by the attribution of hostile intent to others. Scoring high on this form of social perception meant that one was more likely to behave aggressively, and a low score meant that one was less likely to behave aggressively. Thus, one plausible conclusion is that whether early physical punishment leads to later aggressive behavior is very much a function of whether the former (along with other factors) induces a particular kind of social perception. Similarly, whether early abuse is likely to lead to general distress and some form of personality disorder is, in part, a function of the degree to which such abuse (along with other factors) results in particular insecure attachment patterns.

Not addressed, nor intended to be addressed, by either the Alexander et al. (1995) study or the Dodge et al. (1990) study is the critical question of the factors that account for when early abuse (in the Alexander et al., 1995 study) and physical punishment (in the Dodge et al., 1990 study) lead to insecure attachment and when they do not. In other words, if attachment status mediates the effects of early traumatic experiences on later adaptive versus maladaptive behavior, then it is extremely important to know what determines attachment status. Why does one child who has been abused develop secure attachment; another child, a preoccupied attachment status; and still another child, a dismissing attachment status? Similarly, why does one child who has been subjected to physical punishment "learn" to attribute hostile intent to others and then behave aggressively, contrasted with another child who has also been physically punished but who neither characteristically attributes hostile intent to others nor behaves aggressively?

The attribution of hostile intent to others can be understood as one aspect of the individual's internal working model of the other. It would have been interesting to know the attachment status of the participants in the Dodge et al. (1990) study. One would predict that those individuals who did not develop a form of social perception in which they attribute hostile intent to others would be more likely to be securely attached than those individuals who characteristically attribute hostile intent to others. If this were true, one could see the Dodge et al. (1990) and Alexander et al. (1995) studies as quite related. In both cases, the long-term effects of early untoward experiences would be mediated by the individual's attachment status.

It will be recognized that what I refer to above as the critical question is critical in accounting for the development of the resilient or "stress-resistant" child (e.g., Garmezy, 1985). What is it that enables some children who have been subjected to trauma, deprivation, and abuse to develop in a relatively intact way, and in what ways do these children differ from children who "succumb"?

Although it cannot be dealt with in this chapter, one needs to take into account the factor of temperamental predispositions in addressing these questions. There is a good deal of controversy in the attachment literature regarding the influence of temperament on the child's attachment status. On the one hand, there is evidence for a modest but significant relation between temperament and attachment status (e.g., Goldsmith & Alansky, 1987; Vaughn et al., 1992). On the other hand, a number of findings appear to contradict the claim of a direct relationship between temperament and variations in security of attachment. For example, Belsky, Fish, and Isabella (1991) found that almost 25% of 148 infants studied showed changes in level of negativity as a function of quality of parenting and personality and of marital characteristics of parents. A number of studies (e.g., van den Boom, 1990) have reported changes in infants' attachment status following an intervention designed to heighten maternal sensitivity. There is not sufficient space to pursue the issue further. However, as Belsky, Rosenberger, and Crnic (1995) noted, the relationship between temperament and attachment, as well as the relationship between other factors (e.g., quality of marriage of parents and degree of social support) and infant attachment status, is likely to be mediated "by impacting more proximal processes of parent–child interaction" (p. 175). It follows that the role of any factor, including temperament, will vary according to the degree of impact that that factor has on parent–child interaction. (For a further discussion of this issue, see Eagle, 1995.)

Before leaving the Alexander et al. (1995) study, I want to note that, in accord with the findings of other studies noted earlier (e.g., Adam et al., 1995), in contrast to an avoidant/dismissing pattern of insecure attachment, a preoccupied pattern of insecure attachment tends to be most closely associated with psychopathology. However, these results need to be interpreted cautiously. If measures of both pattern of attachment and degree of pathology are based on self-report questionnaires, the results might be somewhat artifactual. That is, the avoidant/dismissing individual may deny or minimize degree of distress experienced as well as other indications of psychopathology (see Shedler, Mayman, & Manis's, 1993 discussion of "illusory mental health" and recent work on "repressive style" [e.g., Weinberger, 1990]). In any case, this issue needs further investigation.

Returning to the relation between borderline pathology and attachment status, according to Melges and Swartz (1989), the borderline person's high level of anxiety about attachment leads to an enmeshed dependence on the attachment figure. West et al. (1993) administered a series of self-report questionnaires, including the Reciprocal Attachment Questionnaire (RAQ) to 146 consecutively admitted female patients to an outpatient psychiatric clinic. Their main purpose was to determine how well these questionnaires, particularly the RAQ, could identify BPD. They found that of the various instruments administered—the Borderline Personality Disorder scale of the MCMI, the SCL-90, the Interpersonal Dependency Questionnaire (IDQ), and the RAQ—only four scales from the RAQ yielded significant results, that is, were significantly correlated with BPD. These scales were Feared Loss, Secure Base (negatively correlated), Compulsive Care Seeking, and Angry Withdrawal. Feared Loss showed the strongest relationship. Taken together, these results suggest that certain forms and degrees of anxious attachment, specifically compulsive care-seeking and angry withdrawal, characterize BPD in female patients.

West et al. (1993) presented a scenario in which these patients "attempt to confirm their security with their attachment figure in a concrete manner by displaying urgent and frequent care-seeking behavior. However, the search for security is repeatedly frustrated and gives rise to angry withdrawal" (p. 820). Thus, for West et al. (1993), angry withdrawal is largely a reaction to the repeated frustrations of the person's need for security. Elsewhere, West and Keller (1994) wrote that in accord with Bowlby's (1963) claim, at the core of insecure attachment and neurotic difficulties is a pathological mourning characterized by "the person's inability to master the loss of a longed for but never fully experienced tender relationship to the caretaker" (p. 321). The avoidantly attached individual deals with such loss by avoiding dependency and intimacy and cultivating fantasies of self-sufficiency, whereas the enmeshed/preoccupied individual "seems not to believe that it is obligatory to say goodbye to a lost attachment relationship. Rather, there is a persistent effort to recover the lost relationship, accompanied by intense anger and reproach. . . . The inability to break from an enmeshed dependence on an ambivalently regarded parent necessarily compromises the individual's ability to form authentic ties to new attachment figures" (p. 321). This latter pattern, as noted, particularly characterizes BPD.

West et al. (1993) implied, but did not explicitly state, that the borderline patient's search for security may frequently be so compulsive and so intense that it is unlikely to be satisfied by anyone. They emphasized nevertheless the failure of significant others to satisfy the borderline patient's need for security. Also, little was said about the borderline patient's inner conflict between desire for and fear of closeness and attachment (which can be experienced as engulfment) and consequent anger toward and withdrawal from the other. Buie and Adler (1982–1983, p. 52) have described this pattern, which they believed characterizes borderline patients, as a "need-fear dilemma" (p. 52). One is also reminded of Guntrip's (1969) "in–out" pattern, in which the schizoid person's need for contact with and support from the object pushes them toward the object (the "in" phase) and fear of closeness and engulfment pushes them away from the object (the "out" phase).

It is unlikely that many psychoanalytic clinicians or theorists believe that the conflict described by Buie and Adler (1982–1983) or Guntrip (1969) is limited to borderline and schizoid individuals. The conflict between—or perhaps one should say, the need to integrate—needs for intimacy and closeness on the one hand and needs for autonomy and separateness on the other is an issue that everyone confronts, and the ubiquitousness of this issue has long been recognized in the psychoanalytic and nonpsychoanalytic literature. The various terms used to refer to some variation of these two dimensions include agency and communion (Bakan, 1966); self-definition and relatedness (Blatt, 1992); symbiosis and separation–individuation (Angyal, 1941; Mahler, 1968); effectiveness and safety (Greenberg, 1991); and, of course, exploration and attachment (Bowlby, 1963). Contemporary psychoanalytic theories are characterized partly by the centrality they assign to these two dimensions and to the conflicts and vicissitudes surrounding them. These two dimensions are also central in contemporary psychoanalytic formulations of psychopathology.

Attachment Patterns and Metacognitive Functioning

According to attachment theory, different representations (e.g., different internal working models) underlie and correspond to different attachment patterns. There is also evidence that different metarepresentational or metacognitive processes are also systematically related to different attachment patterns. Main (1991) distinguished between representational and metarepresentational as "thinking" versus "thinking about thought" (p. 128) or in terms of "possessing a mental representation of an experience versus being able to reflect on its validity, nature and source" (p. 128).

There is evidence that securely and insecurely attached children differ in regard to both cognitive and metacognitive functioning. Grossmann and Grossmann (1991) reported that securely attached children performed better in Piagetian perspective-taking tests than did insecurely attached children. Secure children engaged in longer periods of solitary play and were less distracted than insecure children (Main, 1983; Suess, Grossman, & Sroufe, 1992). With regard to metacognitive functioning, self-directed speech occurred more often in secure than in insecure toddlers (Main, 1983). Kaplan (as cited in Main, 1991) reported that 6-year-old secure children spontaneously acknowledged experiencing more than one feeling at a time and were more capable of describing feelings conditional on different situations.

Why should there be a relationship between children's cognitive and metacognitive functioning on the one hand and attachment status on the other? There are a number of possible answers to this question. One possibility is that "secure children are more likely to be able to devote more attention to exploration (or, more generally, to 'epistemic activity . . .') than insecure children, since less attentional monitoring need be devoted to the parent" (Main, 1991, p. 145). In a related observation, Main (1991) suggested that "the secure child may also have more epistemic 'space' in which to review her actions, situations, or thinking processes . . . [while] insecurity of attachment may lead to the development of defensive thinking processes—processes which are likely from the first to distort, disorganize, or limit access to memories, feelings, intentions and recognition of options" (Main, 1991, p. 146).

Related to this argument, Main (1991) also suggested that capacity for metacognitive functioning may play a "protective" role in the formation of a working model of the self. As she put it, a child capable of metacognitive functioning "can 'operate upon' or meta-represent a proposition such as 'I am a bad person' as follows: 'I *may* be a bad person because my attachment figure seems to think so, but on the other hand, she has been found with false beliefs in other circumstances'"(pp. 136–137). Note that this is still another case (the first was the earlier-discussed relationship between mothers' coherence of narrative and secure attachment in their infants) in which Main argued that metacognitive capacity, that is, the ability to reflect on one's experiences, serves a benevolent or protective role in personality functioning. As we shall see, Fonagy and his coworkers (e.g., 1995) further developed this idea in their investigation of what they called the *reflective-self function*. (This will be discussed later in this section.)

The set of findings indicating that the ability to reflect on one's experiences, memories, feelings, and so on serves a protective role in

personality functioning is eminently compatible with the classic psychoanalytic emphasis on the "curative" role of awareness, insight, and
self-understanding. As I have noted elsewhere (Eagle, 1995), "So many
years after Freud's (1920/1955) and Santayana's claim that those who
do not remember are destined to repeat the past, the best systematic
evidence for that assertion comes . . . from attachment research that
investigates the intergenerational transmission of maternal patterns of
behavior that are associated with [infant] insecure attachment" (p. 129).

These findings tend to support the basic psychoanalytic assumption
that adequate functioning is facilitated by remembering and coming
to terms with one's early experiences—particularly negative and traumatic experiences—with parental figures and with the feelings, conflicts, defenses, and emotional beliefs that these early experiences
helped shape. Whatever other theoretical differences exist among different psychoanalytic theories of psychoanalytic treatment, a basic
assumption they all hold in common is the therapeutic importance of
coming to terms with one's past, of understanding that who one is
now is, in important ways, a function of that past, and of establishing
a sense of continuity between one's past and one's present. In an
important sense, from a psychoanalytic point of view, a wide range of
psychopathology can be characterized partly as a radical discontinuity between past and present. Defenses such as repression, denial, and
splitting represent specific expressions of such discontinuity. In an
equally important sense, a therapeutic goal common to different psychoanalytic perspectives is the gradual replacement of discontinuity
with a sense of continuity.

I want to take a brief excursion here and consider an issue that
appears to be glossed over in the attachment literature. In that literature, a coherent and plausible narrative on the AAI is a criterion for
secure attachment. Indeed, as I have shown, "autobiographical competence," (Holmes, 1993, p. 82), that is, the coherence and plausibility
of the mother's narrative in the AAI is operationally defined as secure
attachment by Main and her colleagues. However, the main evidence
given is the *infant's* secure attachment. Now although it is plausible to
assume that a securely attached mother is more likely to have a
securely attached child, no direct evidence has been presented indicating that these mothers are securely attached.

It is conceivable that an insecurely attached mother, particularly one
who has come to terms with her insecure attachment, is just as likely
to have a securely attached infant as is a securely attached mother. The

assumption that a more coherent and plausible narrative (autobiographical competence) *defines* secure attachment begs the question. In order for the question not to be begged, one would need to show that autobiographical competence is positively and strongly associated with an independent measure indicating secure attachment status.

It may well be that the class of mothers whose narratives are plausible and coherent, and who are characterized by Main and her colleagues as securely attached, in fact includes a heterogeneous group with regard to attachment status (i.e., both securely and insecurely attached individuals), but who have in common a greater degree of success in remembering, working through, and coming to terms with their early attachment experiences (as well as coming to terms with their current attachment status, including a relatively insecure attachment status). Furthermore, it may well be that their infants' secure attachment status is not a function of the mothers' secure attachment but rather of the mothers' greater awareness, greater self-reflection, and greater self-acceptance—*whatever her attachment status.*

It seems to me that when Main and others use autobiographical competence as a measure of secure attachment, they are taking a variable that may be empirically correlated with or even serve to facilitate secure attachment and treating it as a defining criterion of secure attachment (and similarly for the relationship between autobiographical incompetence and insecure attachment). Furthermore, that certain narrative features (e.g., coherence, plausibility) are taken to define secure attachment on the AAI is often overlooked in the literature, and they are discussed as if they were found to characterize the AAI narratives of women judged to be securely attached through independent measures. For example, West, Sheldon, and Reiffer (1989), in referring to the AAI, wrote that "adults rated as secure appeared comfortable in discussing attachment and were able, when constructing their attachment history, to appreciate and integrate both positive and negative aspects of it" (p. 372). This, misleadingly, reads as if adults independently rated as secure also appear comfortable in discussing attachment (and also were able to integrate positive and negative aspects of their attachment history). The fact is, however, that being able to integrate positive and negative aspects in one's attachment narrative *serves as a defining criterion for being classified as securely attached.*

As another example, in a recent paper briefly summarizing research on adult attachment, Alexander et al. (1995) wrote that "secure adults . . . are coherent in their memories of the past. . . . Dismissive adults

. . . tend to idealize or fail to recall their childhood. . . . Preoccupied adults . . . focus excessively on memories of the past. . . ." (p. 3). This is misleading because it implies that the research shows that adults who were independently rated as secure, dismissing, or preoccupied on one measure *also* were found, respectively, to be coherent, dismissing, or overly focused on the past in their AAI narratives. It fails to inform the reader that being coherent, dismissing, or overly focused on the past are *defining criteria* for one's attachment categorization as secure, dismissing, or preoccupied. The two examples I have given are representative of a practice common in the attachment literature. I would question whether—from a theoretical and clinical point of view—telling a coherent and plausible narrative should be viewed as an integral and central component of secure attachment. Rather, its relationship to secure attachment status is that of *empirical correlate*. This raises the question of what should be viewed as integral and central to conceptualizing secure and insecure attachment.

An examination of attachment theory and research provides a reasonably clear answer. Secure attachment lies primarily in such markers as a confident expectation that the attachment figure will be available when needed, a capacity to experience one's attachment needs openly, a capacity for relatively anxiety-free exploration, the ability to derive security from and to use the attachment figure as a secure base from which to explore, the later internalization of the secure base that frees one from requiring the physical presence of the attachment figure, and a number of other factors. Based on the logic of attachment theory, these are the primary criteria for secure attachment. That these characteristics are positively correlated with the capacity to tell a coherent narrative or with self-reflection and metacognitive monitoring is very important, both clinically and theoretically. However, it is confusing to view these capacities as part of the definition of secure attachment.

I would expect that Main (and perhaps Fonagy) would respond to these observations by arguing that an integral aspect of one's attachment status is the nature of one's internal working model and therefore that any significant change in one's internal working model constitutes a change in one's attachment status. I agree with that conclusion but would argue that formal features of the AAI narrative, such as coherence and plausibility, or metacognitive monitoring, do not necessarily constitute changes in one's internal working model (of self, attachment figure, and prototypic interactions between the two).

Rather, metacognitive monitoring better enables one to reflect on one's working model and modulate one's impulses, feelings, and actions. I would take as evidence of significant change in the internal working model itself and associated attachment status changes in such areas as expectations and feelings regarding the attachment figure, degree of internalization of a secure base, and the other characteristics noted earlier.

I believe that in successful treatment there is a mixture of some change both in internal working models and attachment status and an increased capacity to reflect on one's working models, feelings, and expectations, even in areas where they may not have changed significantly. Such increased self-reflective capacity (and the increased self-understanding and self-awareness it generates) serve to modulate one's impulses, feelings, and interactions.

Let me return now to the relationship between metacognitive functioning and attachment status. As noted earlier, Fonagy and his colleagues (e.g., 1995) have extended Main's work with the AAI in some very fruitful and exciting ways that provide closer links with psychoanalytic theory.

Based on the AAI interviews, Fonagy and his colleagues developed a "reflective-self scale" intended to measure the clarity of the interviewee's representation of his or her own and others' mental states (Fonagy, Moran, & Target, 1993; Fonagy, Steele, Steele, Higgitt, & Target, 1994). They found not only that ratings on this scale were reliable but that parental scores on this scale predicted the behavior of their child in the Strange Situation. Fathers and mothers who were rated high in reflective-self functioning were three or four times more likely to have secure children than were parents with poor reflective-self capacity. This also held for mothers in high-stress and deprived groups (e.g., single-parent families, unemployed parents, overcrowded living quarters). Fonagy et al. (1995) found that 10 out of 10 mothers in the high-stress deprived group with high reflective-self ratings had securely attached children, whereas 1 out of 17 of high-stress deprived mothers with low reflective-self ratings had a securely attached child. Fonagy et al. (1995) concluded that "these results confirm the prediction that the capacity to reflect on ideas related to attachment serves a protective, resilience-enhancing function, reducing the likelihood of intergenerational transmission of insecurity" (p. 255). They went on to speculate that the mother's ability to take a "mentalizing" or "intentional" stance toward the child—that is, her ability to understand the child's mental states—gives the child an opportunity to internalize a representation of him or her as "mentalizing, desiring, and believing" (p. 257), that is, to experience oneself as a "mentalizing individual" (p. 257).

Fonagy et al. (1995) have extended the focus on reflective-self functioning to an understanding of borderline personality organization. Among other characteristics, the AAIs of borderline individuals were distinguished by significantly lower ratings on the reflective-self function scale than other personality-disordered patients. The AAI narratives of borderline patients also reported significantly more sexual abuse and significantly less resolution of abuse. According to Fonagy et al. (1995), all these findings taken together "are consistent with the assumption that individuals with experience of severe maltreatment in childhood who respond to this experience by an inhibition of reflective-self function are less likely to resolve this abuse, and are more likely to manifest borderline psychopathology" (p. 260).

Attachment and Feeling Understood

Let me turn now to some additional intriguing suggestions proposed by Fonagy et al. (1995) regarding the repetition of maladaptive relationship patterns. They maintained that wanting to be understood by the caregiver is a critical factor in the child's development of attachment and that a subjective sense of being understood is a critical factor in experiencing security. They argued further that the maltreated child may feel understood when he or she "masochistically submits to the caregiver's groundless attacks or criticisms and internalizes the blame" (Fonagy et al., 1995, p. 268). Indeed, the child may use "provocative or sadomasochistic behaviors with the goal of maintaining a familiar relationship system through which the individual [experiences] subjective closeness (union) to the maltreating caregiver" (p. 268).

I think that Fonagy et al. (1995) are describing an extremely important pathogenic dynamic in which the child is "willing" to undergo distortions in character structure and styles of interaction in order to remain connected to the attachment figure and to experience whatever degree of closeness and security is available from the attachment figure. One is reminded here of both Fairbairn's (1952) notion of the child internalizing the bad object and Winnicott's (1965) concept of the "false self." For Winnicott, the essential process in the development of the false self is children's *compliance* with the caregiver's demands at the expense of following and experiencing their own spontaneous and organic impulses and gestures. Fonagy et al. (1995) added to Winnicott's account the idea that the children comply because they need to feel some objective closeness to and derive some security from the attachment figure.

With regard to Fairbairn's (1952) idea of the child's internalizing the bad object, he wrote that an important part of the child's internalization of the bad object is the need to take in the object's badness in order to perceive the environment as tolerable. Note how similar this is to Fonagy et al.'s (1995) reasoning that the child "submits to the caregiver's groundless attacks or criticisms and internalizes the blame" (p. 268). Fairbairn emphasized the child's need to experience the caregiver as a "good object," which is certainly consistent with the common clinical observation of the rejected or abused child's idealization of the rejecting or abusing parent. Fonagy et al. (1995) added the idea that an important motive underlying the child's internalization of blame and continued idealization of the abusing parent is the need to experience a subjective sense of being understood by the object.

The dynamic identified by Fonagy et al. (1995), in which the child is willing to undergo certain compliance-based deformations in character structure in order to feel understood by, remain connected to, and experience closeness to the attachment figure, seems to me to also be potentially present in the treatment situation. I will discuss this later. I turn now to the implications of attachment research for psychodynamic psychotherapy.

Implications of Attachment Research and Theory for Psychotherapy

I believe that attachment theory provides a valuable framework for conceptualizing core elements of psychoanalytic treatment. Recall that from an attachment theory perspective, the availability of a secure base (and the later internalization of a secure base) makes possible and facilitates exploration, both of the external world and of one's inner world. In effective treatment, the therapist serves as a secure base from which patients may feel freer to explore and confront warded-off and anxiety-laden aspects of their inner worlds. This relatively simple idea does much to resolve the false dichotomy between the therapeutic relationship on the one hand and increased insight and self-understanding on the other. As Spence (1992) noted, it is likely that how a therapist's intervention is received by the patient will be greatly influenced by the existing relationship between the patient and the therapist. Thus, it is likely that an "objectively" accurate interpretation in the context of a poor therapeutic alliance will have less therapeutic impact than an "inexact" interpretation (Glover, 1955) made in the context of a good therapeutic alliance. It is also likely to work in the opposite direction—namely, that an accurate and empathic interpretation will tend to strengthen the therapeutic alliance and the therapeutic relationship. Thus, interpretation and the therapeutic relationship will be related to each other in a circular way: An accurate and empathic interpretation contributes to the strengthening of the therapeutic alliance, which, in turn, will make it more likely that the patient will "receive" and make use of the therapist's interpretations.

One would expect that many patients in psychotherapy, particularly those with personality disorders, are insecurely attached in one way or another. These patients have a history of difficulties in forming and maintaining close affectional bonds. As West and Keller (1994) noted, "Disturbed or impoverished interpersonal relationships are the hallmark of most personality disorders" (p. 314). From the perspective of attachment theory, insecurely attached individuals are likely to desire yet fear close relationships and often consciously deny their need for them or make intensive and excessive demands from the attachment figure and become rageful when their demands are not met. Clearly, these patterns will be enacted in the transference and will often elicit countertransference responses from the therapist.

It is all well and good to say that the therapist needs to represent a secure base for the patient. However, given the insecurely attached individual's internal working model of attachment figures and close relationships, this is easier said than accomplished. In a sense, from the perspective of attachment theory, a central task of psychodynamic psychotherapy is to alter, slowly and cumulatively, the internal working model of the patient, based both on repeated "corrective emotional experiences" (Alexander & French, 1946) with the therapist, and on awareness of and reflection on the internal working model. One can expect that insecurely attached patients will experience the therapist in accord with their internal working model—which is another way of saying that transference will occur—and will repeatedly test the therapist to determine whether he or she is really different from the patient's internal representation of their attachment figure (see Weiss, Sampson, & Mt. Zion Psychotherapy Research Group, 1986 for a discussion of the issue of the patient's presentation of tests to the therapist). One can expect that this continuous testing will elicit strong countertransference responses from the therapist. It is imperative that therapists become aware of their own countertransference responses in order to avoid contributing to the repetition of the insecurely attached patient's history of failed relationships—which would constitute a form of retraumatization—and instead represent a secure base for the patient.

Therapists' awareness of their countertransference responses also serves another important therapeutic function, namely, as a guide to the kinds of responses the patient tends to elicit from significant others, which in turn tend to reinforce and perpetuate maladaptive internal working models. As Strupp and Binder (1984) pointed out, the therapist frequently experiences the kinds of affective cues the patient "pulls for." However, instead of acting on these cues—which, as noted above, could constitute a retraumatization—the therapist invites the patient to examine this entire process. In the language of attachment theory, the therapist encourages an examination of the patient's internal working model of self, other, and self–other interactions. Furthermore, the therapist's response that is constructively different from what the patient "pulls for" can be understood as contributing to a "corrective emotional experience." Thus, there is a convergence of the interpretive insight-promoting and therapeutic relationship functions of the therapist. In effective therapy, both functions serve to alter the patient's maladaptive and distress-producing internal working model.

According to Bowlby (1980), there are a group of insecurely attached individuals who characteristically use "defensive exclusion" of attachment cues, signals, and feelings. They are not open to information and feelings concerning attachment needs and feelings. Instead, they show an avoidant and dismissive attitude toward attachment needs and tend to be compulsively self-reliant. That their avoidant and dismissive attitude toward attachment is indeed defensive is supported by Dozier and Kobak's (1992) finding that when attachment themes were elicited during the AAI, avoidant/dismissive individuals showed heightened physiological arousal while denying the experience of negative affect. In this regard, they behave precisely the same as individuals with a "repressive style" (e.g., Weinberger,

1990), who show a heightened physiological response to stress while reporting low anxiety.[6]

It is obvious that Bowlby's term *defensive exclusion* is essentially synonymous with Freud's concept of repression, save that Freud was concerned with the banishment of forbidden sexual and aggressive wishes from consciousness, whereas Bowlby focused on attachment needs. However, it would seem that the general therapeutic goal of modifying repression or defensive exclusion would be the same in both cases. In addition, in both cases, the patient's conflicts and defenses in regard to sex and aggression in the one case and attachment needs in the other would likely be expressed in the transference relationship. If Bowlby (1977) is correct, the false self-sufficiency of the avoidant/dismissive individual is a defensive response to early and persistent unavailability of the attachment figure and covers "unexpressed yearning for love and support" (p. 207). What the avoidant/dismissive individuals who use defensive exclusion need to recognize and name in the course of treatment are the cutoff feelings of loss, sadness, and anger in response to severe disappointment in their relationship with their attachment figure, resulting in a relative inability to experience attachment emotions or any kind of deep feeling.

As West and Keller (1994) pointed out, although defensive exclusion may characterize the avoidant/dismissive individual, it does not especially characterize the enmeshed/preoccupied pattern of insecure attachment. As the terms *enmeshed* and *preoccupied* suggest, these individuals do not defensively exclude attachment cues, information, or feelings. On the contrary, they are almost always intensely preoccupied with attachment concerns. In contrast to the avoidant/dismissive individual's deactivation of the attachment system, the enmeshed person's attachment system is chronically overactivated. Clinically, this may be seen as intense separation anxiety and "overreactions to anticipated or actual separations from their attachment figures" (West & Keller, 1994, p. 320). The problem with these patients does not seem at all to be the excessive use of defensive exclusion, but rather the rel-

---

[6]An obvious research question is whether avoidant/dismissive individuals defensively exclude primarily attachment-related information or show a general repressive style in regard to a wide range of distressing information and affects. One of my students is currently addressing this issue.

ative *absence* of defense in the face of intense anxieties, longings, rages, and despair linked to close relationships—the kind of pattern one is more likely to see in borderline individuals (Livesley & Schroeder, 1991; West et al., 1993). Hence, lifting repression or undoing defensive exclusion of attachment cues and needs would hardly seem to be the primary therapeutic goal for patients with enmeshed/preoccupied attachment patterns.

What, then, should the primary therapeutic goal be for such patients? As noted earlier, West and Keller (1994) described the enmeshed/preoccupied individual as seeming "not to believe that it is obligatory to say goodbye to a lost attachment relationship. Rather, there is a persistent effort to recover the lost relationship, accompanied by intense anger and reproach expressed toward the parent" (p. 321). They went on to note that "the inability to break free from an enmeshed dependency on an ambivalently regarded parent necessarily compromises the individual's ability to form authentic ties to new attachment figures" (p. 321). If this is correct, a central therapeutic task in working with these patients is to help them relinquish the fantasy of recovering a lost relationship, or, to put it more accurately, to help them relinquish the fantasy of recovering a lost relationship that never was, that is itself a fantasy. As Waelder (1960) noted a long time ago, the relinquishment of infantile wishes and fantasies—according to him, a critical and necessary step in successful psychoanalytic treatment—is always accompanied by mourning—as if one had given up a vital need, the fulfillment of which made life worth living. Such relinquishment requires considerable ego resources, including adequate means of regulation of dysphoric affect, which are often in short supply among severely enmeshed/preoccupied patients who show marked borderline characteristics. For such patients, the availability of the therapist as a reliable attachment figure and a secure base becomes especially critical. Concretely, this means that it is primarily the patient's negative transference reactions that are attended to and interpreted. The positive transference is in part an aspect of the background safety and security provided by the therapeutic situation. Interestingly enough, from a different perspective, Kernberg (1984) and Kernberg, Selzer, Koenigsberg, Carr, and Appelbaum (1989) took a similar stance in their treatment approach to borderline patients.

In the previous discussion, two basic elements in the therapeutic situation have been emphasized: (a) the secure base and corrective emotional experience linked to the therapeutic relationship and (b) patients' reflections on their representational worlds, including the connections between past attachment experiences and current internal working models. Before closing this section, I want to refer once again to the findings discussed earlier indicating that an increased capacity to reflect on one's own "ghosts in the nursery" (Fraiberg, Adelson, & Shapiro, 1975) mitigates against the intergenerational transmission of maladaptive attachment patterns and is associated with positive therapeutic outcome. As I noted earlier, these findings support the basic psychoanalytic assumption that remembering, coming to terms with one's past, and replacing discontinuity with a sense of continuity between one's past and present are critical elements in positive therapeutic outcome and positive functioning.

Recall Fonagy et al.'s (1995) hypothesis that the mother who is able to take a mentalizing or intentional stance toward her child, that is, who understands her child's mental states, gives the child an opportunity to internalize a representation of himself or herself as "mentalizing, desiring, and believing" (p. 257). Fonagy et al. also reported that after one year of intensive inpatient psychotherapy, a significant proportion of borderline patients show "a clear improvement in reflective self function" (p. 267), which, they contended, "equips them with a kind of self-righting capacity which, through being able to operate upon their working models, the latter can become an object of review and change" (p. 267). As I noted earlier, this description states in the language of attachment theory the classical psychoanalytic idea that one of the basic accomplishments in successful psychoanalytic treatment is the strengthening of the observing function of the ego. As I also stated earlier, it is especially important to highlight this point during a period in psychoanalytic history in which the therapeutic value of insight, remembering, and self-reflection has been radically deemphasized.

I would speculate that it is not simply the accuracy of the therapist's interpretations and insights that lead to an increase in the patient's reflective-self function, but also the fact that the therapist—analogous to the mother in relation to the child—takes a mentalizing stance toward the patient, that is, attempts to understand the patient's mental states and thereby encourages the patient to internalize representations of himself or herself as "mentalizing, desiring, and believing."

According to Fonagy et al. (1995), secure attachment consists not only in a confident expectation that the attachment figure will be reliable, but also in the child's subjective sense of being understood by the caregiver.

I noted earlier that the need to feel understood and to maintain a connection with the attachment figure are also likely to be present in the treatment situation. Let me now elaborate on that point. I think there is a risk in the treatment situation that in subtle ways the patient may "deform" his or her character and comply—at the potential expense of his or her own nature—in order to generate a subjective sense of feeling understood by and to maintain a connection with the therapist. Because it is often so subtle, such deformation and compliance can be taken as evidence of real insight and that the patient has really been empathically understood. However, it seems to me to be imperative, for good therapeutic outcome, that the two phenomena be adequately distinguished. Complying with the therapist's expectations is essentially a repetition of earlier experiences, which reinforces a new edition of a false self that needs to be distinguished from true self-understanding and a genuine corrective emotional experience needed to alter internal working models.

It is relatively easy to make this distinction conceptually but often difficult to perceive in the ongoing treatment situation, particularly because therapists may have their own agendas in regard to such issues as adherence to this or that theoretical "school," diagnostic categories, and general conceptions of what patients are supposed to be like. Peterfreund (1983) has distinguished between what he called "stereotyped" therapists, who tend to have preset, largely theoretically determined views of what their patients are like, and more open-minded "heuristic" therapists, who slowly form an internal working model of their patients, based primarily on the material the patients present over a long period of time. I am aware that in reality there is no sharp dichotomy between these two types of therapists. However, it is a useful distinction to keep in mind.

Conclusion

I hope that I have demonstrated in this chapter the rich cross-fertilization that is possible and is already occurring between attachment research and theory and psychoanalytic theories. Psychoanalytic theories point to areas and issues that have tended to be overlooked in the formulation of attachment research and theory. Conversely, attachment research and theory have begun to have a constructive and enriching impact on psychoanalytic theory and practice. One of the most important contributions that attachment research and theory can make to psychoanalytic theorizing is to serve as a model of a discipline that is concerned with developing a tradition of accountability and that is carrying out a cumulative and systematic research program.

References

Adam, K. S., Keller, A. E. R., & West, M. (1995). Attachment organization and vulnerability to loss, separation and abuse in disturbed adolescents. In S. Goldberg, R. Muir, & J. Kerr (Eds.), *Attachment theory: Social, developmental, and clinical perspectives* (pp. 309–341). Hillsdale, NJ: Analytic Press.

Ainsworth, M. D. S. (1984). Attachment. In N. S. Endler & J. McV. Hunt (Eds.), *Personality and the behavior disorders* (Vol. I, pp. 559–602). New York: Wiley.

Ainsworth, M. D. S., & Bowlby, J. (1991). An ethological approach to personality development. *American Psychologist, 46,* 333–341.

Ainsworth, M. D. S., Blehar, M. C., Waters, E., & Wall, S. (1978). *Patterns of attachment: A psychological study of the Strange Situation.* Hillsdale, NJ: Erlbaum.

Alexander, F., & French, T. M. (1946). *Psychoanalytic therapy: Principles and applications.* New York: Ronald Press.

Alexander, P. C., Anderson, C., Schaeffer, C. M., Brand, B., Zachary, B., & Kretz, L. (1995). *Attachment as a mediator of long-term effects in survivors of incest.* Manuscript submitted for publication.

Angyal, A. (1941). *Foundations for a science of personality.* New York: Commonwealth Foundation.

Bakan, D. (1966). *The duality of human existence: Isolation and communion in Western man.* Boston: Beacon Press.

Barron, J. W., Eagle, M. N., & Wolitzky, D. L. (Eds.). (1992). *Interface of psychoanalysis and psychology.* Washington, DC: American Psychological Association.

Bartholomew, K., & Horowitz, L. M. (1991). Attachment styles among young adults: A test for a four-category model. *Journal of Personality and Social Psychology, 61,* 226–244.

Bartholomew, K., & Keelan, P. (1993). *Interpersonal dependency and attachment in adulthood.* Unpublished manuscript, Simon Fraser University, Vancouver, British Columbia, Canada.

Beebe, B., & Lachmann, F. (1988). The contribution of mother–infant mutual influence to the origins of self–object representations. *Psychoanalytic Psychology, 5,* 305–337.

Belsky, J., Fish, M., & Isabella, R. (1991). Continuity and discontinuity in infant negative and positive emotionality: Family antecedant and attachment consequences. *Developmental Psychology, 27,* 421–431.

Belsky, J., Rosenberger, K., & Crnic, K. (1995). The origins of attachment security: "Classical" and contextual determinants. In S. Goldberg, R. Muir, &

J. Kerr (Eds.), *Attachment theory: Social, developmental, and clinical perspectives* (pp. 153–183). Hillsdale, NJ: Analytic Press.

Blatt, S. J. (1992). Relatedness and self definition. In J. Barron, M. Eagle, & D. Wolitzky (Eds.), *Interface of psychoanalysis and psychology* (pp. 399–428). Washington, DC: American Psychological Association.

Bowlby, J. (1963). Pathological mourning and childhood mourning. *Journal of the American Psychoanalytic Association, 11,* 500–541.

Bowlby, J. (1969). *Attachment and loss: Vol. I. Attachment.* New York: Basic Books.

Bowlby, J. (1973). *Attachment and loss: Vol. II. Separation.* New York: Basic Books.

Bowlby, J. (1977). The making and breaking of affectional bonds: Aetiology and psychopathology in the light of attachment theory. *British Journal of Psychiatry, 130,* 201–210.

Bowlby, J. (1980). *Attachment and loss: Vol. III. Loss.* New York: Basic Books.

Bowlby, J. (1988a). Developmental psychiatry comes of age. *American Journal of Psychiatry, 45,* 1–10.

Bowlby, J. (1988b). *A secure base: Clinical application of attachment theory.* London: Routledge.

Buie, D. H., & Adler, G. (1982–1983). Definitive treatment of the borderline personality. *International Journal of Psychoanalytic Psychotherapy, 9,* 57–87.

Cicchetti, D. (1989). How research on child maltreatment has informed the study of child development: Perspectives from developmental psychopathology. In. D. Cicchetti & V. Carlson (Eds.), *Child maltreatment: Theory and research on the causes and consequences of child abuse and neglect* (pp. 377–431). New York: Cambridge University Press.

Cowen, E. L., Pederson, A., Barbigian, H., Izzo, L. D., & Frost, M. A. (1973). Long-term follow-up of early detected vulnerable children. *Journal of Consulting and Clinical Psychology, 41,* 438–446.

Dodge, K. A., Bates, J. E., & Pettit, G. S. (1990). Mechanisms in the cycle of violence. *Science, 250,* 1678–1683.

Dozier, M., & Kobak, R. R. (1992). Psychophysiology and adolescent attachment interviews: Converging evidence for repressing strategies. *Child Development, 63,* 1473–1480.

Eagle, M. (1982). Interests as object relations. In J. Masling (Ed.), *Empirical studies in psychoanalytic theories* (Vol. 1, pp. 159–188). Hillsdale, NJ: Erlbaum.

Eagle, M. (1984). *Recent developments in psychoanalysis: A critical evaluation.* Cambridge, MA: Harvard University Press.

Eagle, M. (1995). The developmental perspectives of attachment and psychoanalytic theory. In S. Goldberg, R. Muir, & J. Kerr (Eds.), *Attachment theory: Social, developmental, and clinical perspectives* (pp. 123–150). Hillsdale, NJ: Analytic Press.

Erdelyi, M. H. (1985). *Psychoanalysis: Freud's cognitive psychology.* New York: Freeman.

Erwin, E. (1996). *A final accounting: Philisophical and empirical issues in Freudian psychology.* Cambridge, MA: MIT Press.

Fairbairn, W. R. D. (1952). *Psychoanalytic studies of the personality.* London: Tavistock/Routledge & Kegan Paul.

Fonagy, P., Moran, G. S., & Target, M. (1993). Aggression and the psychological self. *International Journal of Psychoanalysis, 74,* 471–485.

Fonagy, P., Steele, H., & Steele, M. (1991). Maternal representations of attachment during pregnancy predict the organization of infant–mother attachment at one year of age. *Child Development, 62,* 891–905.

Fonagy, P., Steele, M., Steele, H., Higgitt, A., & Target, M. (1994). The theory and practice of resilience. *Journal of Child Psychology and Psychiatry, 35,* 231–257.

Fonagy, P., Steele, M., Steele, H., Leigh, T., Kennedy, R., Mattoon, G., & Target, M. (1995). Attachment, the reflective self, and borderline states. In S. Goldberg, R. Muir, & J. Kerr (Eds.), *Attachment theory: Social, developmental, and clinical perspectives* (pp. 233–278). Hillsdale, NJ: Analytic Press.

Fraiberg, S., Adelson, E., & Shapiro, V. (1975). Ghosts in the nursery: A psychoanalytic approach to the problem of impaired infant–mother relationships. *Journal of the American Academy of Child Psychiatry, 14,* 387–422.

Freedman, D. G., & Gorman, J. (1993). Attachment and the transmission of culture: An evolutionary perspective. *Journal of Social and Evolutionary Systems, 19,* 297–329.

Freud, S. (1953). Analysis terminable and interminable. In J. Strachey (Ed. and Trans.), *The standard edition of the complete psychological works of Sigmund Freud* (Vol. 23, pp. 209–254). London: Hogarth Press. (Original work published 1937)

Freud, S. (1955). Beyond the pleasure principle. In J. Strachey (Ed. and Trans.), *The standard edition of the complete psychological works of Sigmund Freud* (Vol. 18, pp. 3–64). London: Hogarth Press. (Original work published 1920)

Freud, S. (1964). An outline of psychoanalysis. In J. Strachey (Ed. and Trans.), *The standard edition of the complete psychological works of Sigmund Freud* (Vol. 23, pp. 144–215). London: Hogarth Press. (Original work published 1940)

Garmezy, N. (1985). Stress resistant children: The search for protective factors. In J. Stevenson (Ed.), *Recent research in developmental psychopathology* (pp. 213–233). Elmsford, NY: Pergamon Press.

George, C., Kaplan, N., & Main, M. (1985). *The Berkeley Adult Attachment Interview.* Unpublished protocol, Department of Psychology, University of California, Berkeley.

Glover, E. (1955). *The technique of psychoanalysis.* Madison, CT: International Universities Press.

Goldsmith, H. H., & Alansky, J. A. (1987). Maternal and infant temperamental predictors of attachment: A meta-analytic review. *Journal of Consulting and Clinical Psychology, 55,* 805–816.

Greenberg, J. (1991). *Oedipus and beyond: A clinical theory.* Cambridge, MA: Harvard University Press.

Grossmann, K., & Grossmann, K. (1991). Attachment quality as an organizer of emotional and behavioral responses in a longitudinal perspective. In C. M. Parker, J. Stevenson-Hinde, & P. Marris (Eds.), *Attachment across the life cycle* (pp. 93–114). New York: Tavistock/Routledge.

Guntrip, H. (1969). *Schizoid phenomena, object relations and the self.* Madison, CT: International Universities Press.

Hazan, C., & Shaver, P. (1987). Romantic love conceptualized as an attachment process. *Journal of Personality and Social Psychology, 52,* 511–524.

Hinde, R. A. (1959). Behavior and speculation in birds and lower vertebrates. *Biological Review, 34,* 85–128.

Holmes, D. S. (1990). The evidence for repression: An examination of sixty years of research. In J. L. Singer (Ed.), *Repression and dissociation* (pp. 85–102). Chicago: University of Chicago Press.

Holmes, J. (1993). *John Bowlby and attachment theory.* New York: Routledge.

Horowitz, M. J., Wilner, N., & Alvarez, W. (1979). Impact of Events Scale: A measure of subjective stress. *Psychosomatic Medicine, 41,* 209–216.

Jacobson, J. L., & Wille, D. R. (1986). The influence of attachment pattern on developmental changes in peer interaction from the toddler to the pre-school period. *Child Development, 57,* 338–347.

Kaplan, N. (1987, May). *Internal representations of attachment in six-year-olds.* Paper presented at the biennial meetings of the Society for Research in Child Development, Baltimore.

Karen, R. (1994). *Becoming attached.* New York: Warner Books.

Kernberg, O. (1984). *Severe personality disorders: Psychotherapeutic strategies.* New Haven, CT: Yale University Press.

Kernberg, O. F., Selzer, M. A., Koenigsberg, H. W., Carr, A. C., & Appelbaum, A. H. (1989). *Psychodymanic psychotherapy of borderline patients.* New York: Basic Books.

Kitcher, P. (1992). *Freud's dream: A complete interdisciplinary science of mind.* Cambridge, MA: MIT Press.

Kohut, H. (1971). *The analysis of the self.* Madison, CT: International Universities Press.

Kohut, H. (1977). *The restoration of the self.* Madison, CT: International Universities Press.

Kohut, H. (1984). *How does analysis cure?* Chicago: University of Chicago Press.

Lamb, M. E. (1987). Predictive implications of individual differences in attachment. *Journal of Consulting and Clinical Psychology, 55,* 817–824.

Levine, L. V., Tuber, S. B., Slade, A., & Ward, M. J. (1991). Mother's mental representations and their relationship to mother–infant attachment. *Bulletin of the Menninger Clinic, 55,* 454–469.

Livesley, W. J., & Schroeder, M. L. (1991). Dimensions of personality disorders: DSM-III-R cluster B diagnoses. *Journal of Nervous and Mental Disease, 179,* 320–328.

Livesley, W. J., Schroeder, M. L., & Jackson, D. N. (1990). Dependent personality disorder and attachment problems. *Journal of Personality Disorders, 4,* 131–140.

Mahler, M. (1968). *On human symbiosis and the vicissitudes of individuation: Vol. I. Infantile psychosis.* Madison, CT: International Universities Press.

Main, M. (1983). Exploration, play and cognitive functioning related to infant–mother attachment. *Infant Behavior and Development, 6,* 167–174.

Main, M. (1985, April). *An adult attachment classification system: Its relation to infant–parent attachment.* Paper presented at the Biennial Meeting of the Society for Research in Child Development, Toronto, Ontario, Canada.

Main, M. (1991). Metacognitive knowledge, metacognitive monitoring, and singular (coherent) versus mutiple (incoherent) models of attachment: Findings and directions for future research. In C. M. Parkes, J. Henenson-Hinde, & P. Marris (Eds.), *Attachment across the life cycle* (pp. 127–159). London: Routledge.

Main, M., & George, C. (1985). Responses of abused and disadvantaged toddlers to distress in agemates: A study in a day care setting. *Developmental Psychology, 21,* 407–412.

Main, M., & Goldwyn, R. (1984). Predicting rejection of her infant from mother's representation of her own experience: Implications of the abused–abusing intergenerational cycle. *Child Abuse and Neglect, 8,* 203–217.

Main, M., & Hesse, E. (1990). Parents' unresolved traumatic experiences are related to infant disorganized attachment status: Is frightened/frightening parental behavior the mechanism? In M. Greenberg, D. Cichetti, & E. M. Cummings (Eds.), *Attachment in the preschool years* (pp. 161–182). Chicago: University of Chicago Press.

Main, M., Kaplan, N., & Cassidy, J. (1985). Security in infancy, childhood, and adulthood: A move to the level of representation, In I. Bretherton & E. Waters (Eds.), *Monographs of the Society for Research in Child Development, 50,* 66–104.

Main, M., & Solomon, J. (1990). Procedures for identifying infants as disorganized/disoriented during the Ainsworth Strange Situation. In M. Greenberg, D. Cichetti, & E. M. Cummings (Eds.), *Attachment in the preschool years* (pp. 121–160). Chicago: University of Chicago Press.

Melges, F., & Swartz, M. (1989). Oscillations of attachment in borderline personality disorder. *American Journal of Psychiatry, 146,* 1115–1120.

Millon, T. (1987). Concluding commentary. *Journal of Personality Disorders, 1,* 110–112.

Mitchell, S. (1988). *Relational concepts in psychoanalysis: An integration.* Cambridge, MA: Harvard University Press.

Modell, A. (1984). *Psychoanalysis in a new context.* Madison, CT: International Universities Press.

Nguyen, T. D., Attkisson, C. C., & Stegner, C. (1983). Assessment of patient satisfaction: Development and refinement of a service evaluation questionnaire. *Evaluation and Program Planning, 6,* 299–314.

Passman, R. H., & Erck, T. W. (1977, March). *Visual presentation of mothers for facilitating play in children: The effects of silent films of mothers.* Paper presented at the Society for Research in Child Development, New Orleans, LA.

Passman, R. H., & Weisberg, P. (1975). Mothers and blankets as agents for promoting play and exploration by young children in a novel environment: The effects of social and non-social attachment objects. *Developmental Psychology, 11,* 70–77.

Peterfreund, E. (1983). *The process of psychoanalytic therapy.* Hillsdale, NJ: Analytic Press.

Piaget, J. (1952). *The origins of intelligence.* Madison, CT: International Universities Press.

Rajecki, D. W., Lamb, M. E., & Obmascher, P. (1978). Toward a general theory of infantile attachment: A comparative review of aspects of the social bond. *Behavioral and Brain Sciences, 3,* 417–464.

Rapaport, D. (1942). *Emotions and memory.* Madison, CT: International Universities Press.

Riviere, J. (1927). Contribution to symposium on child analysis. *International Journal of Psychoanalysis, 8,* 373–377.

Sears, R. R. (1944). Experimental analysis of psychoanalytic phenomena. In J. McV. Hunt (Ed.), *Personality and the behavior disorders* (Vol. 1, pp. 306–332). New York: Ronald Press.

Shaver, P. R., & Clark, C. L. (1994). The psychodynamics of adult romantic attachment. In J. Masling & R. F. Bornstein (Eds.), *Empirical perspectives on object relations theory* (pp. 105–156). Washington, DC: American Psychological Association.

Shedler, J., Mayman, M., & Manis, M. (1993). The illusion of mental health. *American Psychologist, 48,* 1117–1131.

Spence, D. P. (1992). Interpretation: A critical perspective. In J. W. Barron, M. N. Eagle, & D. L. Wolitzky (Eds.), *Interface of psychoanalysis and psychology* (pp. 558–572). Washington, DC: American Psychological Association.

Sroufe, L. A. (1986). Appraisal: Bowlby's contribution to psychoanalytic theory and developmental psychology. *Journal of Child Psychology and Psychiatry, 27,* 841–849.

Sroufe, L. A. (1990). An organizational perspective on the self. In D. Cichetti & M. Beeghly (Eds.), *The self in transition* (pp. 281–307). Chicago: University of Chicago Press.

Sroufe, L. A., & Waters, E. (1977). Attachment as an organizational construct. *Child Development, 48,* 1184–1189.

Stern, D. (1985). *The interpersonal world of the infant.* New York: Basic Books.

Strupp, H. H., & Binder, J. L. (1984). *Psychotherapy in a new key.* New York: Basic Books.

Suess, G. J., Grossmann, K. E., & Sroufe, L. A. (1992). Effects of infant attachment to mother and father on quality of adaptation in preschool: From dyadic to individual organisation of self. *International Journal of Behavioral Development, 15,* 43–65.

van den Boom, D. (1990). Preventive intervention and the quality of mother–infant interaction and infant exploration in irritable infants. In W. Koops (Ed.), *Developmental psychology behind the dikes* (pp. 249–270). Amsterdam: Eburon.

Vaughn, B. E., Stevenson-Hinde, J., Waters, E., Kotsaftis, A., Lefeber, G. B., Shouldice, A., Trudel, M., & Belsky, J. (1992). Attachment security and temperament in infancy and early childhood: Some conceptual clarifications. *Developmental Psychology, 28,* 463–473.

Wachtel, P. (1982). Vicious circles: The self and the rhetoric of emerging and unfolding. *Contemporary Psychoanalysis, 18,* 259–272.

Wachtel, P. L. (1987). *Action & insight.* New York: Guilford Press.

Wachtel, P. L. (1993). *Therapeutic communication: Principles and effective practice.* New York: Guilford Press.

Waelder, R. (1960). *Basic theory of psychoanalysis.* Madison, CT: International Universities Press.

Wakefield, J. (1992). Freud and cognitive psychology: The conceptual interface. In J. W. Barron, M. N. Eagle, & D. L. Wolitzky (Eds.), *Interface of psychoanalysis and psychology* (pp. 77–98). Washington, DC: American Psychological Association.

Weinberger, D. A. (1990). The construct validity of the repressive coping style. In J. L. Singer (Ed.), *Repression and dissociation* (pp. 337–386). Chicago: University of Chicago Press.

Weiss, J., Sampson, H., & Mt. Zion Psychotherapy Research Group. (1986). *The psychoanalytic process.* New York: Guilford Press.

West, M. L., & Keller, A. E. R. (1994). Psychotherapy strategies for insecure attachment in personality disorders. In M. B. Sperling & W. H. Berman (Eds.), *Attachment in adults* (pp. 313–330). New York: Guilford Press.

West, M., Keller, A., Links, P., & Patrick, J. (1993). Borderline disorder and attachment pathology. *Canadian Journal of Psychiatry, 38*(Suppl. 1), 516–522.

West, M., Sheldon, A. E. R., & Reiffer, L. (1989). Attachment theory and brief psychotherapy: Applying current research to clinical interventions. *Canadian Journal of Psychiatry, 34,* 369–375.

West, M. L., & Sheldon-Keller, A. E. R. (1994). *Patterns of relating.* New York: Guilford Press.

Winnicott, D. W. (1965). *The maturational process and the facilitating environment.* Madison, CT: International Universities Press.

5

Psychoanalysis and the Study of Adult Lives

Bertram J. Cohler and David S. deBoer

So long as we trace the development from its final outcome backwards, the chain of events appears continuous, and we feel we have gained an insight which is completely satisfactory or even exhaustive. But if we proceed the reverse way, if we start from premises inferred from the analysis and try to follow these up to the final result, we no longer get the impression of an inevitable sequence of events which could not have been otherwise determined. . . . The synthesis is thus not so satisfactory as the analysis; in other words from a knowledge of the premises we could not have foretold the nature of the results.

—Sigmund Freud
"The Psychogenesis of a Case of Homosexuality in a Woman"

The study of lives has been founded on the assumption that experiences earlier in the course of life are cumulative in directing later life outcomes and that development follows a course in which the negotiation of expectable tasks at particular points over time, in a sequential manner, is presumed to foster continued adjustment (Bibring, 1959). This assumption regarding the cumulative nature of psychological development portrayed by Rapaport and Gill (1959) as the genetic point of view was founded largely on a particular reading of psychoanalysis, principally Sigmund Freud's (1905/1953b) *Three Essays on the Theory of Sexuality*, Karl Abraham's (1921/1953, 1924/1953) influential essays, and Erik Erikson's (1950/1963) reformulation of this epigenetic model. However, findings from the study of lives among persons followed over periods of several decades have challenged many of these assumptions regarding such a linear portrayal of lives (Shanok, 1993).

Even when, as in Zetzel and Meissner's (1973) reformulation, the present is included as "coactive" with the past, it is assumed that past memories and associated feelings are recalled in the present, in circumstances experienced as historically similar. Erikson (1950/ 1963) may be credited with extending this epigenetic perspective to the study of the adult years; however, Erikson still assumed that earlier experiences largely determined the outcome of such issues posed for adults as work attainments and management of the capacity for intimacy (Gould, 1993; Vaillant & Koury, 1993; Vaillant & Milofsky, 1980). Controversy continues regarding the nature of contributions that clinical psychoanalysis might make toward an understanding of the course of life, particularly the years of middle and later adulthood.

Much of traditional psychoanalytic study, particularly that of Abraham and his protégé, Melanie Klein, was founded on the belief that the most significant aspects of psychological development are completed during the first years of life and that the rest of life is simply the amplification of psychological issues connected with the "family romance" taking place during those first years. This genetic point of view, representing the dominant intellectual position of psychoanalysis regarding development, poses problems in grasping the significance of psychoanalysis as a means for understanding adult lives. This chapter reviews contemporary perspectives within psychoanalysis that suggest (a) additional understandings of personal change across the course of life and (b) reconsider psychoanalysis as a particularly relevant method of inquiry into continuity and change in the experience of self and others across the adult years.

The Epigenetic Perspective and the Study of Lives

Appraisal of the value of psychoanalytic contributions for the study of development over time may be founded in confusion regarding both the concept of development within psychoanalysis and the means used to study of developmental processes. George Klein (1976) has posited two theories of psychoanalysis: (a) a worldview based on the philosophy of science relevant in the late 19th century and (b) a clinical theory founded on Sigmund Freud's detailed observations within the consulting room. The former theory deals with such concepts as fixation and regression in developmental study, whereas the latter theory deals with such questions as the significance of silence within the psychoanalytic hour, momentary forgetting and remembering, and the experience of analyst and analysand working together within what Gill (1994) has termed a "two-person" psychology (Hoffman, 1991). As Cohler and Galatzer-Levy (1995) have suggested, following George Klein's pioneering reformulation of Freud's contribution, Freud's scientific worldview has too often been confused with the clinical theory founded on the basis of intervention.

The Epigenetic Approach and Freud's Scientific Worldview

Sulloway (1979) and Gay (1988) have observed that much of Freud's discussion of human development was argued by analogy to his laboratory study and was not founded on clinical study. Freud introduced the study of wish and intent into psychoanalysis while striving to remain within the new laboratory psychological and neuroscientific perspectives of the school of Helmholtz. From the mid-19th century, Helmholtz's emphasis on demonstration and experiment in science epitomized positivist Enlightenment thinking within the biological sciences and medicine. Freud was deeply affected by the views of Helmholtz and his followers while he worked in the University of Vienna laboratory of Brücke (1819–1892), whom Helmholtz called "our ambassador to the East" (Bernfeld, 1941, 1951; E. Jones, 1953; Sulloway, 1979).

As Sulloway (1979) has observed, even when Freud was a student, he had been attracted to Haeckel's (1868/1968) concept of the fundamental biogenetic law, which proposed that ontogeny recapitulates phylogeny. Haeckel, and Freud following in this tradition, had argued that the human fetus passes on its way to development through all the evolutionary phases from the simplest one-cell organism to full human development. Although little credence has been given to Haeckel's speculation regarding the course of evolution, this position was particularly attractive to Freud, who, working under Brücke's supervision, initiated laboratory exploration of Haeckel's proposition, working with the brook lamprey. Freud (1910/1957b, 1915/1957) noted that his later discussion of fixation and regression was founded in part on this scientific study early in his career. Indeed, Freud used findings from this early laboratory study as an analogy for his speculations regarding the course of human development, but he did not embed this analogy within clinical study except for the speculative effort to reconstruct the experiences of Leonardo da Vinci in a literary experiment (Jackson, 1969; Stengel, 1963).[1]

Writing in the essay on Leonardo, Freud (1910/1957b) commented that "(i)mpressive analogies from biology have prepared us to find that the individual's mental development repeats the course of human development in abbreviated form" (p. 97). Freud (1913/1958) relied on this analogy rather than on clinical observation alone as the foundation for his genetic psychology. Indeed, Freud was not able to move beyond the scientific worldview first formulated in Brücke's laboratory and further supported through his reading of Darwin's work (Ritvo, 1990) and other 19th-century natural philosophy. This experience-distant perspective seeks to discover possible connections between present psychological states and modes of experiencing earlier maturational processes that at certain "critical periods," particularly in the first years of life, are believed to have been formative in shaping such later outcomes as the capacity for intimate relations with others or the ability to resolve troubling tension states.

---

[1]Problems arise to the extent that clinical observation from the psychoanalytic setting is used as a means of confirming assumptions regarding the relationship of past and present that may have been derived from biological analogy. Viewed from a life-course perspective, the formulation of metapsychology may have permitted Freud to realize an increased sense of meaning and direction in his own life, integrating his prepsychoanalytic laboratory study and his later clinical work, maintaining a coherent narrative of his career that was consistent with biological knowledge available to him at the end of the 19th century (Bernfeld, 1941, 1949; Pribram & Gill, 1976; Sulloway, 1979).

The genetic point of view assumes that it is possible to show

"how the past is contained in the present." Genetic propositions describe why, in past situations of conflict, a specific solution was adopted; why the one was retained and the other dropped, and what causal relation exists between these solutions and later development. Genetic propositions refer to the fact that in an adult's behavior, anxiety may be induced by outdated conditions, and they explain why these conditions may still exercise influence. (Hartmann & Kris, 1945, p. 14)

This (epi)genetic perspective, based on analogy to Freud's prepsychoanalytic study and later extended by Abraham (1924/1953), Erikson (1950/1963), and Rapaport (1960/1967), is founded on assumptions regarding the course of development similar to both ethology and social learning theory[2] and has become the foundation for a general understanding of Freud's contribution to the study of development. This second perspective was widely disseminated in texts and the popular press, where it was appropriately discredited as being unable to account for the subtlety of the human condition. However,

---

[2]The genetic approach, systematized in psychoanalysis by Abraham (1921/1953, 1924/1953) and Erikson (1950/1963), received apparent support from animal studies of "critical periods," or moving windows in development when the occurrence or absence of events permanently affects functions of the evolving organism. Critical periods were clearly demonstrated for certain animal behaviors, for example, imprinting in ducks (Lorenz, 1937/1957; Tinbergen, 1951). The concept was generalized to human development without adequate empirical evidence. In the same manner, both social learning approaches and Piaget's genetic epistemology emphasize the developmental primacy of early over later experiences (N. Miller & Dollard, 1941; Murphy, 1947/1966). Furthermore, although the Piagetian model shares the functionalism implicit in Freud's own mechanistic metapsychology (Basch, 1977; Cohler, 1989; Wolff, 1966), it is at least partially consistent with contemporary views of development in emphasizing at least some discontinuity of thought between earlier and later points in development.

The epigenetic model of psychological development presumes a necessary, causal connection between earlier and later states. However, this rigid connection has been questioned by both clinical and systematic empirical studies of lives over time. For example, imprinting plays a minimal role in human learning and development: Ethological models are largely irrelevant to the study of human infant development (Berenthal & Campos, 1987; Cohler, 1987; Colombo, 1982; Emde, 1981; Kagan, Kearsley, & Zelazo, 1978). Longitudinal studies of personality from childhood through middle and late life demonstrate that lives are less continuous and predictably ordered than is assumed in epigenetic models (Clarke & Clarke, 1976; Emde, 1981; Gergen, 1994; Kagan, 1980; Neugarten, 1969, 1979; Skolnick, 1986).

this exposition of the genetic perspective failed to recognize Freud's signal contribution to the study of development—the concept of the past as presently coactive with the present and enacted, often outside of awareness, in the form of wish or intent (Klein, 1976). Furthermore, this portrayal of Freud's views regarding the past failed to account for his own caution (S. Freud, 1920/1955) that it is easier to reconstruct the past than to predict forward from earlier to later developmental stages.

The genetic point of view both poses problems and offers promise for study of the manner in which the past is used in understanding present wishes and intents. Despite the undeniable relevance of the genetic point of view for these more detailed works outlining, in effect, the natural evolution of individual development, Freud's concern with the genesis of behavior also reflects concern with a mode of historical inquiry and understanding distinctive of psychoanalysis. As Freud (1920/1955) noted, historical explanation is not simply prediction "turned upside down" (Scriven, 1959); rather, it is predicated on an autonomous mode of understanding that is fundamentally different from those linked to prospective inquiry. For this reason, although problematic for the realization of psychoanalysis as a human science, Freud's concern with the genetic approach provides the conceptual foundation for the study of life history as a narrative of experience.

Shifting Perspectives Within Psychoanalysis: From Epigenesis to the Study of Lives

Although findings from experimental psychology have led to substantial revision in dynamic and economic metapsychological approaches (Applegarth, 1977; Gill, 1976; Holt, 1975; Horowitz, 1977; Rosenblatt & Thickstun, 1970, 1977; Swanson, 1977a, 1977b; Wallerstein, 1977), findings from normative developmental study have had much less impact in fostering revision of the genetic approach (Abrams, 1978; Escoll, 1977). To the extent that developmental psychology has been viewed as relevant to psychoanalytic theory and practice, findings emerging from scientific study have too often been viewed as verification of specific assumptions derived from genetic propositions about the origins of behavior in earlier infancy (Basch, 1977, 1982, 1985; Lichtenberg, 1983; Silver, 1985) together with assumptions regarding the consequences of particular early experiences for psychological development and adjustment across the life course (Sternschein, 1973; Tolpin & Kohut, 1980).

Remaining preoccupied with Freud's scientific worldview rather than with his clinical theory emphasizing wish and intent (Wallerstein, 1990), psychoanalysis has largely ignored the findings from study of lives over time into oldest age, suggesting that the course of development may not be as predictable or genetically ordered as previously maintained (Gergen, 1977, 1980; Grunes, 1980; Kagan, 1980; Kohlberg, Ricks, & Snarey, 1984). These reports, based on the long-term study of lives, suggest that changes taking place across the course of life—often in response to unexpected, generally adverse life changes—pose significant challenges to personal adjustment, which may be difficult to predict according to a cumulative theory of development. For such theories fail to acknowledge the possibly transformative impact of later experiences on earlier experiences and the significance of a presently maintained portrayal of the course of life as critical in understanding the experience of self and others (Emde, 1981; Emde & Harmon, 1984).

Gergen (1977) has suggested that much of the course of adult lives may be understood as the response to chance events. In a recent report following up on the study of adult lives over a period of more than a decade, Marjorie Fiske and David Chiriboga (1990) have provided findings confirming the significance of these chance events as determining the subsequent course of life. Although the men and women in their 10-year longitudinal study (across four interview points) were generally able to maintain a sense of coherence and to use a continuing conception of self and personal style in responding to adversity, chance events such as sudden life-threatening illness early in adulthood or illness and other adversity among adult offspring and other close relatives markedly disrupted adjustment. Particularly among middle-aged and older adults, physical illness, even if expectable, ushers in a series of other, secondary consequences, such as an increased sense of personal vulnerability and an accelerated sense of aging.

Fiske and Chiriboga (1990) observed that the very diversity of decisions and opportunities available in contemporary society leaves many persons bewildered regarding life choices. Their observations tally with those of Kaufman (1986) and Gergen (1990), suggesting that the very flexibility of personal options and choices takes a continuing toll on adult adjustment. In short, there are just too many options for people to comprehend; sudden adversity appears to impose further limits on the ability to deal with this adversity. At the same time, it is always tempting to assume that present times are the worst of times; historical evidence tends to raise questions regarding the privileged status of any particular time as presenting unusual challenges for personal adjustment.

Findings from life-course developmental study pose questions regarding either the extent to which there are *specific* effects of early adversity in development that are maintained over time (Emde, 1981) or whether particular intervention techniques provide a "buffering" effect, beyond that due to time itself, against the impact of early adversity in development (Anthony & Cohler, 1987; Cohler & Musick, 1984). This question of the impact of earlier on later experience was systematically studied in the several studies merged into one at Berkeley's Institute of Human Development (Eichorn, Clausen, Haan, Honzik, & Mussen, 1981; Elder, 1974; M. Jones, Bayley, MacFarlane, & Honzik, 1971) and in the report by Kagan and Moss (1962), based on the data from the Fels longitudinal study in Ohio. Significantly, findings from these two longitudinal studies have suggested that little variance of later outcomes can be explained on the basis of childhood factors, including child-rearing attitudes and practices.

In a manner parallel to the situation with the critical-period hypothesis, disappointing findings from longitudinal studies of child development have increasingly led investigators to wonder if the case for the continuity of childhood and adult experience in human development has not been overstated (Brim, 1976; Neugarten, 1969). Indeed, as findings from both longitudinal reports across the adult years and clinical reports have suggested (Colarusso & Nemiroff, 1981; Kohlberg et al., 1984; Moss & Sussman, 1980; Nemiroff & Colarusso, 1985), a primary question in the study of adulthood concerns factors accounting for continuity or change in personality and adjustment from early adulthood through oldest age rather than simply assuming the primacy of either childhood or adult experiences (Neugarten, 1969, 1979; Stevens-Long, 1990).

Personal Development and Life Course: Social Time and Expectable Transitions

The study of lives must always account for the fact that people live within particular social and historical circumstances (Dannefer, 1984; Elder, 1992). The very bright women experiencing social discrimination who consulted Freud in the 1880s and 1890s in Vienna lived at a time very different from the present. Although some critics of contemporary society (Lasch, 1979; A. Miller, 1981) have suggested that current society produces unique and particularly harsh circumstances for personal and social development, a comparative perspective suggests that each era presents unique challenges for both children and adults (Aries, 1962; Harringdon, 1993). Historical study cautions against generalizations across times that differ in social demands on particular lives. For example, as Easterlin (1987) and Guttentag and Secord (1983) have shown, people growing up within particularly large birth cohorts face enhanced competition lifelong for resources ranging from places in preschool programs to realizing adequate medical and social services in later life.

Meanings of personal experience are shaped by these generation-linked experiences as reenacted anew in the context of the family, the larger society, and the psychoanalytic process. Analyst and analysand are both members of this larger society and share particular lived experiences. Differences in ages of these two participants in the psychoanalytic process through which such experiences as the Vietnam War were experienced contribute to somewhat different understandings, which must be collaboratively understood within the context of each session. Hartmann (1939/1958) initially realized both the problems and promise for psychoanalysis posed by considering lives in terms of social contexts. Although phrased in terms of the biological concept of "adaptation," the problem of understanding interpretations of lives in terms of social contexts—including that within the psychoanalytic process itself—remains one that challenges the experience-near perspective of psychoanalysis and the formation of these experience-near meanings of self and experience within larger social contexts.

Across the past three decades there has been a dramatic shift in the study of lives over time from a life span or life-cycle to a life-course perspective. Whereas the concept of life cycle focuses on particular individuals who are understood as transformed from a predefined period to another period in an ordered, cyclical sequence, the concept of the life course presumes an open system recognizing social and historical process and understanding lives over time within the context of both expectable and eruptive changes (Elder, 1992, in press; Neugarten & Hagestad, 1976). The life-course perspective portrays people within a much larger context of socially constructed transitions that are reflected in conceptions of self and other within particular societies at particular times. Particular lives are reflective of these shared conceptions as modified through uniquely ordered circumstances taking place in a particular, unpredictable manner.

The concept of generation is central in understanding life-course perspectives on personal development. Troll (1970) and Bengtson, Furlong, and Laufer (1974) have discussed three age-linked characteristics: (a) place in society within a cluster of four or five groups alive at the same time, (b) period or point in the course of life such as youth or middle age, and (c) cohort or persons of a given birth year who have experienced similar social and historical events. The very age distribution in society leads to groups of persons with understandings of self, others, and experience shaped largely by experience of particular historical events, which, together with the timing of expectable and eruptive life changes, largely determine individual life circumstances and morale (Cohler & Boxer, 1984; Dannefer, 1984; Pearlin, 1980; Pearlin & Lieberman, 1979; Pearlin, Menaghan, Lieberman, & Mullan, 1981; Pearlin & Schooler, 1978).

Finally, the concept of generation also includes the concept of *cohort*, or group of persons who are of a particular age when they experience these same social and historical events (Cain, 1964; Riley, 1973; Ryder, 1965; Schaie, 1984). A preschool child will respond quite differently to such catastrophes as war or natural disaster than will a teenager or a middle-aged adult (Tuttle, 1993). Being of a particular age at the time of such an experience leads to some shared understanding of the subsequent course of life that is different from that of a different age group when the event took place. This perspective suggests that it is not easy to talk about expectable timetables for life transitions except in the context of a particular sociohistorical cohort. Similarly, it is hard to portray modal personality patterns for individuals of particular ages or of particular points in the course of life such as adolescence or midlife, except as qualified by generation understood in terms of particular sociohistorical changes taking place for people born at about the same time and traveling through the course of life as a cohort. However, it is also important to recognize Rosow's (1978) caution that it is difficult to determine the boundaries of a cohort or to know how many years' difference constitutes a significant cohort difference.

These aspects of generation determine the manner in which persons understand sequence and timing of both expectable and eruptive events across the course of life. Neugarten and her colleagues (Neugarten, Moore, & Lowe, 1965) have shown that among generations alive at any point, there is shared agreement regarding the definition of age. Although older adults are somewhat more tolerant than younger adults of larger variation in the time for the occurrence of particular role transitions, there is broad agreement on what constitutes childhood, adolescence, adulthood, and later life. Following Durkheim's (1915/1961) discussion of time and the ritual life of the community, Sorokin and Merton (1937), J. Roth (1963), Neugarten and Hagestad (1976), Hagestad and Neugarten (1985), and Hagestad (1990, 1994) have suggested that individuals maintain an internal timetable for expectable role transitions and associated life changes.

Across the life course, people continually compare their own developmental achievements with that shared definition of being on time or either early or late "off time." Even very young children learn the sequence of expectable events taking place across the course of life from first entrance into school through school leaving, first job, marriage or partnership, advent of parenthood or generative care for another, retirement, widowhood, and death (Farnham-Diggory, 1966). These expectable life changes represent the background of personal experience. Particular, generally unpredictable life circumstances, both adverse and positive, occur in the context of these expectable life changes. Eruptive life changes, such as widowhood in the fourth rather than in the eighth decade of a woman's life pose particular problems both because there are few consociates with whom to share burdens and to provide assistance and also because there has been little time to rehearse this life change through observation of others who have confronted and managed such adversity (Neugarten, 1979).

Seltzer (1976) and Cohler and Boxer (1984) have suggested that the experience of positive morale or life satisfaction is largely determined by the sense of being "on time" for expectable role transitions or life changes. The sense that life changes and role transitions occur in an expected manner and that one is on time for these events, consistent with other members of a cohort or generation, may be associated with an enhanced sense of personal congruence. At the same time, it is important to recognize that there may be differences in definition of timing role transitions, both *within* and *across* cohorts. It is particularly on this latter point that the dynamic we are describing relates to Festinger's (1954) work on social comparison theory, in that people are driven to compare their own developmental achievements with a timetable that can be said to be collectively constructed, not by the entire culture, but by others of similar education, class, generation, and so on.

Within the generation of young adults who were born roughly in the late 1960s through the early 1970s, the so-called Generation X, problems in finding employment in an economy experiencing serious dislocation have led to realization that the first job may not take place until the late twenties, leading to further postponement of such expectable role transitions as marriage and parenthood (Hogan, 1981, 1984; Marini, 1978, 1985). Comparing their own place in the course of life with that of preceding generations, these young adults experience lowered morale and particular frustration from the sense of being late off time for this particular role transition. However, when comparing their own lives with those of other members of their generation, things appear much less bleak and there is improvement in morale.

Being early off time poses particular disadvantages because of lack of preparation for the change, together with lack of others who are experiencing similar changes with whom one can realize enhanced support. Furstenberg, Brooks-Gunn, and Morgan (1987) have suggested that persons in later life may overcome at least some of the problems associated with such early off-time transitions as advent of parenthood during adolescence. However, being late in the shared timetable for life changes has particular advantages. As Nydegger (1980, 1981) and Daniels and Weingarten (1982) have observed, men who make the transition to parenthood late are more settled in their career and more comfortable with themselves than are men who make this transition on time but often are simultaneously concerned with career and other early adult concerns.

Schaie's (1984) summary of his work on the Seattle Longitudinal Study highlights the significance of generation, understood as cohort, on psychometric test findings. Particular sociohistorical events shape the life course of those born at about the same time. It is very difficult to make any statements regarding lives apart from this recognition of the fundamental impact of events experienced in common (Schaie & Hertzog, 1983). The work of Elder and his colleagues, summarized in Elder and Caspi (1990), has clarified the manner in which these events shape the course of lives over time. Using the data collected at Berkeley's Institute of Human Development, Elder (1974) was able to show the differential impact of the Great Depression on the adjustment of groups of preschool and adolescent boys and girls. Elder's work has helped to understand the manner in which people born at about the same time, experiencing particular events in common, share similar effects from events on the subsequent course of life. As Elder and Caspi (1990) observed, age understood as an index of birth year serves to locate people in history and provides an index of the range of events likely to have an impact on particular lives.

Considering that at any one time there may be several cohorts alive and at different ages when a series of linked social and historical events occur, the dynamics of response by these cohorts to both particular events and succeeding events becomes a major factor in understanding both social change and conflicts between generations or cohorts at particular times. Furthermore, just as maturational factors and changing social context are important determinants of personality development across the childhood years, role changes, including losses and exits of the older years, provide continuing challenges and opportunities for the maintenance of a sense of self and well-being (Bibring, 1959). In sum, although it may not be possible a priori to rule out continuity, it should be recognized as something that is *achieved*, a function of modes of experience that are *maintained* across the life course. Continuity is not something that just happens, with the present as a natural outcome of earlier discrete, apparently unconnected past effects. Rather, continuity experienced within lives over time reflects a continuing effort to make the best possible sense out of the totality of life experiences, with the goal of preserving a life history reflecting perceptible meaning.

Dannefer (1984) has suggested that the interplay of persona and social context is critical in understanding the very process of development. As Dannefer (1984) observed,

> The organism is *constituted* as a human being in interaction with the environment, and continually sustained and reconstituted in an ongoing way across the life course. Through this interaction, characteristics that appear to "develop" are actually produced, sustained, or modified. (p. 107)

The concept of point or period in the life course suggests that people experiencing similar social circumstances represent a convoy of consociates who interpret expectable role transitions associated with particular transition points in common, expectable ways. From school leaving to the advent of parenthood, retirement, or widowhood, response to transitions cannot be understood apart from a life history of particular events taking place over time. It is the very attribute of living within a particular time with a particular group of people who have throughout life experienced similar sociohistorical events and who have interpreted them in particular ways at particular ages that is the foundation of the very concept of personal development and that also determines the manner in which lives are to be understood and studied. The very definition of continuity or change portrayed at a particular time is a consequence of these shared meanings regarding person, the passage of time, and both social and historical context, as well as the patterns of human relationships that they generate (Geertz, 1966/1973a, 1966/1973b).

To the extent that normative findings from developmental psychology are used in this process of "postdiction," it may be that both psychoanalysis and developmental psychology suffer in the process. Most certainly, it is neither possible, nor even necessarily desirable, to determine events in infancy and early childhood that, on the basis of retrospective data obtained from clinical psychoanalysis, may provide a comprehensive explanation of adult conduct. The problem involved in reconstructing childhood events based on the analysand's retrospective accounts is that in the first place, continuity may be assumed between childhood and adulthood, an assumption that is not warranted on the basis of empirical study in areas such as personality and adjustment (Brim, 1976; Emde, 1981; Kagan, 1980; Neugarten, 1969; Rutter, 1972, 1984; Skeels, 1966).

In the second place, and of even greater importance, the attempt to reconstruct childhood events may overlook the fact that the analysand's account as an adult is the outcome of a complex process in which the life biography is successively rewritten at transition points in the life course in order to achieve the consistency necessary for continued adaptation (Cohler, 1980, 1982). There is continuing concern within psychoanalysis that the legitimacy of the field will be compromised by recognizing the impossibility of attaining much predictability within lives over time. At least a part of the problem is the continued reliance within psychoanalysis, as in the popular mind, on a conception of lifetimes as cumulative rather than as transformative.

Not only expectable, socially governed changes, such as those connected with role entrances and exits, but also those connected with unexpected life changes—generally adverse and difficult to overcome—continue to shape the course of life. Finally, the very elements of the life story that are highlighted in an effort to provide a link between present and past must necessarily change over time, including that within the analysis itself. So-called events presumed significant in determining present story of lived experiences coconstructed within the analytic setting may change over time and across the course of the analysis. The only enduring aspect of study of the life history that survives is recognition of the context within which the life history is constructed, including the analyst's own ever-changing framework for understanding, founded on changes within psychoanalysis itself.

Life Course and Personal Development: Beyond Epigenetic Perspectives

Until the past two decades, psychoanalysis paid little attention to the expectable changes taking place in self and in society across the adult years and, particularly, in the second half of life. Personal struggles and challenges across the years of middle and later adulthood were viewed as similar to those of the first half of life (Rangell, 1961). Clinical psychoanalysis was believed not appropriate for middle-aged and older adults, and the peer review manual of the American Psychoanalytic Association even cautioned against psychoanalysis as a treatment of choice among middle-aged and older adults.[3] This recommendation assumed that aging was equivalent to decline and that it was not possible to foster change among older adults, who were believed most likely to be set in their ways. At least in part, this view was based on a misconception of increased cognitive and personal

---

[3]Freud himself had little interest in the older patient. Indeed, he was terrified of his own aging (Gay, 1988). His worry that he would die at the same age as his father and his lifelong preoccupation with his hypochondriasis has been documented. It is less well known that Freud had a nursemaid when he was about 3 and that this nursemaid appears to have been a particular source of terror. Freud remembered her as old and as taking him regularly to Catholic Mass, which he experienced as frightening. This early experience led him both to dislike older persons (S. Freud, 1900/1958) and also to maintain an abiding distaste for religion. As a consequence, Freud (1905/1953a, 1906/1953) explicitly cautioned against taking older patients into analysis both because older adults (over 50!) had too much previous history and because the length of remaining life was not sufficient for them to enjoy the newly attained personal freedom uniquely made possible through psychoanalysis.

rigidity among older adults, a notion founded on study of earlier cohorts that were overly represented by immigrants from southern and eastern European cultures who had not had the benefit of formal education and who were still reacting to the experience of geographic dislocation and resettlement in a new land.

Psychoanalysis and the Study of Lives Over Time

Nemiroff and Colarusso (1985) have reviewed much of the literature on psychoanalysis and the clinical study of adult lives. Although clinical reports from early accounts by Abraham (1919/1927) and Fenichel (1945) were enthusiastic regarding the positive outcome of psychoanalytic intervention in work with middle-aged and older adults, the approach in this early study was explicitly informed by a traditional view of nuclear neurosis reenacted in a form not modified through later experience as the foundation of psychoanalytic intervention. More recent reports by analysts reporting on psychoanalytic intervention with older adults (Kahana, 1979; Sandler, 1978) are considerably more optimistic regarding the possibility of changes taking place across the course of the later adult years. Recognizing that in developed countries, more than one third of life is left to be lived after retirement, psychoanalytic intervention with older adults may have influence over several decades of improved quality of life.

Although Erikson's (1982) focus on the course of life as a whole has helped shift the terms of discussion from childhood to the entire course of life through oldest age, continued reliance on an epigenetic rather than on a transformational view of the life course maintains undue emphasis on childhood, as contrasted with adult experiences, in understanding the particular experiences of the adult years.

Vaillant's (1974a, 1974b, 1975, 1977, 1978, 1979, 1993; Vaillant & McArthur, 1972) contribution to psychoanalytic life-course study is particularly difficult to evaluate. In both his work on defenses or means of personal protection against adversity (Vaillant, 1993) and his portrayal of the course of life (Vaillant, 1976, 1977, 1993; Vaillant & Milofsky, 1980), Vaillant endorsed the epigenetic model as portrayed in the work of Abraham and Erikson. Indeed, although Anna Freud (1936/1966) explicitly rejected a notion that the defenses were chronologically organized hierarchically, Vaillant's concept of so-called psychotic, neurotic, immature, and mature defenses not only pathologized the manner in which people seek refuge from painful aspects of life—rather than viewing such efforts as adaptive attainments or coping efforts of a particular sort (Winnicott, 1953, 1960)—but also presumed a temporal rigidity that other study (Swanson, 1961) has explicitly questioned. Finally, Vaillant was forced to rely on retrospective reports of childhood experience because that was the manner in which baseline information was obtained for a group of men first identified as college sophomores. The Berkeley Institute of Human Development studies are more fortunate because at least some of this study focused on lives followed from earliest childhood. As a consequence, Vaillant looked for and reported greater stability within lives over time based on correlational data than has been reported in the Berkeley studies.

At least in part, this reported enhanced stability may stem from the relatively shorter interval between time of reporting on childhood experience and later outcome as well as from the retrospective adult focus that is interwoven with the contemporary adult reports of experience of self and others. As Schuman and Scott (1989), Greene (1986, 1990), and Clausen (1993) have suggested, the adolescent years appear particularly significant in shaping the experience of adulthood. However, in his anecdotal accounts, Vaillant (1977) reported being surprised at the variation shown within lives over time and the quite different routes taken by men in seeking sense of satisfaction and vitality, and he was increasingly concerned with the life history. Furthermore, there appears to be little association between accounts of the childhood years provided by these men in college and when interviewed again in adulthood.

This finding of a disparity in telling about the past as a consequence of place in the course of life demonstrates the significance of understanding any account of the life story in terms of the present temporal context and life circumstances related to both telling and listening (Mishler, 1986). Finally, at least in the forward study of these men from middle to later adulthood, Vaillant focused very much on lived experience, particularly as related to physical and mental health outcomes, and provided important comparative findings regarding aspects of work and intimacy related to continued sense of personal integrity. Even in the work of Livson and Peskin (1980), of Peskin and Livson (1981), of Gould (1993), and of Vaillant (1993), the concurrent, coactive impact of early childhood experiences was presumed to echo across the adult years in a manner not necessarily modified by adult experiences. In a number of pioneering publications, Nemiroff and Colarusso

(Colarusso & Nemiroff, 1981; Nemiroff & Colarusso, 1985, 1990) have systematically reconsidered this earlier perspective.

While recognizing the significance, although not necessarily primacy, of issues stemming from earlier life experience for adult lives, these pioneer investigators of psychoanalysis and adult development also recognized the significant and transforming contributions of the adult years to the experience of self and others. Their seven basic hypotheses regarding adult psychological development (Colarusso & Nemiroff, 1979, 1981) emphasize that the adult past is as significant as the past of early childhood in understanding the manner in which middle-aged and older adults experience self and others. Expected and eruptive adverse changes across the adult years are particularly significant factors shaping the course of adult personality development, as is the experience of changes in body image and physical health.

Changing perspectives regarding the course of life within psychoanalysis have important implications both for method of study and for understanding studies of adult lives followed over time. To date, these findings, founded on six projects and often combined in reports providing contrasts according to gender and generation, have been particularly informative in the effort to understand lives over time. The first to report longitudinal data, the Fels Institute report on a group of midwestern men and women (Kagan & Moss, 1962), was followed by reports emerging from earlier studies, which were combined as the longitudinal study of Berkeley's Institute of Human Development. This was based on earlier collaborative investigation of middle-aged and older men and women in the East San Francisco Bay area who were followed from childhood during the 1920s through to later life (Clausen, 1993; Eichorn et al., 1981). Reports from another project, begun nearly two decades later than the Berkeley studies, have been reported in Vaillant's (1977, 1993) continuing investigation of the lives of a group of psychologically and physically robust sophomore men attending Harvard College during World War II.

A fourth project has been based on the repeated study of men and women in the midst of expectable life changes, living in the San Francisco area, and followed for a decade in the San Francisco area. This analysis has focused on issues of the meaning of transitions in adult lives (Fiske, 1980; Fiske & Chiriboga, 1990; Lowenthal, Thurnher, Chiriboga, & Associates, 1975). A fifth study has undertaken another round of interviews (Sears, 1984) of a group of men and women in the South San Francisco Bay area, initially identified by Louis Terman

(1925) as intellectually gifted (Sears, 1977, 1984; Sears & Barbee, 1977). Finally, study has continued of two Boston-area groups of adolescent offenders from less advantaged circumstances and their nondelinquent counterparts, followed forward from about the time of World War II to the present (Glueck & Glueck, 1950; McCord, 1979, 1980, 1984).

Findings from Vaillant's work and from the Berkeley studies are particularly relevant because they focused on issues of change within lives over a period of many decades from childhood or adolescence to later life. These projects not only provided important questions for study and intervention in the lives of middle-aged and older men and women but also offered additional hope for more effective collaboration of psychoanalysis and the other human sciences to understand the dynamics of continuity and change in lives over time. Vaillant's study initially posed the problem of being founded on the study of some of the most advantaged men in contemporary society, making generalization particularly difficult. Vaillant's discovery of the comparison group for the initial Glueck and Glueck (1950) delinquency study, representing a working-class cohort comparable in age and life circumstances to the Harvard group, and his more recent inclusion of the gifted women from the Terman (1925) study—although from a somewhat older cohort than the Harvard and working-class groups—further extended the range of comparisons founded on gender and on difference in social origins.

The Berkeley studies benefited from especially rich interview and projective test data—collected by many of the initial investigators—on a group of geographically stable men and women over a period of more than half a century. The Berkeley studies also had the advantage of available records on their participants from early childhood through later life. For information about early life circumstances, Vaillant has relied on interviews from the mothers of Harvard cohort and from the participants' self-reports at the time of recruitment into the study. The women from the Terman (1925) study were first identified only in grammar school on the basis of teacher nominations; the nominations reflected the biases of teachers against children from differing ethnic origins or who were less personally attractive and responsive. These children constituted a group of psychologically robust persons similar in many respects to the men in the Harvard group. The working-class group in Vaillant's study was followed from midadolescence and included boys whose life circumstances were exactly like those of the delinquent group, except there was no history of status offenses. As Vaillant (1993) has observed, although these men were not particularly talented at the outset, they have managed to overcome early adversity and become reasonably successful on their own. Snarey's (1993) report on these men and their offspring further documents the success of their life attainments.

Constancy and Change in Development

In contrast with the epigenetic formulation, which reflected the Enlightenment belief that early life events shape the experiential world of later life, findings from longitudinal and cross-sectional studies show little developmental predictability over time (Clarke & Clarke, 1976; Emde, 1981; Kagan, 1980; Skolnick, 1986). Consistent with Freud's (1897/1958) early speculations regarding the course of development, lives might better be portrayed as a series of transformations leading to the dramatic reordering of the meaning of time (Colarusso, 1987; Eisenbud, 1956; Kafka, 1973; Loewald, 1962, 1972; Wessman & Gorman, 1977) and the use of memory in accounting for present perception of prior experience (Carney & Cohler, 1993; Cohler, 1982; Cohler & Freeman, 1993; Fine, Joseph, & Waldhorn, 1959; Schachtel, 1947), presenting a "crisis" requiring resolution (Bibring, 1959), rather than as a series of well-ordered stages.[4] These transformations successively present individuals with a sense of disruption and discontinuity that requires narrative resolution to preserve meaning and a sense of continuity of self. Potentially useful mathematical models of such drastic transformation are available from a branch of mathematics called *catastrophe theory* (Galatzer-Levy, 1978), which postulates that apparently disorderly change often contains an underlying deep structure.

Nuclear neurosis as characteristic transformation. The view that development is a series of drastically reorganizing crises producing distress over the loss of continuity and calling for the reparation of this distress through reconstruction of the narrative of the self is consistent with *clinical* psychoanalytic formulations about development. The "nuclear neurosis" is regarded by many analysts as the cornerstone of psychoanalytic thought. In resolving this epochal struggle (A.

---

[4]In the cognitive realm, Piaget explored how schemas are progressively stretched as new aspects of experience and are "assimilated" until the schema can no longer contain the new information, so that the underlying organizational structure is reorganized and the structure itself "accommodates" (see, e.g., Piaget, 1975/1985).

Freud, 1958; S. Freud, 1900/1958, 1909/1959, 1910/1957a; Shapiro, 1977, 1981)—a resolution that is itself part of a larger transformation that White (1965) named the "five-to-seven" shift—children become amnesiac about the past and more concerned with the present and with instrumental mastery (Erikson, 1950/1963). Psychoanalytic accounts of the tumultuous appearance and resolution of the infantile neurosis (Nagera, 1966) are consistent with experience-near observational descriptions. For example, Piaget's description of the transformation from preoperational to operational thought includes the child's anguish as he or she tries to make sense of the world in new ways (Berlin, 1974; Piaget, 1975/1985).

Adolescence and identity. Later transformations (including those from middle childhood to adolescence, young adulthood to midlife and, possibly, early old age to late old age) share the common characteristic of dramatic alteration in both the sense of time and the use of memory. The five-to-seven shift has been most extensively documented, but there is also profound reordering of sense of time at the onset of adolescence (Cottle, 1977; Cottle & Klineberg, 1974; Erikson, 1950/1963, 1958; Greene, 1986, 1990). For the adolescent, the important time is the future. Memories of the personal past are now devoted to fostering goals based on presently understood personal past and both family and community traditions, the attainment of which is imagined in the future. The goal of the transformation from early to middle childhood is to forget the past, with its unacceptable wishes. The task of adolescence is to anticipate the future and, at the same time, maintain a sense of personal integrity that preserves the connection of past, present, and future. Erikson's (1958) study of Luther documents the problems inherent in maintaining a sense of personal integrity in adolescence in the face of necessary developmental reorganization of experience, which in adolescence involves so dramatically a repudiation of the past, as in Blos's (1967) concept of the second individuation process.

Middle age and interiority. Whereas the adolescent looks forward to the future, remembering the personal past in ways believed to be consistent with future attainments, persons at midlife begin to use memory of the past as a guide to solving problems (Lieberman & Falk, 1971). This third transformation of the life course, characteristically occurring sometime during the sixth decade of life, is significant not just for its changing use of memory but also for the experience of time, now felt as foreshortened with the accompanying personalization of death (Neugarten & Datan, 1974) or awareness of finitude (Munnichs,

1966).[5] Increasing interest in the study of midlife over the past two decades has provided findings that support the view that a personality transformation portrayed by Neugarten and Datan (1973; Neugarten, 1979) as "interiority" takes place sometimes during the sixth decade of life, which has impact similar to that reported both for the five-to-seven shift from early to middle childhood and the adolescent transformation. One particularly significant aspect of change in the sense of time across the second half of life concerns shared agreement regarding the expected duration of finitude of life (Munnichs, 1966), including one's own present belief of expectable longevity. Neugarten (1979) and Neugarten and Datan (1974) have portrayed the experience, generally occurring at some point during the fifth decade of life, of realizing that there is less time to be lived than has been lived already. This crisis of finitude, a consequence of the comparison of the trajectory of one's own life in terms of shared expectations of the duration of life,[6] is fostered by increased awareness of mortality through

---

[5]Although it has sometimes been maintained that the advent of parenthood may lead to the reordering of memory (Benedek, 1959, 1970, 1973), study of the assumption of this new adult social role does not suggest that it leads to new ways in which past memories are used or to the reordering of time perspectives. Although the transition to parenthood often leads to disruption of present adjustment (Cohler, 1994; Goldberg & Michaels, 1988; Rossi, 1968), it does not appear to transform the sense of self in the manner of such life-course transformations as the nuclear neurosis or the midlife crisis of finitude.

[6]Consistent with the perspective provided by Durkheim (1912/1961), Sorokin and Merton (1937), J. Roth (1963), Neugarten and Hagestad (1976), Hazan (1980), Cohler and Boxer (1984), Hagestad and Neugarten (1985), and persons' understanding of the course of their own lives follows a socially structured, symbolic "timetable." From early childhood through later life, individuals continually monitor their own lives in terms of expectable milestones. Although expected timing or expected attainment of particular transitions varies with social status, ethnicity, gender, and other factors, within groups of persons defined in terms of particular historical circumstances, or cohorts (Elder, 1974, 1979, in press; Ryder, 1967), findings from survey studies have shown marked agreement among people regarding the expectable structure or placement of events across the course of life (Cain, 1964; Hogan, 1981; Neugarten & Moore, 1968), as well as significant changes over historical time in the placement and distance between milestones marking the life course (Cherlin, 1981; Glick, 1977; Hareven, 1982, 1986; Kohli & Meyer, 1986; Uhlenberg, 1979, 1988). The nature and significance of personal experience is portrayed in the context of these shared definitions of the timing and direction of lives. People continually compare themselves in terms of particular attainments at particular ages, both as more or less "on" or "off" time for expectable transi-

experience with the deaths of parents and other family members and, increasingly, consociates as well (Jaques, 1965, 1993; Pollock, 1980). The timing of this crisis of finitude is clearly shaped by such life circumstances as social class and ethnicity.

Heightened awareness of one's own mortality, portrayed by Munnichs (1966) as increased "awareness of the finitude of life" and elaborated by Marshall (1975, 1986), Jaques (1965, 1993), Neugarten (1979), and Sill (1980), results in a transformation in emphasis in time from that lived already to that remaining to be lived, and in memory to increased involvement with the past and reminiscence. At first, this reminiscence is used actively in the service of coping with life changes associated with career and family (Lieberman & Falk, 1971; Lieberman & Tobin, 1983; Tobin, 1991; Tobin & Lieberman, 1976). At some point during the late forties or early fifties, people begin looking backward to the past for inspiration and meaning rather than finding such meaning through anticipation of the future. Deaths of friends and family members, particularly of parents, not only personalizes death but also emphasizes the extent to which life has limited duration, with generations succeeding each other (Marshall, 1986).

Lieberman and Tobin (1983), Lieberman and Cohler (1975), and Cohler and Lieberman (1979) have reported findings from a systematic study showing that people in their mid-to-late forties and early fifties experience particular disharmony, lowered morale, increased concerns about health, and increased feelings of anxiety and depression. Although especially characterizing men, marked distress and increased awareness of finitude accompanied this transformation to midlife in both men and women. At least in part, these heightened concerns appeared in many instances, accounting for first experience of psychiatric illness (Gutmann, Griffin, & Grunes, 1982). With advancing age, reminiscence activity becomes increasingly important as a part of taking stock of one's own life, in mourning dreams never realized, and in settling accounts with the past (Butler, 1963; Coleman, 1974, 1986; Coleman & McCullough, 1985; Kaminisky, 1984; McMahon & Rhudick,

---

tions and life changes and as experiencing these changes in a more or less "ordered" or "disordered" manner. The timing of transformations such as those portrayed here assumes the usual ordered nature of timing. However, there may be marked variation at the point in life at which the crisis of finitude is experienced, depending on time of role changes and losses and on such unanticipated adversity as death of spouse or children.

1964, 1967; Moody, 1986; Woodward, 1984). In general, it reflects the development of a more inward orientation, earlier portrayed by Jung (1933) as introversion and, more recently, by Neugarten and Datan (1973; Neugarten, 1979) as interiority. The primary focus of this midlife transformation is with the impact of a changing sense of time and use of memory of the past in the effort to maintain a continued sense of continuity and integrity or coherence of self.

Findings reported by Back (1974), Gutmann (1975, 1987), and Sinnott (1982) also suggest gender-related differences in this midlife transition. Men at midlife become increasingly concerned with issues of personal comfort and seeking succorance from others, moving away from reliance on active mastery in solving problems at home and in the workplace, whereas women may become more oriented toward active mastery and "instrumental–executive" activities, moving away from their earlier involvement in caring for others as wife, mother, and kin-keeper (Cohler & Grunebaum, 1981; Firth, Hubert, & Forge, 1970; Gilligan, 1982; Gutmann, 1987). Back's (1974) study suggests that, with the advent of midlife, women begin to see themselves less in terms mediated through such relationships as wife and mother, and more directly in terms of present involvements beyond those of home and family.

As a consequence of an increased awareness of the finitude of life, both men and women appear to show increased concern with self and to have lessened patience for demands on time and energy, which are increasingly experienced as in "short supply" (Back, 1974; Cohler & Grunebaum, 1981; Cohler & Lieberman, 1980; Erikson, 1982; Erikson, Erikson, & Kivnick, 1986; Hazan, 1980; Kernberg, 1980; Lowenthal et al., 1975; Neugarten, 1979; Rook, 1984, 1989). Concern with the realization of personal goals and with reworking the presently understood life course to maintain a sense of personal coherence becomes particularly salient in later middle age, requiring time and energy that is then less available for other pur-suits (Cohler & Galatzer-Levy, 1990). The ability to mourn goals not attained and to accept the finitude of life without despair provides some evidence of the realization of the success of this effort (Pollock, 1971a, 1971b, 1980).

Other findings comparing the first and second half of life point to differences in personality organization. Gutmann et al. (1982) have described first episodes of psychiatric illness at midlife among individuals previously not experiencing personal distress. Lieberman and Tobin (1983) have shown that a more paranoid adaptation in later life predicts increased longevity among people relocated to institutional care. According to Gutmann (1987), individuals reporting the highest levels of morale are more likely to externalize sources of problems. Although such externalization may hamper adjustment at younger ages, it appears to be important in maintaining adjustment across the later adult years. Memory may also begin to serve a new function with the attainment of midlife. As Lieberman and Falk (1971) have shown, persons at midlife may increasingly rely on the past as a guide to solving problems in the present. Somewhat later in life there is an additional shift from using memories to solve problems to using memory to attain enhanced solace, which become so important as older adults experience the loss of family members and friends through death.

Old age and the crisis of survivorship. There may be a fourth such transformation, a crisis of survivorship, beginning sometime during the eighth decade of life, as people begin to outlive their cohort and to replace time–space relations (Novey, 1968/1985) with memories. Accompanying the life review (Butler, 1963; Kaufman, 1986; Prosen, Martin, & Prosen, 1972; McMahon & Rhudick, 1964), or in settling accounts with the past, there may be increased mythological activity— reconciling previous conflicts and controversies in favor of desired outcomes that provide a particular sense of solace. Consistent with Kearl's observation regarding the importance of maintaining a sense of meaning and personal coherence across the life course, Marshall (1986) has portrayed this reworking of the personal or developmental narrative in order to justify to oneself decisions and actions over the course of a lifetime as the "legitimation of biography."

Furthermore, as both Keith (1982) and Marshall (1986) have noted, if people can believe that time was well spent in the past, then there is hope that remaining time can be put to good use, leading to the conviction that a sense of personal coherence and integration can be maintained, even with recognition of the nearness of death. People tend to remain depressed from a sense of life not fully lived, whereas they usually are able to grieve successfully the loss of a fully lived life. If people at midlife begin to look backward to the past for inspiration rather than forward into the future, older people appear to live principally within the time frame of the particular day. To date, there has been little detailed study of this crisis of survivorship; although the comparison may be unwelcome, this experience of time is similar to that of prisoners or those held hostage. When faced at the end of life with acute "creature" or death anxiety, the only way of coping may be to look at the moment right at hand (Becker, 1973; Shabad, 1996). However, changing population demographics have further increased interest in the second half of life.

Persons over age 80 constitute the most rapidly growing sector of the population, and yet less is known about the means that they use to preserve a sense of personal coherence, and the significance of the experience of others in maintaining meaning, than for other parts of the adult life course (Nemiroff & Colarusso, 1985). For example, although as Lee (1979) has shown, the presence of a few confidants is important in preserving morale in later life, Matthews (1983, 1986) suggested that quite different meanings may be attributed to friends known lifelong and to those first encountered later in life. However, there has been little study of differences for preservation of coherence in later life as a result of the time at which confidants were first met. There is urgent need for increased study of personality and adjustment within this group of frail elderly persons, including study of the struggle with problems of survivorship, which includes both feelings of guilt at having outlived a cohort—sometimes including one's own offspring—and resolution of grief and feelings of loss accompanying the deaths of spouse and friends (Butler, 1963; Erikson et al., 1986; Kaminsky, 1984; Myerhoff, 1979, 1992; Woodward, 1984).

In very late life, largely as a result of the crisis of survivorship, reminiscence virtually supplants time–space social ties, providing important consolation in living from day to day. Partly because of inevitable restrictions on physical mobility, partly as a result of reduced concern with the future, and partly because of the inherent richness and value of past experience, very old people obtain particular comfort from reminiscence based on a lifetime of memories. Reminiscence is too often mistaken for withdrawal, depression, regression, or loneliness. To date, little is known about how continuing morale and sense of personal integration is supported through such reminiscence activity. Particular problems are presented for a continued sense of coherence with the change in focus to living day by day. However, it appears that evocation of memories of shared activities with consociates no longer alive, and even with the family of childhood, is important in maintaining a sense of coherence that overcomes possible despair. Clearly, particular problems are posed for those older adults, such as those suffering Alzheimer's disease, who are no longer able to call on memories of the past as solace. At least a part of the agitation and anxiety experienced by patients in the first stages of Alzheimer's disease may be a consequence of this difficulty in calling on the past as a means of realizing an enhanced sense of solace.

From Natural Science to Human Science Study of Lives Over Time

Much contemporary human science focuses on how coherence is collectively maintained and on the personal significance of these shared meanings for particular life experiences (Geertz, 1966/1973a, 1966/1973b; Obeyesekere, 1981, 1990).[7] Psychoanalysis focuses primarily on how people construct meanings to guide their lives and the social order. The communication of the analysand's life story to the analyst; the analyst's effort to understand this story and to foster a revised, more coherent narrative of the presently remembered past; the experienced present; and the anticipated future are elements of a collaborative search for meaning (Ricoeur, 1971, 1977, 1984a, 1984b; Schafer, 1980, 1981, 1982, 1992). The central subject of psychoanalysis is the way one personally and culturally deals with experience and makes meanings (Kakar, 1985, 1989).

Psychoanalysis and the Study of Meanings

Focus on the meaning for individuals of life experience, as exemplified by the human science approach of Habermas (1968/1971, 1983), Ricoeur (1971, 1977), Geertz (1973, 1983), and others, may be more consistent with the interpretive perspective distinctive of psychoanalysis than is the "natural science" approach, at least to the extent that it makes assumptions about the relationship of past and present based on experience-distant data and assumes the consequent aims of prediction and control. Nevertheless, much of the interest in findings from devel-

---

[7]Obeyesekere (1990) observed that the *work of culture* is to construct and maintain meanings that lead to a sense of collective and personal coherence and continuity. This experience of coherence is founded in the stories that are told—not on another level of reality beyond belief, not on some invisible "foundation." There is no reality above and beyond the world of meanings as realized in stories, including the life history itself.

opmental psychology continues to be focused on the specific problem of validating certain psychoanalytic interpretations, particularly those concerned with reenactment of developmental deficits presumed to have been acquired in earliest childhood. Although there is at present some controversy in psychoanalysis regarding the therapeutic efficacy of these genetic interpretations, as contrasted with those limited to the transference itself (Leites, 1977), concern with the possible origins of these later outcomes is always present in the collaboration of analysand and analyst to understand the origins of present distress.

The significance of communication of the life story for restoration of personal energy and well-being has shifted from Freud's early emphasis on catharsis through reliving the past. Contemporary analysts focus more on the analysand's use of the analyst to attain a greater sense of self structure and vitality (Kohut, 1977). A range of intermediate positions is evident in current thought about the nature of the analytic process (Meissner, 1991). In each version of the use of the life story in psychoanalysis, logic and rhetoric are inseparably connected. The core of analytic work is not rational explanation based on external fact or observation. The distinctive change realized through psychoanalysis is a revised view of the life story (Nasser, 1994; P. A. Roth, 1991a, 1991b; Schafer, 1980). This revision is achieved through the relationship of analyst and analysand, in which the analysand reenacts with the analyst the cumulative life history (S. Freud, 1914/1958; Gill, 1982). The analytic situation differs from other enactments based on the analysand's life story because analyst and analysand collaborate to observe and interpret enactments in a context designed to support observation and interpretation.

The analyst experiences the analysand's life story through empathic listening (Kohut, 1971, 1959/1978). Ideally, the analyst tolerates the pain and anxiety this story may induce, aided by personal and self-analysis (Calder, 1980; Gardner, 1983; Ticho, 1967; Whitaker & Malone, 1953). The analyst tries to attend to all aspects of the way the life story is recurrently told in shifting enactments. Collaborative study of the life history allows new understandings of the analysand's experience of self and others and the construction of a new life history that fosters an enhanced sense of personal well-being and spontaneity (Kohut, 1959/1978; Novey, 1968/1985; Ricoeur, 1977; Schafer, 1980, 1981). Psychoanalysis resolves personal distress through a new, more coherent, useful, and complete narrative that explains present life experiences and memories.

Therefore, the sort of knowledge about people that is most significant may not be contained in general principles. Even if they had the
enormous predictive powers of fundamental concepts of physics,
broad principles would likely prove unsatisfactory for thinking about
lives. This is true, first, because one tends to value most "local knowledge," the ways people construct meaning in their lives in particular
circumstances (Geertz, 1974/1983) and second, because psychological
theories in Western bourgeois culture are supposed to make sense of
wish and intention in terms of readily understandable meanings and
motives. (One wants to be able to say, "Oh, now I see why she acted as
she did" [Brown, 1986].)

Lived Experience and Social Context

The life story and the experience of oneself as coherent over the course
of time, from early childhood through oldest age, occurs in the context
of particular times and places. This recognition of social surround was
assumed by Freud in his work with analysands in the bourgeois, Jewish sector of Vienna in which he lived (Oxaal, 1988). Freud had difficulty conceiving of places and times different from his own, believing
that the "family romance" (S. Freud, 1909/1959) characterizing the
bourgeois family of Vienna was universal. As psychoanalysis developed in Western Europe and the United States, little consideration was
given to issues of place and time as relevant in the study of adult lives.
However, within the social sciences, it was equally difficult to understand social change and to integrate personal and social change.

The reality of a changing world, particularly in the mid-1960s, which
may have marked a social and intellectual watershed in contemporary
culture, intruded on the constancy of the postwar period, when psychoanalysis became an accepted focus within psychiatry and within
arts and letters and demanded recognition of the complex interplay
between life history and history. Popularity of perspectives within psychoanalysis that challenged a more traditional view, from the work of
Melanie Klein and her colleagues in London to the emergence of the
object relations tradition in the United States, suggested that personal
characteristics of patients seeking analysis had changed; contemporary
analysands appeared less personally focused and stable than in previous times. A theory focusing on the nuclear neurosis, and the conflict
psychology that it had fostered, did not appear relevant for these more
troubled adults. Lasch (1979) suggested that the times had indeed

changed in the direction of increased preoccupation with self and the experience of personal coherence in a troubled world.

Pressures within psychoanalysis to encompass a broader range of psychopathology were paralleled within the social sciences by demand for changes in perspectives on social life stressing the function of social institutions for maintaining social cohesion and by demand for theories that might more effectively account for the dynamics of social change. The struggle to understand the antiwar activism and the social upheaval in the wake of major political assassinations of the mid-1960s forced the social sciences to take seriously the reality of social change. The focus on the concept of generation or historical cohort (Cain, 1967; Hagestad & Neugarten, 1985; Mannheim, 1923/1952; Neugarten & Hagestad, 1976; Neugarten et al., 1965; Riley, 1973; Schaie, 1984) suggested that sociohistorical events had a broad impact within society, uniquely affecting both those of particular ages (cohort) and all those alive at a particular time (period). For example, the Vietnam buildup and conflict affected all those alive in the mid-to-late 1960s, but in very different ways for those young adults who were draft-age eligible and their own parents.

This perspective on the interplay of life history and history has been most dramatically illustrated in the work of Elder and his colleagues (Elder, 1974, 1992; Elder & Caspi, 1990; Elder & Rockwell, 1979). Studying the lives through middle adulthood of men and women who were either preschoolers or adolescents at the time of the Great Depression as well as the loss of family income so often a consequence of this economic dislocation, Elder was able to show that particular historical experiences are differently interpreted by persons over time as a consequence of their age at the time of these experiences. Furthermore, just as Schaie (1984) had demonstrated that intellectual functioning across the adult years is a function of social circumstances across the course of life, Elder was able to show long-term personal consequences of the manner in which individuals made meaning of earlier adversity as a function of the intersect of age at the time of particular social and historical changes.

The implication for psychoanalytic study of lives of this approach to the study of social change based on concepts of generation has not been fully appreciated. In the first place, the concept of a social timetable governing the manner in which people evaluate the course of their own life in terms of being a particular age at a particular time suggests that morale is in part determined by the continuing appraisal of self in terms of expectable life changes. Furthermore, the life story told by persons of particular ages cannot be understood apart from the impact of social circumstance, including such generation-defining events as the Great Depression, World War II, or the political and social turmoil of the 1960s. Issues posed for the larger society particularly influence the manner in which people experience their own place within the course of life. Furthermore, with the passage of time, individuals of different ages at the time of the events come to view these events differently. The relationship between life history and history is dynamic. Subsequent changes in particular historical narratives such as the purpose and significance of the Vietnam conflict affect the manner in which persons of differing age cohorts experiencing this event subsequently come to understand it.

The Clinical Method and the Study of Lives Over Time

Traditional understanding of lives, focused on an experience-distant view of lives as constructed from traits and motives presumed stable over time, is inadequate to understand either changes within lives over time or the complex interplay between personal and social change. The clinical method of psychoanalysis provides an important means for understanding the interplay of person and social life. This clinical method is founded on the concept of vicarious introspection or empathy (Fliess, 1953; Greenson, 1960; Kohut, 1959/1978) in which the analyst, listening to reports of lived experience (Schutz & Luckmann, 1973, 1989), "tastes" these accounts of lived experience, which then become a part of an emerging and enlivened shared account of the analysand's life story (Schafer, 1980, 1981).

The contribution of psychoanalysis may be as significant for providing a method for studying personal and social change as for the attention it has focused on understanding action as the outcome of the effort to satisfy particular wishes or intentions. The experiences of a lifetime, together with the presently understood meanings attached to these experiences, are relived within the context of the psychoanalytic interview. Analyst and analysand may join in applying the presently understood significance of life events in managing the adversity of such experiences as stigma or immigration. Social change takes place in context but is experienced by particular persons, who respond to crisis and challenge related to these larger social changes. To date, there has been little use of this empathic method (Greenson, 1960;

Kohut, 1959/1978, 1971; Schafer, 1959) according to reports of change studied through psychoanalysis. Assumptions founded on the clinical method have been used in reports as varied as understanding the impact of harsh environments on the management of feelings (Briggs, 1970), headhunting (Rosaldo, 1993), mourning in a nonliterature culture (Kracke, 1981), migration from the former Soviet Union to Israel (Lieblich, 1993), or the interplay of personal distress and social stigma as determinants of social activism (Cole, in press).

Experience and enactment. The significance of these modes of experiencing becomes the focus of particular study. The concept of transference (Breuer & Freud, 1893–1895/1955; S. Freud, 1900/1958, 1905/1953a, 1914/1958) is founded on the inevitability of the reenactment of intentions emerging over the course of a lifetime within the context of the psychoanalytic hour. The analyst's own capacity to bear his or her own distressing feelings emerging reciprocally to those of the analysand (Flarsheim, 1974; Gardner, 1983; Racker, 1968) makes it possible for him or her to attend the conversation even while continuing to taste the analysand's reports. This empathic method permits increased understanding of the analysand's experience of personal and social change and is reflected in a parallel manner in terms of changes taking place within the psychoanalytic process itself. At the same time, the nature of these enactments must be understood both in terms of the generation-linked experience and present place within the life course of each participant in the psychoanalytic process.

Part of Freud's singular understanding of the human condition was his recognition that the experience of all relationships provides a disguised effort toward the satisfaction of the nuclear wish. The ideal type of such efforts toward satisfaction was the psychoanalytic situation itself, in which the analyst become the equivalent of the "day residue," forming the apparently neutral point of attachment in everyday life for the transference of the energy attached to the nuclear wish across the culturally constructed repression barrier (S. Freud, 1900/1958). Within the analytic situation, because the analyst is not ordinarily involved in the analysand's daily life, this neutrality provides a point of attachment for partial satisfaction in disguised form of the nuclear wish. The process of psychoanalytic treatment is designed to provide an interpretation of this nuclear wish experienced anew in the here and now of the psychoanalytic situation. Through acknowledgment of this wish, its intensity is diminished, alleviating the search for satisfaction in a disguised manner and thereby reducing the consequent conflict, frustration, and disappointment. Freud (1912/1958) cogently defined transference as

> the process by which a patient . . . repeats and re-lives in the present of the psychoanalytic relationship, unconscious conflicts, traumas, and pathological phantasies from his past, and re-experiences them together with affects, expectations, and wishes appropriate to those past situations and relationships, in relation to his analyst, who is then felt to be the person responsible for whatever distress he is re-experiencing. In this way, the symptoms of the patient's illness are given a new transference meaning and his neurosis is replaced by a "transference-neurosis" which can then be cured by the therapeutic work. The transference thus creates an intermediate region between illness and real life through which the transition from the one to the other is made. (p. 154)

The psychoanalytic situation is but one of many aspects of life in which effort is made to satisfy the nuclear wish. Indeed, from the perspective of Freud's theory of psychological conflict, every situation provides fresh opportunity for satisfying the nuclear wish. For example, Katz (1976) and Cohler and Galatzer-Levy (1992) have noted the power of education, from primary school through postdoctoral study, as a means for the expression of transference.[8] A series of reports (Blos, 1980; King, 1980; Kahana, 1985; Neubauer, 1980) have suggested that these transference enactments shift across the course of life. Neubauer (1980) observed that the particular developmental organization in middle childhood shapes the expression of the earlier experienced

---

[8]Kohut (1959/1978, 1971, 1977, 1984) has reformulated the understanding of the continuing impact of childhood across the adult years in terms of an expectable effort lifelong to re-create the comfort and caring associated in a nonspecific manner with the years of infancy and early childhood. Kohut argued both for the experience of shame and disavowal, as well as guilt and repression, as an important sector of personality, and also for the study and interpretation of these "transference-like" enactments of idealization, mirroring, and experience of merger or twinship. These enactments are important responses, both to expectable life changes such as retirement and to unexpected adversity such as personal illness or the illness or loss of beloved family members. Malinowski's (1914–1918/1989) posthumous diary reflects these transference-like enactments within the ethnographic situation as he portrayed his longing for comfort from family and close friends during his ordeal in the field. The activity of calling on or evoking memories of past care and comfort was able to sustain Malinowski through difficult times of trying to understand a culture different from his own.

nuclear neurosis. The nature of enactments within the psychoanalytic interview reflects the interplay of progressive maturation and present understanding of the nuclear conflict of early childhood.

Blos (1980) echoed this theme, noting the intertwined quality of developmentally salient struggles in adolescence and later understandings of the meaning of past satisfactions and frustrations. Endorsing the significance of transference enactments as a method of developmental study, Blos (1980) observed that the psychoanalytic study of adolescence can reveal much regarding the dynamics of characteristic points such as adolescence over the course of life. For example, Blos explored the significance of the teenager's effort to idealize adults, evident in characteristic transferences as the adolescent struggles to resolve issues of activity and passivity and the nuclear neurosis itself. Study of characteristic adolescent transferences permits increased understanding of the determinants of the characteristic rapid mood shifts reported normatively across the adolescent decade (Csikszentmihalyi & Larson, 1984).

From the present perspective, however, it is the transference enactments of middle and later life that are of particular interest in understanding expectable changes in experience of self and others across the second half of life. Whereas earlier reports had focused primarily on the repetition of the nuclear neurosis in the enactments of older analysands toward their analyst, as Nemiroff and Colarusso (1985), Galatzer-Levy and Cohler (1993), and others have noted, additional issues are posed across the course of life. Enactments of older adults toward their analyst reflect expectable changes in the experience of self and others, including such issues as the life review (Butler, 1963), enhanced personalization of death (Neugarten & Datan, 1974), and the crisis of survivorship (Myerhoff, 1979, 1992). King (1980) noted also that enactments of older patients reflect concerns regarding issues of loss of function, enhanced awareness of aging, and concern for the welfare of offspring. King emphasized the significance of enactments reflecting experiences with others over as many as five generations.

Particularly in the analysis of middle-aged men and women, King (1980) maintained that issues stemming from adolescence are once again salient. For example, the experience of leaving home as an adolescent may be reenacted as one's own young adult offspring prepare to live independently (Blos, 1967); losses experienced as a result of the death of parents and friends may also evoke struggles of loss and change across the years of middle and late adolescence. Furthermore, as Cohler (1982) and Greene (1986, 1990) have noted, midlife shares with adolescence a point in the course of life at which concepts of time and memory are reorganized. Indeed, viewed from this perspective, the transition to midlife shares with adolescence points of transformation across the course of life. If adolescence represents a time at which a realistic connection between an expectable future and past is first attained, middle age in American society represents a time at which the past disappointments are acknowledged and in which this new peace with the past may first be attained.

Freud's own distaste for aging has influenced the hesitance of analysts to work with older adults. Even among those analysts willing to work with older analysands, issues posed by middle and later life may be too readily understood in terms of the nuclear neurosis. Freud had suggested that fear of death was itself merely another expression of the castration complex. Although some analysts were able to recognize enactments among older adults, and reciprocal counterenactments among analysts working with these older adults, reflecting the distinctive place in the course of life of these older adults, too often analyses of older adults have been reported as merely extensions of the nuclear complex. Earlier formulations of aging placed particular emphasis on the reverberations of the nuclear conflict across the course of life. The struggles of an older adult facing the loss of the work role through retirement was presumed to be experiencing anew conflicts first engendered six or seven decades earlier with parents during the transition from early to middle childhood. The loss of a spouse through death was similarly assumed to be the reenactment of these early life struggles. In fact, it may be more accurate to understand these interpretations as complementary countertransference enactments (Racker, 1968), reflecting the analyst's own nuclear conflict aroused anew by work with older patients who may evoke parental reactions and countertransferences, and reflecting also the analyst's own fear of aging and death as evoked by such patients.

Additional enactments observed across the course of analysis, such as the grandchild transference of an older adult analysand working with a much younger analyst (Rappaport, 1958) must be understood as more than another enactment stemming from the oedipal neurosis. Indeed, increased recognition of finitude of life, portrayed in the work of Munnichs (1966) and of Marshall (1975, 1986) represents a fundamental shift in the understanding of self and is experienced across the adult years.[9] Shared understandings regarding the expectable course of human life generally leads to increased awareness of the finitude of life and to the personalization of death (Neugarten & Datan, 1974). This enhanced awareness of finitude leads to a shift in the experience of self and place in the world and to an understanding of the role of the past in personal experience, first termed the *life review* by Butler (1963). Although experiences taking place earlier in life may indeed color the manner in which integration of past within present is understood, distinctive and unique experiences across the adult years further influence this life review.

Extension of the concept of transference from its original definition as the satisfaction of the nuclear wish in a disguised manner as a compromise formation, to include longing for childhood security and coherence, suggests the need for a more inclusive term. Most recently, the concept of enactment has been proposed in a number of clinical and theoretical reports by Jacobs (1986, 1991), McLaughlin (1988, 1991), Chused (1991), and a panel report of a meeting of the American Psychoanalytic Association (Johan, 1992). Based on Jacobs' (1986) discussion, emphasizing the effort to satisfy unconscious (oedipal) wishes outside of awareness, the 1989 panel emphasized both the dramatic quality of enactments and also the extent to which these dramatizations determine the response of the other to the situation.[10]

---

[9]Realization of the significance of the "crisis of finitude" stems from Jung's (1933) reflections on the course of life. Work with older patients represents an avenue of rapprochement between existential analysis (May, Angel, & Ellenberger, 1958) and those perspectives on wish and intention concerned with the impact of forces outside of awareness on lives over time. Existential perspectives provide a complementary focus to those more traditionally understood within psychoanalysis. At the same time, although middle-aged adults are focused to a greater extent than younger adults on issues of mortality and the finitude of life (Neugarten & Datan, 1974), it is important to understand this experience within the totality of the life course, including the presently remembered past and anticipated future.

[10]The significance of the analyst's capacity for self-observation as the foundation of "analyzing instrument" following Freud (1900/1958, 1912/1958) was initially portrayed by Isakower (Jaffe, 1986; New York Psychoanalytic Insitute, 1963a, 1963b) in terms of the significance of the analysts' continuing attention to their own experience as a source of information regarding the psychoanalytic process. This capacity for self-observation, elaborated by Gardner (1983) and by Jacobs (1986, 1991), may be the most essential contribution of psychoanalysis as a method of study within the human sciences. Continuing self-observation on the part of the analyst within the discourse of

McLaughlin (1991) has reformulated this concept, recognizing the extension of the concept of the enactment as transference in the most extended sense of that term, expressed as the experience of relationships with others. Underlying the formulation of this concept is recognition that all relationships are endowed with meanings based on the totality of experienced life circumstances and that people enact these meanings in fantasy, word, and deed. These meanings include the variety of ways in which individuals experience others, not only in the realm of competition but also as a source of sustenance, comfort, and solace.

Countertransference and enactment. Just as each person enacts a variety of culturally prescribed intents in fantasy and actuality, so within the therapeutic situation the therapist reciprocally enacts intentions based on a particular life history. Extending Freud's (1912/1958, 1914/1958) use of the concept of transference to include the clinical psychoanalytic setting, the psychoanalyst Annie Reich (1951/1973) further extended the term *countertransference* to refer explicitly to intents and sentiments relevant to the analyst's own resolution of the nuclear neurosis stimulated by the experience of the analysand. As initially used, this term did not refer to all manifestations of the therapist's personality as expressed within the therapeutic relationship, but only to those aspects of the experience of the analysand stimulated reciprocally to the analysand's own unresolved nuclear neurosis. Issues of ambivalence regarding the analysand's successful life attainments, feelings of competitive struggle engendered following the analysand's report of a love affair, and rivalry

---

the psychoanalytic process (Bakhtin, 1986a, 1986b; Todrov, 1984) is the foundation of the capacity for empathy as the means of tasting (Fliess, 1944) the experience of the other through vicarious introspection (Kohut, 1959/1978) and is also an essential element not only in gathering information for a life history but also in the subsequent study of both ethnographies and personal documents or life stories transcribed and rendered as texts. This "double dialogic" perspective, in which the reader's present understanding of the text is informed by vicarious introspection founded on the tasting of the text, is essential in understanding the foundations of "reader-response" theory within criticism and the human sciences (Fish, 1977; Freund, 1987; Good, 1994; Iser, 1978; Mattingly, 1989; Phelan, 1989; Rabinowitz, 1987, 1994). The interplay of empathy as vicarious introspection founded on the analyst's own presently understood life story enacted not only within the context of the psychoanalytic situation but also in gathering and interpreting ethnographies and stories is an important next step in the study of both lives and texts.

with other persons in the analysand's life for the analysand's affections would all be examples of countertransference evoked by particular analytic experiences.[11]

Just as with the analysand's enactment in word and deed of experiences taking place across a lifetime, the analyst's own response to the analysand's material reflects the analyst's own lived experience. King (1980) has noted the significance of a developmentally salient countertransference in the analysis of middle-aged adults who may be struggling with very similar midlife issues; the analyst may be particularly vulnerable to feelings of sadness and loss due to the concurrent experience of loss through death of parents and friends in ways that parallel the analysand's own experience. Those aspects of the analyst's own experience that are not previously the subject of self-inquiry and understanding and that are presently out of awareness may be reciprocally evoked by the collaboration of analyst and analysand. The analysand's bid for a mirroring or idealizing relationship may lead to the analyst's own feelings of lowered self-esteem and unworthiness in the face of such emulation.

Enactment, empathy, and the study of adult lives. The analyst's enhanced awareness of the analysand's lived experience within the analytic collaboration may lead to a counterenactment, including the more narrowly defined countertransference responses that are reciprocal to the analysand's transference neurosis. However, enhanced awareness of the analyst's own lived experience may lead to enhanced empathic response. The extent to which enactments reciprocally evoked within the analyst as a response to hearing the analysand's life story lead to an impasse or interfere in the distinctive mode of listening that characterizes psychoanalysis, and psychoanalytically informed inquiry is closely related to the analyst's capacity for continu-

---

[11]The concept of countertransference as used in discussions of the analyst's responses focuses on responses to the analysand's enactments, both those understood in the very limited sense of transference (S. Freud, 1900/1958; Kohut & Seitz, 1963/1978) and the more extended concept of transference-like enactment (Kohut, 1971), may have very limited value in discussions of the therapeutic process. The term is often used in a derogatory sense to refer to the analyst's unwarranted personal response to the analysand. In part, this most narrow understanding of the term stems from the assumption of the analyst merely as a day residue for transference of the nuclear wish apart from the relationship that most directly characterizes the therapeutic relationship.

ing self-inquiry. Evocation of a variety of meanings of others for one-self is intrinsic within all relationships. Indeed, there is no "other" apart from one's own present experience of that other in terms of one's own lived experience.[12] The use of one's own vicarious intro-spection (Kohut, 1959/1978) or empathy provides a means for trans-forming meanings evoked by this "essential other" (Galatzer-Levy & Cohler, 1993) into enhanced understanding of oneself and for main-taining the capacity to bear the lived experiences of another.

The concept of empathy is one of the least understood concepts within the human sciences. Although the experience of "fellow-feeling" or empathy has informed inquiry in fields ranging from the humanities to psychiatry, the term as used in psychoanalysis has much more specific application. Fliess (1944, 1953) and Jaffe (1986) have suggested that the activity of the analyst involves the experience of tasting the experiences of another and then forming an intervention based on this experience. This process, sometimes known as *counter-identification* (Fliess, 1944, 1953) or *concordant identification* (Racker, 1968), represents an encounter with another's world of lived experi-ence, has also been termed *empathy* and has been more fully described by Schafer (1959), Greenson (1960), and Kohut (1959/1978, 1971). Kohut noted that empathy is a method of study that may be used in a variety of contexts from interrogation to psychotherapy and repre-sents a method of study distinctive to the human sciences.

As the fundamental method of clinical psychoanalysis, the capacity to taste or experience and interpret the variety of enactments within the clinical situation facilitates personality change through bringing previously unacceptable sentiments and intents into awareness and

---

[12]The issue of self and other is particularly crucial within the human sci-ences. Much of recent discussion within anthropology and psychology (Ros-aldo, 1993) has questioned the assumption of an "other" existing apart from one's particular construction of the other. Dialogic perspectives pose the ques-tion of whether there can ever be an other existing apart from oneself and whether the construction of the other, as in fascination with "primitive" lives instructive for one's own culture, is but a representation of an other con-structed by ethnologists living within particular cultures at particular times. One dramatic example of this perspective is Margaret Mead's (1928, 1930) fas-cination with the relative lack of conflict among Micronesian youth regarding issues of sexuality, which represented an other constructed within a Puritan culture.

thereby making them available for change.[13] Freud's (1900/1958, 1914/1958) original concept of "evenly hovering attention" implicitly assumed an experience-near collaborative process similar to that more thoroughly explored by Schafer (1959), Kohut (1959/1978, 1971), and Schwaber (1981, 1983) rather than the more experience-distant and scientific role so often assumed as the ideal for psychoanalysis. Described by Kohut as "vicarious introspection," this cryptic description was later extended by Schwaber (1983). Optimally, the analyst is attuned to the wishes, thoughts, and feelings of the analysand as a consequence of a process of listening to the analysand's narrative. The analyst tastes, or "vicariously introspects," on the pain and joy of the analysand's life world, fostering the analysand's enhanced self-awareness through integration, organization, and focus of this narrative, leading to an "interpretation" that further extends the analysand's range of self-observation and capacity for self-inquiry (Gardner, 1983, 1993; Poland, 1993).

While recognizing the salience of earlier life experiences, focus on the present manner in which adults understand lived experience provides an opportunity for understanding childhood experiences in the enlarged concept of the life story as a whole, from earliest childhood to oldest age. While recognizing the important role of the family romance, particularly across the first half of life, it is important to gain

---

[13]Kohut (1984) and Jackson (1992) have suggested that the experience of being listened to and of the effort by another to understand one's experience has itself the potential to create personality change in psychoanalysis. Since Alexander's (1956) pioneering formulation, the concept of the "corrective emotional experience" has been a controversial issue within psychoanalysis, founded on the assumption that bringing other than rational aspects of thought and action under conscious control represents that mode of change which is distinctive of psychoanalysis. The view that aspects of the psychoanalytic setting might itself foster such change (Stone, 1961) has too often been viewed as antithetical to psychoanalysis as a therapeutic modality. Much is missing from this critique. First, there is no recognition of the significance of another as an evoked or "essential other" (Galatzer-Levy & Cohler, 1993). Also missing is an understanding of the significance of the therapist's ability to maintain an empathic mode of listening, possible only as a consequence of the analyst's own personal analysis and continuing self-inquiry (Gardner, 1983), confronted by the variety of the analysand's enactments within the psychoanalytic setting that might ordinarily inspire enactment of intents and sentiments counter to those introduced by the analysand. The parallel of these issues for research within ethnographic settings or when listening to life stories must be explored through additional study.

a better perspective on the continuing impact of the variety of developmental factors, subsequent life experience, and social surround, all of which contribute to the experience of self and personal integrity over time. This perspective has been particularly clearly portrayed in the concept of self, as used by Hartmann (1950/1964), Winnicott (1953, 1960), and Klein (1976) and through the work of Kohut and his associates (Kohut, 1971, 1977, 1984, 1985a, 1985b; Kohut & Wolf, 1978; Wolf, 1988).

Kohut's seminal work in understanding the psychology of the self originated in an innovation in psychoanalytic method. The received method of psychoanalytic investigation takes a positivistic, external view of the patient. In this view, a patient's ideas about his or her own psychology merely informs the analyst of the particular ways that the patient disguises unconscious materials. The analyst's subjective response to the patient, understanding the patient through empathy, putting himself or herself in the patient's shoes, misleads the analyst. The analyst's own needs to disguise unacceptable psychological realities leads him or her to avoid painful and anxiety-arousing unconscious material in the patient. Thus, the analyst should adopt the position of the observing scientist, putting aside personal resonance with the patient's thoughts and feelings (Fenichel, 1945; Hartmann, 1927). From this standpoint an analyst may be tactful and humane but must always be wary of being misled by the patient.

Kohut (1959/1978) characterized the analytic situation differently. He asserted that the central method of psychoanalysis is empathic understanding. The analyst adopts the perspective of empathic attunement and immersion within the lived experience of the analysand.[14] Kohut's view of the distinctively psychoanalytic method of protracted empathic emergence in the psychological world of the patient is consistent with Klein's (1976) view that a cardinal contri-

---

[14]Prior to Kohut's formulation, the idea that empathy is *the* characteristic mode of psychoanalytic investigation was not only not formulated but actively rejected. Many analysts continue to regard empathy as a poor guide to understand psychology and regard Kohut's methods as not psychoanalytic (Read, 1994; Wallerstein, 1986). Others (Atwood & Stolorow, 1984; Goldberg & Michaels, 1988; Lichtenberg, Bornstein, & Silver, 1984; Schwaber, 1981, 1983) have attempted to characterize the empathic stance more precisely. Problems with an empathic position range from its inevitable challenge to naive visions of an absolute reality to the stress and strains experienced by the analyst who tries to see the world (including himself or herself) through the patient's eyes.

bution of psychoanalysis is the clinical theory, not metapsychology. Kohut's interest in the self, intentions, and motives rather than in drives, structures, and mechanisms is a rigorous departure from the received analytic conceptualization of psychoanalytic investigation.[15] The experience-near perspective initially formulated by Kohut (1959/1978, 1971, 1984) addresses questions of maintaining meaning, coherence, vitality, and solace that have become central also in the human sciences. Furthermore, each discipline has evidence that the presence of other people can help in times of crisis. For example, simply being with others affects positively psychophysiological measures of stress (Schachter, 1959). Kohut's studies of the intrapsychologic use of others represents an important effort to understand the basis of such findings.

The experience that others are trying to understand one appears to be an important source of the comfort engendered by being with others. To date, the empathic method has not been widely used to study adult lives. The shifting use of the analyst as a source of solace and support in the effort to maintain a sense of personal integrity across the course of life provides important information regarding the experience of self and others at all points in the life course. There is some evidence from survey reports, descriptions of psychoanalytic psychotherapies, and psychoanalyses of older adults regarding the manner in which the experience of relating to others may help to maintain meaning across expected adult transformations.

Limited conclusions may be drawn from these studies of the meaning of social ties across the course of adult lives. The literature on social ties in adulthood focuses largely on issues of social network and functional assistance rather than on the meaning of this assistance to the recipient. There are few detailed clinical case reports regarding the

---

[15]There were certainly empathically gifted and intuitive therapists before Kohut. Many analysts appreciated the central role of empathy in support in the analytic process (Gitelson, 1962; Loewald, 1960, 1978, 1986). Other analysts appreciated that the specifically human qualities of the analyst could contribute to understanding the patient, but these modalities were quite different from empathy. Reik (1952), for example, described a process of creative association on the part of the analyst, whose greater access to unconscious mental processes allowed him or her to better understand the patient's unconscious. Racker (1968), among others, recommended the systematic exploration of countertransference as a way to understand the patient's unconscious.

manner in which adults use the experience of the therapist in resolving characteristic transformations of middle and later adulthood. Freud's own deep resistance to issues of aging and his own mortality initiated an institutional bias against the clinical application of psychoanalysis to the aging population, which persists to the present day. This pessimism about analytic work with middle-aged and older adults, partly motivated by such intense countertransference issues as we have noted, becomes a self-fulfilling prophecy in which the lack of analytic experience with these patients provides clinicians little experience or understanding for undertaking such analyses.

This perspective on the changing significance of the evoked or essential other throughout life has important implications for both study and intervention within the lives of middle-aged and older adults. From the perspective of psychoanalytic self psychology, focus shifts from adjustment in the time–space world to the intrapsychologic world. It is difficult to determine the manner in which persons endow relationships with meaning simply on the basis of observation of interpersonal relations. Many older people *appear* to have impoverished ties with others, but this appearance may not reflect intrapsychic reality. As the opportunities for concrete social ties diminish, people replace actuality with reminiscence, preserving the comfort formerly obtained from continuing interpersonal relations with spouse, close friends, and family members. Indeed, beginning with middle age, people often seek to obtain less from interpersonal relationships, particularly those accompanied by feelings of obligation and required reciprocity, in favor of increased time for self; a narrowing of social focus may be expectable and reflects the priorities of this point in life.

Much of the study of psychological development across the second half of life fails to consider the changing nature of the experience of life itself. Precisely because the meaning of time, memory, and others changes across the second half of life, the significance of externally observable behaviors and reports requires different interpretation at different points in life. Reminiscence, for example, may not be principally a defensive regression from current reality, but rather a highly adaptive mode of problem solving in middle age and, later in life, a mode of evoking experiences that provide solace and a continued sense of personal integration and meaning of one's life to date, as well as a mode of beginning more intensely to grieve one's own mortality.

As a consequence of the detailed clinical and developmental study of the past decade, enhanced by the contributions of the humanities, it is now recognized that the process of empathic listening, attuned to the analysand's narrative, does not take place in a vacuum and that, clearly, the analyst's experience is of a jointly constructed actuality or dialogic actuality (Erikson, 1962/1964; Schafer, 1980, 1981). Winnicott (1953, 1960) has well portrayed the manner in which the child constructs an actuality based both on the reality of the person of the caregiver and on the child's construction of caregiver attunement. The concept of intersubjectivity fostering experience of attunement of child with caregiver (Kohut, 1977) as portrayed both in the developmental study of Trevarthan and others (Cohn & Tronick, 1983, 1987a, 1987b; Stern, 1985, 1989; Stolorow & Atwood, 1992; Trevarthan, 1980, 1989; Trevarthan & Hubley, 1978) and in social phenomenology (Husserl, 1960; Schutz, 1957/1966) emphasizes the inherently social nature of the psychoanalytic process.

The impact of the work of Vygotsky and, most recently, Bakhtin, has shown the inherently social nature of all thought that is dialogically or jointly constructed within shared discourse (Wilson & Weinstein, 1992a, 1992b). The dialogic process leads to the rewriting or refashioning of such narratives as that of the analysand over the course of the collaborative work, which in turn leads to the creation of a new narrative as a consequence of the analysand's life story reenacted within the context of the analytic process. Placing the activity of analyst and analysand within a dialogic context suggests first that any life story (re)constructed across the course of an analysis reflects a shared construction of two participants, fostering the analysand's enhanced sense of personal congruity and vitality as contrasted with the analysand's life at the beginning of the analysis (Schafer, 1980, 1981).

In the second place, analyst and analysand, like any teller and listener, live within the context and constraints of the larger social order. The life story presently constructed within analysis differs significantly from that which would have been told at the inception of psychoanalysis in America or at the conclusion of World War II. The history of psychoanalysis parallels the history of the person—later developments have significantly transformed the contributions of Freud's pioneering work and have enhanced the contributions of psychoanalysis as one of the premier approaches to the study of both history and the life history or narrative of the personal past.

Conclusion

The psychoanalytic study of development emerged principally from Freud's scientific worldview and his own effort to link his prepsychoanalytic concern focused on evolution, including both Darwin and Haeckel's (1868/1968) biogenetic "law" with the presumed origins of particular drive dispositions. As Sulloway (1979) has conclusively shown, such concepts as fixation and regression have little foundation in clinical psychoanalytic study and are important primarily as metaphor in understanding the impact of past on present (S. Freud, 1910/1957b, 1925/1959). However, the reality that these concepts do not exist within lives but only within theory need not lead to the conclusion implied in Sulloway's argument that the foundation of these concepts is a now dated scientific worldview, rendering the clinical theory invalid.

Gill (1976) and Klein (1976) both have noted that the fundamental contribution of psychoanalysis has been to renew concern with meaning and intention within lives over time rather than with phenomena beyond the experience-near observational perspective of the clinical interview. To view psychoanalysis as a theory of development is to misunderstand the signal nature of Freud's initial contributions, together with those contributions of contemporary psychoanalysis across so-called theoretical schools emphasizing a two-person psychology (Gill, 1994). It is primarily as a consequence of the unique collaboration between analyst and analysand and of this collaboration's influence on the analysand's present account of lived experience that a foundation exists for understanding the concept of psychological development over time.

The clinical psychoanalytic situation is founded on the analyst's own continuing capacity for self-inquiry (Gardner, 1983), which makes possible continuing attention to the experience of listening to the analysand's life story. This continuing concern regarding the impact of the analysand's life story is uniquely possible as a consequence of the analyst's own prior personal analysis, which fosters increased capacity for self-understanding and the mode of reflective listening so central to the psychoanalytic process (S. Freud, 1912/1958, 1914/1958). Rather than responding with anxiety to the analysand's account of experience and own enactment of this lived experience within the context of the "new" relationship with the analyst—who is friendly but not otherwise involved in the analysand's life—the analyst assists the analysand to observe the impact of particular experiences on wish and action in ways not previously recognized.

The distinctive aspect of psychoanalysis as a mode of listening to lived experience involves the analyst's capacity to taste (Fliess, 1944, 1953) or vicariously introspect (Kohut, 1959/1978) the analysand's accounts of experience and to use this experience of the narrative as a distinctive means of gathering information regarding the interplay of life experiences, social circumstances, and time or point in the course of life as factors shaping meaning and intention. The analyst's continuing focus on resonance with the analysand's reports fosters a listening stance in which the analyst's anxiety in response to the analysand's reports do not interfere in the process of listening or in maintaining an empathic perspective (Devereux, 1967).

So-called countertransference, sometimes used as a means for portraying the analyst's counterenactments to the analysand's experiences and based on unrecognized anxiety and interference in continuing self-inquiry, might better be understood in the terms initially used by Racker (1968) as *concordant* rather than as *complementary*. This phenomenon occurs when the analyst becomes anxious or personally threatened, is unable to listen reflectively, and uses projective identification in order to avoid having to bear the analysand's painful affects. An analogous process takes place more generally in the life-history interview, such as when the interviewer discussing the experience of incarceration in the camps and its aftermath with survivors of *Shoah* experiences anxiety in response to the story and seeks to avoid the discomfort induced by the participant's account of the experience.

Psychoanalysis may be best understood as a means of gathering evidence rather than a particular theory of wish and action; the process of psychoanalysis is one of recurring attention to the manner in which the life story is told (Schafer, 1958, 1980, 1981) within the context of the present relationship. This focus on relationship as the context within which the life story is constructed, reflecting a so-called constructionist perspective so often seen as opposed to an "essentialist" perspective, does not disregard the reality of life experiences. Rather, it is concerned with the meanings that are presently fashioned regarding these life experiences, recognizing that these meanings shift over time and with age. Reports regarding expectable transference enactments across the course of life (Blos, 1980; King, 1980; Neubauer, 1980) provide important information regarding the meaning that persons give to this lived experience across the years of childhood to later life. As clinical reports of the follow-through of child analysis so clearly show, the very meaning of this clinical contact itself shifts with the passage of time and with age (Cohen & Cohler, in press).

The very significance of the life story that is told across the years of clinical psychoanalytic collaboration shows a shift over time as a consequence of the manner in which analysand and analyst experience each other. The history of lived experience recounted in the first weeks of this analytic collaboration may bear little relationship to that recounted several years later at the conclusion of the formal psychoanalytic collaboration. What is interesting is understanding precisely those factors founded in the individual's interaction with the larger symbolic world that might account for the change, rather than simply the change itself. Study of the dynamics of this change will provide important information more generally regarding the determinants of both personal and social change.

Viewed from the perspective of clinical psychoanalysis such as that described in this chapter as well as that given in discussions by Ricoeur (1977) and Schafer (1980, 1981, 1994), the emphasis of psychoanalysis as a mode of study and personality change is on the process of revising the life story through transference rather than on issues of reconstruction of a presumed past. As Wolff (1988), Schafer (1982, 1994), and Cohler (1994) have suggested from somewhat different perspectives, the past as presented is necessarily unreliable except as understood within the context of the relationship between analysand and analyst. Extended more generally to the study of the personal and collective past within the human sciences, the important issue remains the context of the telling and listening of both life history and history rather than the accuracy of the account. The question is less whether a past event took place than the significance of the present telling about this past within a particular context or situation. It is important that study focus on the contexts of telling and listening in the manner initially recommended by Ricoeur (1977), understood within the relationship between teller and listener in inquiry ranging from ethnography (Kracke, 1987; Rosaldo, 1993) to oral history (Tonkin, 1992).

Whereas one consequence of the collaborative work between analyst and analysand is a life story that fosters the analysand's enhanced sense of personal integrity and vitality, another consequence of this work is enhanced understanding of those forces within society that shape the jointly constructed narrative. Not only one's present relationship to mode of production but also the particular social and historical forces ever active in society and experienced by both analyst and analysand work powerfully to shape this narrative, although probably in varying ways at different points in the course of life or within different cohorts (Dannefer, 1984; Elder, 1974, 1992; Schaie, 1984; Troll, 1970). Joint focus on the social context of the telling and the listening among these participants, together with concern with the meaning of these social and historical consequences, provides information regarding not only personal change but also social change. Social forces, including the relation to means of production, organize the very understanding of the course of life itself. The method of clinical psychoanalytic study should explicitly include this social focus at the same time that it is uniquely able to provide information regarding the dynamics or personal meanings based on particular life experiences of both personal and social change. It is in this sense that psychoanalysis is a method of significance not only for clinical intervention but also for understanding lives in time and over time.

References

Abraham, K. (1927). The applicability of psychoanalytic treatment to patients at an advanced age. In K. Abraham (Ed.), In *Selected papers on psychoanalysis* (pp. 312–316). London: Hogarth Press. (Original work published 1919)

Abraham, K. (1953). Contribution to a discussion on tic. In *Selected papers on psychoanalysis* (pp. 323–325). New York: Basic Books. (Original work published 1921)

Abraham, K. (1953). A short study on the development of the libido, viewed in the light of mental disorders. In *Selected papers on psychoanalysis* (pp. 418–501). New York: Basic Books. (Original work published 1924)

Abrams, S. (1978). The teaching and learning of psychoanalytic developmental psychology. *Journal of the American Psychoanalytic Association, 26*, 387–406.

Alexander, F. (1956). *Psychoanalysis and psychotherapy.* New York: Norton.

Anthony, E. J., & Cohler, B. (Eds.). (1987). *The invulnerable child.* New York: Guilford Press.

Applegarth, A. (1977). Psychic energy reconsidered. *Journal of the American Psychoanalytic Association, 25*, 599–602.

Aries, P. (1962). *Centuries of childhood: A social history of family life* (R. Baldick, Trans.). New York: Vintage Books.

Atwood, G., & Stolorow, R. (1984). *Structures of subjectivity: Explorations in psychoanalytic phenomenology.* Hillsdale, NJ: Analytic Press.

Back, K. W. (1974). Transition to aging and the self image. In E. Palmore (Ed.), *Normal aging* (Vol. II, pp. 207–216). Durham, NC: Duke University Press.

Bakhtin, M. M. (1986a). The problem of speech genres. In M. M. Bakhtin (Ed.), *Speech genres and other late essays* (pp. 60–102). Austin, TX: University of Texas Press.

Bakhtin, M. M. (1986b). The problem of the text in linguistics, philology, and the human sciences: An experiment in philosophical analysis. In M. M. Bakhtin (Ed.), *Speech genres and other late essays* (pp. 103–132). Austin, TX: University of Texas Press.

Basch, M. (1977). Developmental psychology and explanatory theory in psychoanalysis. *Annual of Psychoanalysis, 5,* 229–263.

Basch, M. (1982). The significance of infant development studies for psychoanalytic theory. In M. Mayman (Ed.), *Infant research: The dawn of awareness* (pp. 731–738). Madison, CT: International Universities Press.

Basch, M. (1985). Some clinical and theoretical implications of infant research. In D. Silver (Ed.), *Commentaries on Joseph Lichtenberg's psychoanalysis and infant research* (pp. 509–516). Hillsdale, NJ: Analytic Press.

Becker, E. (1973). *The denial of death.* New York: Free Press.

Benedek, T. (1959). Parenthood as a developmental phase: A contribution to the libido theory. *Journal of the American Psychoanalytic Association, 7,* 389–417.

Benedek, T. (1970). Parenthood during the life-cycle. In E. J. Anthony & T. Benedek (Eds.), *Parenthood: Its psychology and psychopathology* (pp. 185–206). Boston: Little, Brown.

Benedek, T. (1973). Discussion: Parenthood as a developmental phase. In T. Benedek (Ed.), *Psychoanalytic investigations* (pp. 401–407). New York: Quadrangle Press.

Bengtson, V., Furlong, M., & Laufer, R. (1974). Time, aging and the continuity of social structure: These and issues in generational analysis. *Journal of Social Issues, 30,* 1–30.

Berenthal, B., & Campos, J. (1987). New directions in the study of early experiences. *Child Development, 58,* 560–567.

Berlin, R. (1974). *A developmental analysis of the coping process.* Unpublished doctoral dissertation, University of Chicago, Chicago, IL.

Bernfeld, S. (1941). Freud's earliest theories on the school of Helmholtz. *Psychoanalytic Quarterly, 13,* 341–362.

Bernfeld, S. (1949). Freud's scientific beginnings. *Imago, 6,* 163–196.

Bernfeld, S. (1951). Sigmund Freud, M.D., 1882–1885. *International Journal of Psycho-Analysis, 32,* 204–217.

Bibring, G. (1959). Some considerations of the psychological processes in pregnancy. *Psychoanalytic Study of the Child, 14,* 113–121.

Blos, P. (1967). The second individuation process of adolescence. *Psychoanalytic Study of the Child, 22,* 162–186.

Blos, P. (1980). The life cycle as indicated by the nature of the transference in the psychoanalysis of adolescents. *International Journal of Psycho-Analysis, 61,* 145–151.

Breuer, J., & Freud, S. (1955). Studies in hysteria. In J. Strachey (Ed. and Trans.), *The standard edition of the complete psychological works of Sigmund Freud* (Vol. 2, pp. 1–305). London: Hogarth Press. (Original work published 1893–1895)

Briggs, J. (1970). *Never in anger.* Cambridge, MA: Harvard University Press.

Brim, O. G., Jr. (1976). Life-span development of the theory of oneself: Implications for child development. In H. Reese & L. Lipsitt (Eds.), *Advances in child development and behavior* (Vol. II, pp. 241–251). New York: Academic Press.

Brown, R. (1986). *Social psychology* (2nd ed.). New York: Free Press.

Butler, R. (1963). The life-review: An interpretation of reminiscence in the aged. *Psychiatry, 26,* 65–76.

Cain, L. (1964). Life-course and social structure. In R. Faris (Ed.), *Handbook of modern sociology* (pp. 272–309). Chicago: Rand McNally.

Cain, L. (1967). Age status and generational phenomena: The new old people in contemporary America. *The Gerontologist, 7,* 83–92.

Calder, K. (1980). An analyst's self-analysis. *Journal of the American Psychoanalytic Association, 28,* 5–20.

Carney, J., & Cohler, B. (1993). Developmental continuities and adjustment in adulthood: Social relations, morale, and the transformation from middle to late life. In G. Pollock & S. Greenspan (Eds.), *The course of life: Vol. 6. Late adulthood* (Rev. ed., pp. 199–226). Madison, CT: International Universities Press.

Cherlin, A. (1981). *Marriage, divorce, remarriage.* Cambridge, MA: Harvard University Press.

Chused, J. (1991). The evocative power of enactments. *Journal of the American Psychoanalytic Association, 39,* 615–639.

Clarke, A., & Clarke, A. D. B. (Eds.). (1976). *Early experience: Myth and evidence.* New York: Free Press.

Clausen, J. (1993). *American lives: Looking back at the children of the Great Depression.* New York: Free Press.

Cohen, J., & Cohler, B. (in press). *The psychoanalytic study of lives over time: Clinical and research perspectives on children who return to analysis as adults.* New Haven, CT: Yale University Press.

Cohler, B. (1980). Developmental perspectives on the psychology of the self. In A. Goldberg (Ed.), *Advances in self psychology* (pp. 69–115). Madison, CT: International Universities Press.

Cohler, B. (1982). Personal narrative and life-course. In P. Baltes & O. G. Brim, Jr. (Eds.), *Life span development and behavior* (Vol. 4, pp. 205–241). New York: Academic Press.

Cohler, B. (1987). Approaches to the study of development in psychiatric education. In S. Weissman & R. Thurnblad (Eds.), *The role of psychoanalysis in psychiatric education: Past, present and future* (pp. 225–270). New York: International Universities Press.

Cohler, B. (1989). Psychoanalysis and education: III. Motive, meaning and self. In K. Field, B. Cohler, & G. Wool (Eds.), *Learning and education:*

Psychoanalytic perspectives (pp. 11–84). Madison, CT: International Universities Press.

Cohler, B. (1994). Memory recovery and the use of the past: A commentary on Lindsay and Read from psychoanalytic perspectives. *Applied Cognitive Psychology, 8,* 365–378.

Cohler, B., & Boxer, A. (1984). Middle adulthood: Settling into the world. Person, time and context. In D. Offer & M. Sabshin (Eds.), *Normality and the life course: A critical integration* (pp. 145–203). New York: Basic Books.

Cohler, B., & Freeman, M. (1993). Psychoanalysis and the developmental narrative. In G. Pollock & S. Greenspan (Eds.), *The course of life: Vol. 5. Early adulthood* (Rev. ed., pp. 99–177). Madison, CT: International Universities Press.

Cohler, B., & Galatzer-Levy, R. (1990). Self, meaning, and morale across the second half of life. In R. Nemiroff & C. Colarusso (Eds.), *New dimensions in adult development* (pp. 125–169). New York: Basic Books.

Cohler, B., & Galatzer-Levy, R. (1992). Psychoanalysis and the classroom: Intent and meaning in learning and teaching. In N. Szajnberg (Ed.), *Educating the emotions: Bruno Bettelheim and psychoanalytic development* (pp. 41–91). New York: Plenum.

Cohler, B., & Galatzer-Levy, R. (1995). *What kind of a science is psychoanalysis?* Manuscript submitted for publication.

Cohler, B., & Grunebaum, H. (1981). *Mothers, grandmothers and daughters: Personality and child care in three generation families.* New York: Wiley-Interscience.

Cohler, B., & Lieberman, M. (1979). Personality change across the second half of life: Findings from a study of Irish, Italian and Polish-American men and women. In D. Gelfand & A. Kutznik (Eds.), *Ethnicity and aging* (pp. 227–245). New York: Springer.

Cohler, B., & Lieberman, M. (1980). Social relations and mental health: Middle-aged and older men and women from three European ethnic groups. *Research on Aging, 2,* 454–469.

Cohler, B., & Musick, J. (1984). Psychopathology of parenthood: Implications for mental health of children. *Infant Mental Health Journal, 4,* 140–164.

Cohn, J., & Tronick, E. (1983). Three-month-old infants' reaction to stimulated maternal depression. *Child Development, 54,* 185–193.

Cohn, J., & Tronick, E. (1987a). Mother–infant face-to-face interaction: The sequence of dyadic states at 3, 6, and 9 months. *Developmental Psychology, 23,* 68–77.

Cohn, J., & Tronick, E. (1987b). Specificity of infants' response to mothers' affective behavior. *Journal of the American Academy of Child and Adolescent Psychiatry, 28,* 242–248.

Colarusso, C. (1987). The development of time sense: From object constancy to adolescence. *Journal of the American Psychoanalytic Association, 35,* 119–144.

Colarusso, C., & Nemiroff, R. (1979). Some observations and hypotheses about the psychoanalytic theory of adult development. *International Journal of Psycho-Analysis, 60,* 59–71.

Colarusso, C., & Nemiroff, R. (1981). *Adult development: A new dimension of psychodynamic theory and practice.* New York: Plenum.

Cole, T. (in press). *No color is my kind: The life of Eldrewey Stearns and the integration of Houston, Texas.* Austin, TX: University of Texas Press.

Coleman, P. (1974). Measuring reminiscence characteristics from conversation as adaptive features of old age. *International Journal of Aging and Human Development, 5,* 281–294.

Coleman, P. (1986). *Ageing and reminiscence: Social and clinical implications.* New York: Wiley.

Coleman, P., & McCulloch, A. (1985). The study of psychosocial change in late life: Some conceptual and methodological issues. In J. Munnichs, P. Mussen, E. Olbrich, & P. Coleman (Eds.), *Life-span and change in a gerontological perspective* (pp. 239–256). New York: Academic Press.

Colombo, J. (1982). The critical period concept: Research, methodology, and theoretical issues. *Psychological Bulletin, 91,* 260–275.

Cottle, T. (1977). *Perceiving time: A psychological investigation.* New York: Wiley.

Cottle, T., & Klineberg, S. (1974). *The present of things future.* New York: Free Press.

Csikszentmihalyi, M., & Larson, R. (1984). *Being adolescent: Conflict and growth in the teenage years.* New York: Basic Books.

Daniels, P., & Weingarten, K. (1982). *Sooner or later: The timing of parenthood in adult lives.* New York: Norton.

Dannefer, D. (1984). Adult development and social theory: A paradigmatic reappraisal. *American Sociological Review, 49,* 100–116.

Devereux, G. (1967). *From anxiety to method in the behavioral sciences.* The Hague, The Netherlands: Mouton.

Durkheim, E. (1961). *The elementary forms of the religious life* (J. S. Swain, Trans.). New York: Free Press. (Original work published 1912)

Easterlin, R. (1987). *Birth and fortune: The impact of numbers on personal welfare* (2nd ed.). Chicago: University of Chicago Press.

Eichorn, D., Clausen, J., Haan, N., Honzik, M., & Mussen, P. (1981). *Present and past in middle life.* New York: Academic Press.

Eisenbud, J. (1956). Time and the Oedipus. *Psychoanalytic Quarterly, 25,* 373–384.

Elder, G., Jr. (1974). *Children of the Great Depression.* Chicago: University of Chicago Press.

Elder, G., Jr. (1979). Historical change in life patterns and personality. In P. Baltes & O. G. Brim, Jr. (Eds.), *Life-span development and behavior* (pp. 117–159). New York: Academic Press.

Elder, G. (1992). Life course. In E. Borgatta & M. Borgatta (Eds.), *Encyclopedia of sociology* (Vol. 3, pp. 1120–1130). New York: Macmillan.

Elder, G. (in press). Time, human agency, and social change: Perspectives on the life course. *Social Psychology Quarterly.*

Elder, G., & Caspi, A. (1990). Studying lives in a changing society: Sociological and personological explorations (Henry A. Murray Lecture Series). In A. Rabin, R. A. Zucker, R. Emmons, & S. Frank (Eds.), *Studying persons and lives* (pp. 201–247). New York: Springer.

Elder, G., & Rockwell, R. (1979). The life-course and human development: An ecological perspective. *International Journal of Behavioral Development, 2,* 1–21.

Emde, R. (1981). Changing the models of infancy and the nature of early development: Remodeling the foundation. *Journal of the American Psychoanalytic Association, 29,* 179–219.

Emde, R., & Harmon, R. (1984). Entering a new era in the search for developmental continuities. In R. Emde & R. Harmon (Eds.), *Continuities and discontinuities in development* (pp. 1–11). New York: Plenum.

Erikson, E. H. (1958). *Young man Luther: A study in psychoanalysis and history.* New York: Norton.

Erikson, E. H. (1963). *Childhood and society.* (Rev. ed.). New York: Norton. (Original work published 1950)

Erikson, E. (1964). Psychological reality and historical actuality. In E. Erikson, *Insight and responsibility* (pp. 159–256). New York: Norton. (Original work published 1962)

Erikson, E. (1982). *The life-cycle completed: A review.* New York: Norton.

Erikson, E., Erikson, J., & Kivnick, H. (1986). *Vital involvement in old age: The experience of old age in our time.* New York: Norton.

Escoll, P. J. (1977). The contribution of psychoanalytic developmental concepts to adult analysis. *Journal of the American Psychoanalytic Association, 25,* 219–234.

Farnham-Diggory, S. (1966). Self, future, and time: A developmental study of the concepts of psychotic, brain injured, and normal children. *Monographs of the Society for Research in Child Development, 33*(Serial No. 103).

Fenichel, O. (1945). The psychoanalytic theory of neurosis. New York: Norton.

Festinger, L. (1954). A theory of social comparison processes. *Human Relations, 7,* 117–140.

Fine, B., Joseph, E., & Waldhorn, H. (1959). *Recollection and reconstruction/reconstruction in psychoanalysis* [Monograph IV of the Kris Study Group]. Madison, CT: International Universities Press.

Firth, R., Hubert, J., & Forge, A. (1970). *Families and their relatives: Kinship in a middle class sector of London.* New York: Humanities Press.

Fish, B. (1977). Neurologic antecedents of schizophrenia in children: Evidence for an inherited, congenital neurointegrative deficit. *Archives of General Psychiatry, 34,* 1297–1313.

Fiske, M. (1980). Tasks and crises of the second half of life: The interrelationship of commitment, coping, and adaptation. In J. Birren & R. B. Sloane (Eds.), *Handbook of mental health and aging* (pp. 337–373). Englewood Cliffs, NJ: Prentice Hall.

Fiske, M., & Chiriboga, D. (1990). *Change and continuity in adult life.* San Francisco: Jossey-Bass.

Flarsheim, A. (1974). The therapist's collusion with the patient's wish for suicide. In P. Giovacchini, A. Flarsheim, & B. Boyer (Eds.), *Tactics and technique in psychoanalytic therapy: Vol. II. Countertransference* (pp. 155–195). New York: Science House-Aronson.

Fliess, R. (1944). The metapsychology of the analyst. *Psychoanalytic Quarterly,* *11,* 211–227.

Fliess, R. (1953). Countertransference and counteridentification. *Journal of the American Psychoanalytic Association, 1,* 268–284.

Freud, A. (1958). Child observation and prediction of development: A memorial lecture in honor of Ernst Kris. *Psychoanalytic Study of the Child, 13,* 92–116.

Freud, A. (1966). *The ego and the mechanisms of defense* (Rev. ed.). Madison, CT: International Universities Press. (Original work published 1936)

Freud, S. (1953a). Fragment of an analysis of a case of hysteria. In J. Strachey (Ed. and Trans.), *The standard edition of the complete psychological works of Sigmund Freud* (Vol. 8, pp. 7–124). (Original work published 1905)

Freud, S. (1953b). Three essays on the theory of sexuality. In J. Strachey (Ed. and Trans.), *The standard edition of the complete psychological works of Sigmund Freud* (Vol. 7, pp. 130–243). London: Hogarth Press. (Original work published 1905)

Freud, S. (1953). My views on the part played by sexuality in the aetiology of the neuroses. In J. Strachey (Ed. and Trans.), *The standard edition of the complete psychological works of Sigmund Freud* (Vol. 7, pp. 271–282). London: Hogarth Press. (Original work published 1906)

Freud, S. (1955). The psychogenesis of a case of homosexuality in a woman. In J. Strachey (Ed. and Trans.), *The standard edition of the complete psychological works of Sigmund Freud* (Vol. 18, pp. 147–172). London: Hogarth Press. (Original work published 1920)

Freud, S. (1957a). Five lectures on psychoanalysis. In J. Strachey (Ed. and Trans.), *The standard edition of the complete psychological works of Sigmund Freud* (Vol. 11, pp. 3–55). London: Hogarth Press. (Original work published 1910)

Freud, S. (1957b). Leonardo da Vinci and a memory of his childhood. In J. Strachey (Ed. and Trans.), *The standard edition of the complete psychological works of Sigmund Freud* (Vol. 11, pp. 63–138). London: Hogarth Press. (Original work published 1910)

Freud, S. (1957). The unconscious. In J. Strachey (Ed. and Trans.), *The standard edition of the complete psychological works of Sigmund Freud* (Vol. 14, pp. 159–195). London: Hogarth Press. (Original work published 1915)

Freud, S. (1958). Letter of December 6, 1896. In J. M. Masson (Ed. and Trans.), *The complete letters of Sigmund Freud to Wilhelm Fliess, 1887–1904* (pp. 207–215). Cambridge, MA: Harvard University Press. (Original work published 1897)

Freud, S. (1958). The interpretation of dreams. In J. Strachey (Ed. and Trans.), *The standard edition of the complete psychological works of Sigmund Freud* (Vols. 4–5). London: Hogarth Press. (Original work published 1900)

Freud, S. (1958). Recommendations to physicians practicing psychoanalysis. *Standard edition of the complete psychological works of Sigmund Freud* (Vol. 12, pp. 109–120). London: Hogarth Press. (Original work published 1912)

Freud, S. (1958). The claims of psychoanalysis to scientific interest. In J. Strachey (Ed. and Trans.), *The standard edition of the complete psychological works of Sigmund Freud* (Vol. 13, pp. 165–192). London: Hogarth Press. (Original work published 1913)

Freud, S. (1958). Further recommendations to physicians practicing psychoanalysis: II. Remembering, repeating and working-through. In J. Strachey (Ed. and Trans.), *The standard edition of the complete psychological works of Sigmund Freud* (Vol. 12, pp. 146–156). London: Hogarth Press. (Original work published 1914)

Freud, S. (1959). Family romances. In J. Strachey (Ed. and Trans.), *The standard edition of the complete psychological works of Sigmund Freud* (Vol. 9, pp. 235–244). London: Hogarth Press. (Original work published 1909)

Freud, S. (1959). An autobiographical study. In J. Strachey (Ed. and Trans.), *The standard edition of the complete psychological works of Sigmund Freud* (Vol. 20, pp. 7–74). London: Hogarth Press. (Original work published 1925)

Freund, E. (1987). *The return of the reader: Reader-response criticism.* New York: Methuen.

Furstenberg, F., Brooks-Gunn, J., & Morgan, S. (1987). *Adolescent mothers in later life.* New York: Cambridge University Press.

Galatzer-Levy, R. (1978). Qualitative change from quantitative change: Mathematical catastrophe theory in relation to psychoanalysis. *Journal of the American Psychoanalytic Association, 26,* 921–936.

Galatzer-Levy, R., & Cohler, B. (1993). *The essential other: A developmental psychology of the self.* New York: Basic Books.

Gardner, R. (1983). *Self-inquiry.* Boston: Little, Brown/Atlantic Monthly Press.

Gardner, R. (1993). On talking to ourselves: Some self-analytical reflections on self-analysis. In J. Barron (Ed.), *Self-analysis: Critical inquiries, personal visions* (pp. 147–170). Hillsdale, NJ: Analytic Press.

Gay, P. (1988). *Freud: A life for our times.* New York: Norton.

Geertz, C. (1973a). The impact of the concept of culture on the concept of man. In C. Geertz (Ed.), *The interpretation of cultures* (pp. 33–54). New York: Basic Books. (Original work published 1966)

Geertz, C. (1973b). Person, time and conduct in Bali. In C. Geertz (Ed.), *The interpretation of cultures* (pp. 360–411). New York: Basic Books. (Original work published 1966)

Geertz, C. (1973). *The interpretation of cultures.* New York: Basic Books.

Geertz, C. (1983). "From the native's point of view": On the nature of anthropological understanding. In C. Geertz (Ed.), *Local knowledge: Further essays in interpretive anthropology.* New York: Basic Books. (Original work published 1974)

Geertz, C. (1983). Local knowledge: Fact and law in comparative perspective. In C. Geertz (Ed.), *Local knowledge: Further essays in interpretive anthropology* (pp. 167–234). New York: Basic Books.

Gergen, K. (1977). Stability, change and chance in understanding human development. In N. Datan & H. Reese (Eds.), *Life-span developmental psychology: Dialectical perspectives on experimental research* (pp. 32–65). New York: Academic Press.

Gergen, K. (1980). The emerging crisis in life-span development theory. In P. Baltes & O. G. Brim, Jr. (Eds.), *Life-span development and behavior* (Vol. 3, pp. 31–65). New York: Academic Press.

Gergen, K. (1990). Social understanding, and the inscription of self. In J. Stigler, R. Shweder, & G. Herdt (Eds.), *Cultural psychology* (pp. 569–606). Cambridge, England: Cambridge University Press.

Gergen, K. (1994). *Realities and relationships: Soundings in social construction.* Cambridge, MA: Harvard University Press.

Gill, M. (1976). Metapsychology is not psychology [Psychological Issues Monograph 71]. In M. Gill & P. Holzman (Eds.), *Psychology versus metapsychology* (pp. 71–105). Madison, CT: International Universities Press.

Gill, M. (1982). *Analysis of the transference: Volume I. Theory and technique.* Madison, CT: International Universities Press.

Gill, M. (1994). *Psychoanalysis in transition: A personal view.* Hillsdale, NJ: Analytic Press.

Gilligan, C. (1982). *In a different voice: Psychological theory and women's lives.* Cambridge, MA: Harvard University Press.

Gitelson, M. (1962). The first phase of psychoanalysis: Symposium on the curative factors in psycho-analysis. *International Journal of Psycho-Analysis, 43,* 194–205.

Glick, P. (1977). Updating the family life-cycle. *Journal of Marriage and the Family, 39,* 5–13.

Glueck, S., & Glueck, E. (1950). *Unraveling juvenile delinquency.* New York: Commonwealth Foundation.

Goldberg, W., & Michaels, G. (1988). Conclusion. The transition to parenthood: synthesis and future directions. In G. Michaels & W. Goldberg (Eds.), *The transition to parenthood: Current theory and research* (pp. 342–360). New York: Cambridge University Press.

Good, B. (1994). *Medicine, rationality, and experience: An anthropological perspective.* New York: Cambridge University Press.

Gould, R. (1993). Transformational tasks in adulthood. In G. H. Pollock & S. Greenspan (Eds.), *The course of life: Vol. VI. Late adulthood* (pp. 23–68). Madison, CT: International Universities Press.

Greene, A. L. (1986). Future time perspective in adolescence: The present of things future revisited. *Journal of Youth and Adolescence, 15,* 99–113.

Greene, A. L. (1990). Great expectations: Constructions of the life-course during adolescence. *Journal of Youth and Adolescence, 19,* 289–306.

Greenson, R. (1960). Empathy and its vicissitudes. *International Journal of Psycho-Analysis, 41,* 418–424.

Grunes, J. (1980). Reminiscences, regression, and empathy—A psychotherapeutic approach to the impaired elderly. In S. Greenspan & G. Pollock (Eds.), *The course of life: Vol. III. Adulthood and the aging process* (pp. 545–548). Washington, DC: U.S. Government Printing Office.

Gutmann, D. (1975). Parenthood: Key to the comparative study of the life-cycle. In N. Datan & L. Ginsberg (Eds.), *Life-span developmental psychology: Normative life-crises* (pp. 167–184). New York: Academic Press.

Gutmann, D. (1987). *Reclaimed powers: Towards a psychology of men and women in later life*. New York: Basic Books.

Gutmann, D., Griffin, B., & Grunes, J. (1982). Developmental contributions to the late-onset affective disorders. In P. Baltes & O. G. Brim (Eds.), *Life-span development and behavior* (pp. 244–263). New York: Academic Press.

Guttentag, M., & Secord, P. (1983). *Too many women: The sex ratio question*. Beverly Hills, CA: Sage.

Habermas, J. (1971). *Knowledge and human interests*. Boston: Beacon Press. (Original work published 1968)

Habermas, J. (1983). Interpretive social science vs. hermeneuticism. In N. Haan, R. Bellah, P. Rabinow, & W. Sullivan (Eds.), *Social science as moral inquiry* (pp. 251–270). New York: Columbia University Press.

Haeckel, E. (1968). *Natural history of creation* [Naturaliche Schopfungsgesichte]. Berlin: George Reimer. (Original work published 1868)

Hagestad, G. (1990). Social perspectives on the life course. In R. Binstock & L. K. George (Eds.), *Handbook of aging and the social sciences* (3rd ed., pp. 151–168). New York: Academic Press.

Hagestad, G. (1994). *On-time, off-time, and out of time*. Paper presented at the annual meeting of the Gerontological Society of America, Atlanta, GA.

Hagestad, G., & Neugarten, B. (1985). Age and the life-course. In R. Binstock & E. Shanas (Eds.), *Handbook of aging and society* (2nd ed., pp. 35–61). New York: Van Nostrand Reinhold.

Hareven, T. (1982). *Family time and industrial time*. New York: Cambridge University Press.

Hareven, T. (1986). Historical changes in the construction of the life-course. *Human Development, 29*, 171–180.

Harringdon, D. (1993). Child-rearing antecedents of suboptimal personality development: Exploring aspects of Alice Miller's concept of poisonous pedagogy. In D. Funder, R. Parke, C. Tomlinson-Keasey, & K. Widaman (Eds.), *Studying lives through time: Personality and development* (pp. 289–313). Washington, DC: American Psychological Association.

Hartmann, H. (1927). Understanding and explaining. In H. Hartmann, *Essays on ego psychology* (pp. 369–404). Madison, CT: International Universities Press.

Hartmann, H. (1958). *Ego psychology and the problem of adaptation*. (D. Rapaport, Trans.). Madison, CT: International Universities Press. (Original work published 1939)

Hartmann, H. (1964). Comments on the psychoanalytic theory of the ego. In H. Hartmann (Ed.), *Essays on ego psychology* (pp. 113–141). Madison, CT: International Universities Press. (Original work published 1950)

Hartmann, H., & Kris, E. (1945). The genetic approach in psychoanalysis. *Psychoanalytic Study of the Child, 1*, 11–30.

Hazan, H. (1980). *The limbo people: A study of the constitution of the time universe among the aged*. London: Routledge & Kegan Paul.

Hoffman, I. (1991). Towards a social-constructivist view of the psychoanalytic situation. *Psychoanalytic Dialogues, 1*, 74–105.

Hogan, D. (1981). *Transitions and social change: The early lives of American men.* New York: Academic Press.

Hogan, D. (1984). The demography of life-course transitions: Temporal and gender considerations. In A. Rossi (Ed.), *Gender and the life-course* (pp. 65–78). New York: Aldine/Atherton.

Holt, R. R. (1975). The past and future of ego psychology. *Psychoanalytic Quarterly, 44,* 550–576.

Horowitz, M. (1977). The quantitative line of approach in psychoanalysis: A clinical assessment of its current status. *Journal of the American Psychoanalytic Association, 25,* 559–580.

Husserl, E. (1960). *Cartesian meditations: An introduction to phenomenology* (D. Cairns, Trans.). The Hague, The Netherlands: Martinus Nijoff.

Iser, W. (1978). *The act of reading: A theory of aesthetic response.* Baltimore: Johns Hopkins University Press.

Jackson, S. (1969). The history of Freud's concepts of regression. *Journal of the American Psychoanalytic Association, 17,* 743–784.

Jackson, S. (1992). The listening healer in the history of psychological healing. *American Journal of Psychiatry, 149,* 1623–1632.

Jacobs, T. (1986). On countertransference enactments. *Journal of the American Psychoanalytic Association, 34,* 289–307.

Jacobs, T. (1991). *The use of the self: Countertransference and communication in the analytic situation.* Madison, CT: International Universities Press.

Jaffe, D. (1986). Empathy, counteridentification, countertransference: A review with some personal perspectives on the "analytic instrument." *Psychoanalytic Quarterly, 55,* 215–243.

Jaques, E. (1965). Death and the midlife crisis. *International Journal of Psycho-Analysis, 46,* 502–514.

Jaques, E. (1993). The midlife crisis. In S. Greenspan & G. Pollock (Eds.), *The course of life: V. Early adulthood* (pp. 201–232). Madison, CT: International Universities Press.

Johan, M. (1992). Enactments in psychoanalysis [Report on panel discussion]. *Journal of the American Psychoanalytic Association, 40,* 827–841.

Jones, E. (1953). *The life and work of Sigmund Freud* (Vol. 1). New York: Basic Books.

Jones, M., Bayley, N., MacFarlane, J., & Honzik, M. (1971). *The course of human development.* Waltham, MA: Xerox College Publishing.

Jung, C. G. (1933). *Modern man in search of a soul.* New York: Harcourt, Brace & World.

Kafka, J. (1973). The experience of time [Report on panel discussion]. *Journal of the American Psychoanalytic Association, 21,* 65–667.

Kagan, J. (1980). Perspective on continuity. In O. G. Brim, Jr. & J. Kagan (Eds.), *Constancy and change in human development* (pp. 26–74). Cambridge, MA: Harvard University Press.

Kagan, J., Kearsley, R., & Zelazo, P. (1978). *Infancy: Its place in human development.* Cambridge, MA: Harvard University Press.

Kagan, J., & Moss, H. (1962). *From birth to maturity.* New York: Wiley.

Kahana, R. (1979). Strategies of psychotherapy with the wide range of older individuals. *Journal of Geriatric Psychiatry, 12,* 71–100.

Kahana, R. (1985). The ant and the grasshopper in later life. In R. Nemiroff & C. Colarusso (Eds.), *The race against time: Psychotherapy and psychoanalysis in the second half of life* (pp. 263–292). New York: Plenum.

Kakar, S. (1985). Psychoanalysis and non-western cultures. *International Review of Psycho-Analysis, 12,* 441–448.

Kakar, S. (1989). The maternal–feminine in Indian psychoanalysis. *International Journal of Psychoanalysis, 16,* 355–362.

Kaminsky, M. (1984). The uses of reminiscence: A discussion of the formative literature. In M. Kaminsky (Ed.), *The uses of reminiscence: New ways of working with older adults* (pp. 137–156). New York: Haworth Press.

Katz, J. (1976). Development of the mind. In J. Katz & R. T. Hartnett (Eds.), *Scholars in the making: The development of graduate and professional students* (pp. 107–126). Cambridge, MA: Ballinger.

Kaufman, S. (1986). *The ageless self: Sources of meaning in late life.* Madison, WI: University of Wisconsin Press.

Keith, P. (1982). Perceptions of time remaining and distance from death. *Omega, 12,* 269–280.

Kernberg, O. (1980). Normal narcissism in middle age. In O. Kernberg (Ed.), *Internal world and external reality: Object relations theory applied* (pp. 121–153). Northvale, NJ: Jason Aronson.

King, P. (1980). The life cycle as indicated by the nature of the transference in the psychoanalysis of the middle-aged and elderly. *International Journal of Psycho-Analysis, 61,* 153–160.

Klein, G. (1976). *Psychoanalytic theory: An exploration of essentials* (M. Gill, Ed.). Madison, CT: International Universities Press.

Klineberg, S. (1967). Changes in outlook on the future between childhood and adolescence. *Journal of Personality and Social Psychology, 7,* 185–193.

Kohlberg, L., Ricks, D., & Snarey, J. (1984). Childhood development as a predictor of adaptation in adulthood. *Genetic Psychology Monographs, 110,* 91–172.

Kohli, M., & Meyer, J. (1986). Social structure and social construction of life stages. *Human Development, 29,* 145–180.

Kohut, H. (1971). *The analysis of the self: A systematic approach to the psychoanalytic treatment of narcissistic personality disorders* [Monograph]. Madison, CT: International Universities Press.

Kohut, H. (1977). *The restoration of the self.* Madison, CT: International Universities Press.

Kohut, H. (1978). Introspection, empathy and psychoanalysis: An examination of the relationship between mode of observation and theory. In P. Ornstein (Ed.), *The search for the self: Selected writings of Heinz Kohut, 1950–1978* (Vol. I, pp. 205–232). Madison, CT: International Universities Press. (Original work published 1959)

Kohut, H. (1984). *How does analysis cure?* Chicago: University of Chicago Press.

Kohut, H. (1985a). On the continuity of the self and cultural selfobjects. In C. Strozier (Ed.), *Self psychology and the humanities: Reflections on a new psychoanalytic approach by Heinz Kohut* (pp. 232–243). New York: Norton. (Original work published 1981)

Kohut, H. (1985b). *Self psychology and the humanities: Reflections on a new psychoanalytic approach by Heinz Kohut* (Charles Strozier, Ed.). New York: Norton. (Original work published 1981)

Kohut, H., & Seitz, P. (1978). Concepts and theories of psychoanalysis. In P. Ornstein (Ed.), *The search for the self: Selected writings of Heinz Kohut, 1950–1978* (Vol. 1, pp. 337–374). Madison, CT: International Universities press. (Original work published 1963)

Kohut, H., & Wolf, E. (1978). The disorders of the self and their treatment: An outline. *International Journal of Psychoanalysis, 59,* 413–425.

Kracke, W. (1981). Kagwahiv mourning: Dreams of a bereaved father. *Ethos, 9,* 258–275.

Kracke, W. (1987). Encounter with other cultures: Psychological and epistemonological aspects. *Ethos, 15,* 3–8.

Lasch, C. (1979). *The culture of narcissism: American life in an age of diminishing expectations.* New York: Norton.

Lee, G. (1979). Children and the elderly. *Research on Aging, 1,* 335–360.

Leites, N. (1977). Transference interpretations only? *International Journal of Psycho-Analysis, 58,* 275–287.

Lichtenberg, J. (1983). *Psychoanalysis and infant research.* Hillsdale, NJ: Analytic Press.

Lichtenberg, J., Bornstein, M., & Silver, D. (1984). *Empathy* (Vol. 1 & 2). Hillsdale, NJ: Analytic Press/Erlbaum.

Lieberman, M., & Cohler, B. (1975). *Constructing personality measures for older people* (Report to the Administration on Aging). Chicago: Committee on Human Development, University of Chicago.

Lieberman, M., & Falk, J. (1971). The remembered past as a source of data for research on the life cycle. *Human Development, 14,* 132–141.

Lieberman, M., & Tobin, S. (1983). *The experience of old age: Stress, coping and survival.* New York: Basic Books.

Lieblich, A. (1993). Looking at change: Natasha, 21: New immigrant from Russia to Israel. In R. Josselson & A. Lieblich (Eds.), *The narrative study of lives* (pp. 92–129). Thousand Oaks, CA: Sage.

Livson, N., & Peskin, H. (1980). Perspectives on adolescence from longitudinal research. In J. Adelson (Ed.), *Handbook of adolescent psychology* (pp. 47–96). New York: Wiley.

Loewald, H. (1960). The therapeutic action of psychoanalysis. *International Journal of Psycho-Analysis, 41,* 16–33.

Loewald, H. (1962). The super-ego and the ego-ideal: II. Super-ego and time. *International Journal of Psycho-Analysis, 43,* 264–268.

Loewald, H. (1972). The experience of time. *Psychoanalytic Study of the Child, 27,* 401–410.

Loewald, H. (1978). *Psychoanalysis and the history of the individual.* New Haven, CT: Yale University Press.

Loewald, H. (1986). Transference–countertransference. *Journal of the American Psychoanalytic Association, 34,* 275–287.

Lorenz, K. (1957). The nature of instinct. In C. Schiller (Ed.), *Instinctive behavior* (pp. 129–175). Madison, CT: International Universities Press. (Original work published 1937)

Lowenthal, M. F., Thurnher, M., Chiriboga, D., & Associates. (1975). *Four states of life*. San Francisco: Jossey-Bass.

Malinowski, B. (1989). *A diary in the strict sense of the term*. Stanford, CA: Stanford University Press. (Original work published 1914–1918)

Mannheim, K. (1952). The problem of generations. In K. Mannheim, *Essays on the sociology of knowledge* (pp. 276–322). London: Routledge & Kagan Paul. (Original work published 1922)

Marini, M. (1978). The transition to adulthood: Sex difference in educational attainment and age at marriage. *American Sociological Review, 43*, 483–507.

Marini, M. (1985). Age and sequencing norms in the transition to adulthood. *Social Forces, 63*, 229–244.

Marshall, V. (1975). Age and awareness of finitude in developmental gerontology. *Omega, 6*, 113–129.

Marshall, V. (1986). A sociological perspective on aging and dying. In V. Marshall (Ed.), *Later life: The social psychology of aging* (pp. 125–146). Thousand Oaks, CA: Sage.

Matthews, S. (1983). Definitions of friendship and their consequences in old age. *Ageing and Society, 3*, 144–155.

Matthews, S. (1986). *Friendships through the life course*. Newbury Park, CA: Sage.

Mattingly, C. (1989). *Thinking with stories: Story and experience in a clinical practice*. Unpublished doctoral dissertation, Massachusetts Institute of Technology, Cambridge, MA.

May, R., Angel, E., & Ellenberger, H. (Eds.). (1958). *Existentialism: A new dimension in psychiatry and psychology*. New York: Basic Books.

McCord, J. (1979). Some child-rearing antecedents of criminal behavior in adult men. *Journal of Personality and Social Psychology, 37*, 1477–1486.

McCord, J. (1980). Patterns of deviance. In S. B. Wells, R. Crandall, M. Roff, J. Strauss, & W. Pollin (Eds.), *Human functioning in longitudinal perspective* (pp. 157–165). Baltimore: Williams & Wilkins.

McCord, J. (1984). Longitudinal study of personality development. In S. Mednick, M. Harway, & K. Finello (Eds.), *Handbook of longitudinal research: Vol. II. Teenage and adult cohorts* (pp. 522–531). New York: Praeger.

McLaughlin, J. (1988). The analyst's insights. *Psychoanalytic Quarterly, 57*, 370–389.

McLaughlin, J. (1991). Clinical and theoretical aspects of enactment. *Journal of the American Psychoanalytic Association, 39*, 595–614.

McMahon, A., & Rhudick, P. (1964). Reminiscing: Adaptational significance in the aged. *Archives of General Psychiatry, 10*, 292–298.

McMahon, A., Rhudick, P. (1967). Reminiscing in the aged: An adaptational response. In S. Levin & R. Kahana (Eds.), *Psychodynamic studies on aging: Creativity, reminiscing, and dying* (pp. 64–78). Madison, CT: International Universities Press.

Mead, M. (1928). *Coming of age in Samoa: A psychological study of primitive youth for Western civilization*. New York: Morrow.

Mead, M. (1930). *Growing up in New Guinea: A comparative study of primitive education*. New York: Morrow.

Meissner, W. (1991). *What is effective in psychoanalytic therapy: The move from interpretation to relation.* Northvale, NJ: Jason Aronson.

Miller, A. (1981). *Prisoners of childhood.* (R. Ward, Trans.). New York: Basic Books.

Miller, N., & Dollard, J. (1941). *Social learning theory and imitation.* New Haven, CT: Yale University Press.

Mishler, E. (1986). *Research interviewing: Context and narrative.* Cambridge, MA: Harvard University Press.

Moody, H. (1986). The meaning of life and the meaning of old age. In T. Cole & S. Gadow (Eds.), *What does it mean to grow old: Reflections from the humanities* (pp. 9–40). Durham, NC: Duke University Press.

Moss, H., & Sussman, E. (1980). Longitudinal study of personality development. In O. G. Brim, Jr. & J. Kagan (Eds.), *Constancy and change in human development* (pp. 530–595). Cambridge, MA: Harvard University Press.

Munnichs, J. (1966). *Old age and finitude: A contribution to psychogerontology.* New York: Karger.

Murphy, G. (1966). *Personality: A biosocial approach to organization and structure.* New York: Basic Books. (Original work published 1947)

Myerhoff, B. (1979). *Number our days.* New York: Dutton.

Myerhoff, B. (1992). *Remembered lives: The work of ritual, storytelling, and growing older* (M. Kaminsky, Ed.). Ann Arbor, MI: University of Michigan Press.

Nagera, H. (1966). *Early childhood disturbances, the infantile neurosis, and the adulthood disturbances* [Monograph]. Madison, CT: International Universities Press.

Nasser, A. (1994). Psychoanalysis after representation: The philosophical framework. *Psychoanalysis and Contemporary Thought, 17,* 179–214.

Nemiroff, R., & Colarusso, C. (Eds.) (1985). *The race against time: Psychotherapy and psychoanalysis in the second half of life.* New York: Plenum.

Nemiroff, R., & Colarusso, C. (1990). Frontiers of adult development in theory and practice. In R. Nemiroff & C. Colarusso (Eds.), *New dimensions in adult development* (pp. 97–124). New York: Basic Books.

Neubauer, P. B. (1980). The life cycle as indicated by the nature of the transference in the psychoanalysis of children. *International Journal of Psycho-Analysis, 61,* 137–144.

Neugarten, B. (1969). Continuities and discontinuities of psychological issues into adult life. *Human Development, 12,* 121–130.

Neugarten, B. (1979). Time, age, and the life-cycle. *American Journal of Psychiatry, 136,* 887–894.

Neugarten, B., & Datan, N. (1973). Sociological perspectives on the life-cycle. In P. Baltes & K. W. Schaie (Eds.), *Life span developmental psychology: Personality and socialization* (pp. 53–69). New York: Academic Press.

Neugarten, B. L., & Datan, N. (1974). The middle years. In S. Arieti (Ed.), *American handbook of psychiatry: Vol. 1. The foundations of psychiatry* (pp. 592–608). New York: Basic Books.

Neugarten, B., & Hagestad, G. (1976). Age and the life course. In R. Binstock & E. Shanas (Eds.), *Handbook of aging and the social sciences* (pp. 35–55). New York: Van Nostrand Reinhold.

Neugarten, B., & Moore, J. (1968). The changing age-status system. In B. Neugarten (Ed.), *Middle-age and aging: A reader in social psychology* (pp. 5–20). Chicago: University of Chicago Press.

Neugarten, B., Moore, J., & Lowe, J. (1965). Age norms, age constraints, and adult socialization. *American Journal of Sociology, 70*, 710–717.

New York Psychoanalytic Institute. (1963a). *Minutes of the faculty meeting of October 14.*

New York Psychoanalytic Institute. (1963b). *Minutes of the faculty meeting of November 20.*

Novey, S. (1985). *The second look: The reconstruction of personal history in psychiatry and psychoanalysis.* Madison, CT: International University Press. (Original work published 1968)

Nydegger, C. (1980). Role and age transitions: A potpourri of issues. In C. Fry & J. Keith (Eds.), *New methods of old age resesarch: Anthropological alternatives* (pp. 127–145). Chicago: Loyola University of Chicago, Center for Urban Studies.

Nydegger, C. (1981). On being caught up in time. *Human Development, 24*, 1–12.

Obeysekere, G. (1981). *Medusa's hair: An essay on personal symbols and religious experience.* Chicago: University of Chicago Press.

Obeysekere, G. (1990). *The work of culture: Symbolic transformation in psychoanalysis and anthropology.* Chicago: University of Chicago Press.

Oxaal, I. (1988). The Jewish origins of psychoanalysis reconsidered. In E. Timms & N. Siegel (Eds.), *Freud in exile: Psychoanalysis and its vicissitudes* (pp. 37–54). New Haven, CT: Yale University Press.

Pearlin, L. (1980). Life strains and psychological distress among adults. In E. Erikson & N. Smelser (Eds.), *Themes of work and love in adulthood* (pp. 174–192). Cambridge, MA: Harvard University Press.

Pearlin, L., & Lieberman, M. (1979). Social sources of emotional distress. In R. Simmons (Ed.), *Research in community and mental health* (Vol. I, pp. 217–248). Greenwich, CT: JAI Press.

Pearlin, L., Menaghan, B., Lieberman, M., & Mullan, J. (1981). The stress process. *Journal of Health and Social Behavior, 22*, 337–356.

Pearlin, L., & Schooler, C. (1978). The structure of coping. *Journal of Health and Social Behavior, 19*, 2–21.

Peskin, H., & Livson, N. (1981). Use of the peat in adult psychological health. In D. Eichon, J., Clausen, N. Haan, M. Honzik, & P. Mussen (Eds.), *Present and past in middle-life* (pp. 154–183). New York: Academic Press.

Phelan, J. (1989). *Reading people, reading plots: Character, progression and the interpretation of narrative.* Chicago: University of Chicago Press.

Piaget, J. (1985). *The equilibration of cognitive structures: The central problem of cognitive development* (T. Brown & K. J. Thampy, Trans.). Chicago: University of Chicago Press. (Original work published 1975)

Poland, W. (1993). Self and other in self-analysis. In J. Barron (Ed.), *Self-analysis: Critical inquiries, personal visions* (pp. 219–240). Hillsdale, NJ: Analytic Press.

Pollock, G. (1971a). On time and anniversaries. In M. Kanzer (Ed.), *The unconscious today: Essays in honor of Max Schur* (pp. 233–257). Madison, CT: International Universities Press.

Pollock, G. (1971b). On time, death, and immortality. *Psychoanalytic Quarterly,* *40,* 435–446.

Pollock, G. (1980). Aging or aged: Development or pathology. In S. Greenspan & G. Pollock (Eds.), *The course of life: Vol. 3. Adulthood and the aging process* (pp. 549–585). Washington, DC: U.S. Government Printing Office.

Pribram, K., & Gill, M. (1976). *Freud's "Project" reassessed.* New York: Basic Books.

Prosen, H., Martin, R., & Prosen, M. (1972). The remembered mother and the fantasized mother: A crisis of middle age. *Archives of General Psychiatry,* *27,* 791–794.

Rabinowitz, P. (1987). *Before reading: Narrative conventions and the politics of interpretation.* Ithaca, NY: Cornell University Press.

Rabinowitz, P. (1994). Reader-response theory and criticism. In M. Groden & M. Kreiswith (Eds.), *The Johns Hopkins guide to literary theory and criticism* (pp. 606–609). Baltimore: Johns Hopkins University Press.

Racker, H. (1968). *Transference and countertransference.* Madison, CT: International Universities Press.

Rangell, L. (1961). The role of early psychic functioning in psychoanalysis. *Journal of the American Psychoanalytic Association, 9,* 595–609.

Rapaport, D. (1967). On the psychoanalytic theory of motivation. In M. Gill (Ed.), *The collected papers of David Rapaport* (pp. 853–915). New York: Basic Books. (Original work published 1960)

Rapaport, D., & Gill, M. (1959). The points of view and assumptions of metapsychology. *International Journal of Psycho-Analysis, 40,* 153–162.

Rappaport, E. (1958). The grandparent syndrome. *Psychoanalytic Quarterly, 27,* 518–538.

Read, G. (1994). *Transference neurosis and psychoanalytic experience.* New Haven, CT: Yale University Press.

Reich, A. (1973). On countertransference. In A. Reich (Ed.), *Annie Reich: Psychoanalytic contributions* (pp. 136–154). Madison, CT: International Universities Press. (Original work published 1951)

Reik, T. (1952). *Listening with the third ear.* New York: Dutton.

Ricoeur, P. (1971). The model of the text: Meaningful action considered as text. *Social Research, 38,* 529–562.

Ricoeur, P. (1977). The question of proof in Freud's psychoanalytic writings. *Journal of the American Psychoanalytic Association, 25,* 835–872.

Ricoeur, P. (1984a). *The reality of the historical past.* Milwaukee, WI: Marquette University Press.

Ricoeur, P. (1984b). *Time and narrative* (Vol. 1; K. McLaughlin & D. Pellauer, Trans.) Chicago: University of Chicago Press.

Riley, M. (1973). Aging and cohort succession: Interpretations and misinterpretations. *Public Opinion Quarterly, 37,* 35–49.

Ritvo, L. (1990). *Darwin's influence on Freud: A tale of two sciences.* New Haven, CT: Yale University Press.

Rook, K. (1984). The negative side of social interaction: The impact of psychological well-being. *Journal of Personality and Social Psychology, 46,* 1097–1108.

Rook, K. (1989). Strains in older adults' friendships. In R. Adams & R. Blieszner

(Eds.), *Old adult friendship: Structure and process* (pp. 166–192). Thousand Oaks, CA: Sage.

Rosaldo, R. (1993). *Culture and truth: The remaking of social analysis* (2nd ed.). Boston: Beacon Press.

Rosenblatt, A., & Thickstun, J. (1970). A study of the concept of psychic energy. *International Journal of Psycho-Analysis, 51,* 265–278.

Rosenblatt, A., & Thickstun, J. (1977). Energy, information and motivation: A revision of psychoanalytic theory. *Journal of the American Psychoanalytic Association, 25,* 537–558.

Rosow, I. (1978). What is a cohort and why? *Human Development, 21,* 65–75.

Rossi, A. (1968). Transition to parenthood. *Journal of Marriage and the Family, 30,* 26–39.

Roth, J. (1963). *Timetables: Structuring the passage of time in hospital treatment and other careers.* Indianapolis, IN: Bobbs-Merrill.

Roth, P. A. (1991a). Interpretation as explanation. In D. Hiley, J. Bohman, & R. Shusterman (Eds.), *The interpretive turn: Philosophy, science, culture* (pp. 179–196). Ithaca, NY: Cornell University Press.

Roth, P. A. (1991b). Truth in interpretation: The case of psychoanalysis. *Philosophy of the Social Sciences, 21,* 175–195.

Rutter, M. (1972). Relationships between child and adult psychiatric disorders: Some research considerations. *Acta Psychiatric Scandinavica, 48,* 3–21.

Rutter, M. (1984). Continuities and discontinuities in socio-emotional development: Empirical and conceptual perspectives. In R. Emde & R. Harmon (Eds.), *Continuities and discontinuities in development* (pp. 41–68). New York: Plenum.

Ryder, N. (1965). The cohort as a concept in the study of social change. *American Sociological Review, 30,* 843–861.

Sandler, A. M. (1978). Psychoanalysis in later life: problems in the psychoanalysis of an aging narcissistic patient. *Journal of Geriatric Psychiatry, 11,* 5–36.

Schachtel, E. (1947). Memory and childhood amnesia. *Psychiatry, 10,* 1–26.

Schachter, S. (1959). *The psychology of affiliation.* Stanford, CA: Stanford University Press.

Schafer, R. (1958). How was this story told? *Journal of Projective Techniques, 22,* 181–210.

Schafer, R. (1959). Generative empathy in the treatment situation. *Psychoanalytic Quarterly, 28,* 342–373.

Schafer, R. (1980). Narration in the psychoanalytic dialogue. *Critical Inquiry, 7,* 29–53.

Schafer, R. (1981). *Narrative actions in psychoanalysis.* Worcester, MA: Clark University Press.

Schafer, R. (1982). The relevance of the "here and now" transference interpretation to the reconstruction of early development. *International Journal of Psycho-Analysis, 63,* 77–82.

Schafer, R. (1992). *Retelling a life: Narration and dialogue in psychoanalysis.* New York: Basic Books.

Schafer, R. (1994). The contemporary Kleinians of London. *Psychoanalytic Quarterly, 63,* 409–432.

Schaie, K. W. (1984). The Seattle longitudinal study: A 25-year exploration of the psychometric intelligence of adulthood. In K. W. Schaie (Ed.), *Longitudinal studies of personality* (pp. 64–135). New York: Guilford Press.

Schaie, K. W., & Hertzog, C. (1983). Fourteen-year cohort-sequential studies of adult development. *Developmental Psychology, 19*, 532–543.

Schuman, H., & Scott, J. (1989). Generations and collective memory. *American Sociological Review, 54*, 359–381.

Schutz, A. (1966). The problem of transcendental intersubjectivity in Husserl. In A. Schutz (Ed.), *Collected papers: III. Studies in phenomenological philosophy* (pp. 51–84). The Hague, The Netherlands: Martinus Nijhoff. (Original work published in 1957)

Schutz, A., & Luckmann, T. (1973). *The structure of the life-world* (Vol. 1; T. Luckmann, Trans.). Evanston, IL: Northwestern University Press.

Schutz, A., & Luckmann, T. (1989). *The structures of the life-world* (Vol. 2; R. M. Zaner & D. J. Parent, Trans.). Evanston, IL: Northwestern University Press. (Original work published 1983)

Schwaber, E. (1981). Empathy. *Psychoanalytic Inquiry, 1*, 357–392.

Schwaber, E. (1983). A particular perspective on analytic listening. *Psychoanalytic Study of the Child, 38*, 519–546.

Scriven, M. (1959). Truisms as the grounds for historical explanations. In P. Gardiner (Ed.), *Theories of history* (pp. 443–475). New York: Free Press.

Sears, R. (1977). Sources of life satisfactions of the Terman gifted men. *American Psychologist, 32*, 119–128.

Sears, R. R. (1984). The Terman Gifted Children Study. In S. Mednick, M. Harway, & K. Finello (Eds.), *Handbook of longitudinal research* (pp. 398–411). New York: Praeger.

Sears, R. R., & Barbee, A. (1977). Career and life-satisfactions among Terman's gifted women. In J. C. Stanley, W. George, & C. Solano (Eds.), *The gifted and the creative: A fifty year perspective* (pp. 27–65). Baltimore: Johns Hopkins University Press.

Seltzer, M. (1976). Suggestions for examination of time-disordered relationships. In J. Gubrium (Ed.), *Times, roles, and self in old age* (pp. 111–125). New York: Human Sciences Press.

Shabad, P. (1996). *The echo of inner truth.* Manuscript in preparation.

Shanok, R. (1993). Toward an inclusive adult developmental theory: Epigenesis reconsidered. In G. H. Pollock & S. Greenspan (Eds.), *The course of life: Vol. VI. Late adulthood* (pp. 243–259). Madison, CT: International Universities Press.

Shapiro, T. (1977). Oedipal distortions in severe character pathologies: Developmental and theoretical considerations. *Psychoanalytic Quarterly, 46*, 559–579.

Shapiro, T. (1981). On the quest for the origins of conflict. *Psychoanalytic Quarterly, 50*, 1–21.

Sill, J. (1980). Disengagement reconsidered: Awareness of finitude. *The Gerontologist, 37*, 587–594.

Silver, D. (1985). (Ed.). *Commentaries on Joseph Lichtenberg's psychoanalysis and infant research.* Hillsdale, NJ: Analytic Press.

Sinnott, J. (1982). Correlates of sex roles of older adults. *Journal of Gerontology, 37,* 587–594.

Skeels, H. M. (1966). Adult status of children from contrasting early life experiences: A follow-up study. *Monographs of the Society for Research in Child Development, 3* (Whole No. 105).

Skolnick, A. (1986). Early attachment and personal relationships across the life course. In P. B. Baltes, D. Featherman, & R. Lerner (Eds.), *Life-span development and behavior* (Vol. 7, pp. 173–206). Hillsdale, NJ: Erlbaum.

Snarey, J. (1993). *How fathers care for the next generation.* Cambridge, MA: Harvard University Press.

Sorokin, P., & Merton, R. (1937). Social time: A methodological and functional analysis. *American Journal of Sociology, 42,* 615–629.

Stengel, E. (1963). Hughlings Jackson's influence on psychiatry. *British Journal of Psychiatry, 109,* 348–355.

Stern, D. (1985). *The interpersonal world of the infant.* New York: Basic Books.

Stern, D. (1989). The representation of relational patterns: Developmental considerations. In A. Sameroff & R. Emde (Eds.), *Relationship disturbances in early childhood* (pp. 52–69). New York: Basic Books.

Sternschein, I. (1973). The experience of separation-individuation in infancy and its reverberations through the course of life: III. Maturity, senescence, and sociological implications [Report on panel discussion]. *Journal of the American Psychoanalytic Association, 21,* 633–645.

Stevens-Long, J. (1990). Adult development: Theories past and future. In R. Nemiroff & C. Colarusso (Eds.), *New dimensions in adult development* (pp. 125–169). New York: Basic Books.

Stolorow, R., & Atwood, G. (1992). *Contexts of being: The intersubjective foundations of psychological life.* Hillsdale, NJ: Analytic Press.

Stone, L. (1961). *The psychoanalytic situation: An examination of its development and essential nature.* Madison, CT: International Universities Press.

Sulloway, F. (1979). *Freud, biologist of the mind.* New York: Basic Books.

Swanson, G. (1961). Determinants of the individual's defense against inner conflict. In J. Glidewell (Ed.), *Parental attitudes and child behavior* (pp. 5–41). Springfield, IL: Charles C Thomas.

Swanson, D. (1977a). On force, energy, entropy, and the assumptions of metapsychology. *Psychoanalysis and Contemporary Science, 5,* 137–153.

Swanson, D. (1977b). The psychic energy concept—A critique. *Journal of the American Psychoanalytic Association, 25,* 603–634.

Terman, L. (1925). *Genetic studies of genius* (Vol. 1). Stanford, CA: Stanford University Press.

Ticho, G. (1967). On self-analysis. *International Journal of Psycho-Analysis, 48,* 308–318.

Tinbergen, N. (1951). *The study of instinct.* Oxford, England: Clarendon Press.

Tobin, S. (1991). *Personhood in advanced old age: Implications for practice.* New York: Springer.

Tobin, S., & Lieberman, M. (1976). *Last home for the aged: Critical implications of institutionalization.* San Francisco: Jossey-Bass.

Todrov, T. (1984). *Mikhail Bakhtin: The dialogical principle* (W. Godzich, Trans.). Minneapolis, MN: University of Minnesota Press.

Tolpin, M., & Kohut, H. (1980). The disorders of the self: The psychopathology of the first years of life. In S. Greenspan & G. Pollock (Eds.), *The course of life: Vol. 1. Infancy and early childhood* (pp. 425–442). Washington, DC: U.S. Government Printing Office.

Tonkin, E. (1992). *Narrating our pasts: The social construction of oral history.* New York: Cambridge University Press.

Trevarthan, C. (1980). The foundations of intersubjectivity: Development of interpersonal and cognitive understanding in infants. In D. Olson (Ed.), *The social foundations of language and thought: Essays in honor of Jerome Bruner* (pp. 316–342). New York: Norton.

Trevarthan, C. (1989, Autumn). Origins and directions for the concept of infant intersubjectivity. *Society for Research in Child Development Newsletter,* 1–4.

Trevarthan, C., & Hubley, P. (1978). Secondary intersubjectivity: Confidence, confiders, and acts of meaning in the first year. In A. Lock (Ed.), *Action, gesture, and symbol* (pp. 183–230). New York: Academic Press.

Troll, L. (1970). Issues in the study of generations. *International Journal of Aging and Human Development, 1,* 199–218.

Tuttle, W., Jr. (1993). America's home front children in World War II. In G. Elder, J. Modell, & R. D. Parke (Eds.), *Children in time and place: Developmental and historical insights* (pp. 27–46). New York: Cambridge University Press.

Uhlenberg, P. (1979). Demographic change and the problems of the aged. In M. Riley (Ed.), *Aging from birth to death* (pp. 153–166). Boulder, CO: Westview Press.

Uhlenberg, P. (1988). Aging and the societal significance of cohorts. In J. Birren & V. Bengtson (Eds.), *Emergent theories of aging* (pp. 405–425). New York: Springer.

Vaillant, G. (1974a). Antecedents of healthy adult male adjustment. In D. Ricks, A. Thomas, & M. Roff (Eds.), *Life-history research in psychopathology* (Vol. 3, pp. 230–242). Minneapolis, MN: University of Minnesota Press.

Vaillant, G. (1974b). Natural history of male psychological health: II. Some antecedents of healthy adult adjustment. *Archives of General Psychiatry, 31,* 15–22.

Vaillant, G. (1975). Natural history of male psychological health: III. Empirical dimensions of mental health. *Archives and General Psychiatry, 32,* 420–426.

Vaillant, G. (1976). Natural history of male psychological health: V. The relation of choice of ego mechanisms of defense to adult adjustment. *Archives of General Psychiatry, 33,* 533–545.

Vaillant, G. (1977). *Adaptation to life.* Boston: Little, Brown.

Vaillant, G. (1978). Natural history of male psychological health: VI. Correlates of successful marriage and fatherhood. *American Journal of Psychiatry, 135,* 653–659.

Vaillant, G. (1979). Natural history of male psychological health: VIII. Effects of mental health on physical health. *New England Journal of Medicine, 301,* 1249–1254.

Vaillant, G. (1993). *The wisdom of the ego.* Cambridge, MA: Harvard University Press.

Vaillant, G., & Koury, S. (1993). Late midlife development. In G. H. Pollock & S. Greenspan (Eds.), *The course of life: Vol. VI. Late adulthood* (pp. 1–22). Madison, CT: International Universities Press.

Vaillant, G., & McArthur, C. (1972). Natural history of male psychological health: I. The adult life cycle from 18–50. *Seminars in Psychiatry, 4,* 415–427.

Vaillant, G., & Milofsky, E. (1980). Natural history of male psychological health: IX. Empirical evidence for Erikson's model of the life cycle. *American Journal of Psychiatry, 137,* 1348–1359.

Wallerstein, R. (1977). Psychic energy reconsidered—Introduction. *Journal of the American Psychoanalytic Association, 25,* 529–536.

Wallerstein, R. (1986). *Forty-two lives in treatment: A study of psychoanalysis in psychotherapy.* New York: Guilford Press.

Wallerstein, R. (1990). Psychoanalysis: The common ground. *International Journal of Psycho-Analysis, 71,* 3–20.

Wessman, A., & Gorman, B. (1977). The emergence of human awareness and concepts of time. In B. Gorman & A. Wessman (Eds.), *The personal experience of time* (pp. 4–56). New York: Plenum.

Whitaker, C., & Malone, T. (1953). *The roots of psychotherapy.* New York: Blakiston.

White, S. H. (1965). Evidence for a hierarchical arrangement of learning processes. In L. Lipsitt & C. Spiker (Eds.), *Advances in child development and behavior* (pp. 187–220). New York: Academic Press.

Wilson, A., & Weinstein, L. (1992a). An investigation into some implications of a Vygotskian perspective on the origins of the mind: Psychoanalysis and Vygotskian psychology. Part I. *Journal of the American Psychoanalytic Association, 40,* 349–379.

Wilson, A., & Weinstein, L. (1992b). Language and the psychoanalytic process: Psychoanalysis and Vygotskian psychology, Part II. *Journal of the American Psychoanalytic Association, 40,* 725–760.

Winnicott, D. W. (1953). Transitional objects and transitional phenomena. In D. W. Winnicott (Ed.), *Collected papers: Through pediatrics to psychoanalysis* (pp. 229–242). New York: Basic Books.

Winnicott, D. (1960). The theory of the parent–infant relationship. *International Journal of Psycho-Analysis, 41,* 585–595.

Wolf, L. (1988). *Postcards from the end of the world: Child abuse in Freud's Vienna.* New York: Atheneum.

Wolff, P. (1966). The causes, controls, and organization of behavior in the neonate [Monograph 17]. *Psychological Issues, 5.*

Wolff, P. (1988). The real and reconstructed past. *Psychoanalysis and Contemporary Thought, 11,* 379–414.

Woodward, K. (1984). Reminiscence and the life review: Prospects and retrospects. In T. Cole & S. Gadow (Eds.), *What does it mean to grow old: Reflections from the humanities* (pp. 135–162). Durham, NC: Duke University Press.

Zetzel, E., & Meissner, W. (1973). *Basic concepts of psychoanalytic psychiatry.* New York: Basic Books.

6

Clinical Applications
of Attachment Theory:
Empirical and Theoretical Perspectives

Lisa Sandow Lyons and Michael B. Sperling

Attachment theory has had a major impact within psychoanalytic theory and practice in recent years. It provides a theoretical foundation and a developmental underpinning for the paradigm shift that has begun to move psychoanalytic thinking from a one-person to a two-person psychology, and from a focus on internal fantasy to a focus on the formative power of relational experiences (Beebe, 1986, 1993; Bowlby, 1988; Cramer & Stern, 1988; Stern, 1988).

A basic assumption of attachment theory is that infants are born with a biologically based survival system that compels them to seek help from caretakers when threatened, anxious, or in need of protection. According to Bowlby (1969), the attachment system consists of specific behaviors (e.g., signaling distress by crying, seeking the proximity of caretakers) that are activated in times of need and that, ideally, result in the infant's getting protection from real dangers as well as relief from the anxiety and stress of both real and imagined dangers. The situations that activate the attachment system, as well as the specific care-seeking behaviors it triggers, change over the course of normal development. This change occurs both in response to normally occurring developmental changes and in response to the ongoing interaction of experiences in relationships and previously formed representations of attachment. By "representations of attachment," we are referring to an individual's assumptions and expectations concerning the role of interpersonal relationships in satisfying needs for caretaking and protection. These assumptions are believed to be formed from early relational experiences and then to influence the perception of later interpersonal experiences as well as to be open to modification in the face of disconfirming experience. Of importance here is that attachment theory considers the *attachment system* (by which we are referring both to the biologically based need as well as to the proximity-seeking behaviors evoked by it) to be a pivotal factor in human experience, and one that is critical to the organization and perception of relationships throughout the life span.

A central hypothesis that runs throughout Bowlby's writings on attachment, and that forms an important link between attachment theory and psychoanalytic theories, is that after infancy, the behaviors and affects generated by activation of the attachment system are mediated by the individual's mental representations of attachment. Bowlby suggested that although an individual's *internal working models* of attachment (the term he used for mental representations of attachment) begin to be formed at birth, they are "working models." In other words, although to a certain extent they shape both the perception of attachment relationships and the behaviors elicited by the activation of attachment needs, they also are subject to development and modification throughout the life span in response to actual experiences (Bowlby, 1980).

Internal working models are understood to be personal theories about behavior in interpersonal relationships. They are believed to be formed from actual experience and determine subsequent attachment behaviors (Bowlby, 1977; Holmes, 1993). They provide models both for interpreting interpersonal events and for perceiving the self in relation to others. They include information about past and present attachment figures, concepts and evaluations of the self formed from attachment experiences, concepts of the self in relation to attachment figures, affects associated with attachment and attachment figures, and schemas for handling situations in which the attachment system is activated (Bowlby, 1980). Simply put, internal working models provide templates that guide the individual in interpreting attachment-related experiences as well as the information necessary for an individual to respond to situations that activate the attachment system.

One of the ways that internal working models are different from mental representations, as the term is understood within both psychoanalytic and cognitive theory, is that in addition to functioning as templates, internal working models are considered to be "dynamic mental structures on which the individual can operate in order to conduct small scale experiments or simulations in the head" (Bretherton, 1990, p. 239). Mental manipulations of the internal working model allow the individual to assess the possible consequences of attachment-related behaviors, access a repertoire of tactics for managing interpersonal situations, and handle the affects that arise when the attachment system is activated (Bowlby, 1973).

Bowlby (1969) further postulated that when the attachment system is activated, the behaviors associated with it take precedence over behaviors that promote exploration, independence, and cognitive growth. From an attachment theory perspective, a central issue in development is how the individual negotiates the continuing dialectic between activation of the attachment system and the related proximity-seeking behaviors on the one hand and independence and exploration on the other. This tension is an implicit issue in other theories of development (e.g., Erikson, 1963; Mahler, Pine, & Bergman, 1975). However, attachment theory is distinguished by the focus on the biological roots of this dialectic, the centrality given the relationship between attachment-related behaviors and exploration and cognitive growth, the assumption that real relational experiences have a pivotal role in forming representations of attachment, and the assumption that the attachment system is important to normal development throughout the life span.

Attachment theory (Bowlby, 1969, 1980) has provided the foundation for a growing body of empirical research. Initially, the focus of this work was on categorizing styles of behavior within close relationships. Through the systematic ethological studies of Ainsworth (Ainsworth, Blehar, Waters, & Wall, 1978) and others, what has emerged as the "gold standard" of attachment categories is a tripartite system. For children, this system reveals characteristic behavioral categories of *secure, insecure/avoidant,* and *insecure/resistant–ambivalent.* For adults, the corresponding labels are *secure, insecure/dismissing,* and *insecure/preoccupied*. The construct of internal working models of attachment, the relationship of these models to early experiences and behavior, and the developmental sequelae that may be influenced by attachment style have formed the core of the next generation of empirical work that has emerged around attachment theory. Much of this research has attempted to understand the ongoing role in development of mental representations of attachment (e.g., Beebe, 1993; Main, Kaplan, & Cassidy, 1985; Shaver & Clark, 1994), explore the range of behavioral responses to activation of the attachment system (e.g., Ainsworth et al., 1978; Elicker, Englund, & Sroufe, 1992; Sable, 1983), document the intergenerational transmission of attachment style (Beebe & Lachmann, 1988; Main & Hesse, 1990), and examine the personality and behavioral correlates of different attachment styles and representations (e.g., Beebe & Lachmann, 1988; Cramer & Stern, 1988; Main et al., 1985).

Attachment theory is rich in clinical implications in that it suggests that the earliest relational experiences have tremendous significance for later development. Although there is a growing body of empirical work that looks at the developmental sequelae of attachment patterns, explicit clinical applications of attachment theory and supporting empirical work have only recently begun to be reported in the literature. The task of this chapter is to examine some of the clinical implications and applications of attachment theory, especially as viewed through the frame of mental representations. This will involve a review of some of the empirical literature concerning the relationship between attachment dynamics and personality functioning, a brief reexamination of some more familiar approaches to clinical work from the perspective of attachment theory, a review of the salient literature concerned with explicit clinical applications of attachment theory, and exploration of some ideas concerning the possible future directions that both clinical and empirical work might follow.

Attachment and Personality

In the broadest sense, much of the empirical work that has grown out of attachment theory can be construed as relating to personality development. However, there is a growing body of empirical work that explicitly relates attachment style to personality variables. The following review is by necessity brief, but the goal here is not to review the field but to look explicitly at studies that elucidate the relationship between attachment and aspects of personality that are typically targets of clinical intervention and change.[1]

The classifications suggested by the Strange Situation (Ainsworth et al., 1978) have been shown to be reliable, continuous, and related in predictable ways to behaviors in childhood. Waters (1978) found that 96% of a group of middle-class children rated at 12 and 18 months received the same classification at each rating. Main and Weston (1981) found that 73% of infant classifications were stable over several months. Grossmann and Grossmann (1991) have followed a sample of children for 10 years. Using a behavioral measure derived from the Strange Situation but suitable for older children (Main & Cassidy, 1988), as well as other measures of social adaptation, they have found differences between secure and insecure children in interpersonal functioning and stress management skills that are strikingly congruent with the children's original classification. At age 10, children rated as secure reported having one or more good friends whom they considered reliable and trustworthy; children rated as insecure reported either having good friends about whom they were unable to provide such basic information as a name, or having no good friends at all. The insecure children also reported being exploited, ridiculed, and excluded by peers. Not surprisingly, given the differences mentioned above between secure and insecure children with relation to peer support networks, the secure children reported turning to others for help when dealing with negative feelings; the insecure children classified as avoidant reported dealing with negative feelings alone.

Elicker et al. (1992) observed the social functioning at a summer camp of a group of children whose attachment category had been measured in infancy. They found that the secure children were more healthy emotionally, more self-assured, and more competent; the insecure children were more dependent on adults and had a negative bias when evaluating others. Other studies have shown a positive relationship between secure attachment at 18 months and ego resiliency at 4 to 5 years (Arend, Gove, & Sroufe, 1979), with securely attached children showing more flexibility, persistence, and resourcefulness, and becoming less disorganized when stressed, when compared with inse-

---

[1]The reader is referred to Rothbard and Shaver (1994) and Shaver and Clark (1994) for more complete reviews of the attachment literature.

curely attached children. Waters, Wippman, and Sroufe (1979) also demonstrated advantages for secure children on measures of leadership, empathy, self-directedness, and curiosity. Studies looking at the relationship between attachment category and aggressive behavior in preschool children have demonstrated significant correlations between insecure/avoidant attachment and aggressive behavior in boys (Egeland & Sroufe, 1981; Renkin, Egeland, Marvinney, Manglesdorf, & Sroufe, 1989; Sroufe, 1983). Early attachment classification has also been shown to correlate significantly with school functioning. Insecure children are more likely than secure children to be rated by observers to be withdrawn, have attentional problems, act out, and be rated by teachers to be more hostile, impulsive, and withdrawn (Erickson, Sroufe, & Egelund, 1985). Anxious/ambivalent children were evaluated in this study to be lacking in assertiveness and confidence.

Attachment style has also been associated with concurrent measures of personality variables in children. Matas, Arend, and Sroufe (1978) found that among a group of 2-year-olds whose attachment style had been categorized at 18 months, those rated secure were more imaginative, enthusiastic, persistent, and compliant. They were also better able to use their mother's suggestions, displayed more positive and less negative affect, and were less aggressive. These findings were replicated by Frankel and Bates (1990).

Overall, anxious/ambivalent children have been shown to be somewhat preoccupied with attachment figures, clingy, tearful, and angry (Ainsworth et al., 1978). They have been shown to be victimized often by other children (Fury as cited in Shaver & Clark, 1994) and less versed in interpersonal skills (Elicker et al., 1992). Avoidant children have been shown to be highly anxious (Sroufe & Waters, 1977) and less responsive to peers (Pancake, as cited in Shaver & Clark, 1994) during the preschool years. During later childhood, they have been shown to have worse peer relations than secure children, poorer social understanding and skills, more jealousy, and less personal agency in soliciting social contacts (Sroufe, 1983). Secure infants and children are more confident in themselves and their caretakers (Elicker et al., 1992), more easygoing and cooperative (Arend et al., 1979), more empathic (Sroufe & Fleeson, 1988), more creative (Elicker et al., 1992), better able to establish and maintain friendships (Elicker et al., 1992), and better able to collaborate and cooperate (Arend et al., 1979).

In assessing the research on personality functioning and attachment classification, it is important to consider that attachment style and related personality characteristics may be the consequence of temperament rather than, at least in significant measure, relational experiences. Shaver and Clark (1994) argued for attachment style as an environmentally determined variable, citing studies from three areas of research. First, in studies that look at the discontinuity of attachment styles, attachment classification of infants has been shown to be different with each parent (Main et al., 1985). Second, studies have demonstrated changes in a child's attachment category in predictable directions in response to changes in family relationships and environment (Erickson et al., 1985), and the mother's economic security and relationship stability (Egelund, Kalkoske, Gottesman, & Erickson, 1990). Finally, studies have begun to emerge demonstrating changes in attachment style as a function of therapeutic interventions. Van den Boom (as cited in Shaver & Clark, 1994) demonstrated that babies deemed "difficult" were more likely to be rated as secure at 12 months if their mothers were trained to be more sensitive to their babies' cues, relative to the babies of mothers who were not trained. Outcome studies from two infant–parent treatment programs that target high-risk dyads (Erickson, Korfmacher, & Egeland, 1992; Lieberman, Weston, & Pawl, 1991) have demonstrated changes in attachment style in the direction of greater security as one outcome of intervention.

Although attachment theory has been used principally to describe individual differences within the frame of normal personality development (Bartholomew, 1994), generating treatments based on it requires an understanding of what an attachment perspective suggests about abnormal functioning and psychopathology. The groundbreaking studies of Ainsworth et al. (1978) and the empirical and integrative work of Beebe (1986) and Beebe and Lachman (1988) suggest that attachment behaviors associated with insecure attachment may for a very young child be reasonable solutions to relationship or caretaking dilemmas. However, the evidence for correlations between insecure attachment and later relationship and school difficulties suggests that attachment style may play a significant role in the emergence of difficulties later in life. A few studies have looked explicitly at this connection. Lyons-Ruth, Alpern, and Repacholi (1993) looked at the relationship between (a) infant attachment, development, maternal psychosocial problems, and maternal behavior at home, assessed when the infant was 18 months old, and (b) child behavior problems at 5 years old. They found that a strong predictor of peer-directed hostile behavior at age 5 was a disorganized/disoriented attachment sta-

tus at 18 months, suggesting that attachment status may be a significant predictor of later maladaption (Lyons-Ruth et al., 1993). Benoit,
Zeanah, and Barton (1989) looked at the attachment status of mothers
of 25 hospitalized failure-to-thrive infants and found that 96% were
classified as insecure, compared with 60% of mothers in a control
group of infants. West and colleagues have looked at the relationship
of anxious attachment and psychopathology in a population of adult
psychiatric outpatients (West, Rose & Sheldon, 1993) and at the relationship of attachment pathology and borderline personality disorder
(BPD; West, Keller, Links, & Patrick, 1993). They found that scores on
a measure of anxious attachment can differentiate between psychiatric
outpatients and nonpatients (West, Rose, & Sheldon, 1993) and that
high scores on measures of four dimensions of attachment (feared
loss, secure base, compulsive caregiving, and angry withdrawal) identified patients who also scored high on a measure of BPD (West,
Keller, et al., 1993).

Attachment Theory and Established Clinical Perspectives

Representational process is one of the fundamental mechanisms governing mental functioning, and it has generated interest within several theoretical domains. Attachment, psychoanalytic, and cognitive
theories, principally, and systems and social constructionist theories,
secondarily, have all provided avenues of investigation. The descrip-
tors for representations of attachment within psychoanalytic theory
(*internal object representation*), attachment theory (*internal working
model*), cognitive theory (*schema*), and social theory (*narrative*) refer to
constructs that, although distinct, demonstrate considerable conceptual overlap. Although our principal concern here is not the degree to
which different schools of personality theory and psychotherapy overlap, some discussion of this may help to illuminate the richness and
uniqueness of attachment theory and the contribution that the construct of internal working models of attachment has to offer clinical
theory and practice.

The focus of attachment theory on internal working models of
attachment provides an important link between attachment theory
and the many other well-established clinical approaches that focus on
mental representations of relationships (e.g., object relations theory).

For the purposes of this discussion, the construct of mental representations refers to a system of internal expectations and organizing mechanisms regarding interpersonal experiences with an attachment valence. These representations of attachment are formed from actual interpersonal experiences, yet may or may not retain conscious memories of these experiences (Sperling & Lyons, 1994). The difference between remembered experience and internal representations may be understood with reference to the distinction between episodic and semantic memory, proposed by Tulving (as cited in Bowlby, 1980). Memories stored episodically are stored as events or episodes in a person's life. They are stored as sequential stories, usually retain their perceptual properties, and are integrated into an individual's conscious sense of self. Semantically stored information "exists as generalized propositions about the world" (Bowlby, 1980, p. 62). Following this model, memories of specific incidents with caretakers are stored as episodic memories; generalizations about the quality of caretaking relationships, abstracted from experiences, are stored semantically. The process of forming representations of attachment is part of the semantic memory system. The distinction between semantic and episodic memory is especially important from a treatment perspective, as an individual may have gross inconsistencies between episodic and semantic memories about caretakers, and these inconsistencies may be a source of conflict (Bowlby, 1980).

With its derivation in cognitive developmental theory (Bartlett, 1932; Piaget, 1955), *schema* has come to be adopted by many current researchers as the term of choice in referring to representational process. Within psychoanalytic theory, schema has proved to be a useful construct in the attempt to move away from a structural, drive theory model and toward a multidetermined view of personality formation, behavior, and pathology that takes into account the ongoing interplay both between conscious and unconscious material and between intrapsychic and interpersonal events. When schemas— operating out of awareness—interfere with an individual's conscious, integrated sense of self, plans, talents, and values, the consequence is what a more classical approach would call neurotic behavior (Slap & Slap-Shelton, 1991).

Within cognitive theory, schemas provide a basic model of the storage, selection, association, and retrieval of information, and they are the direct target of assessment and therapeutic change. A schema is a cognitive structure that acts "as a pattern for selecting, encoding, retrieving, and interpreting the stimuli that confront an individual" (Greenberg & Beck, 1990, p. 179). Schemas provide a filter through which (interpersonal) information is selected for processing, stored, recalled, and interpreted. Greenberg and Beck (1990) suggested that "an important consequence of the continuous operation of schemas is biased and distorted information processing" (p. 180). Within a schema-focused model, pathology is then defined with reference to specific schemas that distort reality so as to lead to maladaptive thinking and behavior.

Particularly noteworthy from an integrative perspective is the research of McAdams (e.g., 1993) focusing on the iteration of "personal myths" and their structuring impact on how people define themselves, the work of Horowitz (e.g., 1991) on person schemas, and the attempts of Horowitz (1988) to combine this notion with psychoanalytic constructs. Horowitz (1991) suggested that person schemas "are structures of meaning that integrate knowledge about self and others. These mental structures may operate consciously and unconsciously to organize thought, complex mood states, self-appraisal, and interpersonal actions" (p. 1). This sensibility is consistent with McAdams' concept of personal myths, or life narratives. Schemas and personal myths thus are mental representations, both conscious and unconscious, of intrapsychic and interpersonal events. Representations of the self within an individual include multiple self-schemas that are differentially expressed in different states of mind. Furthermore, within an individual, person schemas can operate defensively "to avoid expressing derivatives of some other more dreaded person schema" (Horowitz, 1991, p. 2). Schemas are also used to track and describe the perceptions of reality in transference responses during therapy (Luborsky, Crits-Christoph, Friedman, Mark, & Schaffler, 1991) to diagram complex patterns in interpersonal relationships (Horowitz, 1991) and to study and redefine diagnostic classifications (Horowitz, 1991).

Such discussions of the divergences and commonalities among different schools of personality development and psychotherapy come to varying conclusions, depending on the level of abstraction at which each model is discussed (Arkowitz & Hannah, 1989). Messer and Winoker (1984, 1986) have suggested that at the most abstract, different schools of psychotherapy represent widely divergent visions of reality and of human nature. These divergent visions of reality by definition limit any attempts at theoretical or clinical integration. Yet on a much more concrete level, a comparison by Arkowitz and Hannah

(1989) of the interpersonal element in behavioral, cognitive, and psychodynamic psychotherapy suggested that "all three approaches emphasize providing patients with new experiences (which may be accompanied by affective arousal), disconfirmation of dysfunctional expectancies through these experiences, and a corresponding change in behavior in relevant situations outside of therapy" (p. 156).

The construct of representations of attachment falls in a middle ground of abstraction somewhere between a "vision of reality" and a concrete clinical technique. Representations of attachment may be viewed as important elements of an individual's "inner disposition," a major component in the development of "dysfunctional expectancies," and a mediator of the ability to engage in new experiences. Although usually not specifically named, representations of attachment are one of the most common targets of assessment and change in both psychoanalytic and cognitive approaches to psychotherapy. It is an interesting paradox in the field that this construct is so fundamental both clinically and theoretically, yet, outside of projective personality assessment, has remained somewhat secondary theoretically and, in many models of psychotherapy, often unattended to clinically.

Explicit Clinical Applications of Attachment Theory

The application of an attachment-theory perspective to the clinical situation remains relatively unexplored. Some of the rich implications of attachment theory for clinical work were addressed by Bowlby, both in general outline (Bowlby, 1977) and specifically in relationship to mourning, which Bowlby treated both theoretically and clinically as an intense and distilled expression of attachment dynamics (Bowlby, 1977, 1980). Additional valuable contributions have been made by Sable (1992), Holmes (1993), Shaver and Clark (1994), and, with regard to family treatment, Byng-Hall (1995).

Bowlby suggested that in early life, the most significant loss an infant has to negotiate is that of the mother or primary caretaker (Bowlby, 1980). Loss is viewed as occurring on a continuum from the normal fluctuations in availability that might be experienced in the course of a day to profound loss through death or abandonment. He suggested that it is not the actual experience of loss that determines later attachment behavior but rather the ways in which the attachment needs activated by the loss are handled, by both the child and the environment. One goal of attachment behavior is to maintain the bond with the primary caretaker. When that bond is threatened, behaviors are triggered that are meant to preserve or reestablish it. Bowlby suggested that the more serious the threat to the bond is perceived to be, the more intense and varied the behaviors will be that are used to try to preserve the bond. When the behaviors are successful in restoring the bond, the anxiety and stress associated with the loss resolves. However, if the behaviors do not succeed, they may intensify and come to occupy a disproportionate place in the child's life. Eventually, if the behaviors are unsuccessful in restoring the loss and relieving the stress, the child will stop trying. When that occurs, the child may defend against the internal stress associated with the loss by showing an apparent lack of interest in attachment relationships. Over time, the ways the child comes to negotiate both the intrapsychic and interpersonal experiences of loss become the foundations of the developing adult's internal working models of attachment and will profoundly influence patterns of behavior in intimate relationships.

Among attachment researchers, behaviors associated with separation from and reunions with significant others have become the microcosm through which attachment behavior and representations of attachment are viewed. Empirical work has clarified distinct categories of attachment behavior patterns in small children. Although initially a child develops a pattern of attachment behaviors as the best possible adaptation to interpersonal and attachment dilemmas, those patterns often become maladaptive in later life. Secure attachment is considered to be the attachment style most enhancing of development. Securely attached children evidence distress when separated from their mother, explore freely in her presence, and come to her for comfort when distressed. After stressful separations, they are easily comforted and return quickly to exploration. Children classified in the other categories, all categories of insecure attachment, show alterations of this pattern that ultimately may interfere with cognitive and emotional development. The children may act as if they do not notice either the separation or reunion (considered maladaptive because they are denying part of the experience), may become inconsolable when distressed at separation, may be excessively clingy at reunion, and may respond in confused and contradictory ways when stressed by a separation. The implication of these less adaptive patterns is that there has not been the opportunity to develop ways of dealing with the activation of the attachment system that allow reasonable expression of distress, relatively efficient comforting, and speedy return to exploratory behaviors.

With adults, the behavioral picture is more complicated, but similar patterns emerge. Adults who are securely attached are able to form trusting intimate relationships, are able to use those relationships for comfort when their attachment needs are activated, and are able to experience and work through loss of attachment figures without extreme or prolonged disruptions in functioning. Adults labeled as insecurely attached are less able to form and sustain intimate relationships, may find their lives profoundly disrupted by losses of important relationships, and may show more angry and avoidant behaviors in intimate relationships. In the extreme, such adults may dismiss the need for intimate relationships altogether.

The defense mechanism most active in insecurely attached individuals is exclusion of attachment-related information (Bowlby, 1980; West, Sheldon, & Reifer, 1987). This tends to occur when attachment needs experienced in the context of environmental stressors have chronically gone unmet, leading to intolerable and unrelieved suffering. Rather than let those needs be experienced, along with the accompanying painful feelings, they are defensively excluded. Bowlby (1969) suggested that this defensive deactivation of attachment needs is most likely to happen during early childhood, because it is then that the needs are most intense and the suffering associated with unmet needs the greatest. If, for instance, a child is repeatedly unsuccessful in getting comfort from a caretaker when threatened, the need for comfort will eventually be excluded from awareness. Bowlby suggested that the exclusion from awareness of environmental threats and associated needs for comfort and protection can happen at any point in the process of perception and memory. Thus, events and needs may actually not be perceived, or they may be perceived but not remembered. In the latter instance, information is either processed out of awareness or processed in awareness, compared with expectancies based on past experiences and then excluded from awareness (Bowlby, 1980).

Defensive behaviors can take many different forms. Behavior aimed at restoring attachment relationships, such as proximity seeking or crying, can become partially or completely deactivated. Frequently, a set of affective and behavioral responses may become disconnected from the person or situation that elicits them and redirected elsewhere, resulting in the individual's being unaware of the true origin of the responses. Bowlby (1980) suggested that responses to others can also be diverted to the self (e.g., in depression), leaving the individual unaware of the interpersonal situation that triggered the experienced affects. Bowlby also stressed that defensive exclusion is often incomplete. Fragments of deactivated behaviors or feelings that have been blocked may reach awareness, through moods, memories, or dreams, and fragments of responses may be directed at different people, leading to something akin to splitting.

In treatment, the task initially is to understand how information can be selected and then excluded, what information the individual is likely to exclude, what leads to the long-term exclusion, and the advantages and disadvantages of the exclusion for the individual (Bowlby, 1977). The therapy is viewed as providing the patient with a "secure base"— a protected environment in which relationships can be explored (Bowlby, 1977; Byng-Hall, 1995; Holmes, 1993; Shaver & Clark, 1994). The therapist's task is to facilitate exploration of current relationships in the patient's life, explore representations of attachment as they emerge in the transference, and explore and understand how current relationship patterns may have developed from responses to early experiences with attachment figures (Bowlby, 1977; West et al., 1987). Eventually, the therapy must help the patient experience the attachment needs and associated feelings that had been defensively excluded (West et al., 1987). Bowlby (1977) suggested that interruptions in treatment (including patient or therapist vacations) can often be used productively both in this final task and to help understand the patient's characteristic responses to separation and reunion experiences. An additional task of attachment-focused treatment is to help the patient integrate both multiple and conflicting models of attachment and to explore and integrate inconsistencies between internal representations of attachment and more conscious beliefs and social functioning. The goal of this task is greater awareness of semantic memories (or schemas) and a more coherent understanding of attachment feelings and experiences (Shaver & Clark, 1994).

Although much attention has been paid to measuring attachment styles in both children and adults (e.g., Ainsworth et al., 1978; Main et al., 1985; Sperling, Berman, & Fagen, 1992; Sperling, Foelsch, & Grace, in press), scant attention has been paid to the treatment implications of different styles of attachment. In a recent discussion, Shaver and Clark (1994) suggested some expectations and directions for treatment of adults with differing styles of insecure attachment. The authors suggested that individuals who are dismissing of attachment will have particular difficulty trusting a therapist and that they will need to explore very specific negative feelings and experiences with attachment figures. Individuals who are preoccupied with attachment relationships will have to explore their assumptions about the need for vigilance and clinging behavior in relationships and will have to look at the origins of their jealousy in relationships. Whereas the goal for the first group (dismissing of attachment) is greater trust and engagement in relationships, the goal for the second group (preoccupied with attachment) is greater independence from attachment figures. The authors also suggested that it is the second group who are most likely to fall in love with the therapist and to become overly reliant on the therapy relationship.

An attachment-informed therapy model contains elements of cognitive, object relations, and interpersonal approaches to treatment. However, the centrality of providing the patient with a secure base in therapy, the use of interpretations that concentrate on the role of real experiences rather than primitive fantasies, and the focus on the past and current behavior of attachment figures as well as the patient's responses to attachment-related situations all set this approach to treatment apart.

Outside of somewhat general discussions about the role of attachment theory in psychotherapy (e.g., Bowlby, 1977, 1988; Byng-Hall, 1995; Sable, 1992) and the attention of attachment, psychoanalytic, and cognitive theories to representational process as a metapsychological and interpersonal variable, specific discussions about modes of psychotherapy that use representations of attachment as a central element in defining pathology, and that focus therapy on correcting dysfunctional representations, appear infrequently in the literature. Those modes of therapy focusing directly, albeit not exclusively, on correcting dysfunctional representations of attachment fall into four fundamental but not mutually exclusive categories: (a) therapy that works to provide alternative representations of attachment and interpersonal functioning through relational modeling within the therapist–patient attachment bond (e.g., Cramer & Stern, 1988; Lanyado, 1988; Leifer, Wax, Leventhal-Belfer, Fouchia, & Morrison, 1989; Sable, 1983; Wright, 1986); (b) a more specific application of relational modeling that attempts to reparent through establishing a corrective attachment bond with the therapist, or between a child and the primary caretaker, that competes with and substantially alters dysfunctional representations (e.g., Frischer, 1985; Jernberg, 1989; Watanabe, 1987); (c) therapy that aims to analyze cognitively and emotionally, reassess, and thereby change representations of attachment and the defenses that maintain them (e.g., Slap & Slap-Shelton, 1991; West et al., 1987); and (d) a variant of the reassessment technique that focuses on reconstruction of representational narratives of attachment experiences (e.g., White & Epston, 1990). The first two categories generally incorporate more traditional applications of psychoanalytic or developmental theory. The latter two categories offer some relatively novel approaches that integrate cognitive theory with more traditional dynamic approaches and offer some interesting and novel possibilities.

What follows is a sampling of important material within each of these areas. This review is necessarily selective, given the volume of work within some of these areas. A problem in constructing such a review is the difficulty of demarcating the notion of representations of attachment, and a representational focus in therapy, from the vast literature that focuses on the more general construct of relationships as a foundation concept or intervention technique (e.g., psychoanalytic object relations and interpersonal theories). We have attempted to limit the material covered here to that which has direct implications for attachment and representational process.

Relational Modeling

Although many of the clinical applications of object relations and attachment theory focus on the therapeutic use of the bond with the patient, several clinicians have written both theoretical discussions and case histories that directly address efforts to help a patient reexperience and correct attachment relationships with the original caretaker as a means of changing mental representations of attachment. Following Bowlby, the therapeutic relationship is conceived as an opportunity for the patient to experience a secure attachment relationship (Sable, 1983), and the therapeutic bond is reconceptualized as "providing an atmosphere in which to experience a temporary attachment relationship . . . the therapist becomes a safe base from which to explore one's attachment behavior patterns" (Sable, 1983, p. 379). Implied here is a view of personality development and pathology that gives primary importance to "real life experiences, especially those of separation or loss, that may have been, or are now, painful, frightening, or unhappy" (Sable, 1983, p. 381). Consistent with object relations and attachment theories, the need for close relationships and normal dependency is seen as healthy; evaluations of personality disorder are made with relation to an individual's degree of emotional detachment from others and the impact of that detachment on real-life experiences.

Lanyado (1988) described work with an avoidantly attached child who was unable to respond to his mother's newly found ability to meet his attachment needs. She found it necessary for the therapist to relive with the child the disturbed attachment experiences, and the accompanying feelings, with the therapist as a stand-in for the original attachment figure. It was only after a long process of reexperiencing the avoidant relationship that the child was able to develop a secure attachment to the therapist. He was then finally able to enter into secure attachment relationships outside of therapy. Lanyado theoretically related this treatment to Bowlby's (1988) belief that the role of the therapist is not primarily to interpret experience but to be a guide and companion as the patient explores himself or herself and his or her experience. One qualification to be considered when generalizing from Lanyado's (1988) approach is that the child whose treatment she described had probably experienced a secure attachment relationship with his father before the father's death. The task of the therapeutic work then was to help the child remember and revalue those early experiences of secure attachment, rather than to do the much more difficult task of supplanting and replacing long-standing avoidant or anxious attachment patterns with newly constructed secure attachment patterns.

Another approach treats the parent (usually mother)–child dyad as a unit and attempts both to treat dysfunctional attachment history in the parent and, at the same time, to intervene correctively in the ongoing mother–child relationship. Dysfunctional attachment is seen to result from the interaction between the child's personality, the parent's own attachment history, and the parent's resulting projective identifications onto the child. Empirical support for this approach comes from a one-case pilot study by Cramer and Stern (1988). The authors operationalized a mother's mental representations of her child and then showed how changes in her mental representations were reflected in interactional changes within the dyad and in changes in the child's behavior. In another study, Leifer et al. (1989) described a 2-year treatment of an avoidantly attached 2-year-old and mother, using a multitreatment approach. They provided individual treatment for the mother and Parent–Infant Relationship Treatment (PIRT) for the dyad. The PIRT included both interventions focused directly on changing observed interactions between the mother and child (such as teaching the mother to read the child's cues more accurately and therapist-modeled caretaking and play activities) and dynamic work focused on helping the mother connect her difficulties relating to the child to her own attachment experiences, fears of rejection by the child, and feelings of helplessness as a parent.

In a more analytically focused discussion, Wright (1986) suggested that becoming a parent "reactivates repressed internalized relationships" and that only when parents confront the pain from their own childhood will they be able to avoid re-creating their own painful attachment relationships with their children. He presented three basic distortions in the parent–child relationship, which are seen to result from parental projective identifications: (a) an avoidant relationship, in which the parent is neglectful, and deeply conflicted about caretaking, and in which the parent may be trying to protect the child from the parent's own rage; (b) a symbiotic relationship, in which the parent is enacting his or her own need for and early deprivation of a symbiotic relationship; and (c) a rejecting relationship, where the baby is seen as the bad half of the parent's split internal object representations. The goals of therapy are for the parent to recognize the projective identification as a product of the parent's own early deprivation and to be able to replace it with empathy for the baby. According to Wright (1986), the therapy process involves observing and intervening in the parent–child relationship. Parents are made aware of how they use the baby as a transference object and of the extent to which this reflects their own pain and deprivation. Additionally, the therapist directly intervenes in parent–child interactions during home visits, where positive interactions with the child are modeled.

Reparenting

A somewhat related approach to relational modeling attempts to change internal representations of attachment through reparenting. Within a psychoanalytic nosology, this tactic might also be described as a radical form of transferential enactment, or abreaction. Ann Jernberg (1989) described using a reparenting model called "theraplay" with self-contained individuals. The model involves first exploring the patient's early attachment history to understand what sorts of dysfunctional interactions might have taken place. The therapist then begins by relating to the patient as a parent to a small child, at the level at which the patient's emotional growth became derailed. Jernberg suggested that patients' resistances to establishing intimate relationships be dealt with by a "gradually intensifying intrusiveness" from the therapist. With children, this involves using games and caretaking behaviors (including putting on lotion, washing, holding popsicles for the patient to lick) to intrude with intimacy on the patients' self-enforced distance. With adults, reparenting in this model involves (a) focus in therapy on the relationship with the therapist and (b) the therapist's relating consistently and over a long period with empathy and affective attunement. More specifically, Jernberg (1989) suggested that with adults as with children, the therapist draw out memories of childhood deprivations of affective attunement and supply corrective experiences. This might include responding as a caring parent to memories of past events in which the patient felt deprived; responding with affective attunement to childhood pictures of the patient; and responding as a caring parent to current real-life events, including, for example, offering phone calls and cards on birthdays and other important occasions.

More aggressive attempts at reparenting have involved regressing the child to the time when attachment with the primary caretaker became faulty, and then teaching the mother and child to respond to each other in ways that correct the earlier dysfunctional bonding (Frischer, 1985; Watanabe, 1987). Frischer (1985) described treatment with infants and young children who had been diagnosed in multiple evaluations as suffering from severe developmental disturbances in the ability to relate. The goal of this treatment was to help the children overcome inborn deficits that had created barriers to developing attachment relationships. Through careful observation, she analyzed and learned to understand each infant's individual and atypical cues and styles of communication. Using this information, as well as an understanding of each mother's difficulties in "reading" her child, she designed preverbal sensory experiences for the mother–child dyad that were geared to each child's individual difficulties. Using these nonverbal experiences between mother and child, she was able to teach the mothers to understand and respond to their children's cues. Given the children's level of impairment, the outcomes of the treatment ($n = 4$) were unexpectedly favorable. The children were able to form stronger attachments with their primary caretakers, and over the time that they were followed, appeared to develop more normally than had been predicted from their early lack of relatedness. A similar approach was described by Watanabe (1987), who used regression with older children as a means for the child and mother to reexperience crucial developmental periods, correcting interactional patterns that had been dysfunctional the first time around.

Reassessment

As noted earlier, Bowlby (1988) is one of the very few theorists or clinicians who has explicitly discussed the clinical implications of mental representations. With regard to representations of attachment, he stated that

> A therapist applying attachment theory sees his role as being one of providing the conditions in which his patient can explore his representational models of himself and his attachment figures with a view to reappraising and restructuring them in the light of the new understanding he acquires and the new experiences he has in the therapeutic relationship. (p. 138)

Consistent with this, Bowlby described five main roles that the therapist adopts toward the patient: (a) providing a secure base; (b) encouraging exploration of relationships and expectations with significant figures; (c) encouraging examination of the relationship with the therapist; (d) fostering consideration of how relational perceptions, expectations, feelings, and actions (i.e., working models) may be the product of parental experiences and expectations; and (e) enabling the patient to recognize that these models may or may not be appropriate to present and future circumstances.

West et al. (1987) have proposed a model for brief psychotherapy that specifically integrates attachment and psychoanalytic theory and that closely follows Bowlby's model of treatment. Their treatment focuses on understanding and then correcting patients' mental representations of attachment figures. Awareness of representations is developed through analysis of the ways they are reflected in the relationship with the therapist—essentially analyzing the transference—and then later through exploration of the relationship between the attachment to the therapist and early caretaking experiences. Although this work sounds little different from a typical brief dynamic psychotherapy, the focus on representations of attachment, albeit through the transference, remains paramount and increasingly a focus of intervention as the therapy progresses. Following Bowlby, West et al. looked at the defensive operations that maintain a patient's representations of attachment, giving the most attention to the defense of exclusion of attachment relevant information.

According to this model, behavior patterns and affects associated with distressing interpersonal experiences may be excluded from an individual's representations of attachment because they cause pain; similar information continues to be excluded as the individual evaluates and internalizes subsequent experiences. For instance, they suggest that if attachment figures were consistently unavailable when needed, awareness of the need for attachment would shut off because the experience of not having the need met is too painful. According to this model, the principal transformative process in therapy is the recognition and acceptance of denied and dissociated feelings of anger, yearning, sadness, and loss relevant to attachment.

Treatment based on a psychoanalytic schema model also aims to reassess mental representations of attachment, although the task is accomplished differently than in treatment based on a structural or relational model. In the model, the task is not to analyze the transference in order to uncover defenses that mask unacceptable impulses or interpersonal desires. Rather, the task is to examine the hidden internal schemas that influence behavior and to "enable the patient to recognize the existence and activity of such an organization; to see how pervasive, often in subtle ways, are its influences on his mental set, perceptions, and behavior; and to enable him to struggle to erode the disruptive effects of this schema and replace the continual acting out of old tableaus with mature, adaptive reason and judgment" (Slap & Slap-Shelton, 1991, pp. 99–100). According to the model proposed by Slap and Slap-Shelton (1991), this is accomplished by using the patient's ego in the service of understanding the "content and activity of the disruptive residues of his traumatic past" (p. 101) and the controlling effects of past experience on current functioning. This model does use transference within the therapy relationship to explore the manifestations of disruptive schemas from the past and expects that the therapist will reflect on and provide appropriate interpretations of the material presented. However, it is also expected that the therapist's personality will emerge during treatment and that nontransferential aspects of the relationship between therapist and patient will be important in treatment.

In schema-based therapies drawn from cognitive models, mental representations of attachment are assessed and modified through cognitive reassessment, role playing, and carefully designed "experiments" in relating, both within the therapy relationship and in the real world. An early model for this work, and one that has many implications for work explicitly focused on representations of attachment, comes from Kelly (1955). Although not explicitly focused on attachment, the representational focus includes representations of early relationships. He asserted that interactions with others are shaped by personal constructs about the world and that the vision of reality created by these constructs determines the experience of reality. These constructs are dichotomous theoretical beliefs about the world that, according to Kelly, exert a deterministic control over lives in that they lead to predictions and interpretations of events and relationships. These predictions and interpretations are then used to further validate the constructs from which they were derived. Unlike psychodynamically focused theories, Kelly was not concerned, either theoretically or clinically, with the historical or interpersonal details of how an individual's construct system developed; his therapy focused on analyzing a person's personal construct system and on finding techniques to change its dysfunctional and self-limiting components.

Constructs are analyzed on a number of dimensions, including the extent to which a construct is symbolized verbally; whether both ends of the dichotomy are in awareness; the degree to which constructs are constricted (*constriction* refers to the narrowing of constructs in order to eliminate inconsistencies between experience and the construct); the degree to which a construct uses other constructs to define itself; the number and kinds of events a construct can subsume; the degree to which a construct is essential to an individual's maintenance of a sense of self; and the tightness or looseness of the construct (loose constructs are those that can lead to alternative predictions; tight constructs cannot). This analysis is achieved by directly questioning patients about their experiences and how they interpret them, analysis of interactions within the therapy relationship, and the use of specialized techniques developed by Kelly and his associates. Among these techniques are the use of the Repertory Grid Analysis (Fransella & Bannister, 1977), a personality assessment tool aimed at analyzing constructs, and detailed third-person self-characterizations written by the patient. The goals of personal construct therapy include knowledge of the ways in which one's construct system shapes relationships and choices, the revision of constructs so as to allow for greater flexibility in predicting and interpreting events in the here and now, and the inclusion of more reality-based information (Kelly, 1955).

Within cognitive therapy based on a schema model, treatment focuses on assessment and change of the patient's underlying schemas about the self, the world, and the future (Greenberg & Beck, 1990). This is accomplished through examination of past and current relationships, behavior, and assumptions, often tracked by ongoing assessments with self-report questionnaires (e.g., the Beck Depression Inventory [Beck & Steer, 1987]; the Hopelessness Scale [Beck, Weissman, Lester, & Trexler, 1974]). The therapist's task is to help patients understand how their schemas influence their perceptions of themselves, events, and the world; promote understanding of how schemas that were accurate representations of reality in the past may no longer represent reality accurately and may negatively influence current functioning; and help change the schemas themselves. Change is accomplished through logical analysis, use of imagery, thought stopping, reality testing, and analysis of the recursive relationship of thought patterns and behavior.

Representational Narratives

The significance and self-reifying quality of representational narratives has been interesting for some time to social historians and personality and social psychologists (e.g., recent contributions by Bruner, 1987; Cohler, 1988; Gergen & Gergen, 1984; McAdams, 1993; Sarbin, 1986). Recently, some psychologists have become interested in the question of historical truth versus narrative/subjective truth (e.g., Schafer [1983]; Spence [1982]). In their focus on narrative construction, these writers advocate the growing trend of constructivism, as opposed to logico-scientific positivism, in the psychological disciplines. Sarbin (1986) referred to a narrative, or story, as "a symbolized account of actions of human beings that has a temporal dimension" (p. 3) and suggested that narratives provide the "root metaphors" for psychological science. Bruner's (1987) argument distills the nature of the extensive sociohistorical focus on representational life narratives:

> Eventually the culturally shaped cognitive and linguistic processes that guide the self-telling of life narratives achieve the power to structure perceptual experience, to organize memory, to segment and purpose-build the very "events" of a life. In the end, we become the autobiographical narratives by which we "tell about" our lives. (p. 15)

The connection between hermeneutic and therapeutic applications of representational narrative constructions has not been adequately studied. As with most areas in the representational domain, there are related endeavors within personal construct and psychoanalytic theories, but few writers have attempted to articulate a specific and systematic approach to the integration of representational narratives within psychotherapy. It is interesting, however, that narrative construction, albeit with a spiritual rather than a theoretical foundation, is a basic element underlying the assumptions of self-help programs based on 12-step models, such as Alcoholics Anonymous.

One such effort to apply narrative construction psychotherapeutically within systems theory (White & Epston, 1990) addressed the interrelated triad of story (or narrative), knowledge (or known "truths"), and power (or interpersonal cybernetics) and its influence on representations. They examined the narrative representational basis for therapy with the assumption that

> Persons experience problems, for which they frequently seek therapy, when the narratives in which they are "storying" their experience, and/or in which they are having their experience "storied" by others, do not sufficiently represent their lived experience, and that, in these circumstances, there will be significant aspects of their lived experience that contradict these dominant narratives. (pp. 14–15)

So it is the discrepancy between lived experience and self- or other-constructed storied experience that constitutes the basis for the representational conflict that often leads one to seek therapy.

As with family therapies that operate from a general systems theory understanding, therapy operating from a narrative stance is less a matter of technique and more a matter of perspective. What is helpful with a patient is primarily a function of the representational sensibility that one brings to the clinical situation, whereas therapies dominated by logico-scientific thinking focus more on the application of specific technique derived from linear, causal understandings of human relationships. White and Epston's (1990) suggestions for a psychotherapy organized around narrative/representational change were therefore more paradigmatic than technical. They emphasized the sense of authorship and reauthorship in the retelling of one's lived experience, and invited "a reflexive posture and an appreciation of one's participation in interpretive acts" (p. 83).

Attachment-Representational Change in Psychotherapy: Outcome Studies

Mental representations are assumed to be fairly stable over time, especially with regard to their manifestations in particular types of interpersonal relationships, whereas interpersonal behavior is likely to vary in different types of relationships and across situations within a relationship. This representational stability within categories of relationships may be most true in individuals who are psychologically healthy, as they have developed more differentiated, articulated, and integrated representations (Blatt, Brenneis, Schimek, & Glick, 1976). In contrast, those with severe psychopathology have been found to have more global, generalized mental representations, which may promote a kind of rigid as opposed to dynamic consistency to the representational world (Blatt, Wein, Chevron, & Quinlan, 1979). This global quality of representations characterizes childhood more than adulthood (Sperling et al., 1992), and in normal development tends to evolve into more fluid, dynamic, and differentiated representations. Certain conditions may also promote adaptive evolution and differentiation in mental representations, in addition to the normally occurring periods of developmental transition, such as adolescence and young adulthood. Evolution in the representations of adults, which implies major structural changes in object relations, may be one of the principal goals of an intensive psychotherapy and might be used as a measure of psychotherapeutic change (Gruen & Blatt, 1990).

Although few published studies to date within attachment or cognitive theories have documented psychotherapeutically mediated changes in representations of attachment, some psychoanalytic empirical studies support the notion of changes in object relations during psychotherapy, with a few of these further addressing the notion of representational change. This body of work derives primarily from two sources: the Yale Object Representation Research Group and the Menninger Psychotherapy Research Project.

From the Yale group, Diamond, Kaslow, Coonerty, and Blatt (1990), Gruen and Blatt (1990), and Blatt, Wiseman, Prince-Gibson, and Gatt (1991) all offer related systematic small sample studies tracking changes in object representations over the course of 1- to 3-year psychoanalytically oriented psychotherapy. Participants were 4, 2, and 8 adolescent/young adult inpatients, respectively, diagnosed with a variety of Axis I and Axis II disorders. These studies make use of the Object Representation Inventory (ORI; Blatt et al., 1979), which assesses the level and quality of object representations through open-ended descriptions of parents, friends, significant others, and therapist, and the subsequent inquiry into adjectives used in these descriptions. The ORI assesses 12 scorable attributes in these descriptions (affectionate, ambitious, malevolent–benevolent, cold–warm, degree of constructive involvement, intellectual, judgmental, negative–positive ideal, nurturant, punitive, successful, and strength), as well as the conceptual (i.e., developmental) level of the object representations.

Diamond et al. (1990) found that over the course of psychotherapy, the patients' representations of self and others demonstrated a clearer sense of boundaries and separateness, as well as increased empathic relatedness and intersubjectivity. The latter dynamics are tied in to the attainment of object constancy by the end of treatment. Gruen and Blatt (1990) found that changes in representational structures over time were closely linked with changes in the transference relationship and that "the integration and consolidation of conflicting self-images is dependent on the resolution of central psychological conflicts involving parental representations" (p. 399). Like Diamond et al., they also found that the capacity for empathy was important in this process. Blatt et al. (1991) found significant correlations between changes in clinical functioning (global assessment scores) during treatment and both the conceptual level and scorable attributes of mother and father, but not therapist, representations.

On the basis of data from the Menninger project, Kavanagh (1985) investigated changes in object representations during psychoanalysis and psychotherapy, using both the Mutuality of Autonomy Scale (Urist, 1977) and the Concept of the Object Scale (Blatt et al., 1976), which are scored from Rorschach data. His findings, for a sample of 33 outpatients of varying diagnoses, indicated significant pre- to posttreatment differences on both scales for those treated with psychoanalysis (16) or psychoanalytic psychotherapy (17), but only the Concept of the Object Scale significantly differentiated the two types of treatment. Specifically, by the end of treatment, the psychoanalysis patients produced more accurately perceived whole human figures, attributed more benevolent content to the figures, and increased report of figures in which the roles were articulated. Both psychoanalysis and psychoanalytic psychotherapy patients reported more human interactions characterized by mature interdependence and characterized inaccurately perceived human figures as less self-motivated. In discussing his findings, Kavanagh (1985) suggested that what may change in psychotherapy is an individual's

> capacity to experience both more mature and more primitive functioning and to move flexibly along the continuum between these two positions; to know what it is to cooperate in a mutually trustful and respectful manner with another separate, unique individual, but also to be able to experience oneself as lost in another (e.g., in passionate love) without the disorganizing fear of being destroyed. (p. 557)

These outcome studies within psychoanalytic theory offer provocative findings, but the first three have unreliable generalizability because of their case analysis or small sample format, and the latter study's findings are limited by the lack of random assignment to one of the two psychodynamic treatment modalities. Furthermore, with the exception of Kavanagh's (1985) work, these studies did not specifically focus on variations of technique as it differentially affects process or outcome. Nonetheless, they all begin the task of empirically integrating the considerable literature on the origins and projective assessment of mental representations with investigation into the factors associated with representational change during psychotherapy—a task that demands further systematic research.

A small number of outcome studies from parent–child intervention projects have directly addressed the relationship of changes in attachment style (as opposed to representation) and treatment process and outcome. Although attachment style is assessed from behavior and thus is not identical to attachment representation, the two constructs are closely related conceptually. This is especially so when children are assessed using the Strange Situation technique (which might be considered equally a representational as well as a style measure). Two interesting studies, a preliminary outcome evaluation of a primary prevention project (Project STEEP; Erickson et al., 1992) and an outcome study from the Infant–Parent Program at San Francisco General Hospital (Lieberman et al., 1991), looked at differences between intervention groups and controls in risk/prevention infant–parent treatment programs and offer some support for the contention that early intervention with the dyad can positively effect change in attachment style. Another study using a single-case format, whose treatment process was described earlier, focuses explicitly on changes in attachment style and representation (Cramer & Stern, 1988).

Leifer et al.'s (1989) multimodal treatment of a mother and her infant demonstrated a change in attachment category over the course of treatment, from avoidant to secure, as measured by the Strange Situation. The participants in this study were an aloof mother with a childhood history of neglect, physical abuse, and significant losses of several attachment figures, and her apathetic, withdrawn, infant son. Pretreatment assessment was used to tailor treatment to the needs of this mother–infant dyad. The choice was made to treat the mother with psychodynamically oriented psychotherapy and the dyad with PIRT. Individual treatment was used to explore the representational issues related to the mother's difficulties forming intimate relationships and her defensive style of keeping aloof rather than forming relationships that she feared losing. In treatment, she explored her past and her difficulties with intimacy both in her marriage and with her therapist. PIRT focused on the interactions between mother and son. The mother learned how to interact with her son through modeling, watching and analyzing videos of herself playing with the child, and learning how to "read" her son's needs. Treatment lasted for 2 years. At the end of treatment, ratings of the mother–infant interactions were significantly improved. The child was more responsive to his mother and was considerably less avoidant of contact with her. The interaction between the two appeared to be more harmonious, with a greater range of affect and more mutual enjoyment. Significantly, the child's attachment style rating on the Strange Situation moved from avoidant to secure.

Summary and Future Directions

The overview of clinical uses of attachment offered in this chapter suggests that an attachment perspective crosses boundaries between dynamic, analytic, and cognitive approaches to treatment and might easily be integrated into formulations from any of these perspectives. The area of representational narrative construction, and its potential for effecting therapeutic change in life narratives, seems to be a particularly intriguing domain deserving of much more attention. It is likely to receive such attention in the future, given its manifold integrative possibilities.

At the broadest and most general psychotherapeutic level in reference to adults, alertness to the recall and enactments of attachment representations as they are expressed both in the transference and in patients' current and past relationships is a sensibility that can inform and enrich a clinician's understanding. This may lead to greater sensitivity toward subtle cues about a patient's enduring attachment style and to changes in attachment behaviors that may signal more basic structural (i.e., representational) changes. A sensibility about attachment issues may put certain defenses (e.g., exclusion of attachment-related information) more in the forefront of treatment and may provide a convenient window through which to view reactions to losses and separations.

Within the field of infant mental health, attachment theory has had a profound and specific influence. We have cited several clinical examples of infant/child treatments that use attachment theory to focus on the caretaker–child relationship. A development of this work that has promise is the creation of community-based risk assessment/primary prevention programs for infants considered at-risk for emotional and developmental problems. These programs are based on empirical work that links microevents between caretaker and infant to both the caretaker's ongoing representations of attachment and the development of the infant's attachment style (Beebe, 1993; Main & Hesse, 1990) and on longitudinal research demonstrating correlations between early attachment experiences and later development (e.g., Main & Cassidy, 1988; Main & Weston, 1981; Matas et al., 1978). The treatments tend to combine relational modeling, reassessment, and reparenting and to integrate attachment theory, psychoanalytically oriented psychotherapy, and community psychology. An important assumption of this work is that changes in the direction of greater security of attachment in a mother's internal working models of attachment will lead to changes in the mother's behavior toward the child. This behavioral change is then expected to lead to changes in the child's internal working models and, ultimately, the child's behavior.

Early corrective intervention in the attachment dynamics between caregiver and child seems to hold promise for the treatment of severe childhood disorders related to the ability to form and sustain emotional ties. However, the currently available outcome results are based on a small number of cases. The clinician is especially directed to use caution in considering modes of treatment that include induced regression as part of the therapeutic intervention (e.g., Watanabe, 1987).

The further development of clinical models that are based on attachment theory seems closely related to developments in the ability both to conceptualize and to measure individual differences in adult attachment. Although the attachment *system*, as described by Bowlby (1969), is well defined, there is limited consensus in the field concerning the dimensions most relevant to understanding categories of attachment and to the measurement of attachment in adults. The construct of attachment is rich and complex. The attachment system gets activated in many different kinds of relationships and situations and may lead the same individual to quite different behaviors in different circumstances. Internal working models, the hypothesized mediators between attachment needs and specific behaviors, are considered to be dynamic mechanisms that may change in response to environmental changes (Bowlby, 1969). As might be expected, designing valid and reliable attachment measures has proved difficult.

A number of adult measures of attachment have been developed, and many of them yield attachment categories that are conceptually similar. Currently, adult attachment is measured using interviews (e.g., Main et al., 1985), forced choice (e.g., Hazan & Shaver, 1987), and self-report (e.g., Sperling et al., 1992; Feeney, Noller, & Hanrahan, 1994). The measures differ in the theoretical premises from which they are generated; in the kinds of relationships (e.g., parents, friendships, sexual relationships) they use to examine attachment; in the domains they consider in categorizing attachment style (e.g., memories of early relationship experiences, current behavior in intimate relationships), in the categories of insecure attachment they yield; and in whether they code behaviors, affective memories, or cognitive characteristics.

There is disagreement in the field concerning how many categories of attachment are relevant and whether differences in attachment behavior are best conceptualized categorically or dimensionally. It is additionally problematic that the construct validity of many of the available measures has not been well established and that many studies assign participants to attachment groups on the basis of responses to only one measure. In order to translate the currently available attachment research into useful clinical models, to validate those models empirically, and to design studies that use attachment as a focus of clinical intervention and a measure of clinical change, it seems critical that future research focus on developing the construct of attachment, both through theoretical expansion and the development of construct valid measures. Questions that future research might profitably consider include the degree to which internal models of attachment are available to conscious processing (Bartholomew, 1994), the specificity of internal models of attachment to specific situations and classes of relationships (Bartholomew, 1994), the degree to which internal models of attachment are stable throughout the life span, the degree to which adult exploratory behaviors are affected by attachment style, and whether attachment style is best viewed as a categorical or a continuous variable.

References

Ainsworth, M. D. S., Blehar, M. C., Waters, E., & Wall, S. (1978). *Patterns of attachment: A psychological study of the Strange Situation.* Hillsdale, NJ: Erlbaum.

Arend, R., Gove, F., & Sroufe, L. A. (1979). Continuity of individual adaptation from infancy to kindergarten: A predictive study of ego-resiliency and curiosity in preschoolers. *Child Development, 50,* 950–959.

Arkowitz, H., & Hannah, M. T. (1989). Cognitive, behavioral, and psychodynamic therapies: Converging or diverging pathways to change? In A. Freeman, K. M. Simon, L. E. Beutler, & H. Arkowitz (Eds.), *Comprehensive handbook of cognitive therapy* (pp. 143–167). New York: Plenum.

Bartholomew, K. (1994). Assessment of individual differences in adult attachment. *Psychological Inquiry, 5,* 23–67.

Bartlett, F. C. (1932). *Remembering: A study in experimental and social psychology.* Cambridge, England: Cambridge University Press.

Beck, A. T., & Steer, R. A. (1987). *The Beck Depression Inventory: Manual.* San Antonio, TX: Psychological Corporation.

Beck, A. T., Weissman, A., Lester, D., & Trexler, L. (1974). The measure of pessimism: The Hopelessness Scale. *Journal of Consulting and Clinical Psychology, 42,* 861–865.

Beebe, B. (1986). Mother–infant mutual influence and precursors of self and object representations. In J. Masling (Ed.), *Empirical studies of psychoanalytic theories* (Vol. 2, pp. 27–48). Hillsdale, NJ: Analytic Press.

Beebe, B. (1993, October). *A dyadic systems view of communication: Contributions from infant research to adult treatment.* Paper presented at the Self Psychology Conference, Toronto, Ontario, Canada.

Beebe, B., & Lachmann, F. M. (1988). The contribution of mother–infant mutual influence to the origins of self- and object representations. *Psychoanalytic Psychology, 5,* 305–337.

Benoit, D., Zeanah, C. H., & Barton, M. L. (1989). Maternal attachment disturbances in failure to thrive. *Infant Mental Health Journal, 10,* 185–202.

Blatt, S. J., Brenneis, C. B., Schimek, J. G., & Glick, M. (1976). Normal development and psychopathological impairment of the concept of the object on the Rorschach. *Journal of Abnormal Psychology, 85,* 364–373.

Blatt, S. J., Wein, S. J., Chevron, E., & Quinlan, D. M. (1979). Parental representations and depression in normal young adults. *Journal of Abnormal Psychology, 88,* 388–397.

Blatt, S. J., Wiseman, H., Prince-Gibson, E., & Gatt, C. (1991). Object representations and change in clinical functioning. *Psychotherapy, 28,* 273–283.

Bowlby, J. (1969). *Attachment and loss: Vol. 1. Attachment.* New York: Basic Books.

Bowlby, J. (1973). *Attachment and loss: Vol. 2. Separation: anxiety and anger.* New York: Basic Books.

Bowlby, J. (1977). The making and breaking of affectional bonds: II. Some principles of psychotherapy. *British Journal of Psychiatry, 130,* 421–431.

Bowlby, J. (1980). *Attachment and loss: Vol. 3. Loss.* New York: Basic Books.

Bowlby, J. (1988). *A secure base: Parent–child attachment and healthy human development.* New York: Basic Books.

Bretherton, I. (1990). Communication patterns, internal working models, and the intergenerational transmission of attachment relationships. *Infant Mental Health Journal, 11,* 237–252.

Bruner, J. (1987). Life as narrative. *Social Research, 54*(1), 11–52.

Byng-Hall, J. (1995). Creating a secure family base: Some implications of attachment theory for family therapy. *Family Process, 34,* 45–58.

Cohler, B. J. (1988, December). The human studies and life history: The *Social Service Review* lecture. *Social Service Review,* 552–575.

Cramer, B., & Stern, D. N. (1988). Evaluation of changes in mother–infant brief psychotherapy: A single case study. *Infant Mental Health Journal, 9,* 20–45.

Diamond, D., Kaslow, N., Coonerty, S., & Blatt, S. J. (1990). Changes in separation-individuation and intersubjectivity in long-term treatment. *Psychoanalytic Psychology, 7,* 363–397.

Egelund, B., Kalkoske, M., Gottesman, N., & Erickson, M. (1990). Preschool behavior problems: Stability and factors accounting for change. *Journal of Child Psychology and Psychiatry, 31,* 891–909.

Egelund, B., & Sroufe, L. S. (1981). Attachment and early maltreatment. *Child Development, 52,* 44–52.

Elicker, J., Englund, M., & Sroufe, L. A. (1992). Predicting peer competence and peer relationships in childhood from early parent–child relationships. In R. Parke & G. Ladd (Eds.), *Family–peer relations: Modes of linkage* (pp. 77–106). Hillsdale, NJ: Erlbaum.

Erickson, M. F., Korfmacher, J., & Egeland, B. R. (1992). Attachments past and present: Implications for therapeutic intervention with mother–infant dyads. *Development and Psychopathology, 4,* 495–507.

Erickson, M., Sroufe, L. A., & Egelund, B. (1985). The relationship of quality of attachment and behavior problems in preschool in a high risk sample. *Child Development Monographs, 50,* 147–166.

Erikson, E. H. (1963). *Childhood and society* (2nd ed.). New York: Norton.

Feeney, J. A., Noller, P., & Hanrahan, M. (1994). Assessing adult attachment: Developments in the concept of security and insecurity. In M. B. Sperling & W. H. Berman (Eds.), *Adult attachment: Conceptual and clinical applications across the life span* (pp. 128–152). New York: Guilford Press.

Frankel, K. A., & Bates, J. E. (1990). Mother–toddler problem solving: Antecedents in attachment, home behavior, and temperament. *Child Development, 61,* 810–819.

Fransella, F., & Bannister, D. (1977). *A manual for repertory grid technique.* New York: Academic Press.

Frischer, L. (1985). Non-verbal psychotherapy with infants. *Infant Mental Health, 6,* 76–88.

Gergen, M. M., & Gergen, K. (1984). The social construction of narrative accounts. In K. J. Gergen & M. M. Gergen (Eds.), *Historical social psychology* (pp. 173–189). Hillsdale, NJ: Erlbaum.

Greenberg, M. S., & Beck, A. T. (1990). Cognitive approaches to psychotherapy: Theory and therapy. In R. Plutchik & H. Kellerman (Eds.), *Emotion: Theory, research, and experience: Vol. 5. Emotion, psychopathology, and psychotherapy* (pp. 177–194). San Diego, CA: Academic Press.

Grossmann, K. E., & Grossmann, K. (1991). Attachment quality as an organizer of emotional and behavioral responses in a longitudinal perspective. In C. M. Parkes, J. Stevenson-Hinde, & P. Marris (Eds.), *Attachment across the lifecycle* (pp. 93–114). London: Tavistock/Routledge.

Gruen, R. J., & Blatt, S. J. (1990). Changes in self and object representation during long-term dynamically oriented treatment. *Psychoanalytic Psychology, 7,* 399–422.

Hazan, C., & Shaver, P. (1987). Romantic love conceptualized as an attachment process. *Journal of Personality and Social Psychology, 52,* 511–524.

Holmes, J. (1993). Attachment theory: A biological base for psychotherapy. *British Journal of Psychiatry, 163,* 430–438.

Horowitz, M. J. (1988). *Introduction to psychodynamics.* New York: Basic Books.

Horowitz, M. J. (1991). *Person schemas and maladaptive interpersonal patterns.* Chicago: University of Chicago Press.

Jernberg, A. M. (1989). The theraplay approach to the self-contained patient. In E. Mark Stern (Ed.), *Psychotherapy and the self-contained patient* (pp. 85–93). Binghamton, NY: Haworth Press.

Kavanagh, G. G. (1985). Changes in patients' object representations during psychoanalysis and psychoanalytic psychotherapy. *Bulletin of the Menninger Clinic, 49,* 546–564.

Kelly, G. A. (1955). *The psychology of personal constructs* (Vols. 1 and 2). New York: Norton.

Lanyado, M. (1988). Variations on the theme of transference and countertransference in the treatment of a ten year old boy. *Journal of Child Psychotherapy, 15,* 85–101.

Leifer, M., Wax, L. C., Leventhal-Belfer, L., Fouchia, A., & Morrison, M. (1989). The use of multitreatment modalities in early intervention: A quantitative case study. *Infant Mental Health Journal, 10,* 100–115.

Lieberman, A. F., Weston, D. R., & Pawl, J. H. (1991). Preventive intervention and outcome with anxiously attached dyads. *Child Development, 62,* 199–209.

Luborsky, L., Crits-Christoph, P., Friedman, S. H., Mark, D., & Schaffler, P. (1991). Freud's transference template compared with the Core Conflictual

Relationship Theme (CCRT): Illustrations by the two specimen cases. In M. Horowitz (Ed.), *Person schemas and maladaptive interpersonal patterns* (pp. 167–195). Chicago: University of Chicago Press.

Lyons-Ruth, K., Alpern, L., & Repacholi, B. (1993). Disorganized infant attachment classification and maternal psychosocial problems as predictors of hostile–aggressive behavior in the preschool classroom. *Child Development, 64,* 572–585.

Mahler, M., Pine, F., & Bergman, A. (1975). *The psychological birth of the human infant.* New York: Basic Books.

Main, M., & Cassidy, J. (1988). Categories of response to reunion with the parent at age 6: Predictable from infant attachment classifications and stable over a 1 month period. *Developmental Psychology, 24,* 415–426.

Main, M., & Hesse, E. (1990). Parents' unresolved traumatic experiences are related to infant disorganized status: Is frightened and/or frightening parental behavior the linking mechanism? In M. T. Greenberg, D. Cicchetti, & E. M. Cummings (Eds.), *Attachment in the preschool years* (pp. 161–184). Chicago: University of Chicago Press.

Main, M., Kaplan, N., & Cassidy, J. (1985). Security in infancy, childhood, and adulthood: A move to the level of representation. *Child Development Monographs, 50,* 66–104.

Main, M., & Weston, D. (1981). Quality of attachment to mother and to father: Related to conflict behavior and the readiness for establishing new relationships. *Child Development, 52,* 932–940.

Matas, L., Arend, R., & Sroufe, L. A. (1978). Continuity of adaptation in the second year: The relationship between quality of attachment and later competence. *Child Development, 49,* 547–556.

McAdams, D. P. (1993). *The stories we live by.* New York: William Morrow.

Messer, S. B., & Winokur, M. (1984). Ways of knowing and visions of reality in psychoanalytic and behavior therapy. In H. Arkowitz & S. B. Messer (Eds.), *Psychoanalytic therapy and behavior therapy: Is integration possible?* (pp. 63–100). New York: Plenum.

Messer, S. B., & Winokur, M. (1986). Eclecticism and the shifting visions of reality in three systems of psychotherapy. *International Journal of Eclectic Psychotherapy, 5,* 115–124.

Piaget, J. (1955). *The language and thought of the child.* New York: Harcourt Brace.

Renkin, B., Egelund, B., Marvinney, D., Manglesdorf, S., & Sroufe, L. A. (1989). Early childhood antecedents of aggression and passive-withdrawal in early elementary school. *Journal of Personality, 57,* 257–281.

Rothbard, J. C., & Shaver, P. R. (1994). Continuity of attachment across the life span. In M. B. Sperling & W. H. Berman (Eds.), *Attachment in adults: Clinical and developmental perspectives.* New York: Guilford Press.

Sable, P. (1983). Overcoming fears of attachment in an adult with a detached personality. *Psychotherapy: Theory, Research and Practice, 20,* 376–382.

Sable, P. (1992). Attachment theory: Application to clinical practice with adults. *Clinical Social Work Journal, 20,* 271–283.

Sarbin, T. (1986). *Narrative psychology: The shared nature of human conduct.* New York: Praeger.

Schafer, R. (1983). *The analytic attitude.* New York: Basic Books.

Shaver, P. R., & Clark, C. L. (1994). The psychodynamics of adult romantic attachment. In J. M. Masling & R. F. Bornstein (Eds.), *Empirical perspectives on object relations theory* (pp. 105–156). Washington DC: American Psychological Association.

Slap, J., & Slap-Shelton, L. (1991). *The schema in clinical psychoanalysis.* Hillsdale, NJ: Analytic Press.

Spence, D. P. (1982). *Narrative truth and historical truth: Meaning and interpretation in psychoanalysis.* New York: Norton.

Sperling, M. B., Berman, W. H., & Fagen, G. (1992). Classification of adult attachment: An integrative taxonomy from attachment and psychoanalytic theories. *Journal of Personality Assessment, 52,* 239–247.

Sperling, M. B., Foelsch, P., & Grace, C. (in press). Measuring adult attachment: Are self-report instruments congruent? *Journal of Personality Assessment.*

Sperling, M. B., & Lyons, L. S. (1994). Representations of attachment and psychotherapeutic change. In M. S. Sperling & W. H. Berman (Eds.), *Attachment in adults: Clinical and developmental perspectives* (pp. 331–347). New York: Guilford Press.

Sroufe, L. A. (1983). Infant–caregiver attachment and patterns of adaptation in pre-school: The roots of maladaptation and competence. In M. Perlmutter (Ed.), *Minnesota symposia in child psychology* (Vol. 16, pp. 41–83). Hillsdale, NJ: Erlbaum.

Sroufe, L. A., & Fleeson, J. (1988). The coherence of family relationships. In R. S. Hinde & J. Stevenson-Hinde (Eds.), *Relationships within families: Mutual influences* (pp. 27–47). Oxford, England: Oxford University Press.

Sroufe, L. A., & Waters, E. (1977). Heart rate as a convergent measure in clinical and developmental research. *Merrill-Palmer Quarterly, 23,* 3–27.

Stern, D. N. (1988). The dialectic between the "interpersonal" and the "intrapsychic": With particular emphasis on the role of memory and representation. *Psychoanalytic Inquiry, 8,* 503–512.

Urist, J. (1977). The Rorschach Test and the assessment of object relations. *Journal of Personality Assessment, 41,* 3–9.

Watanabe, H. (1987). Establishing emotional mutuality not formed in infancy with Japanese families. *Infant Mental Health Journal, 8,* 398–408.

Waters, E. (1978). The reliability and stability of individual differences in infant–mother attachment. *Child Development, 49,* 483–494.

Waters, E., Wippman, J., & Sroufe, L. S. (1979). Attachment, positive affect, and competence in the peer group: Two studies in construct validation. *Child Development, 50,* 821–829.

West, M., Keller, A., Links, P., & Patrick, J. (1993). Borderline disorder and attachment pathology. *Canadian Journal of Psychiatry, 38,* 16–21.

West, M., Rose, M. S., & Sheldon, A. (1993). Anxious attachment as a determinant of adult psychopathology. *Journal of Nervous and Mental Disease, 181,* 422–427.

West, M., Sheldon, B. A., & Reifer, L. (1987). Attachment theory and brief psychotherapy: Applying current research to clinical interventions. *Canadian Journal of Psychiatry, 34,* 369–374.

White, M., & Epston, D. (1990). *Narrative means to therapeutic ends.* New York: Norton.

Wright, B. M. (1986). An approach to infant–parent psychotherapy. *Infant Mental Health Journal, 7,* 247–263.

7

Reconsidering the Role of Hostility in Completed Suicide:
A Life-Course Perspective

Paul R. Duberstein, Larry Seidlitz, and Yeates Conwell

The ego can kill itself only if, owing to the return of the object-cathexis, it can treat itself as an object—if it is able to direct against itself the hostil-ity which relates to an object and which represents the ego's original reac-tion to objects in the external world.

—Sigmund Freud
Mourning and Melancholia
(emphasis added)

Suicidal individuals are profoundly aggressive.

D. H. Buie and J. T. Maltsberger
"The Psychological Vulnerability to Suicide"
(emphasis added)

This project was financially supported in part by Public Health Service grants T32-MH18911 and K07-MH01135 from the Mental Disorders of Aging Branch of the National Institute of Mental Health.

We wish to extend our appreciation to Jane Pearson, Nancy Talbot, Otto Thaler, and the editors for their thoughtful comments on previous versions of this manuscript; and to Susan Tollers, Diana Carroll, and Sarah Smith for their library and editorial assistance.

257

Mourning and Melancholia has profoundly influenced generations of clinicians and theorists interested in the dynamics of suicide and self-destruction. Like Freud, many have assumed that suicidal people are hostile (Buie & Maltsberger, 1989; Hendin, 1991; Klein, 1935; Menninger, 1938/1985; Schmideberg, 1936; Zilboorg, 1936, 1937). More recently, aggression has become a central construct in a highly influential psychobiological model (Brown & Goodwin, 1986). Although much has been written about the psychodynamics of suicidal behavior, there are few empirically based psychodynamic formulations of completed suicide. Facile acceptance of the notion that suicide victims are profoundly hostile has negative consequences for both theory and practice, leading clinicians and theorists alike to place undue emphasis on that affect, independent of other psychological features and risk factors.

This chapter provides the first review of the empirical evidence bearing on the role of hostility in completed suicide. It has three aims. First, we elucidate the relationship between hostility and suicide in younger and older suicide victims. We conclude that hostility, although relevant to suicide in younger victims, does not appear to characterize older victims. Second, we review the roles of other clinically significant affects in suicide, including depression, anxiety, helplessness/hopelessness, and self-consciousness. Older and younger victims appear to be characterized by different patterns of affects. The interrelationship of these affects with age, hostility, and each other has not been addressed either theoretically or empirically. Our third aim, therefore, is to present models of psychological vulnerability to completed suicide in the two age groups based on these affective patterns.

Having outlined our aims, we hasten to add a few disclaimers. As Havens (1965) put it, suicide represents "the final common pathway of diverse circumstances, of an interdependent network rather than an isolated cause, a knot of circumstances tightening around a single time and place." (p. 401). We will not provide a comprehensive review of risk factors for suicide in different age groups. Interested readers may consult McIntosh, Santos, Hubbard, and Overholser (1994); Berman and Jobes (1991); Blumenthal and Kupfer (1990); and Maris, Berman, Maltsberger, and Yufit (1992). We will not focus on major psychiatric illness, or "Axis I" psychopathology, in the parlance of the fourth edition of the *Diagnostic and Statistical Manual of Mental Disorders* (American Psychiatric Association, 1994). Although much attention has been allocated to the role of psychiatric illness in suicide, there has been comparatively little attention given to the role of prior psychological vulnerability, a state of affairs that apparently has not changed much since Zilboorg (1936) discussed the "current misconception . . . that suicide is caused by mental disease" (p. 1354). Readers are urged to consult informative reviews of the literature on suicide in patients with affective disorders (Sainsbury, 1986), bipolar disorder (Goodwin & Jamison, 1990), schizophrenia (Caldwell & Gottesman, 1990), and alcoholism (G. E. Murphy, 1992). Whereas most retrospective studies show that close to 90% of completed suicides have a diagnoseable Axis I condition at the time of death (Clark & Horton-Deutsch, 1992), we believe that psychological vulnerability precedes the diagnoseable psychopathology observed in completed suicides.

This chapter is divided into five sections. First, as an introduction, we review Freud's formulation of suicide set forth in *Mourning and Melancholia* and compare it with contemporary perspectives on the relations between affect, life circumstances, and psychopathology. Second, we provide a brief overview of the epidemiology of suicide. Third, we examine important conceptual and methodological issues in suicide research. We explain our rationale for focusing exclusively on studies of completed suicide that have used either a prospective design or a particular type of retrospective method called the *psychological autopsy*. Fourth, we review the literature on hostility and other affects in completed suicides. Fifth, we discuss the strengths, limitations, and main findings of the review. We provide two psychodynamic formulations of psychological vulnerability to suicide, one for younger adults, the other for older adults. We also consider the implications of the review for psychodynamic theories of suicide, integrative psychobiological theories of suicide, programmatic empirical research, and clinical practice. Finally, in an attempt to connect this review with broader themes in psychodynamics and biomedical research, we conclude by raising a question that psychodynamic scholars interested in the dynamics of aging and suicide must consider: Do psychological characteristics confer risk of death from specific causes, such as suicide, or death from all causes?

Theoretical Background

Although Sigmund Freud never wrote a paper exclusively focused on suicide and he did not intend to characterize all suicides, he was vexed by the act and the problems it posed for his theory. Indeed,

Freud's desire to explain and understand suicide led him to supplement the libido theory by inventing the controversial concept of the death instinct. He never settled on a single psychodynamic formulation of suicide, but the quotation at the beginning of this chapter has left a lasting impression on the field.

In *Mourning and Melancholia*, Freud (1917/1957) discussed suicide as a consequence or concomitant of melancholia that, according to his analysis, resulted from the loss of a narcissistic object choice. In most cases, the withdrawn libido would attach to a new relationship. In melancholic people, however, the free libido, "in accordance with the oral or cannibalistic phase of libidinal development" (p. 249), was withdrawn or incorporated into the ego, where it "served to establish an *identification* with the abandoned object" (p. 249). In that way, "the love-relation need not be given up" (p. 249). Because of its identification with the object, however, the ego was "judged by an agency as though it were an object, a forsaken object" (p. 249). Therefore, "an object loss was transformed into an ego loss and the conflict between the ego and the loved person into a cleavage between the critical activity of the ego and the ego as altered by identification" (p. 249).

> The analysis of melancholia now shows us that the ego can kill itself only if, owing to the return of the object-cathexis, it can treat itself as an object—if it is able to direct against itself the hostility which relates to an object and which represents the ego's original reaction to objects in the external world. . . . The object has, it is true, been got rid of, but it has nevertheless proved more powerful than the ego itself. (p. 249)

Put succinctly, the combination of loss, regression to the oral phase, and hostility can be lethal. The *Mourning and Melancholia* formulation of suicide recognizes the interactive roles of an affect or disposition (hostility), a stressful circumstance (the loss of a narcissistic object choice), and an acute response to that stressor (regression to the oral phase). It therefore has much in common with, but is not identical to, a contemporary perspective on the relations between personality and affect, environment, and mental and physical health. This view assumes that the person–environment relationship is bidirectional: People modify and are affected by the social and physical environment (Caspi & Bem, 1990; Contrada, Leventhal, & O'Leary, 1990; Magnusson, 1990). Moreover, because of their propensities, some people (e.g., those who are hostile) are more affected by specific life events or changing life and environmental circumstances (e.g., loss of a narcissistic object choice) than are others (e.g., nonhostile individuals). This relation, termed *reactive interaction* (Caspi & Bem, 1990) or *congruence* (C. J. Robins, 1990), is analogous to the concept of *stress conditioning* (Lin, Woelfel, & Light, 1985) and may account for the finding that life events prior to suicide are not randomly distributed across psychiatric diagnoses (Duberstein, Conwell, & Caine, 1993; Heikkinen et al., 1994; G. E. Murphy & Robins, 1967; Rich, Fowler, Fogarty, & Young, 1988). Research conducted from this interactionist perspective is aimed less at discovering direct effects of person variables (Magnusson, 1990)—such as personality, emotion, or psychiatric diagnosis—on health outcome than in specifying what combinations of person variables and life circumstances have health implications.

This perspective is perhaps as useful in the nature of the questions it raises as in the answers it provides. A question not even considered from other perspectives here assumes vital importance: Are there differences in the relationship between hostility and suicide as a function of age, a particular life circumstance?[1] The epidemiology of suicide reveals other compelling reasons to examine the relation between affect and suicide in different age groups.

Epidemiology of Suicide Across the Life Course

Completed suicide is the ninth leading cause of death in the United States. Age differences in the suicide rate have been recognized at least since the 1897 publication of Durkheim's (1897/1951) classic multinational study, *Suicide*. He commented that with the exception of Sweden, the highest suicide rate "occurs only in the last or next to last period of life and, everywhere alike . . . the increase to this extreme limit is continuous" (p. 101). Nearly 100 years later in the United States, older people still have the highest suicide rates of any age group. In 1992, for example, the suicide rate for the general population of the United States was 12.0 per 100,000 (National Center for Health Statistics, 1994). The group at highest risk was White men over the age

---

[1]The social connotations of age are frequently overlooked in biological and even social research. This conceptualization of age as a window on life circumstance is based in part on the writings of life-course theorists (Cohler & Jenuwine, 1995; Hagestad & Neugarten, 1985) and is not incompatible with a conceptualization of age as a biological variable, an index of physical maturation or decline.

of 84 years, whose rate of 67.6 per 100,000 was more than five times the nation's age-adjusted rate. The consistency of these findings across nations and time are typically interpreted to mean that factors inherent to the aging process are associated with increased risk for suicide.

In the United States, the suicide rate in elderly men is substantially higher than that observed in elderly women. Rates of male suicide increase throughout adulthood, and rates of female suicide peak in middle age and decrease thereafter. The gender differential is greatest in elderly people (McIntosh, 1992). Whereas the ratio of male to female completed suicides in the total population is approximately 4 to 1, the ratio in those victims aged 85 years and older is up to 12 to 1 (National Center for Health Statistics, 1994), an especially striking statistic given that women greatly outnumber men in that age group at a ratio of 5 to 2 (U.S. Department of Commerce, 1995).

Membership in a particular birth cohort may also increase suicide risk. Adolescents and young adults born over the past three decades currently have higher suicide rates than did their grandparents, born in the 1900s, at the same age. In epidemiologic terms, this is called a *birth-cohort effect*. The risk for suicide varies in individuals constituting different birth cohorts, presumably because the cohorts were exposed differentially to risk factors. The high prevalence of illicit drug use, posited by some to explain the higher suicide rate characteristic of recent young adult cohorts (Miles, 1977), is one such factor.

Given the vast differences in rates of suicide across the life course attributable both to aging and to membership in particular birth cohorts, it is reasonable to hypothesize that there are age-related differences in the psychological (and biological and social) factors associated with suicide, with concomitant implications for theory, risk assessment, and the development of life-stage–specific strategies for prevention and intervention. For example, the notion that suicide victims are hostile may apply only to young adult suicides or to suicides within a particular birth cohort.

Conceptual and Methodological Questions

Why Focus Exclusively on Completed Suicide?

Most past and current psychological theorists do not differentiate attempted suicide from completed suicide. Freud apparently never distinguished between the two. Neither did Menninger (1938/1985), who conceived of certain behaviors, such as antisocial behavior and alcoholism, as "chronic suicides." Such indifference to the distinction between attempted and completed suicide is unique neither to psychodynamics nor to theorists of the early 20th century. In his theoretical explication of the presuicidal cognitive–affective state, the contemporary social psychologist Baumeister (1990) argued persuasively that the theoretical distinction between attempted suicide and completed suicide was "tangential" (p. 90) to his concerns.

Clinicians have also ignored the distinction between attempted and completed suicide, perhaps because the empirical data on the affective and personality characteristics of completed suicides were scarce. There is no longer a paucity of information. New research findings, which have been discussed but not systematically reviewed, suggest the possibility of constructing a preliminary portrait of completed suicides.

We believe it is more valuable to review informative but imperfect studies of completed suicide than to review elegant studies of suicide attempters, not because attempted suicide is an insignificant public health problem, but because discussions of the causes and correlates of completed suicide should not be conflated with discussions of the causes and correlates of other theoretically and clinically compelling behaviors in the suicidal spectrum, such as attempted suicide, suicidal ideation, and attitudes toward suicide. Although a similar psychology may underlie the entire spectrum of suicidal behaviors and attitudes, it is premature to assume this is the case. E. Robins (1981) noted that von Andics (1938) first raised this issue in the psychiatric literature; since that time, it has been repeatedly supported (Dorpat & Ripley, 1960; Linehan, 1986; Maris, 1981; Stengel & Cook, 1958).

Research on attempted suicide is not an adequate proxy for research on completed suicide for at least two reasons. First, while the investigation of suicide attempters has the obvious advantage of providing direct access to the individual for study, data obtained must still be interpreted in the context of potential distortions in self-perception that may characterize suicidal people. (This is not necessarily a problem if the distortions themselves are a focus of study.) Second, the overwhelming majority of suicide attempters included in cross-sectional studies will never complete suicide, and fewer than one third of suicide completers have a previous history of suicide attempts (Dorpat & Ripley, 1960; Fawcett et al., 1987; Rich, Young, & Fowler, 1986; E. Robins, Murphy, Wilkinson, Gassner, & Kayes, 1959). Indeed, the demographic risk factors for attempted suicide and completed suicide are so different that drawing conclusions about attempted suicide from research on completed suicide is analogous to drawing inferences about women's health from studies of men, or vice versa. Such conclusions may be appropriate in some circumstances but not others.

Too often, conclusions regarding personality and suicidal behavior have been drawn primarily from cross-sectional studies of suicide attempters who have sought medical or psychiatric treatment (Goldsmith, Fyer, & Frances, 1990; Perry, 1989). Although many clinicians may have had experience with patients whose suicide attempts were "nearly" fatal had it not been for heroic efforts on the part of rescue or medical personnel, most attempted suicides are not "near misses." Even heroic rescue measures would not have saved the vast majority of completed suicides. Although the available case studies of individuals who, incredibly, survived serious suicide attempts such as gunshot wounds to the chest can be clinically instructive, it seems unlikely that cross-sectional data on affect in suicide attempters will yield a definitive view of people who actually kill themselves.

How Can the Hypothesis That People Who Commit Suicide Are Hostile Be Tested?

Some readers may be skeptical of any attempt to draw meaningful conclusions from research on persons who complete suicide. As Barraclough (1971) put it, "Measuring the personality of the living is hard enough; in the dead one would think it impossible" (p. 96). How can one reach meaningful conclusions about the psychological characteristics of someone in absentia? Several methods have been used, some of which are superior to others. Conclusions drawn in this chapter were derived primarily from studies using either a prospective design or a particular method called the *psychological autopsy* (Clark & Horton-Deutsch, 1992). Neither adequately addresses the possibility that suicide deaths may be underreported,[2] but their strengths out-

---

[2]The possibility that suicides are underreported is an ongoing concern (e.g., Hlady & Middaugh, 1988). Even more disturbing is the possibility that underreporting may not be randomly distributed across gender, socioeconomic status, ethnicity, psychiatric diagnosis, or other important suicide risk factors. Warshauer and Monk (1978) showed that African American suicides are more likely to be underreported because of the use of less lethal suicide methods (e.g., stabbing, carbon monoxide inhalation) in that population. Similarly,

weigh their weaknesses. Rather than reiterate the excellent discussions of these methodological matters (Beskow, Runeson, & Asgard, 1990; Brent, 1989; Clark & Horton-Deutsch, 1992; Monk, 1987; Younger, Clark, Oehmig-Lindroth, & Stein, 1990), we emphasize issues pertaining specifically to the validity of the psychological data obtained in studies of completed suicide.

The prospective design. There is nothing about the prospective design itself that limits the accuracy of psychological data in studies of completed suicide. However, the studies typically used self-report measures, the accuracy of which has been inadequately addressed. Ideally, prospective studies of the relations between psychological constructs (such as hostility) and health outcomes (such as suicide) should be based on multiple psychological assessment methods. For example, hostility could be assessed using self-report, informant report, clinician rating, and projective measures. To our knowledge, no such study has been conducted.[3] To the extent that self-report data are valid and accurate representations of affective experience, there should be little concern about the quality of data generated in prospective studies. Unfortunately, self-report data, as the lone window on affective experience, are somewhat limited. For example, Shedler, Mayman and Manis (1993; see also chap. 2 in this volume) have shown that a substantial proportion of respondents who reported that they were affectively healthy actually were in psychological distress.

Rockett and Smith (1993) demonstrated that there is a good probability that drowning suicides of elderly Japanese women are significantly undercounted and misclassified as unintentional drownings. In 1989, a work group that was established under the auspices of the Centers for Disease Control sought to derive explicit criteria to assist in determining whether a death is a suicide. That endeavor was grounded in skepticism: "Because the extent to which suicides are underreported or misclassified is unknown, it has not been possible to estimate precisely the number of suicides, identify risk factors, or plan and evaluate preventive interventions" (Davidson et al., 1989, p. 360). Other findings, however, indicate that accident victims and suicides can indeed be meaningfully discriminated and that the extent of misclassification is negligible (Kleck, 1988). We are not going to resolve the debate here. We merely wish to warn the reader that all data on completed suicide should be interpreted cautiously.

[3]None of the prospective studies discussed in this chapter have been based on any theory of affect and suicide. Nor were they designed a priori as studies of suicide. Although they may thus be more appropriately termed *cohort studies, follow-up studies,* or *follow-up mortality studies,* we will use the less awkward and more familiar term *prospective studies.*

Prospective investigations of inpatients (ascertained during hospitalization) cannot escape the potential confound that the reason for hospitalization, such as a suicide attempt, may have profound effects on the person's life. For example, the failed suicidal act may have a "cathartic effect" causing symptomatic relief (Bronisch, 1992; Exner & Wylie, 1977). Subsequent medical and psychiatric interventions could transiently or permanently alter the individual's psychological function, for better or worse. In both community and patient samples, unless data are collected on several occasions, it is unclear whether the behaviors and feelings that are observed and reported are attributable to state processes, trait processes, or some combinations thereof. Despite these limitations, prospective studies of completed suicide are invaluable because they minimize the potential for hindsight bias.

The retrospective studies. Retrospective studies of suicide come in many forms. The *psychobiography*, written about extraordinary people such as the poet Sylvia Plath (Alvarez, 1970) or the author Yukio Mishima (Stokes, 1974), who left lengthy paper trails, is perhaps the most compelling. Although it is possible that case reports and biographies have dispassionately clarified the understanding of suicide, it is just as likely that they have also served to confuse the issue, leaving the impression, for example, that suicide is a romantic act, a fitting end to the life of a hero or villain. In the United States, unnecessarily romanticized accounts are less frequently observed in studies based on the *coroner's or medical examiner's report*, which describes the scene and circumstances of a suicide (e.g., Hoberman & Garfinkel, 1988). Stark and chilling, these documents often contain the contents of a suicide note, interviews with neighbors, landlords, and next of kin, as well as detailed physical descriptions of the body, but little reliable psychological information. The British system of coroner's inquest probably yields richer and more accurate information. Another type of retrospective study is based on *record reviews* from hospitals (Farberow & McEvoy, 1966; Kullgren, Renberg, & Jacobsson, 1986; Modestin & Wurmle, 1989; Pokorny, 1960), prisons (Backett, 1987), universities (Seiden, 1966), and other institutions. These records can provide valuable information about suicides in specific high-risk populations, but data are often recorded unsystematically and unreliably. Retrospective analysis of *psychological test data* obtained during hospitalization or outpatient treatment (Blatt & Ritzler, 1974; Exner & Wylie, 1977; Lester, 1971) overcomes this problem but is not generalizable to those who have not been hospitalized or in psychological treatment. Theoretically based empirical studies of *personal documents,* such as diaries and suicide notes (Leenaars, 1988), may help psychodynamically oriented clinicians and theorists even though diaries are recovered in a vanishingly small number of cases, and only approximately 35% of suicide victims leave notes.

Only the *psychological autopsy* method can overcome the problems of generalizability and unsystematic data collection. In a psychological autopsy, relatives, friends, caregivers, and others familiar with the decedent are interviewed and relevant records (e.g., medical, criminal) are reviewed. The measures vary from study to study, but most contemporary psychological autopsies, which attempt to compile a clinically comprehensive understanding of the deceased, include a structured diagnostic interview, a depression inventory, and an assessment of stressful life events. Clark and Horton-Deutsch (1992) provided a concise summary of methodological requirements for defining an adequate psychological autopsy study and a review of its history.[4]

---

[4]We sketch a few of the highlights. In 1939, New York City Mayor Fiorello LaGuardia asked psychoanalyst Gregory Zilboorg of the Committee for the Study of Suicide (CSS) to undertake a study of the case histories of policemen who committed suicide between 1934 and 1940 (P. Friedman, 1967). By that time, Zilboorg had already established himself as one of the few clinical theorists of his generation with a special interest in suicide (Zilboorg, 1936, 1937). He had recently introduced clinicians to the anthropological studies that were so useful in the formulation of his ideas (Zilboorg, 1936) and had begun his activities on the Board of Directors of the CSS. His CSS colleague, Gerald Jameison (1936), had conducted one of the first retrospective studies of suicide in the United States, using data gathered at Bloomingdale Hospital, currently New York Hospital–Cornell Medical Center, Westchester Division. The CSS, influenced by the anthropological field methods so prominent at the time, investigated 93 police suicides. The findings, however, were not published until P. Friedman's (1967) chapter appeared nearly 30 years later. In 1958, apparently without knowledge of the CSS study of completed suicide, the Los Angeles County coroner asked a team of psychologists and psychiatrists to aid in the medicolegal investigation of equivocal deaths (Curphey, 1961). They labeled their method the *psychological autopsy.* It focused "primarily on the personality elements associated with suicide, such as suicidal intention, subtle communication relating to suicidal intent, reactive or psychotic depression, and schizophrenia" (Litman, Curphey, Shneidman, Farberow, & Tabachnik, 1963; Shneidman & Farberow, 1961, p. 118). Whereas the Los Angeles group emphasized *psychological processes in equivocal deaths,* researchers in St. Louis (Robins et al., 1959) and Seattle (Dorpat & Ripley, 1960) were more interested in the role of *psychiatric diagnosis in completed suicide.* Apparently working without knowledge of either the CSS police study or the Los Angeles endeavor, these researchers used psychological autopsy methodology to study

It has been assumed that informant bias has been mitigated by the use of the "best estimate" (Leckman, Sholomskas, Thompson, Belanger, & Weissman, 1982), using all available information, but questions remain about the accuracy of psychological autopsy data. Brent, Perper, Kolko, and Zelenak (1988) demonstrated that neither the presence or severity of parental affective symptoms nor the length of time between the date of their child's death and date of interview influenced the parents' report of suicide intent; the number of psychiatric diagnoses; or the diagnoses of affective, conduct, anxiety, or substance abuse disorder. LeSage and colleagues (1994) reported similar results. Whereas these findings are generally concordant with a substantial body of research on the accuracy of parental reports of psychopathology in their children (Richters, 1992), serious questions remain about informant-based research in the psychological autopsy.

The personality and affective variables identified in psychological autopsies may be enduring dispositions unaffected by the vicissitudes of the decedent's life, but it is important for researchers not to assume that this is the case. Informants may describe the decedent as he or she appeared in the final weeks and months of life, but these descriptions may not accurately depict the victim before the onset of the suicidal crisis. Psychological and epidemiological research converge on the notion that informants may less accurately report traits or affects that are relatively private, such as shyness or self-consciousness, than those that are readily observable, such as hostility (Chapman, Mannuzza, Klein, & Fyer, 1994; Funder & Dobroth, 1987). Other research suggests that certain personal qualities of informants (Masling, Johnson, & Saturansky, 1974; Riso, Klein, Anderson, Ouimette, & Lizardi, 1994) and targets (Colvin, 1993) may affect the quality and quantity of data obtained. Although creative research programs have been developed to determine the level of accuracy of people's personality judgments and to identify the properties of judges and targets associated with accurate judgments, this methodology has not yet been applied to the psychological autopsy. The extent of the overlap between the personality of the victim and the personality of the victim as remembered by the

---

community samples of consecutive suicides. With its emphasis on careful psychiatric diagnosis, the St. Louis study in particular set the standard for subsequent studies. This "painstakingly conceived and executed" investigation was summarized in book-length form more than two decades after its completion (E. Robins, 1981, p. xiii).

informant remains unexamined empirically. Nor have possible determinants of this overlap been fully examined, such as the duration and nature of the relationship between informant and deceased and the informant's verbal ability, personality, and psychiatric symptoms.

Moreover, it is likely that the relationship between informant and researcher affects the quality and quantity of information elicited (Cohler & Jenuwine, 1995), a variant of the problem of examiner behavior in the assessment situation (Masling, 1960). Some interviewers may be more likely than others to elicit angry feelings from informants, who in turn may be more likely to report that the victim was an angry or hostile person. This possibility, consistent with the notion that the act of suicide itself may elicit hatred in care providers (Maltsberger & Buie, 1974) and family members, remains an unexamined potential confounding variable that must be acknowledged. Despite these potential limitations, the psychological autopsy provides researchers with a unique opportunity to learn about the role of hostility and other affects in completed suicide.

Empirical Review

This review examines the relationship between hostility and completed suicide in different age groups. It provides a framework from which we can begin to develop, test, and refine empirically based psychodynamic formulations of completed suicide. Although developmental tasks shift dramatically in the first decades of adulthood (Erikson, 1950; Levinson, Darrow, Klein, Levinson, & McKee, 1978), the available data will not allow us to discriminate people who commit suicide in their third decade from those who take their lives in their fifth decade. Nor are we able to distinguish people who commit suicide in their sixth decade from victims who die in their eighth or ninth decade. However, we are able to distinguish suicide victims in two age groups, corresponding roughly to younger and older adulthood, using the end of the fifth decade as the approximate divide.

Although it would have been preferable to examine Freud's (1917/1957) notion that the combination of hostility and regression to the oral phase increases psychological vulnerability to suicide in the context of actual or threatened loss, the available data will not allow it. This review is guided by the structure of the *Mourning and Melancholia* formulation, if not its content. The *Mourning and Melancholia* formulation makes it clear that a review of the role of hostility in suicide without an examination of the role of other important psychological constructs is of limited utility, both conceptually and clinically. We therefore sought to include all prospective (see Tables 1 and 2) and psychological autopsy (see Table 3) studies of affect in completed suicide.[5] In addition to hostility, the following sets of affect-related constructs have been associated with suicide: hopelessness, helplessness and dependency, anxiety, depression, and social disengagement and self-consciousness. We were struck not only by the constructs that have been implicated in suicide, but also by those that have not. We uncovered no evidence linking paranoia, narcissism, or obsessive–compulsive traits to suicide, although it is possible, but unlikely, that these constructs have not been systematically investigated. Therefore, the notion that suicides are characterized by a nonspecific pattern of maladaptive affects or traits is probably inaccurate.

We begin each of the following sections with a brief definition of a construct and discussion of how it has been operationalized in this area of research. The relationships between each construct and completed suicide are reviewed. Those that failed to reach statistical significance, as defined in the original report, are described as negative findings. We recognize the arguments against using tests of statistical significance as both the sole means of hypothesis testing and arbiter of clinical meaningfulness (Bakan, 1967; J. Cohen, 1994; Kupfer, Kraemer, & Bartko, 1994). Meta-analysis can remove some of the arbitrariness or error inherent in null hypothesis significance testing (J. Cohen, 1994; Rosenthal, 1991). By providing estimates of the magnitude of effect (J. Cohen, 1994; Rosenthal, 1991) and exploring sources of heterogeneity

---

[5]Psychological autopsy researchers have typically assessed the presence and nature of personality disorders, rather than particular traits and affects, perhaps because they have been patterned after the initial St. Louis study (Robins et al., 1959), rather than the Committee for the Study of Suicide study of police suicide or Shneidman and Farberow's (1961) approach. Several other psychological autopsy studies have reported data on personality disorders or "abnormalities" (Asgard, 1990; Barraclough, Bunch, Nelson, & Sainsbury, 1974; Chynoweth, Tong, & Armstrong, 1980; Clark, 1991; Dorpat & Ripley, 1960) but provide insufficient detail about the specific characteristics of these abnormalities to warrant inclusion in Table 3. Others have not reported any information at all on personality (e.g., Arató, Demeter, Rihmer, & Somogyi, 1988; Cheng, 1995; E. Robins et al., 1959). A number of prospective studies have observed too few suicides (e.g., Bronisch & Hecht, 1992; Martin, Cloninger, Guze, & Clayton, 1985; Rao, Weissman, Martin, & Hammond, 1993) during the follow-up to reach any definitive conclusion about that outcome. They are not included in Tables 1 and 2.

between studies (Berlin, 1995; Colditz, Burdick, & Mosteller, 1995), meta-analysis can yield a clearer and more useful summary statement than that provided by maintaining a mere "boxscore" of probability values. Still, meta-analysis is not universally embraced (Eysenck, 1978; Lewin, 1996). Moreover, an adequate meta-analysis requires access to raw data as well as detailed information on sampling, measurement, and design issues (Kupfer et al., 1994). Ideally, such a labor-intensive endeavor should be preceded by a conceptual analysis that evaluates the adequacy of the documentation and outlines potential sources of heterogeneity between studies, such as differing lengths of follow-up in prospective cohort studies. Other sources of heterogeneity include covariate measurement, and quality of design and its implementation (Colditz et al., 1995). Although not a substitute for such a conceptual analysis, this boxscore review will lay its foundation. Each section concludes with a summary that integrates the available evidence with findings from investigations not reviewed (e.g., record-linkage or mortality studies) and identifies possible research directions.

Hostility

Definition. The first cluster of emotions and personality dispositions to be examined are those associated with hostility and aggression. These include the constructs of anger, impulsivity, irritability, emotional dyscontrol, and misconduct. One or more of these constructs were measured in a number of prospective studies of suicide with self-report scales or clinician ratings. Antisocial and borderline personality disorders, examined in some psychological autopsy studies of suicide, are also reviewed in this section. Antisocial personality disorder is characterized by overtly hostile behaviors, such as frequently engaging in physical fights, being physically cruel, rape, and theft. It is also associated with impulsive behavior, such as frequent change of residence, job, and relationships. Borderline personality disorder is characterized by emotional instability, including intense and frequent anger, as well as by impulsivity. Self-directed anger or aggression is often evident in behaviors such as self-mutilation and suicidal threats or behaviors.

Evidence from prospective studies. Allebeck, Allgulander, and Fisher (1988) investigated 50,465 conscripts who enrolled in the Swedish military in 1969 and 1970. The conscripts represented all but a small fraction (2–3%) of Swedish men born between 1949 and 1951. An unspecified structured interview and a battery of psychological

Table 1

Prospective Studies of Suicide: Clinical Samples

Site/Study	Publication	Index sample/ Control group (CG)	Suicide subsample	Dates of entry/ Follow-up	Significant (s) and nonsignificant (ns) differences
Houston, VA	Pokorny (1983)	4,800 psychiatric inpatients / CG: nonsuicide subsample	n = 67 100% male age: NR	NR/ NR	s: depression, self-consciousness ns: hostility
Linkoping, Sweden	Borg & Stahl (1982)	2,184 psychiatric inpatients (80%) and outpatients (20%) / CG: nonsuicide subsample	n = 34 gender: NR age: M = 48	1976/ 12/1977	ns: depression, anxiety
Lund, Sweden Lund Alcohol	Berglund (1984)	1,312 inpatient alcoholics / CG: nonsuicide subsample	n = 88 gender: NR age: M = 43	1949–1969/ 12/1980	s: hostility, self-consciousness ns: depression
	Berglund (1986)	1,000 inpatient alcoholics / CG: nonsuicide peptic ulcer subsample	n = 15 with peptic ulcer 100% male age: NR	1956–1969/ 12/1980	s: anxiety
	Berglund, Krantz, & Lundqvist (1987)	1,312 inpatient alcoholics / CG: none, examined relations of affects to autopsy findings	n = 55 with autopsy	1949–1969/ 12/1980	s: self-consciousness
Lund, Sweden Lund Depression	Brådvik & Berglund (1993)	1,206 inpatient depressives / CG: subsample of 89 nonsuicides, matched on age, sex, diagnoses, & year of admission	n = 89 43% male age: NR	1956–1969/ 12/1982	s: self-consciousness
Multisite, U.S. NIMH Psychobiology of Depression	Fawcett et al. (1978)	954 inpatients and outpatients with affective disorders / CG: nonsuicide subsample	n = 25 56% male age: M = 39	1978/ 1/1982	s: hopelessness, self-consciousness

Multisite, U.S. NIMH Psychobiology of Depression	Fawcett et al. (1990)	Same as Fawcett et al. (1987) CG: nonsuicide subsample	$n = 32$ ages: 21–73	1978/1988	s: hopelessness, anxiety
Philadelphia Suicide Ideator	Beck, Steer, Kovacs, & Garrison (1985)	207 inpatients with suicide ideation (46% male, ages: $M = 34$)/ CG: nonsuicide subsample	$n = 14$ gender: NR age: NR	1970–1975/ 5 years after entry	s: hopelessness; ns: depression
	Beck, Brown, & Steer (1989)	141 inpatients with suicide ideation and clinician ratings of hopelessness/ CG: nonsuicide subsample	$n = 10$ gender: NR ages: NR	1970–1975/ 5 years after entry	s: hopelessness
Philadelphia Suicide Attempter	Beck & Steer (1989)	413 inpatient suicide attempters/ CG: nonsuicide subsample	$n = 20$ gender: NR age: NR	1970–1975 12/1982	ns: hopelessness
	Beck, Steer, & Trexler (1989)	161 inpatient suicide attempters with alcoholism/ CG: nonsuicide subsample	$n = 18$ 44% male age: $M = 30$	1970–1975/ 12/1982	ns: hopelessness
Philadelphia Outpatient Study	Beck, Brown, Berchick, Stewart, & Steer (1990)	1,958 cognitive therapy outpatients/ CG: nonsuicide subsample	$n = 17$ 53% male age: $M = 40$	1978–1985/ 12/1985	s: depression, hopelessness
Odense University Odense, Denmark	Nielsen, Wang, & Bille-Brahe (1990)	207 suicide attempters/ CG: nonsuicide subsample	$n = 24$ 50% male $Mdn = 40$	1980–1981/ 5 years after entry	s: depression

Note. NR = not reported; M = mean; Mdn = median. The affects and traits listed in the far right column encompass but are not necessarily identical to the specific psychological constructs measured. See text for information on how these constructs have been operationalized in each study. Studies that have yielded two or more publications have been based on single (nonindependent) samples.

Table 2

Prospective Studies of Suicide: Community Samples

Site/Study	Publication	Index sample/Control group (CG)	Suicide subsample	Dates of entry/Follow-up	Significant (s) and nonsignificant (ns) differences
Sweden Swedish Military	Allebeck, Allgulander, & Fisher (1988)	50,465 military conscripts/CG: nonsuicide subsample	n = 247 100% male ages: 18–34	1969–1970/1983	s: hostility, self-consciousness
	Allebeck & Allgulander (1990)				s: hostility, self-consciousness
Switzerland Swiss Military	Angst & Clayton (1986)	6,315 military conscripts/CG: normal subsample (n = 5,521)	n = 15 100% male age: NR	1971/1983	s: hostility, depression ns: self-consciousness, anxiety
Finland Finnish Twin Study	Romanov et al. (1994)	10,586 male twins/CG: nonsuicide subsample	n = 51 100% male age: NR	1975/1981	s: hostility
Baltimore, MD (U.S.) John Hopkins Precursor Study	Thomas (1971)	1,271 medical students/CG: living and nonsuicide dead subsamples	n = 12 67% male age: M = 31	1948–1964/?	s: self-consciousness ns: hostility, depression
	Epstein, Thomas, Shaffer, & Perlin (1973)	1,198 medical students/CG: nonsuicide subsample (18 matched for age, sex, race, class, and marital status plus 6 others)	n = 9 78% male age: M = 35	1948–1964/NR	s: hostility, depression, anxiety
	Graves & Thomas (1991)	1,046 male medical students/CG: nonsuicide subsample	n = 13 100% male ages: 24–54	1948–1964/1988	s: hostility, self-consciousness

Population	Authors	Sample / CG	n	Dates	Affects and traits
Southern California California Retirement	Ross, Bernstein, Trent, Henderson, & Paganini-Hill (1990)	11,888 retirement community residents / CG: nonsuicide subsample	n = 19 53% male age: NR	1981–1982/ 1/1987	s: depression
Pennsylvania– Harvard Alumni Study I	Paffenbarger & Asnes (1966)	41,266 male college students / CG: nonsuicide subsample	n = 225 100% male	1926–1950/ 1/1965 age: M = 33	s: anxiety, self-consciousness
Pennsylvania– Harvard Alumni Study II	Paffenbarger, King, & Wing (1969)	51,000 male college students / CG: 762 nonsuicide subsample	n = 381 100% male age: M = 38	1916–1950/ 1967	s: anxiety, self-consciousness
Cambridge, MA (U.S.) Harvard Alumni	Paffenbarger, Lee, & Leung (1994)	21,582 male Harvard alumni / CG: nonsuicides	n = 129 100% male age: NR	1962–1977/ 1/1989	s: self-consciousness
California (U.S.) Terman Study	Tomlinson-Keasey, Warren, & Elliot (1986)	672 girls with IQs > 135 / CG: subsample of 32 non-suicides, of whom 15 were matched on age of death and 17 were living	n = 8 0% male ages: 22–55	1917–1928/ 1964	s: anxiety, depression in combination with other predictors
	Lester (1991)	1,528 children with IQs > 135 / CG: 15 nonsuicide completers matched on sex and clinician-ratings of mental health	n = 15 with ratings of mental health 74% male age: NR	1917–1928/ 1987	s: anxiety
4 communities (U.S.) EPESE	Pearson, Simonsick, & Phillips (1993)	>14,000 community dwelling elderly	n = 18 100% male age: M = 74	1981–1984/ ongoing, every 3 years	s: depression

Note. NR = not reported; M = mean; Mdn = median; EPESE = Established Populations for Epidemiologic Studies of the Elderly. The affects and traits listed in the far right column encompass but are not necessarily identical to the specific psychological constructs measured. See text for information on how these constructs have been operationalized in each study. Studies that have yielded two or more publications have been based on single (nonindependent) samples.

Table 3

Psychological Autopsy Studies

Site	Publication	Suicide subsample	Control group
San Diego, CA (U.S.)	Rich, Young, & Fowler (1986)	$n = 204$ 70% male ages: 16–88	None
	Rich & Runeson (1992)	$n = 133$ 74% male ages: 13–29	None
	Carney, Rich, Burk, & Fowler (1994)	$n = 204$ 70% male ages: 16–88	None
Louisville, KY (U.S.)	Shafii, Carrigan, Whittinghill, & Derrick (1985)	$n = 20$ 90% male ages: 12–19	Matched-pair controls (friends of the deceased)
	Shafii, Steltz-Lenarsky, McCue-Derrick, Beckner, & Whittinghill (1988)	$n = 21$ 90% male ages: 11–19	Matched-pair controls (friends of the deceased)
New York, NY (U.S.)	D. Shaffer, Garland, Gould, Fisher, & Trautman (1988)	$n = 114$ 85% male ages: NR–19	Demographically matched normal controls
Pittsburgh, PA (U.S.)	Brent, Perper, Goldstein, et al. (1988)	$n = 27$ 78% male ages: $M = 18$	Suicidal inpatients
	Brent et al. (1993)	$n = 66$ 85% male ages: $M = 17$	Demographically matched normal controls
	Brent, Johnson, et al. (1994)	$n = 43$ 86% male ages: $M = 17.4$	Demographically matched normal controls
	Brent, Perper, et al. (1994)	$n = 63$ 76% male ages: $M = 17$	Community controls with a history of affective disorder
Quebec City/ Montreal, Canada	LeSage et al. (1994)	$n = 75$ 100% male ages: 18–35	Demographically matched normal controls
Finland (national)	Marttunen, Aro, Henriksson, & Lönnqvist (1991)	$n = 83$ 83% male ages: 13–19	None
	Henriksson et al. (1993)	$n = 229$ 75% male ages: 13–NR	None
	Henriksson et al. (1995)	$n = 43$ 79% male ages: 60–NR	None
	Isometsä et al. (1996)	$n = 229$ 75% male ages: 13–NR	None

continues

Table 3 *(continued)*

Site	Publication	Suicide subsample	Control group
Israel (national/ military)	Apter et al. (1993)	$n = 43$ 100% male ages: 18–21	None
Göteborg, Sweden	Runeson (1989)	$n = 58$ 72% male ages: 15–29	None
	Runeson & Beskow (1991)	$n = 58$ 72% male ages: 15–29	None
Rochester, NY (U.S.)	Duberstein, Conwell, & Caine (1994)	$n = 52$ 88% male ages: 21–83	Demographically matched normal controls
Los Angeles (U.S.)	Farberow, Kang, & Bullman (1990)	$n = 41$ gender: NR ages: $Mdn = 32$	Deceased motor vehicle accident victims
Baltimore area, MD (U.S.)	J. Shaffer et al. (1972)	$n = 16$ 100% male ages: 13–65	Deceased motor vehicle accident victims

Note. NR = not reported; M = mean; Mdn = median. Military recruits (Apter et al., 1993) and veterans (Farberow et al., 1990) were examined in two studies. The remainder were conducted on community samples. With the exception of the Pittsburgh investigations, all of the studies that have yielded two or more publications have been based on single samples. This is not a comprehensive listing of the psychological autopsy literature; only those publications reporting data bearing on affect or personality are included.

tests were administered to each recruit. They also collected developmental and family data and conducted a brief psychiatric screening interview. During the 13-year follow-up period, 247 formerly conscripted men committed suicide. Psychiatric assessments of the conscripts based on the interview and questionnaire revealed that three constructs related to hostility-predicted suicide status. These were school misconduct, low emotional control, and a variable that presumably reflected the severity of these problems, early contact with child welfare authorities.

Angst and Clayton (1986) collected medical, personality, and social data on 6,313 Swiss military conscripts in 1971. Approximately one half of these respondents provided data anonymously and thus could not be identified at follow-up 12 years later in an investigation of hospital records and death certificates. Of the remaining respondents ($n =$

3,155), 59 had died (35 accidents, 15 suicides, and 9 other). Examination of their Freiburg Personality Inventory profiles revealed that suicide victims scored higher than controls on aggression, excitability, and dominance (reactive aggression). Interestingly, sociopaths, depressives, and accident victims also obtained higher scores than controls on these indices of aggression.

Thomas (1971) prospectively collected medical, personality, and social data on 1,271 Johns Hopkins University medical students from 1948 to 1964. She used a discriminant function analysis to determine if responses of suicide victims ($n = 12$) to the Habits of Nervous Tension questionnaire would be different from those provided by matched living controls, accidental and natural deaths, and the total living sample. Suicide victims scored higher on the item "irritability with concern as to who is to blame." Graves and Thomas (1991) used survival analysis and replicated this finding ($N = 13$ suicide victims). They noted that irritability was one of the two strongest predictors of suicide, the other being urinary frequency, perhaps an indicator of anxiety. In another study on this medical student sample, a blind reviewer examined the substantial clinical data that had been collected on 33 of the medical students (Epstein, Thomas, Shaffer, & Perlin, 1973). Nine of the students had committed suicide, 18 were matched nonsuicide controls, and 6 others were included as distractors. Informed that the subjects included at least one suicide and suitable controls, the reviewer was asked to rate the subjects on a number of standardized instruments and to rank the subjects according to suicide potential. The 9 suicides correctly received the nine highest ranks on suicide potential, and they received significantly higher scores on the "anger–hostility" factor of a standard mood scale.

Romanov and colleagues (1994) used a prospective design to examine the relationship between suicide and hostility, measured by self-report, in a sample of 10,586 Finnish male twins aged 24 to 59 years. The sample was divided into three groups—most hostile, moderately hostile, and least hostile—and the relative risks of suicide among the three groups were calculated. Suicide risk was higher among men with both moderate and high levels of hostility. Specifically, compared with men in the least hostile group, men in the most hostile group were 3.6 times more likely to commit suicide, and men in the moderately hostile group were twice as likely to commit suicide. Although age was included in the model, it was not a significant predictor. Data on female participants were collected, but analyses of suicide predictors were not presented because of the small number of suicides among the female subjects.

Evidence from psychological autopsy studies. In a psychological autopsy study of 114 consecutive adolescent suicides in the New York metropolitan area, D. Shaffer, Garland, Gould, Fisher, and Trautman (1988) reported that histories of antisocial behavior were observed in 67% of adolescent boys and 30% of adolescent girls who committed suicide, compared with 17% and 12% of "normal" control boys and girls, respectively. Similarly, Shafii, Carrigan, Whittinghill, and Derrick (1985) noted that 70% of suicide victims in their adolescent sample (N = 20) evidenced antisocial behavior (defined as involvement with law enforcement, constant physical fights, or suspension from school because of disciplinary problems). Further analyses of those data showed no difference between suicides and a matched control group in the proportions having an Axis II diagnosis (Shafii, Steltz-Lanarsky, McCue-Derrick, Beckner, & Whittinghill, 1988), but methodological limitations may have prevented the detection of differences. Specifically, Axis II developmental disorders and personality disorders were not distinguished in the analyses, and the control participants were recruited from among the victims' friends. This recruitment strategy, although effectively matching on such factors as age, sex, race, and education, allowed the possibility that the control sample had elevated rates of disturbance because of assortative friendships with the suicide sample. In a better designed study comparing suicides (n = 38) and accident victims (n = 46), informants reported that the former were more likely to be irritable or to have anger outbursts (Farberow, Kang, & Bullman, 1990).

In a study of 27 adolescent completed suicides and 56 suicidal inpatients who had either attempted or seriously considered suicide, conduct disorder was present in 22% of the completed suicides and 30% of the suicidal inpatients (Brent, Perper, Goldstein, et al., 1988). Both groups had dramatically elevated rates of conduct disorder in comparison to population norms. In a case-control study on another sample, suicide victims (n = 67) had a much higher rate of conduct disorder than did control subjects (Brent et al., 1993). Adolescent suicides also had strikingly high rates of bipolar disorder in these samples (Brent, Perper, Goldstein, et al., 1988; Brent et al., 1993). Recognizing that the "delineation between cyclothymia, bipolar II, and borderline disorders is difficult to establish owing to ambiguities in the diagnostic criteria" (Brent et al., 1993, p. 525), these authors conjectured that the relatively high rates of bipolar disorder in their studies may be mirrored by the relatively high rates of borderline personality disorder in other studies of completed suicides. In a more recent publication, Brent, Johnson, and colleagues (1994) reported that suicides ($n = 43$) obtained higher scores than did controls on parental reports of irritability and aggression. Moreover, 18.9% of the sample of suicide victims and 2.3% of the control sample met diagnostic criteria for either antisocial (11.9%) or borderline (7.0%) personality disorder.

Psychological autopsy studies indicate that antisocial and borderline personality disorders are present in a substantial minority of completed suicides in persons younger than 30 to 35 years of age (LeSage et al., 1994; Marttunen, Aro, Henrikkson, & Lonnqvist, 1991; Rich & Runeson, 1992; Runeson, 1989; Runeson & Beskow, 1991). An investigation of 53 suicide victims between the ages of 13 and 19 in Finland showed that 20% of the victims met criteria for antisocial or borderline personality disorder, and 8% met criteria for conduct disorder (Marttunen et al., 1991). A Canadian study reported that 28% of male suicide victims between the ages of 18 and 35 ($n = 75$) met diagnostic criteria for borderline personality disorder (LeSage et al., 1994). Similarly, 20 of 58 (34%) suicides between the ages of 15 and 29 in Sweden met criteria for the diagnosis of either borderline or antisocial personality disorder, 14 of whom (70%) had a comorbid substance abuse disorder (Runeson, 1989), and 8 of whom met criteria for both personality disorders (Runeson & Beskow, 1991). Whereas the research conducted in Finland, Sweden, and Canada showed that approximately 30% of suicide victims evidenced hostility-related traits, only 13 of 133 (10%) young suicide victims in the San Diego study met criteria for these diagnoses (Rich, Young, & Fowler, 1986). Rich and Runeson (1992) ascribed the variance between the San Diego and Sweden findings to differences in the rates of detection of Axis II disorders, especially borderline personality disorder. In a reexamination of the San Diego data, which was carefully designed to detect borderline personality disorder, Rich and Runeson (1992) observed that 41% of young victims met their newly developed criteria for borderline personality disorder. Isometsä and colleagues (1996) reported that 10.8% of their sample of 185 Finnish suicides across the life course met diagnostic criteria for either antisocial or borderline personality disorder. Note that the prevalence estimates of these disorders in the general population range from 4% to 5% (Weissman, 1993).

Negative findings. An investigation of 43 suicide victims aged 18 to 21 years in Israel revealed a greatly elevated rate of Cluster B personality traits, but in contrast to the borderline and antisocial victims in the Scandinavian and North American samples, most were narcissistic (Apter et al., 1993). Although this was a military rather than a community sample, military service is obligatory in Israel. Brent, Perper, et al. (1994) reported no difference in the rate of conduct disorder observed among suicides and controls who had histories of affective disorder. Brent, Johnson, et al. (1994) reported no difference between suicide victims and controls on the Assault subscale of the Buss-Durkee Hostility-Guilt Inventory. Duberstein, Conwell, and Caine (1994) found no difference between 52 suicide victims aged 20 to 83 and normal controls on impulsivity and hostility, despite observing differences on several other personality dimensions. Rich and colleagues (1986) reported that only 2 of 150 (1.5%) subjects older than 30 had a personality disorder. The prevalence of hostility-related personality disorders among elderly suicides in that sample was therefore quite low. A publication describing the older victims in the San Diego sample tentatively supports this conclusion (Carney, Rich, Burke, & Fowler, 1994). There is no mention of personality disorders—hostility related or not—in that article. Henriksson et al. (1995) reported that 5 of 43 suicide victims over the age of 60 met criteria for personality disorder, only one of whom met criteria for borderline personality disorder.

Negative findings were also obtained in several prospective studies. In his investigation of 4,800 Veterans Administration psychiatric inpatients, Pokorny (1983) reported that suicide attempters, but not completers, obtained high hostility scores. In a comparison of alcoholics who later committed suicide ($n = 88$) with alcoholics who did not commit suicide ($n = 1,224$), Berglund (1984) reported that the groups did not differ in their reported or observed levels of psychopathy and criminality. Angst and Clayton (1986) reported that suicides in their Swiss military sample were more aggressive than controls, but no more aggressive than sociopaths, depressives, or accident victims. Thomas (1971) observed that, although medical students who later died of suicide were more "irritable" than the nonsuicide controls, they were not more "angry."

Comment. The retrospective and prospective studies reviewed in this section provide moderately strong evidence for the role of hostility-related affects and behavior in suicide, and they can be readily integrated with studies that show relatively high rates of suicide in patients with antisocial and borderline personality disorders (Black,

Warrack, & Winokur, 1985; Links, Mitton, & Steiner, 1990; Miles, 1977; Paris, Nowlis, & Brown, 1987; Stone, Hurt, & Stone, 1987). Note, however, that the relationship between hostility-related affects and behaviors had not been demonstrated in studies conducted on a Veterans Administration sample (Pokorny, 1983), alcoholics (Berglund, 1984), and a community-based sample of suicides (Duberstein et al., 1994). Nor has it been demonstrated in samples of older adults (Duberstein et al., 1994; Henriksson et al., 1995; Rich et al., 1986). (These issues are detailed further in the Discussion section.)

Hopelessness, Helplessness, and Dependency

Definition. The term *hopelessness* refers to a condition in which the individual perceives the future as holding little or no satisfaction or pleasure. In prospective studies, hopelessness has typically been assessed by a self-report inventory, although clinician ratings have also been used. Retrospective studies of this construct have been based on informant responses to single items. The related construct of helplessness is "likely to be experienced by the person more manifestly dependent on external objects" (Engel, 1963, p. 284). It was measured in one of the studies reviewed with several questionnaire items. Whereas it is hypothesized that hopelessness and helplessness are discrete affects, it has also been noted that they frequently co-occur (Engel, 1963) and that "helplessness is a necessary component of hopelessness" (Abramson, Metalsky, & Alloy, 1989, p. 359). Hopelessness and helplessness may therefore be conceptualized as closely related to the dependent (Bornstein, 1992), anaclitic (Blatt, 1974), sociotropic (Beck, 1983), or oral-dependent (Masling, 1986) personality orientation.

Evidence from prospective studies. In a prospective investigation of 207 psychiatric inpatients with suicidal ideation, Beck, Steer, Kovacs, and Garrison (1985) examined the Beck Hopelessness Scale (BHS; Beck, Weissman, Lester, & Trexler, 1974) scores in 14 suicide victims and the nonsuicide controls. The suicide victims had obtained higher scores on the BHS. In a study of 1,958 outpatients in cognitive therapy, Beck, Brown, Berchick, Stewart, and Steer (1990) compared suicide victims ($n = 17$), living patients, and patients who died of natural causes. Suicide victims had obtained higher scores than both comparison groups on the BHS. The mean BHS score of the suicide victims was 15.3 ($SD = 4.5$). Impelled in part by the criticism that the

BHS is confounded with social desirability (Cole, 1988), Beck, Brown, and Steer (1989) conducted a 5- to 10-year prospective investigation of 141 suicide ideators for whom *clinical* ratings of hopelessness at the time of inpatient admission were available. Ten people committed suicide during the follow-up period. These individuals had received higher clinical ratings of hopelessness than had the patients who did not commit suicide.

A study conducted on an elderly sample of 11,788 residents of a retirement community showed a strong relationship between a single item measure of hopelessness and suicide (Ross, Bernstein, Trent, Henderson, & Paganini-Hill, 1990). The risk of suicide among those who responded negatively to the question "Are you hopeful about the future?" was 5.6 times greater than those who responded positively. In a multisite prospective investigation of 954 patients in the United States with affective disorder, Fawcett and colleagues (1987) reported that hopelessness was one of 19 variables that distinguished suicide victims ($n = 14$) and controls. Another examination of that data set investigated interactions among risk factors (Young, Fogg, Scheftner, & Fawcett, 1994). Pervasive hopelessness in the intake episode was associated with a greater suicide rate only in participants who did not meet diagnostic criteria for either alcohol or drug abuse. Among those classified as drug or alcohol abusers, the absence of pervasive hopelessness was associated with greater suicide risk. In a follow-up analysis, hopelessness was more closely associated with suicides 2 to 10 years after discharge than within 1 year of hospital discharge (Fawcett et al., 1990). This finding is concordant with the notion that hopelessness is not merely an acutely painful cognitive–affective state to which some people are unpredictably vulnerable, but also implies that such vulnerability may represent an enduring feature of a dependent personality.

Other research provides more direct evidence for the role of dependency in suicide. Berglund, Krantz, Lundqvist, and Therup (1987) compared suicide completers ($n = 67$) with former inpatients who did not complete suicide ($n = 8,046$). Patients with affective disorders and alcoholism were excluded from the analyses. At discharge, those who later committed suicide were more likely than those who did not to have been rated as "easily led, dependent, and immature." Because many divorced and unmarried individuals have this personality style, the authors speculated that a dependent, immature style may lay the foundation for interpersonal disturbances. Epstein and colleagues

(1973) found that medical students who committed suicide were rated as more dependent than a control sample by a blind reviewer of the participants' clinical data collected at the time of the participants' entry into the study.

Evidence from psychological autopsy studies. Informants reported that suicide victims were less likely to be hopeful about the future than were accident victims; 58% of the suicide victims were reportedly hopeless (Farberow et al., 1990). Maris (1981) obtained similar results: Fifty-three percent of the informants in his study reported that the suicide victims were hopeless about the future in the 2 months prior to death.

Negative findings. Importantly, hopelessness does not predict eventual suicide when the intake samples are restricted to suicide attempters (Beck & Steer, 1989) and alcoholic suicide attempters (Beck, Steer, & Trexler, 1989). Of 10 clinical and demographic variables used as predictor variables in a sample of 413 psychiatrically hospitalized suicide attempters, Beck and Steer (1989) observed that only the diagnosis of alcoholism predicted eventual suicide. They concluded that "the role of hopelessness in predicting suicide by attempters is problematic" (p. 208). In a separate report, Beck, Steer, and Trexler (1989) prospectively studied the 161 alcoholics in their sample of 413 suicide attempters. They attempted to differentiate suicide attempters who later completed suicide ($n = 18$) from those who did not later take their own lives ($n = 143$) on 27 psychosocial variables. During the index suicide attempt, those who later committed suicide had taken more precautions to avoid being rescued than had noncompleters. (Similar findings were reported in another analysis [Steer, Beck, Garrison, & Lester, 1988].) No differences were observed on any of the other 26 variables, including hopelessness. As in the previous report (Beck & Steer, 1989), the authors speculated that the suicide attempter's level of hopelessness was diminished by the suicide attempt itself. Alternatively, the range of hopelessness scores in a sample of alcoholics may be too restricted to detect its contribution to suicide. Consistent with this possibility, Berglund (1984) observed no differences between alcoholics who committed suicide and those who did not in their levels of dependency.

Comment. The rigorously designed prospective studies reviewed in this section indicate that hopelessness and related constructs of helplessness and dependency contribute significantly to completed suicide in depressed patients (Beck, Brown, & Steer, 1989; Beck et al.,

1990; Fawcett et al., 1987, 1990) and suicide ideators (Beck et al., 1985). They support the findings from one less well-designed investigation, a retrospective chart review of the role of hopelessness in suicide among schizophrenic patients (Drake & Cotton, 1986). The relationship between hopelessness and suicide has not held up in samples of inpatient alcoholic suicide attempters (Beck & Steer, 1989; Beck, Steer, & Trexler, 1989; Berglund, 1984). No research has been published on the relationship between hopelessness and suicide in a community sample of younger adults or in a sample of older psychiatric patients. Only one prospective study has revealed a link between hopelessness and suicide in an elderly community sample (Ross et al., 1990); it awaits replication.

Depression

Definition. For the purposes of this review, the term *depression* refers to a sad or depressed mood. This definition does not necessarily encompass depressive syndrome. However, it is possible that major depression or another affective disorder (American Psychiatric Association, 1994) was present in a substantial minority of respondents who obtained high scores on the instruments used in prospective studies: the Beck Depression Inventory (BDI; Beck, Ward, Mendelson, Mock, & Erbaugh, 1961), the Center for Epidemiological Studies Depression Scale (CES-D; Radloff, 1977), and the Zung Self-Rating Scale for Depression (Zung, 1965). Like the diagnostic criteria for depressive disorders, these measures define depression by the presence of various symptoms such as depressed mood, anhedonia, guilt, fatigue, and sleep and appetite disturbances. Other studies that were reviewed used one or more items on questionnaires or clinical rating forms to measure depressed mood or related constructs such as life weariness and guilt.

Evidence from prospective studies. Pokorny (1983) reported that among inpatients in a Veterans Administration hospital, eventual suicide victims obtained higher scores on depression, guilt, and self-derogation as measured by clinician ratings on various ratings forms and a structured interview instrument. Epstein and colleagues (1973) showed that medical students who eventually committed suicide were rated by a blind reviewer of their clinical files as being significantly more depressed than a nonsuicide control group. Angst and Clayton (1986) reported that Swiss army conscripts who later completed suicide obtained higher scores on the Depressiveness subscale of the Freiburg Personality Inventory than did the nonsuicide control sample. Ross and colleagues (1990) showed in their study of elderly retirement community residents that depression, as measured by four items from the Zung Self-Rating Scale for Depression (Zung, 1965), was associated with completed suicide in both univariate and multivariate analyses. In a prospective study of 18 suicide victims who had participated in the Established Populations for Epidemiologic Studies of the Elderly, the suicide victims scored higher on the CES-D (M = 13.7) than did elderly persons in other population studies (M = 8–9; Pearson, Simonsick, & Phillips, 1993).

The findings of depression in community studies of suicide are complemented by similar results in clinical samples. In their prospective study of 1,958 cognitive therapy patients, Beck and colleagues (1990) reported that suicide victims had obtained higher scores on the BDI than had controls, whether now living or deceased. Their mean score was 30.6 (SD = 11.5). In a prospective study of 1,312 alcoholics, Berglund (1984) observed that alcoholics who committed suicide (n = 88) were more likely than the nonsuicide comparison sample to be rated by their psychiatrists as "slightly depressed." Brådvik and Berglund (1993) compared suicides with primary diagnoses of melancholic depression, with controls matched for diagnoses, age, gender, and index admission year. Men, but not women, who committed suicide were more likely than control participants to report feeling "weary of life."

Evidence from psychological autopsy studies. Farberow et al. (1990) developed a continuous measure of depression on the basis of the retrospectively reported presence or absence of symptoms associated with the disorder. Vietnam veterans who had completed suicide (n = 38) had significantly higher scores than a nonsuicide control group of Vietnam veterans who died in motor vehicle accidents (MVAs; n = 46). Duberstein et al. (1994) found that both older and younger suicide victims obtained elevated scores on the depression facet of the NEO Personality Inventory Neuroticism factor (Costa & McRae, 1985), and J. Shaffer, Perlin, Schmidt, and Himelfarb (1972) reported that suicide victims were more depressed than MVA controls.

Negative findings. Borg and Stahl (1982) obtained no differences between suicides and age-, gender-, and diagnoses-matched controls in clinician ratings of depression, but it is likely that both the sample size and length of follow-up were inadequate. In another prospective study, inpatients with suicidal ideation who eventually committed suicide could not be distinguished on the basis of their BDI scores from those who remained alive (Beck et al., 1985). Finally, although Thomas and colleagues (Graves & Thomas, 1991; Thomas, 1971) have shown that several items from their Habits of Nervous Tension questionnaire were associated with completed suicide, the item "depressed feelings" was not.

Comment. Psychological autopsy studies have consistently shown that frequently, suicide victims die in the midst of an affective disorder such as major depression (Apter et al., 1993; Barraclough, 1971; Brent, Perper, Goldstein, et al., 1988; Brent et al., 1993; Conwell et al., 1996; Isometsä et al., 1994; LeSage et al., 1994; Rich et al., 1986; Runeson, 1989). Whereas these investigations have focused on depression as a categorical diagnosis, the research reviewed in this section further reinforces the importance of depression in suicide because it has been based on dimensional measures. However, it appears that the relationship between depression and suicide has been demonstrated more consistently in older samples (Pearson et al., 1993; Ross et al., 1990) than younger samples (Beck et al., 1985; Graves & Thomas, 1991; Thomas, 1971). On the basis of their examination of the relationship between age and psychiatric diagnosis in a sample of completed suicides, Conwell and colleagues (1996) have suggested that the risk for suicide increases with age in individuals with a major affective disorder. More research is needed to determine whether indeed depression in older adulthood increases suicide risk more than depression in younger adulthood.

Anxiety

Definition. Symptoms of anxiety, worry, and nervous tension are closely related and are reflected in diagnostic criteria for generalized anxiety disorder and anxiety scales. Anxiety may also be associated with other diagnoses (e.g., schizophrenia, major depression), although not reflected in their criteria. Anxiety symptoms have been measured in prospective studies by specific self-report items or by clinician ratings.

Evidence from prospective studies. Prospective studies conducted on nonpsychiatric samples suggest that anxiety contributes to suicide. In an analysis of data from the Terman Life-Cycle Study, Lester (1991) reported that participants who later took their own lives reported more "nervous symptoms" on their intake form than did "maladjusted" participants who did not later commit suicide. (Using the Terman database, Shneidman [1971] found that completers and controls could be distinguished by their greater "perturbation" and "lethality"; Lester [1991] argued that this early effort was methodologically flawed.)

In the study of John Hopkins medical student suicides, Epstein et al. (1973) found that after examining the clinical data files of suicides and matched controls, the clinicians rated the suicides higher on the overt anxiety factor of a standard personality measure. In a prospective study of college alumni, Paffenbarger and Asnes (1966) compared suicide victims and the nonsuicide control participants for family background and physical, psychological, and sociocultural characteristics. Paffenbarger, King, and Wing (1969) conducted similar analyses on a slightly different sample. Both studies revealed that suicide completers obtained higher scores than did control participants on a self-report measure of worry at the time of intake.

Berglund (1986) found that a greater proportion of alcoholic suicide victims with a peptic ulcer ($n = 15$) were rated as strained and tense than were alcoholics with a peptic ulcer who did not commit suicide ($n = 68$). Fawcett and colleagues (1990) found that depressed suicide victims were more anxious at intake than were depressed patients who did not commit suicide.

Evidence from psychological autopsy studies. D. Shaffer et al. (1988) reported that a subgroup of adolescent suicides with no behavior problems evidenced excessive anxiety. In their psychological autopsy study, Duberstein et al. (1994) reported that informants described suicide victims ($n = 52$) as typically more anxious than age- and gender-matched controls. J. Shaffer et al. (1972) also provide evidence of anxiety in suicide victims.

Negative findings. In his comparison of alcoholics who committed suicide with alcoholics who did not commit suicide, Berglund (1984) found that the groups did not differ in their reported or observed levels of tension and anxiety. In their prospective study of 2,184 Swedish psychiatric inpatients and outpatients, Borg and Stahl (1982) reported no differences between suicides and age-, gender-, and diagnoses-matched controls in their levels of clinician-rated anxiety. Epstein and colleagues (1973) showed that although a clinician distinguished suicides and controls on a personality measure of anxiety, their ratings on an adjective mood scale that measured anxiety and tenseness did not differentiate the two groups. Angst and Clayton

(1986) observed no differences between Swiss military suicide victims and controls on an index of nervousness. Thomas and colleagues found no difference between suicides and nonsuicide controls on several items of the Habits of their Nervous Tension questionnaire pertaining to "uneasy or anxious feelings," "general tension," or "tremulousness or shakiness."

Comment. Prospective studies of psychiatric inpatients with anxiety disorders indicate that approximately 20% of their deaths are suicides (Allgulander, 1994; Allgulander & Lavori, 1991; Coryell, 1988), and at least one psychological autopsy study has documented that diagnosable anxiety disorders are more prevalent in suicide victims than controls (Brent et al., 1993). The data reviewed in this section further confirm that anxiety is an important affect in younger suicide victims (Graves & Thomas, 1991; Lester, 1991; Paffenbarger & Asnes, 1966; Paffenbarger et al., 1969; Thomas, 1971). Of the apparently negative findings (Angst & Clayton, 1986; Borg & Stahl, 1982; Duberstein et al., 1994), at least two might be attributed to insufficient statistical power (Borg & Stahl, 1982; Duberstein et al., 1994). The role of anxiety in late-life suicide has not been studied in sufficient detail to warrant a firm conclusion either way.

Social Disengagement and Self-Consciousness

Definition. *Social disengagement*, the obverse of the construct *sociability*, refers to the tendency to avoid interaction or to have fewer contacts with other people. Self-consciousness and interpersonal sensitivity are akin to the constructs of anxiety and shyness. Although social disengagement might in some cases be unrelated to self-consciousness and interpersonal sensitivity, the latter constructs are likely to contribute to the tendency to avoid social interaction (Crozier, 1990) and may be related to Kagan's (1989) concept of *inhibition*.

Evidence from prospective studies. Prospective studies conducted on nonpsychiatric (Allebeck & Allgulander, 1990; Allebeck et al., 1988; Graves & Thomas, 1991; Lester, 1991; Paffenbarger & Asnes, 1966; Thomas, 1971) and psychiatric (Fawcett et al., 1987; Pokorny, 1983) samples who later committed suicide have shown that they are more socially disengaged than nonsuicidal control samples. They are more likely than control samples to have had few friends (Allebeck et al., 1988; Allebeck & Allgulander, 1990; Fawcett et al., 1987) and to want to be left alone (Graves & Thomas, 1991; Thomas, 1971). They are less likely to socialize (Pokorny, 1983), to confide and seek reassurance (Thomas, 1971), and to participate in extracurricular activities (Paffenbarger & Asnes, 1966).

The lack of social relations among suicide victims might be attributable to their painful self-consciousness and interpersonal sensitivity. In three follow-up reports of college alumni, Paffenbarger and colleagues have shown that self-consciousness, assessed by self-report, is associated with completed suicide (Paffenbarger & Asnes, 1966; Paffenbarger et al., 1969; Paffenbarger, Lee, & Leung, 1994). In their prospective study of depressed inpatients, Brådvik and Berglund (1993) compared suicides with primary diagnoses of melancholic depression with controls matched for diagnoses, age, gender, and index admission year. Men, but not women, who committed suicide were more likely than controls to be rated as brittle and sensitive. Berglund (1984) observed that alcoholics who later committed suicide were more likely to be rated as brittle and sensitive than alcoholics who did not commit suicide.

Evidence from psychological autopsy studies. Farberow et al. (1990) found that 73% of Vietnam veteran suicide victims were "less interested in people," compared with 29% of the control sample of veterans, and Shafii and colleagues (1985) observed that 65% of the adolescent suicide victims in their sample were characterized as extremely quiet, socially aloof, and lonely. Duberstein et al. (1994), using a standardized version of an informant-report personality questionnaire, reported that both younger and older suicide victims were perceived by others as significantly more self-conscious than were control participants. Younger suicide victims were also described as less active and assertive than control participants. Apter et al. (1993) reported that 37% of the suicides in their sample evidenced schizoid personality traits, but the study did not include a control sample.

Negative findings. LeSage and colleagues (1994) found no difference between controls and suicide victims in the prevalence of schizoid personality disorder. Rich and Runeson (1992) reported that only 1 of 191 younger suicide victims met criteria for schizoid personality disorder. Angst and Clayton (1986) found in their prospective study of Swiss military conscripts that suicide victims and control participants did not differ on a self-report measure of extraversion. Duberstein and colleagues (1994) noted in their psychological autopsy study that, whereas younger suicide victims obtained lower extraversion scores than did younger controls, no such differences were observed between older victims and controls.

Comment. The studies reviewed in this section provide strong evidence that self-consciousness and sensitivity are important affects in suicide across the life course, a conclusion consistent with Rorschach research (Blatt & Ritzler, 1974) and psychobiographical speculation (Alvarez, 1970). The studies on social disengagement and schizoid personality are more difficult to interpret, given negative findings and the absence of any evidence of introversion in older victims. We conclude that there is moderately strong evidence of social disengagement in younger victims, but there is no evidence that older victims are more introverted than their same-age peers.

The notion that suicide victims are socially isolated and not integrated into the social milieu goes back at least as far as Durkheim. Whereas researchers have spent much time investigating the role of social "stressors" in suicide, such as the paucity of helpful social support systems or the death of a spouse (Bock & Webber, 1972; Kaprio, Koskenvuo, & Rita, 1987; MacMahon & Pugh, 1965), comparatively little attention has been paid to the personality features that contribute to social isolation. We speculate that it may be attributed, in part, to enduring personality features related to self-consciousness and sensitivity, although the causal direction may be the other way around: Forced social isolation may lead to self-consciousness. We are aware of no research that has addressed this question.

Discussion

Before considering the implications of these findings, we examine several strengths and limitations of this review and area of research. We have attempted to review the most interpretable studies available on the relationship between affect and completed suicide, paying special attention to how that relation may shift across the life course. "Negative findings" were considered, and studies on attempted suicide were excluded to facilitate interpretation. Although we focused on studies with particularly strong design features, we attempted to integrate their findings with those obtained in less well-designed investigations and, where applicable, with studies on major psychiatric illness. These are important strengths. There are several problems, however, that limit any effort to draw firm conclusions.

Limitations of the Review

Constructs and their assessment. Most of the studies discussed in this chapter have not typically been based on any theory of affect and suicide, were not designed a priori as studies of affect and suicide, and did not use multiple methods of affect assessment. Operational definitions of hostility have unfortunately been limited to informant report, self-report, or clinical observation. The clinical ratings were typically made at "face value," without reference to psychodynamic themes or unconscious processes. Definitional complexity and diagnostic complexity have been ignored (Angst & Clayton, 1986). For example, none of the studies reviewed in this chapter attempted to distinguish hostility from irritability, anger, or aggression. Nor have hostile thoughts been distinguished from hostile actions. In this review, we have justified grouping together constructs such as these on both empirical and theoretical grounds. A more refined and differentiated understanding of the psychology of completed suicide will emerge only from studies that empirically attempt to sharpen rather than level the distinguishing characteristics of the important psychological constructs.

Psychological autopsy researchers have typically assessed the presence and nature of personality disorders rather than particular traits and affects that might be implicated in suicide. It is likely, however, that some Axis II diagnoses are virtually indistinguishable from each other and from some Axis I diagnoses (Gunderson & Phillips, 1991; Widiger & Shea, 1991). Furthermore, we know of no attempt to demonstrate the reliability and validity of Axis II diagnoses assessed in the psychological autopsy. Moreover, the applicability of Axis II syndromes to elderly people, the age group with the highest suicide rate, has not been established (Sadavoy & Fogel, 1992).

Role of control sample and sample size. We will illustrate the problems posed by control samples with the following example: A study conducted on a community cohort revealed that hopelessness was significantly associated with suicide (Ross et al. 1990), whereas a study conducted on alcoholics showed no such association (Beck, Steer, & Trexler, 1989). Too often, findings such as these are misinterpreted to mean that hopelessness is important in the former population but unimportant in the latter, or that alcoholics who commit suicide are not hopeless. Assuming that Beck, Steer, and Trexler (1989) failure to reject the null hypothesis is not attributable to insufficient statistical power, it is more accurate to conclude that hopelessness distinguishes community dwellers who commit suicide from those who do not but does not distinguish alcoholics who commit suicide from those who do not. Any comparison of findings from a set of disparate prospective studies that used different index populations, comparison samples, and follow-up periods will lead to this interpretive ambiguity (Monk, 1987).

Ambiguity of interpretation also arises in part because efforts to *describe* victims of completed suicide are frequently confused with efforts to *predict* who in a given population will commit suicide. Psychodiagnostic prediction of suicide is rooted in the mainstream agenda of post–World War II personality psychology: "prediction from personality scales and inventories" (Craik, 1986, p. 21). It is designed to facilitate clinical decision making, an unquestionably important pursuit. Rather than prediction, in this chapter, we have emphasized description of suicide victims in different age groups. Without a comprehensive description of the psychology of suicide victims, predictive efforts will remain limited.

Generalizability of samples. The age ranges in prospective and retrospective studies make it difficult to draw unambiguous conclusions about affect and suicide across the second half of life. Although potentially able to provide valuable information regarding suicide risk in specific index populations, prospective investigations have not studied sociodemographically representative samples of completed suicides. This problem can be surmounted by studying high-risk samples, but this potential has not yet been realized. Prospective investigations of military samples and psychiatric patients have limited generalizability; most persons who complete suicide have been neither in the mental health system nor in the military.

Several publications reviewed in this chapter have not reported participants' ages. The vast majority of victims included in those studies that have reported age were younger than 60 years. Furthermore, the psychological autopsy studies that have observed relatively high rates of personality disorders have been conducted on younger samples; few studies have attempted to provide Axis II diagnoses for suicides across the second half of life. Therefore, the generalizability of available data to elderly men, the sociodemographic group with the highest rate of completed suicide, has not been demonstrated. In particular, there is a striking absence of data on suicide in the "old-old," the fastest growing segment of the population. Whereas much more is known about suicide in younger victims than in older victims, recent data enable us to sketch an empirically based description of the psychological vulnerability to suicide in *both* age groups. Given the heterogeneity of the older population, our formulation of the psychological vulnerability to suicide in the latter half of life may apply particularly to the "young-old," not to the old-old. In order for future reviewers of this literature to go beyond our relatively crude younger–older distinction, researchers must be more explicit about how age mediates the relation between affect and suicide and examine more discrete age groups.

Finally, with respect to gender, men commit nearly 80% of all suicides, yet in published prospective studies, the gender distributions of victims are highly variable. Men constitute more than 90% of Scandinavian samples (Allebeck et al., 1988; Allebeck & Allgulander, 1990; Angst & Clayton, 1986; Berglund, 1984, 1986; Berglund et al., 1987) and close to 50% of American samples (Beck, Steer, & Trexler, 1989; Beck et al., 1990; Fawcett et al., 1987, 1990). Moreover, the available information is inadequate to conduct a systematic literature review, let alone draw firm conclusions about gender differences in the psychology of completed suicide. Several publications have not reported how many men and women constituted the sample. There have been two studies—one retrospective (Asgard, 1990) and one prospective (Tomlinson-Keasey, Warren, & Elliott, 1986)—conducted on samples of women only; detailed data on affect and personality were collected in the latter but not the former. Only one retrospective report examined gender differences, focusing primarily on suicide method (Rich, Ricketts, Fowler, & Young, 1988). We are aware of no prospective study that has investigated gender differences; this lack is perhaps ascribable to the ever-present methodological problem of insufficient statistical power, which plagues even seemingly large prospective cohort studies. For example, Romanov and colleagues (1994) collected baseline data on a sample that included 10,857 women, but "results for women were not tabulated as there were very few cases of . . . suicides" (p. 331) during the follow-up period.

This paucity of information is of significant concern because there are compelling reasons to think that there are gender differences in the psychology of suicide. There are gender differences not only in most areas of personality and emotion research, but in the epidemiology of completed suicide, attempted suicide, and depression as well. Women have substantially higher rates of attempted suicide and recognized clinical depression than men, yet the rate of completed suicide among men is much higher, a seeming paradox that feminist perspectives may explain. Beginning with J. B. Miller (1976), Chodorow (1978), and Gilligan (1982), and continuing more recently both with the development of social–psychological conceptions of the self (Markus & Oyserman, 1989) and with the publication of essays organized around the concept of the self-in-relation (Jordan, Kaplan, Miller, Stiver, & Surrey, 1991), there has been a growing awareness of the salience and importance of *others* in the construction of the self in women. Applying this perspective to the problem of suicide, Kaplan and Klein (1989) speculated that although a man may be "highly invested in an intellectualized belief in his fundamental right to kill himself," a woman is motivated not to commit suicide by a "sense of responsibility to avoid hurting those who would be affected by her death" (pp. 260–261).

Gender differences in the psychology of completed suicide have not yet been reported because they have not been examined systematically. The impact of this neglect on the published literature is unknown but potentially significant. We have already observed that hopelessness scores predict completed suicide status in a population of depressed patients but not in a population of substance abusers. It is just as reasonable to believe that scores on a particular inventory may characterize completed suicides in one sex but not the other. This possibility must not be overlooked.

Hostility and Completed Suicide Across the Life Course

The bulk of the evidence suggests that hostility is related to suicide in younger victims. However, the negative findings and inconsistencies in the literature indicate the relationship is not as unambiguous as may have been assumed. Furthermore, the relationship between hostility and completed suicide must be interpreted in a broader psychological framework.

The relationship between hostility and completed suicide appears to be confined to young people. The titles of articles about the role of "spite" (Zilboorg, 1936) and "rage" (Hendin, 1991) in suicide refer specifically to "the young," an appropriate qualification. Without exception, the retrospective studies (Brent et al., 1988, 1993; LeSage et al., 1994; Marttunen et al., 1991; Rich & Runeson, 1992; Rich et al., 1986; Runeson, 1989; D. Shaffer et al., 1988; Shafii et al., 1985) and prospective studies (Allebeck & Allgulander, 1990; Allebeck et al., 1988; Angst & Clayton, 1986) that have reported a high prevalence of hostility have all been conducted on younger samples. These prevalence estimates may be subject to methodological artifact. For example, with a major methodological modification, the prevalence estimate of borderline personality disorder among young suicides in the San Diego study jumped from 10% (Rich et al., 1986) to 41% (Rich & Runeson, 1992). This does not cast doubt on the notion that young people who commit suicide are hostile. However, in conjunction with negative findings and inconsistencies (Angst & Clayton, 1986; Apter et al., 1993; Berglund, 1984; Duberstein et al., 1994; Pokorny, 1983; Thomas, 1971), it does indicate that the *strength* of the relationship between hostility and completed suicide in young people deserves more study.

Only one study has reported on the prevalence rates of Axis II disorders in a representative sample of completed suicides across the life course (Isometsä et al., 1996). Several reports on the prevalence of Axis II disorders and traits in age-defined subsamples of that population have also been reported (Henriksson et al., 1995; Marttunen et al., 1991; Marttunen, Aro, Henriksson, & Lönnqvist, 1994). Although the Finnish team has not explicitly examined the relationship between age and Axis II disorders in their sample, it appears that the prevalence of hostility-related personality disorders decreased with age. The extent to which this decrease mirrors the decrease in hostility-related Axis II disorders in the community (B. J. Cohen et al., 1994) is unknown. Moreover, hostility has not been implicated in any other studies of older samples that have explicitly examined the issue (Duberstein et al., 1994; Paffenbarger et al., 1994; Rich et al., 1986). Others do not mention hostility, despite paying careful attention to other psychological themes (Barraclough, 1971; Carney et al., 1994; Clark, 1991; M. Miller, 1978; Pearson et al., 1993; Ross et al., 1990). For example, Clark (1991) reported that approximately 9% of his sample of older suicide victims met criteria for a personality disorder, but the nature of the disorder was not specified. However, hostility is not a central construct in Clark's (1993) empirically based theory of vulnerability to late-life suicide, so it is unlikely that these personality disorders were hostility-related. Although the absence of such discussion, by itself, does not mean that hostility is unimportant in suicide in older adults, most evidence indicates that the relationship between hostility and suicide is confined to the young and, perhaps, middle-aged population.

The relationship between hostility and completed suicide must be interpreted in a broader psychological framework. Recommendations for assessment and intervention that are based on the finding that hostility is the only affect consistently associated with suicide would differ substantially from those based on the observation that hostility is one of several interrelated features of individuals who commit suicide. Indeed, the review indicated that in addition to hostility, depressive negativism, anxious worry, painful self-consciousness, and hopelessness were also salient in younger suicide victims. Older suicides, although not characterized by hostility, tended to be plagued by depression, hopelessness, self-consciousness, and perhaps anxiety. Although we are confident that the pattern of affects and traits outlined here are associated with suicide, unfortunately there are no empirical data from which we may draw conclusions about how they covary *within* persons (see Allport, 1937/1961; Magnusson, 1990; Murray, 1981; Runyan, 1983). The formulations that follow are based on the assumption that these constructs do indeed covary within individuals.

Formulations of Psychological Vulnerability to Suicide

The investigations reviewed in this chapter, other research not reviewed in detail, and our experience conducting psychological autopsies on more than 200 suicide victims provide a framework from which we begin to develop psychodynamic formulations of completed suicide in younger and older adults. It is expected that other life-stage–specific conceptualizations will be developed as more is learned about suicide in specific age groups. By focusing on age, we do not mean to imply that formulations organized around other constructs, such as gender or major psychiatric illness, are unnecessary or unimportant.

Younger adults. Most contemporary cognitive or social learning theories would not predict that an identifiable subset of hopeless, anxious, depressed, and self-conscious people will also be hostile. Normative studies reveal no significant relationship between hostility and hopelessness, anxiety, depression, and self-consciousness. In contrast, psychodynamic theory, particularly its constructs of orality and oral aggression (Abraham, 1924/1949; Masling, 1986) can account for these relations and another finding not reviewed in this chapter: Younger people who drink alcohol heavily are at increased risk for suicide (Fawcett et al., 1987, 1990; Fowler, Rich, & Young, 1986; Klatsky & Armstrong, 1993; Nielsen, Wang, & Bille-Brahe, 1990; Romanov et al., 1994; Tomlinson-Keasy et al., 1986; see also G. E. Murphy, 1992).

We hypothesize that younger suicides may be characterized by both oral-dependent affects and oral aggression, although it must be conceded that empirical research has not yet established that these constructs cluster in younger suicide victims.

Psychodynamic theory posits, and empirical research has generally shown, that oral-dependent individuals are vulnerable to feelings of hopelessness, helplessness, anxiety, and depression and to substance abuse (Bornstein, 1992, 1993). Perhaps the two most characteristic features of mildly depressed dependent people is their sense of feeling incomplete and unintegrated and their impoverished capacity to endure solitude (Bornstein, Poynton, & Masling, 1985; Masling, 1986). Younger people who overvalue their need for closeness may believe that they have been or will be abandoned or rejected, activating the fantasy that they cannot live without the yearned-for other. Young adults who are both dependent and hostile aggressively may enact this fantasy.

The notion that younger suicides may be characterized by an unusual blend of affects and attitudes is not new. As already noted, the *Mourning and Melancholia* formulation suggests that oral regression and hostility are important features of the suicidal state. Similarly, Bakan (1967) observed that conflicting affective themes or trends are present in suicidal persons: "Considering the usual sense of the terms 'conforming' and 'psychopathic personality,' putting them together appears a contradiction in terms, yet the suicide seems to be such that both terms apply" (p. 120). One study supports the plausibility of this observation. Shafii and colleagues (1985) reported that 70% of adolescent victims showed evidence of antisocial behavior, and 65% were extremely quiet, socially aloof, and lonely. Clearly, a substantial minority of this sample was characterized by an unusual blend of antisocial *and* inhibited traits and behaviors. Kagan's (1989) observation that some of the most interesting and significant findings are those revealing dimensions that are uncorrelated in one population but correlated in another seems particularly applicable to the notion that younger suicide victims are both oral-dependent and hostile. The following case example, culled from our retrospective psychological autopsy study (Conwell et al., 1996), reveals this possibility and more broadly illustrates the limitations of a psychological formulation of suicide that emphasizes the role of hostility independent of other important affects.

Mr. A was a 36-year-old, separated, White, high-school–educated, self-employed father with one child. He committed suicide by drug ingestion. In the words of his therapist, Mr. A began a "fast, hard, downhill slide" following his mother's death in a motor vehicle accident 5 months earlier. Mr. A's consumption of both alcohol and cocaine increased and apparently remained a severe problem until his own death. This exacerbated the tension in his already strained and abusive relationship with his second wife. Mr. A aggressively beat his wife 2 weeks after his mother's death, prompting Mrs. A to move out of the family home the next day. Mr. A responded by slitting his wrists. After receiving outpatient medical attention, Mr. A was discharged with no follow-up plan. Over the next 4 months, his level of functioning deteriorated dramatically. He binged on cocaine and stopped working. Contacts with health care providers were limited to two conjoint marital therapy sessions and two visits to his physician, during which time he requested Antabuse and Ativan.

Mr. A's lengthy suicide note to his estranged wife revealed significant feelings of loneliness ("My biggest fear in life. . . . The past four months have been unbearable") and grief ("Everything that really mattered to me is gone, mom, you and X [daughter], and my business. These were my whole life."). He concluded with a hostile paragraph designed to instill guilt: "You have the power to destroy another person's life. You have the power over me and always have. Well my life is destroyed. But it's not all your fault. . . . P.S. Remember when I said I wouldn't live without you and X. Guess it was true."

Older adults. The unusual cluster of affects so prominent in younger suicides is not as salient in older victims as are depression, self-consciousness, and hopelessness. Our own psychological autopsy study suggests that older suicide victims are cognitively rigid, showing a preference for the familiar and routine (Duberstein, 1995; Duberstein et al., 1994). Their lives have been rigidly maintained or organized by a goal that is no longer attainable or life-sustaining.

Loss of either a goal or routine can be catastrophic. The roles of younger adulthood—member of the workforce, spouse, parent—are relatively concrete and well structured. Those of older adulthood are not, having evolved over a shorter period of time. As the expected life span has increased in technologically advanced countries, the culturally prescribed roles and tasks of later adulthood have undergone fairly rapid change. Consequently, there is less cultural constraint, less structure, and more ambiguity in the lives of older adults (Kuypers & Bengston, 1973).

The increased ambiguity associated with aging is reflected in Erikson's (1950) concept of "psychosocial tasks," now almost five decades old but perhaps more salient than ever. Ego integrity, the primary life task of older adulthood, refers to a number of constituent affective and attitudinal states, including an "acceptance of one's own and only life cycle as something that had to be had and that, by necessity, permitted of no substitution" and a feeling of "comradeship with the ordering ways of distant times and different pursuits" (p. 268). The latter attitude pertains to an appreciation of one's life in the context of one's familial and social fabric, including one's association to generations past and future. These attitudes probably do not suddenly appear but are a product of fairly intensive life review (Butler, 1963). Accepting one's life as it has been lived allows one to relinquish control over one's eventual death. Difficulty negotiating this task poses a major problem that suicide solves unambiguously and permanently: the fear of not actively participating in one's death (Erikson & Jacobs, 1989). Whereas the yearning for interpersonal closeness may be a central theme in the lives of younger victims, regrets over conceding autonomy may be central to the psychological experience of older victims (cf. Blatt, 1990).

The discursiveness of Erikson's (1950) discussion of late-life tasks mirrors their ambiguity. Although the paucity of research linking them with standard personality traits and affects is thus not surprising, we speculate that people who are depressed, self-conscious about role experimentation, and not open to new experiences are especially vulnerable to malevolent consequences of role ambiguity, including suicide. The following case, investigated as part of our psychological autopsy study (Conwell et al., 1996), illustrates this possibility.

> Mr. B was an 82-year-old White retired construction worker with an eighth-grade education. He had lived alone since his wife's death in 1980. He committed suicide by slashing his neck, leaving no note. Mr. B's son recalled the gradual onset of depressive symptoms over the last year of his life. The syndrome became better defined in the last 2 months. Depressed mood, loss of interest and pleasure in his children and grandchildren, social withdrawal, hypersomnia, fluctuating psychomotor change with periods of retardation and agitation, low self-esteem, and suicidal ideation were prominent symptoms.
>
> Mr. B's life had been relatively stable since his wife's death. His relationship with his children was relatively free of conflict, and he was in generally good health and able to live independently in his own residence. A quiet and methodical man, his sole source of plea-

sure appeared to be his daily 5-mile walk, chiefly "out of habit." Mr. B had few friends outside the family, was involved in no groups, and had no hobbies. He never read for pleasure, was uninterested in art and sports, and was reluctant to make idle conversation, saying, "What's the point? We're not going to change anything." His tolerance of physical illness and pain was low, according to his son, who noted him to be irritable and anxious when anyone around him was sick. A relatively minor back injury suffered 2 months prior to death coincided with the exacerbation of his depressive symptoms and made it impossible for him to take his daily walk.

There were at least two clues to suicide in the weeks prior to death. Although Mr. B had long stopped smoking, a result of his emphysema and bronchitis, his son discovered him smoking in his apartment 10 days prior to death. Mr. B became quite agitated, commenting to his son that he had "nothing left to live for and nothing to do." Anxious about what he felt was confronting his father, and somewhat shocked by his father's unprecedented expression of emotion, the son took no action. A week later, Mr. B visited his urologist, had an uncomplicated urethral dilation, but thereafter refused to have a foley catheter left in place, as was the ordinary procedure for his recurrent urethral strictures, a consequence of gonorrhea as a younger man. Mr. B's physician reported that Mr. B requested arsenic to "put his dog to sleep." Mr. B did not have a dog. In the final contacts with family on the night before his death, he was cheerful and outgoing, seemingly improved. He explained where a key had been hidden outside of his apartment, in case anyone needed to gain entry. He gave his son a birthday card to deliver to his granddaughter, returned home, laid out all of his papers, paid his rent, and took his life the following day.

Implications

We end the chapter by discussing its implications for psychodynamic theory, psychobiological formulations, programmatic empirical research, and clinical assessment.

The role of age and hostility in psychodynamic theories of suicide. Our observation that psychological vulnerability to suicide varies across the life course reinforces the importance of considering the age of the patient in applications of psychodynamic theory. Too often, life course issues have not been considered, perhaps in part because they have not often been explicitly articulated. Whereas Zilboorg (1936) and Hendin (1991) called attention to the life course, Freud (1917/1957) did not. Psychodynamic theories of suicide must systematically consider these issues.

No investigation to date has directly tested Freud's notion that suicide results in part from retroflexed hostility. There is, however, moderately strong evidence of an association between hostility toward others and suicide. Psychodynamic formulations of suicide should consider the strong possibility that retroflexed hostility and hostility toward others are not mutually exclusive phenomena in younger suicidal patients.

Integrative models of the psychobiology of suicide. Abundant evidence supports an association between suicidal behavior and altered function of the central nervous system (CNS) monoamine neurotransmitter, serotonin (5-hydroxytryptamine [5-HT]). Among the earliest findings were diminished levels of 5-HT and its metabolite, 5-hydroxyindoleacetic acid (5-HIAA) in the brains of suicide victims compared with controls (see Stanley, Mann, & Cohen, 1986 for a review). Methodological limitations of working in postmortem tissue with unstable neurochemical compounds subsequently led investigators to study 5-HT receptors. $5-HT_2$ receptors are located on the postsynaptic membrane. With few exceptions (Cheetham, Crompton, Katona, & Horton, 1988; Gross-Isseroff, Salama, Israeli, & Biegon, 1990), studies have repeatedly found increased binding of radiolabeled $5-HT_2$ receptor ligands in the frontal cortex of suicides compared with controls (Arora & Meltzer, 1989; Mann, Stanley, McBride, & McEwen, 1986; Stanley & Mann, 1983). 5-HT reuptake sites are marked by receptors on the presynaptic membrane. Although results have been mixed, several reports have noted significantly decreased binding at these sites in suicides compared with controls (Arató et al., 1991; Crow et al., 1984; Stanley, Virgilio, & Gershon, 1982).

No attempts have been made to correlate changes in central serotonin function with systematic measures of affect or behavior. However, Åsberg, Träskman, and Thoren (1976) noted an association among depressed patients between low cerebrospinal fluid (CSF) levels of 5-HIAA and the incidence of attempted suicide, particularly of a violent and aggressive nature. Prospective follow-up of suicide attempters suggested that those with low CSF 5-HIAA levels were 10 times more likely subsequently to die by their own hand than were attempters with normal or high CSF 5-HIAA levels (Åsberg, Nordström, & Träskman-Bendz, 1986). The association between CSF serotonin metabolites and violent suicidal acts has been repeatedly confirmed (Åsberg et al., 1986). These and similar findings have led to the hypotheses that completed suicide results from hostile tendencies that could be assessed via the Rorschach (Rydin, Åsberg, Edman, & Schalling, 1990) and are the behavioral correlates of altered central serotonin function.

The notion that the psychological vulnerability to suicide differs with age has important implications for theories of the psychobiology of suicide. If hostility characterizes suicide in younger but not older victims, and altered serotonergic function is associated with suicide, then it is possible that (a) altered central 5-HT function may be indirectly related to hostility; (b) hostility may be the behavioral expression of CNS 5-HT abnormalities in earlier life but not later on, perhaps because of its mediation by other aging-related biological, psychological, or social factors; or (c) the biological mechanisms of suicidal behavior may differ as a function of age. In other words, although abnormalities in central serotonin may predispose individuals to suicide at younger ages, other neurochemical systems may play a more prominent role in later years.

Unfortunately, relatively little is known about changes in most neurochemical systems with normal aging. Nor has age been adequately considered as a relevant variable in postmortem tissue studies of suicide victims and controls. The limited available data suggest, however, that the dopamine, γ-aminobutyric, and opiate systems, as well as the hypothalamic–pituitary–adrenal (HPA) axes should be considered potentially significant to suicide in elderly people (see Conwell, Raby, & Caine, 1995, for a review).

Programmatic empirical research. Research examining the relations of hostility and other affects to suicide typically has not considered the role of stressful life circumstances. Instead, it has been designed to answer the question "Are suicide victims more hostile than those who do not commit suicide?" This is a "main effects" question, in contrast to the one that considers interactions with stressful life circumstances: "Are hostile people more likely than nonhostile people to commit suicide when confronted with loss?" Failure to raise this and other issues that bear on the interaction of personality and stressful circumstances is a significant limitation. Psychodynamic writings on suicide (Buie & Maltsberger, 1989; Hendin, 1991), including *Mourning and Melancholia*, offer hypotheses that are "interactions," not main effects. *Mourning and Melancholia* is first and foremost a description of the relations of affect to loss, interpreted in its broadest sense. Loss unleashes the hostility that plays so central a role in the psychodynamic formulation of suicide. Far from being a trivial detail, loss is a necessary component of the formulation.

An ideal test of this and other interaction hypotheses would involve both a premorbid multimethod assessment of hostility (i.e., self-report, informant report, projective ratings), as well as a retrospective examination, using psychological autopsy methodology, of stressful circumstances prior to death. Although no study meets all these requirements, both Essen-Moller's Lundby Study (Hagnell & Rorsman 1978, 1979, 1980) and Weissman's study of childhood depression and suicide (Rao et al., 1993) combined retrospective and prospective design elements. They are thus potentially superior to other published studies. They do not permit firm conclusions about the role of hostility and other affects in completed suicide, however, because of inadequate sample sizes and because premorbid multimethod affect assessments were not conducted. Researchers could use extant longitudinal survey databases linked with the National Death Index and conduct brief retrospective interviews with informants, a relatively inexpensive strategy by which the interaction hypothesis could be tested.

In general, inadequate sample sizes and instrumentation have impeded research on completed suicide, as have the use of samples that are not representative of the population of suicides. Multisite collaborative efforts using psychological assessment methods that are brief yet reliable may eliminate these structural barriers. It is true that meta-analysis may mitigate the problem of small samples and provide an answer to the main effects question: "Are suicide victims more hostile than those who do not commit suicide?" However, it cannot overcome the problems of nonrepresentative samples and inadequate instrumentation. Furthermore, we question whether this main effects question merits consideration and would encourage instead both original research and replications of studies on psychological constructs that increase vulnerability to suicide in particular age groups, especially those constituting the second half of life.

Clinical assessment and intervention. *Younger patients.* The expectation among clinicians that suicidal persons will be hostile is one of Freud's legacies. This review provides support for the position that young people who commit suicide are not only hostile, but have complex dependency-related affects as well. The psychologist assessing suicide potential among aggressive, hostile young adults must conduct a careful psychodynamic interview with special emphasis on dependency issues, or what has been termed "the patient's autonomous capacities to maintain identity and self-worth" (Buie & Maltsberger, 1989, p. 64).

For young adult patients vulnerable to suicide, loved ones are not merely life-sustaining, they are life-defining. Given this dependency, preoccupation with a (lost) loved one may be prominent. Clinically, we have been struck by the proportion of young completed suicides, typically men, who were legally (and quite reasonably) prevented from seeing their partner in the weeks prior to death. Oral-dependent traits may also be evident, manifest as increased drinking, smoking, or substance use when anxiously alone.

Oscillating between activity and passivity, trust and mistrust, naivete and cynicism, hope and hopelessness, rageful attack and fearful cower, it is not unusual for younger suicidal individuals to present a mixed and confusing clinical picture. Rado's (1956) discussion of the "struggle between fear and rage" and Klein's (1935) depiction of the "depressive position" both emphasized the juxtaposition of anger with an amalgam of dependency-related affects, such as sadness and fear. These blends may reflect intrapsychic conflicts and may ultimately result in distorted communication of wishes (Fawcett, Leff, & Bunney, 1969), confounding family members, clinicians, and researchers.

Through the process of projective identification, helpless angry patients induce helplessness and anger in the clinician. The rage experienced by clinicians in response to hopeless, depressed, dependent, and covertly help-rejecting suicidal patients, as well as some nonsuicidal patients, may develop into a profound countertransference hate (Maltsberger & Buie, 1974). Identification and examination of the clinician's countertransference in supervision or consultation can illuminate and enhance the treatment (Talbot, 1995) and aid in the management of suicidal behaviors.

Older patients. The concept of countertransference hate, although applicable to patients across the life course, is perhaps more clinically useful in managing younger than older patients. Whereas aspects of countertransference reactions to older patients have been discussed (Colarusso & Nemiroff, 1987; Grotjahn, 1955), the idiosyncratic aspects of countertransference reactions to older suicidal patients have received far less attention. We will sketch a few tentative ideas. Countertransference errors are not uncommon among clinicians who work with older adults. Perhaps the most pernicious is acting on the belief

that suicide in older adults is nothing more complicated than a rational, sensible response to medical illness, chronic pain, or loss in a person with little time left to live. Because older suicidal patients are
unlikely to seek psychotherapeutic intervention, psychologists are
more likely to see these patients in medical and primary care settings.
Psychologists and other clinicians in these settings who perceive
themselves primarily as curers, saviors, or protectors, and derive
meaning primarily from powerful and prestigious roles no longer
accessible to their elderly patients, may be especially uncomfortable
(Conwell, 1994). They may be more likely than others to believe that
suicide in late life is "reasonable" and perhaps should be assisted or facilitated, not because the patients are old, but because action-oriented
clinicians are unable to bear their own powerlessness when confronted
with patients who hold rigid views concerning their sense of inadequacy and lack of potential for change.[6] Even if such patients do seek

---

[6]It is not our intent here to imply that assisted suicide inevitably results
from health care providers' countertransference errors or unexamined moti-
vations. Nor do we wish to imply that the patient's desire for assisted suicide
and the health care provider's desire to facilitate that process is necessarily
"pathological." Because we do not want to leave the impression that assisted
suicide is merely the product of the inability of action-oriented clinicians to
bear their own powerlessness when confronted with the demands of terminally ill patients, we expand on the assisted-suicide theme in this footnote,
using a case example.

Most assisted suicides in this country are not the public dramatic spectacles
that have come to be expected from Jack Kevorkian. Rather, it is likely that
they are enacted privately, secretly, ambivalently, and even somewhat ambigu-
ously, making it difficult to know exactly who did what to whom, and how.
An open and frank discussion and empirical examination of the psychological
pressures—some subtle, others not—experienced by all participants might be
illuminating.

That is easier said than done. Even when the patients, family members, and
health care providers are psychologically sophisticated, the psychological
state of the dying person can continue to elude understanding. Consider
Freud's death. Conflicting accounts of how Freud died have been published.
Gay's (1988) moving rendering of Sigmund Freud's death reads like an
account of an assisted suicide:

At their first meeting Freud [and his physician] Schur had settled the
delicate matters of frankness, and Freud broached an even more delicate issue: "Promise me also: when the time comes you won't let
them torment me unnecessarily." Schur promised, and the two men
shook hands on it. (pp. 642–643)
[A decade later] Schur was on the point of tears as he witnessed

or are referred for psychotherapy, they may be relatively less receptive to psychodynamically informed therapies or slower to engage in meaningful life review or reminiscence. They may even resist concrete or practical suggestions. Whereas there is no quick fix for this very difficult population, it is possible that family and group methods may be used effectively by clinicians who themselves see the potential for meaning in the lives of their patients who are bereaved, retired, sick, and in pain (Duberstein, 1995).

Conclusion

We are reasonably convinced that completed suicides in different age groups are characterized by distinct patterns of affects and traits. This review of the literature on hostility and suicide from a life-course per-

---

> Freud facing death with dignity and without self-pity. He had never seen anyone die like that. On September 21, Schur injected Freud with three centigrams of morphine—the normal dose for sedation was two centigrams—and Freud sank into a peaceful sleep. Schur repeated the injection, when he became restless, and administered a final one the next day, September 22. Freud lapsed into a coma from which he did not awake. He died at three in the morning, September 23, 1939. . . . The old stoic had kept control of his life to the end. (p. 651)

Gay (1988) defended his iconoclastic hypothesis, meticuously noting the discrepancies between his interpretation of the final act and the received wisdom. He concluded,

> I see Freud's end as a stoic suicide, carried out in his behalf, since he was too weak to act himself, by his loyal and loving physician and reluctantly acquiesced in by his no less loyal and even more loving daughter. (p. 740)

Perhaps it is mere coincidence that Gay's (1988) description of Freud—stoic, independent, headstrong, not religious—bears a striking resemblance to the portraits of less remarkable older men who have taken their own lives with neither the assistance nor acquiescence of others. On the other hand, it is an oversimplification to assume that Freud's desire to die could have been explored in psychotherapy in an effort to prevent any form of suicide—assisted or otherwise. Likewise, it is a mistake to presume Schur's inability to bear his own powerlessness in the face of Freud's requests. Yet without data, one can only presume or assume. The delicate drama enacted by health care providers, their terminally ill patients, and the patients' families ought to be more rigorously examined from a variety of psychological and sociological perspectives. These investigations will uncover issues and dilemmas that are currently obscure and are superior to ignoring the problem, which has been the option preferred until recently. Ignoring the processes and problems associated with end-of-life decision making has not eliminated them.

spective reveals the clinical danger of placing undue emphasis on the affective characteristics of the suicide victim independent of life circumstance, and it suggests the need to consider the possibility that different affective features represent vulnerabilities to suicide at different positions in the life course. Whether these differences represent enduring features of nature or fleeting reflections of birth cohort and historical period remains to be discovered. Too often, psychodynamically oriented clinicians and researchers have overlooked both psychological development beyond young adulthood and its cultural context. Continued development of psychoanalysis as developmental psychology promises to change that and rekindle psychodynamic scholarship on matters of life and death.

Do psychological and social characteristics confer risk for specific causes of death, such as suicide, or death from all causes? We have deliberately (and conveniently) delayed discussion of this issue. But it must be broached at least briefly, if only to connect our review with some broader issues in psychodynamics and biomedical research. Freud (1920/1957) emphasized that manifestations of self-destruction are rarely visible and are highly varied. Menninger's (1938/1985) discussion of partial suicide, focal suicide, and organic suicide expanded on this idea, and Bakan's (1968) notion that "every person has a fatal disease, the decentralization of the telos, from which he must eventually die" (p. 44) is yet another variant of the same theme. The controversial nature of these ideas, the dramatic language ("death instinct," "organic suicide") with which they were conveyed, and the lack of supporting scientific evidence may have impeded their serious consideration at a time when medicine was preoccupied with the doctrine of specific etiology and issues pertaining to death and dying were rarely discussed openly. But these are different times. Although research on the biological limitations of longevity has gained momentum and a public forum (Hayflick, 1994), another area of investigation—less technical but as important and better developed—indicates that there are psychologically determined limits to longevity and that humans currently play a substantial role in precipitating the diseases that bring about their demise. Approximately 25% to 40% of cancer deaths (Doll & Peto, 1981) and 19% of all deaths in the United States (McGinnis & Foege, 1993) could be attributed to tobacco. Alcohol misuse accounts for roughly 5% of the deaths in this country (McGinnis & Foege, 1993); efforts to quantify its effects on physical morbidity and psychological suffering remain major public health challenges.

Overall mortality estimates attributable to hostility are unavailable, but hostility has been associated with deaths due not only to suicide but also to accidents (Romanov et al., 1994) and heart disease (Almada et al., 1991) as well. As epidemiologic research continues to uncover evidence for the notion that psychosocial considerations place individuals at risk for a premature death from a variety of nonspecific causes (Allgulander & Lavori, 1993; Bruce, Leaf, Rozal, Florio, & Hoff, 1994; H. S. Friedman et al., 1995; J. M. Murphy, Monson, Olivier, Sobol, & Leighton, 1987), as neuroscientists continue to postulate mechanisms that mediate this relationship (e.g., Sapolsky, 1992), and as our culture begins open discussion (Nuland, 1994) and vehement debate about death and dying, it is time for psychodynamic scholars to reconsider the psychology of self-determined death, in all its vicissitudes.

References

Abraham, K. (1949). The influence of oral eroticism on character formation. In C. A. D. Bryan & A. Strachey (Eds. and Trans.), *Selected papers of Karl Abraham, M.D.* (pp. 399–406). London: Hogarth Press. (Original work published 1924)

Abramson, L. Y., Metalsky, G. I., & Alloy, L. B. (1989). Hopelessness depression: A theory-based subtype of depression. *Psychological Bulletin, 96,* 358–372.

Allebeck, P., & Allgulander, C. (1990). Suicide among young men: Psychiatric illness, deviant behavior and substance abuse. *Acta Psychiatrica Scandinavica, 81,* 565–570.

Allebeck, P., Allgulander, C., & Fisher, L. (1988). Predictors of completed suicide in a cohort of 50,465 young men: Role of personality and deviant behavior. *British Medical Journal, 297,* 176–178.

Allgulander, C. (1994). Suicide and mortality patterns in anxiety neurosis and depressive neurosis. *Archives of General Psychiatry, 51,* 708–712.

Allgulander, C., & Lavori, P. W. (1991). Excess mortality among 3,302 patients with "pure" anxiety neurosis. *Archives of General Psychiatry, 48,* 599–602.

Allport, G. (1961). *Pattern and growth in personality.* New York: Holt, Rinehart & Winston. (Original work published 1937)

Almada, S. J., Zonderman, A. B., Shekelle, R. B., Dyer, A. R., Daviglus, M. L., Costa, P. T., Jr., & Stamler, J. (1991). Neuroticism and cynicism and risk of death in middle-aged men: The Western Electric Study. *Psychosomatic Medicine, 53,* 165–175.

Alvarez, A. (1970). *The savage god.* New York: Random House.

American Psychiatric Association. (1994). *Diagnostic and statistical manual of mental disorders* (4th ed.). Washington, DC: Author.

Angst, J., & Clayton, P. (1986). Premorbid personality of depressive, bipolar, and schizophrenic patients with special reference to suicidal issues. *Comprehensive Psychiatry, 27,* 511–531.

Apter, A., Bleich, A., King, R., Kron, S., Fluch, A., Kotler, M., & Cohen, D. (1993). Death without warning? A clinical postmortem study of suicide in 43 Israeli adolescent males. *Archives of General Psychiatry, 50,* 138–142.

Arató, M., Demeter, E., Rihmer, Z., & Somogyi, E. (1988). Retrospective psychiatric assessment of 200 suicides in Budapest. *Acta Psychiatrica Scandinavica, 77,* 454–456.

Arató, M., Tekes, K., Tóthfalusi, L., Magyar, K., Palkovits, M., Frecska, E., Falus, A., & MacCrimmon, D. J. (1991). Reversed hemispheric asymmetry of imipramine binding in suicide victims. *Biological Psychiatry, 29,* 699–702.

Arora, R. C., & Meltzer, H. Y. (1989). Serotonergic measures in the brains of suicide victims: 5-HT$_2$ binding sites in the frontal cortex of suicide victims and control subjects. *American Journal of Psychiatry, 146,* 730–736.

Åsberg, M., Träskman, L., & Thoren, P. (1976). 5-HIAA in cerebrospinal fluid: A biochemical suicide predictor? *Archives of General Psychiatry, 33,* 1193–1197.

Åsberg, M., Nordström, P., & Träskman-Bendz, L. (1986). Cerebrospinal fluid studies in suicide: An overview. *Annals of the New York Academy of Sciences, 487,* 243–255.

Asgard, U. (1990). A psychiatric study of suicide among urban Swedish women. *Acta Psychiatrica Scandinavia, 82,* 115–124.

Backett, S. A. (1987). Suicide in Scottish prisons. *British Journal of Psychiatry, 151,* 218–221.

Bakan, D. (1967). *On method: Towards a reconstruction of psychological investigation.* San Francisco: Jossey-Bass.

Bakan, D. (1968). *Disease, pain, and sacrifice: Toward a psychology of suffering.* Boston: Beacon Press.

Barraclough, B. M. (1971). Suicide in the elderly: Recent developments in psychogeriatrics [Special supplement]. *British Journal of Psychiatry, 6,* 87–97.

Barraclough, B. M., Bunch, J., Nelson, B., & Sainsbury, P. (1974). 100 cases of suicide: Clinical aspects. *British Journal of Psychiatry, 125,* 355–373.

Baumeister, R. F. (1990). Suicide as escape from self. *Psychological Review, 97,* 90–113.

Beck, A. T. (1983). Cognitive therapy of depression: New perspectives. In P. J. Clayton & J. E. Barrett (Eds.), *Treatment of depression: Old controversies and new approaches* (pp. 265–290). New York: Raven Press.

Beck, A. T., Brown, G., Berchick, R., Stewart, B., & Steer, R. (1990). Relationship between hopelessness and ultimate suicide: A replication with psychiatric outpatients. *American Journal of Psychiatry, 147,* 190–195.

Beck, A., Brown, G., & Steer, R. (1989). Prediction of eventual suicide in psychiatric inpatients by clinical ratings of hopelessness. *Journal of Consulting and Clinical Psychology, 57,* 309–310.

Beck, A. T., & Steer, R. A. (1989). Clinical predictors of eventual suicide: A 5- to 10-year prospective study of suicide attempters. *Journal of Affective Disorders, 17,* 203–209.

Beck, A. T., Steer, R. A., Kovacs, M., & Garrison, B. (1985). Hopelessness and eventual suicide: A 10-year prospective study of patients hospitalized with suicidal ideation. *American Journal of Psychiatry, 142,* 559–563.

Beck, A. T., Steer, R. A., & Trexler, L. D. (1989). Alcohol abuse and eventual suicide: A 5- to 10-year prospective study of alcohol-abusing suicide attempters. *Journal of Studies on Alcohol, 50,* 202–209.

Beck, A. T., Ward, C. H., Mendelson, M., Mock, J., & Erbaugh, J. (1961). An inventory for measuring depression. *Archives of General Psychiatry, 4,* 561–571.

Beck, A. T., Weissman, A., Lester, D., & Trexler, L. D. (1974). The measurement of pessimism: The Hopelessness Scale. *Journal of Consulting and Clinical Psychology, 42,* 861–865.

Berglund, M. (1984). Suicide in alcoholism: A prospective study of 88 suicides. The multidimensional diagnosis at first admission. *Archives of General Psychiatry, 41,* 888–891.

Berglund, M. (1986). Suicide in male alcoholics with peptic ulcers. *Alcoholism: Clinical and Experimental Research, 10,* 631–634.

Berglund, M., Krantz, P., & Lundqvist, G. (1987). Suicide in alcoholism: A prospective study of 55 cases with autopsy findings. *Acta Psychiatrica Scandinavica, 76,* 381–385.

Berglund, M., Krantz, P., Lundqvist, G., & Therup, L. (1987). Suicide in psychiatric patients: A prospective study of 67 cases without initial signs of severe depression or alcoholism. *Acta Psychiatrica Scandinavica, 76,* 431–437.

Berlin, J. A. (1995). Invited commentary: Benefits of heterogeneity in meta-analysis of data from epidemiologic studies. *American Journal of Epidemiology, 142,* 383–387.

Berman, A. L., & Jobes, D. A. (1991). *Adolescent suicide: Assessment and intervention.* Washington, DC: American Psychological Association.

Beskow, J., Runeson, B., & Asgard, U. (1990). Psychological autopsies: Methods and ethics. *Suicide and Life-Threatening Behavior, 20,* 307–323.

Black, D. W., Warrack, G., & Winokur, G. (1985). The Iowa Record-Linkage Study I. Suicides and accidental deaths among psychiatric patients. *Archives of General Psychiatry, 42,* 71–75.

Blatt, S. J. (1974). Levels of object representation in anaclitic and introjective depression. *Psychoanalytic Study of the Child, 29,* 107–157.

Blatt, S. J. (1990). Interpersonal relatedness and self-definition: Two personality configurations and their implications for psychopathology and psychotherapy. In J. L. Singer (Ed.), *Repression and dissociation* (pp. 299–335). Chicago: University of Chicago Press.

Blatt, S. J., & Ritzler, B. A. (1974). Suicide and the representation of transparency and cross-sections on the Rorschach. *Journal of Consulting and Clinical Psychology, 42,* 280–287.

Blumenthal, S. J., & Kupfer, D. J. (Eds.). (1990). *Suicide over the life cycle: Risk factors, assessment, and treatment of suicidal patients.* American Psychiatric Press.

Bock, E. W., & Webber, I. L. (1972). Suicide among the elderly: Isolating widowhood and mitigating alternatives. *Journal of Marriage and the Family, 34,* 24–31.

Borg, S. E., & Stahl, M. (1982). Prediction of suicide: A prospective study of suicides and controls among psychiatric patients. *Acta Psychiatrica Scandinavia, 65*, 221–232.

Bornstein, R. F. (1992). The dependent personality: Developmental, social, and clinical perspectives. *Psychological Bulletin, 112*, 3–23.

Bornstein, R. F. (1993). *The dependent personality*. New York: Guilford Press.

Bornstein, R. F., Poynton, F. G., & Masling, J. (1985). Orality and depression: An empirical study. *Psychoanalytic Psychology, 2*, 241–249.

Brådvik, L., & Berglund, M. (1993). Risk factors for suicide in melancholia: A case-record evaluation of 89 suicides and their controls. *Acta Psychiatrica Scandinavica, 87*, 306–311.

Brent, D. A. (1989). The psychological autopsy: Methodological considerations for the study of adolescent suicide. In I. S. Lann, E. K. Moscicki, & R. Maris (Eds.), *Strategies for studying suicide and suicidal behavior* (pp. 43–57). New York: Guilford Press.

Brent, D. A., Johnson, B. A., Perper, J., Conolly, J., Bridge, J., Bartle, S., & Rather, C. (1994). Personality disorder, personality traits, impulsive violence, and completed suicide in adolescents. *Journal of the American Academy of Child Adolescent Psychiatry, 33*, 1080–1086.

Brent, D. A., Perper, J. A., Goldstein, C. E., Kolko, D. J., Allan, M. J., Allman, C. J., & Zelenak, J. P. (1988). Risk factors for adolescent suicide. *Archives of General Psychiatry, 45*, 581–588.

Brent, D. A., Perper, J. A., Kolko, D. J., & Zelenak, J. P. (1988). The psychological autopsy: Methodological considerations for the study of adolescent suicide. *Journal of the American Academy of Child and Adolescent Psychiatry, 27*, 362–366.

Brent, D. A., Perper, J. A., Moritz, G., Allman, C., Friend, A., Roth, C., Schweers, J., Balach, L., & Baugher, M. (1993). Psychiatric risk factors for adolescent suicide: A case-control study. *Journal of the American Academy of Child and Adolescent Psychiatry, 27*, 362–366.

Brent, D. A., Perper, J. A., Moritz, G., Baugher, M., Schweers, J., & Roth, C. (1994). Suicide in affectively ill adolescents: A case-control study. *Journal of Affective Disorders, 31*, 193–202.

Bronisch, T. (1992). Does an attempted suicide actually have a cathartic effect? *Acta Psychiatrica Scandinavia, 86*, 228–232.

Bronisch, T., & Hecht, H. (1992). Prospective long-term follow-up of depressed patients with and without suicide attempts. *European Archives of Psychiatry and Clinical Neuroscience, 242*, 13–19.

Brown, G. L., & Goodwin, F. K. (1986). Cerebrospinal fluid correlates of suicide attempts and aggression. *Annals of the New York Academy of Sciences, 487*, 175–188.

Bruce, M. L., Leaf, P. J., Rozal, G. P., Florio, L., & Hoff, R. A. (1994). Psychiatric status and 9-year mortality data in the New Haven Epidemiologic Catchment Area Study. *American Journal of Psychiatry, 151*, 716–721.

Buie, D. H., & Maltsberger, J. T. (1989). The psychological vulnerability to suicide. In D. Jacobs & H. N. Brown (Eds.), *Suicide: Understanding and responding* (pp. 59–72). Madison, CT: International Universities Press.

Butler, R. N. (1963). The life review: An interpretation of reminiscence in the aged. *Psychiatry, 26,* 65–76.

Caldwell, C. B., & Gottesman, I. I. (1990). Schizophrenics kill themselves too: A review of risk factors for suicide. *Schizophrenia Bulletin, 16,* 571–589

Carney, S. S., Rich, C. L., Burk, P. A., & Fowler, R. C. (1994). Suicide over 60: The San Diego Study. *Journal of the American Geriatrics Society, 42,* 174–180.

Caspi, A., & Bem, D. J. (1990). Personality continuity and change across the life course. In L. A. Pervin (Ed.), *Handbook of personality: Theory and research* (pp. 549–575). New York: Guilford Press.

Chapman, T. F., Mannuzza, S., Klein, D. F., & Fyer, A. J. (1994). Effects of informant mental disorder on psychiatric family history data. *American Journal of Psychiatry, 151,* 574–579.

Cheetham, S. C., Crompton, M. R., Katona, C. L. E., & Horton, R. W. (1988). Brain 5-HT$_2$ receptor binding sites in depressed suicide victims. *Brain Research, 443,* 272–280.

Cheng, A. T. A. (1995). Mental illness and suicide: A case-control study in East Taiwan. *Archives of General Psychiatry, 52,* 594–603.

Chodorow, N. (1978). *The reproduction of mothering.* Berkeley, CA: University of California Press.

Chynoweth, R., Tonge, J. I., & Armstrong, J. (1980). Suicide in Brisbane—A retrospective psychosocial study. *Australian and New Zealand Journal of Psychiatry, 14,* 37–45.

Clark, D. C. (1991, January 28). *Suicide among the elderly* [Final report to the AARP Andrus Foundation]. (Available from David C. Clark, PhD, Center for Suicide Research and Prevention, Rush-Presbyterian-St. Luke's Medical Center, 1725 West Harrison St., Suite 955, Chicago, IL 61612.)

Clark, D. C. (1993). Narcissistic crises of aging and suicidal despair. *Suicide and Life-Threatening Behavior, 23,* 21–26.

Clark, D. C., & Horton-Deutsch, S. (1992). Assessment in absentia: The value of the psychological autopsy method for studying antecedents of suicide and predicting future suicides. In R. W. Maris, A. L. Berman, J. T. Maltsberger, & R. I. Yufit (Eds.), *Assessment and prediction of suicide* (pp. 144–182). New York: Guilford Press.

Cohen, B. J., Nestadt, G., Samuels, J. F., Romanoski, A. J., McHugh, P. R., & Rabins, P. V. (1994). Personality disorder in later life: A community study. *British Journal of Psychiatry, 165,* 493–499.

Cohen, J. (1994). The earth is round (*p* <. 05). *American Psychologist, 49,* 997–1003.

Cohler, B., & Jenuwine, M. (1995). Suicide, life-course, and life story. *International Psychogeriatrics, 7,* 199–219.

Colarusso, C. A., & Nemiroff, R. A. (1987). Clinical implications of adult developmental theory. *American Journal of Psychiatry, 144,* 1263–1270.

Colditz, G. A., Burdick, E., & Mosteller, F. (1995). Heterogeneity in meta-analysis of data from epidemiologic studies: A commentary. *American Journal of Epidemiology, 142,* 371–382.

Cole, D. A. (1988). Hopelessness, social desirability, and parasuicide in two college student samples. *Journal of Consulting and Clinical Psychology, 56,* 131–136.

Colvin, C. R. (1993). "Judgable" people: Personality, behavior, and competing explanations. *Journal of Personality and Social Psychology, 64,* 861–873.

Contrada, R. J., Leventhal, H., & O'Leary, A. (1990). Personality and health. In L. A. Pervin (Ed.), *Handbook of personality: Theory and research* (pp. 638–669). New York: Guilford Press.

Conwell, Y. (1994). Physician assisted suicide. *Suicide and Life-Threatening Behavior, 24,* 326–333.

Conwell, Y., Duberstein, P. R., Cox, C., Herrmann, J., Forbes, N. T., & Caine, E. D. (1996). Relationships of age and Axis I diagnoses in victims of completed suicide: A psychological autopsy study. *American Journal of Psychiatry, 153,* 1001–1008.

Conwell, Y., Raby, W. N., & Caine, E. D. (1995). Suicide and aging: II. The psychobiological interface. *International Psychogeriatrics, 7,* 165–181.

Coryell, W. (1988). Panic disorder and mortality. *Psychiatric Clinics of North America, 11,* 433–440.

Costa, P. T., Jr., & McCrae, R. R. (1985). *The NEO Personality Inventory: Manual.* Odessa, FL: Psychological Assessment Resources.

Craik, K. (1986). Personality research methods: An historical perspective. *Journal of Personality, 54,* 19–51.

Crow, T. J., Cross, A. J., Cooper, S. J., Deakin, J. F. W., Ferrier, I. N., Johnson, J. A., Joseph, M. H., Owen, F., Poulter, M., Lofthouse, R., Corsellis, J. A. N., Chambers, D. R., Blessed, G., Pery, E. K., Pery, R. H., & Tomlinson, B. E. (1984). Neurotransmitter receptors and monoamine metabolites in the brains of patients with Alzheimer-type dementia and depression, and suicides. *Neuropharmacology, 23,* 1561–1569.

Crozier, W. R. (1990). *Shyness and embarrassment: Perspectives from social psychology.* New York: Cambridge University Press.

Curphey, T. J. (1961). The role of the social scientist in the medicolegal certification of death from suicide. In N. L. Farberow & E. S. Shneidman (Eds.), *The cry for help* (pp. 110–117). New York: McGraw-Hill.

Davidson, L. E., Berman, A. L., Jobes, D., Buzbee, H., Gantner, G., Moore-Lewis, B., & Mills, D. H. (1989). Operational criteria for determining suicide. *Journal of the American Medical Association, 261,* 360–361.

Doll, R., & Peto, R. (1981). *The causes of cancer: Quantitative estimates of available risks of cancer in the United States today.* New York: Oxford University Press.

Dorpat, T. L., & Ripley, H. S. (1960). A study of suicide in the Seattle area. *Comprehensive Psychiatry, 1,* 349–359.

Drake, R. E., & Cotton, P. G. (1986). Depression, hopelessness and suicide in chronic schizophrenia. *British Journal of Psychiatry, 148,* 554–559.

Duberstein, P. R. (1995). Openness to experience and completed suicide across the second half of life. *International Psychogeriatrics, 7,* 183–198.

Duberstein, P. R., Conwell, Y., & Caine, E. D. (1993). Interpersonal stressors, substance abuse, and suicide. *Journal of Nervous and Mental Disease, 181,* 82–87.

Duberstein, P. R., Conwell, Y., & Caine, E. D. (1994). Age differences in the personality characteristics of suicide completers: Preliminary findings from a psychological autopsy study. *Psychiatry, 57,* 213–224.

Durkheim, E. (1951). *Suicide: A study in sociology.* New York: Free Press. (Original work published in 1897)

Engel, G. L. (1963). Toward a classification of affects. In P. Knapp (Ed.), *Expression of the emotions in man* (pp. 266–294). Madison, CT: International Universities Press.

Epstein, L. C., Thomas, C. B., Shaffer, J. W., & Perlin, S. (1973). Clinical prediction of physician suicide based on medical student data. *Journal of Nervous and Mental Disease, 156,* 19–29.

Erikson, E. (1950). *Childhood and society.* New York: Norton.

Erikson, E., & Jacobs, D. (1989). Foreword: A dialogue with Erik H. Erikson. In D. Jacobs & H. N. Brown (Eds.), *Suicide: Understanding and responding* (pp. xi–xiv). Madison, CT: International Universities Press.

Exner, J. E., & Wylie, J. (1977). Some Rorschach data concerning suicide. *Journal of Personality Assessment, 41,* 339–348.

Eysenck, N. F. (1978). An exercise in mega-silliness. *American Psychologist, 33,* 517.

Farberow, N. L., Kang, H. K., & Bullman, T. A. (1990). Combat experience and postservice psychosocial status as predictors of suicide in Vietnam veterans. *Journal of Nervous and Mental Disease, 178,* 32–37.

Farberow, N. L., & McEvoy, T. L. (1966). Suicide among patients with diagnoses of anxiety reaction or depressive reaction in general medical and surgical hospitals. *Journal of Abnormal Psychology, 71,* 287–299.

Fawcett, J., Leff, M., & Bunney, W. (1969). Suicide: Clues from interpersonal communication. *Archives of General Psychiatry, 21,* 129–139.

Fawcett, J., Scheftner, W., Clark, D., Hedeker, D., Gibbons, R., & Coryell, W. (1987). Clinical predictors of suicide in patients with major affective disorder: A controlled prospective study. *American Journal of Psychiatry, 144,* 35–40.

Fawcett, J., Scheftner, W., Fogg, L., Clark, D., Young, M. A., Hedeker, D., & Gibbons, R. (1990). Time-related predictors of suicide in major affective disorder. *American Journal of Psychiatry, 147,* 1189–1194.

Fowler, R., Rich, C., & Young, D. (1986). San Diego Suicide Study: II. Substance abuse in young cases. *Archives of General Psychiatry, 43,* 962–965.

Freud, S. (1957). Mourning and melancholia. In J. Strachey (Ed. and Trans.), *The standard edition of the complete psychological works of Sigmund Freud* (Vol. 14, pp. 239–260). London: Hogarth Press. (Original work published 1917)

Freud, S. (1957). Beyond the pleasure principle. In J. Strachey (Ed. and Trans.), *The standard edition of the complete psychological works of Sigmund Freud* (Vol. 18, pp. 7–64). London: Hogarth Press. (Original work published 1920)

Friedman, H. S., Tucker, J. S., Schwartz, J. E., Tomlinson-Keasey, C., Martin, L., & Wingard, D. L., & Criqui, M. H. (1995). Psychosocial and behavioral predictors of longevity: The aging and death of the "Termites." *American Psychologist, 50,* 69–78.

Friedman, P. (1967). Suicide among police: A study of ninety-three suicides among New York City policemen, 1934–1940. In E. S. Shneidman (Ed.), *Essays in self-destruction* (pp. 414–449). New York: Science House.

Funder, D. C., & Dobroth, K. M. (1987). Differences between traits: Properties associated with interjudge agreement. *Journal of Personality and Social Psychology, 52,* 409–418.

Gay, P. (1988). *Freud: A life for our time.* New York: Norton.

Gilligan, C. (1982). *In a different voice.* Cambridge, MA: Harvard University Press.

Goldsmith, S. J., Fyer, M., & Frances, A. (1990). Personality and suicide. In S. J. Blumenthal & D. J. Kupfer (Eds.), *Suicide over the life cycle* (pp. 155–176). Washington, DC: American Psychiatric Press.

Goodwin, F. K., & Jamison, K. (1990). *Manic depressive illness.* New York: Oxford University Press.

Graves, P. L., & Thomas, C. B. (1991). Habits of nervous tension and suicide. *Suicide and Life-Threatening Behavior, 21,* 91–105.

Gross-Isseroff, R., Salama, D., Israeli, M., & Biegon, A. (1990). Autoradiographic analysis of [^{3}H]ketanserin binding in the human brain postmortem: Effect of suicide. *Brain Research, 507,* 208–215.

Grotjahn, M. (1955). Analytic psychotherapy with the elderly. *Psychoanalytic Review, 42,* 419–427.

Gunderson, J. G., & Phillips, K. A. (1991). A current view of the interface between borderline personality disorder and depression. *American Journal of Psychiatry, 148,* 967–975.

Hagestad, G. O., & Neugarten, B. L. (1985). Age and the life course. In R. Binstock & E. Shanas (Eds.), *Handbook of society and aging* (pp. 35–61). New York: Van Nostrand Reinhold.

Hagnell, O., & Rorsman, B. (1978). Suicide and endogenous depression with somatic complaints in the Lundby Study. *Neuropsychobiology, 4,* 180–187.

Hagnell, O., & Rorsman, B. (1979). Suicide in the Lundby Study: A comparative investigation of clinical aspects. *Neuropsychobiology, 5,* 61–73.

Hagnell, O., & Rorsman, B. (1980). Suicide in the Lundby Study: A controlled prospective investigation of stressful life events. *Neuropsychobiology, 6,* 319–332.

Havens, L. (1965). The anatomy of a suicide. *New England Journal of Medicine, 272,* 401–406.

Hayflick, L. (1994). *How and why we age.* New York: Ballantine Books.

Heikkinen, M. E., Aro, H. M., Henriksson, M. M., Isometsä, E. T., Sarna, S. J., Kuoppasalmi, K. I., & Lönnqvist, J. K. (1994). Differences in recent life events between alcoholic and depressive nonalcoholic suicides. *Alcoholism: Clinical and Experimental Research, 28,* 1143–1149.

Hendin, H. (1991). Psychodynamics of suicide, with particular reference to the young. *American Journal of Psychiatry, 148,* 1150–1158.

Henriksson, M., Aro, H., Marttunen, M., Heikkinen, M., Isometsä, E., Kuoppasalmi, K., & Lönnqvist, J. (1993). Mental disorders and comorbidity in suicide. *American Journal of Psychiatry, 150,* 935–940.

Henriksson, M. M., Marttunen, M. J., Isometsä, E. T., Heikkinen, M. E., Aro, H. M., Kuoppasalmi, K. I., & Lönnqvist, J. K. (1995). Mental disorders in elderly suicide. *International Psychogeriatrics, 7,* 275–286.

Hlady, W. G., & Middaugh, J. P. (1988). The underrecording of suicides in state and national records, Alaska, 1983–1984. *Suicide and Life-Threatening Behavior, 18,* 237–244.

Hoberman, H. M., & Garfinkel, B. D. (1988). Completed suicide in children and adolescents. *Journal of the American Academy of Child and Adolescent Psychiatry, 27,* 689–695.

Isometsä, E. T., Henriksson, M. M., Aro, H. M., Heikkinen, M. E., Kuoppasalmi, K. E., & Lönnqvist, J. K. (1994). Suicide in major depression. *American Journal of Psychiatry, 151,* 530–536.

Isometsä, E. T., Henriksson, M. M., Heikkinen, M. E., Aro, H. M., Marttunen, M. J., Kuoppasalmi, K. I., & Lönnqvist, J. K. (1996). Completed suicide in personality disorders. *American Journal of Psychiatry, 153,* 667–673.

Jameison, G. R. (1936). Suicide and mental disease: A clinical analysis of one hundred cases. *Archives of Neurology and Psychiatry, 36,* 1–11.

Jordan, J. V., Kaplan, A. G., Miller, J. B., Stiver, I. P., & Surrey, J. L. (1991). *Women's growth in connection: Writings from the Stone Center.* New York: Guilford Press.

Kagan, J. (1989). *Unstable ideas: Temperament, cognition, and self.* Cambridge, MA: Harvard University Press.

Kaplan, A. G., & Klein, R. B. (1989). Women and suicide. In D. Jacobs & H. N. Brown (Eds.), *Suicide: Understanding and responding* (pp. 257–282). Madison, CT: International Universities Press.

Kaprio, J., Koskenvuo, M., & Rita, H. (1987). Mortality after bereavement: A prospective study of 95,647 widowed persons. *American Journal of Public Health, 77,* 283–287.

Klatsky, A. L., & Armstrong, M. A. (1993). Alcohol use, other traits, and risk of unnatural death: A prospective study. *Alcoholism: Clinical and Experimental Research, 17,* 1156–1162.

Kleck, G. (1988). Miscounting suicides. *Suicide and Life-Threatening Behavior, 18,* 219–231.

Klein, M. (1935). A contribution to the psychogenesis of manic-depressive states. *International Journal of Psychoanalysis, 16,* 145–174.

Kullgren, G., Renberg, E., & Jacobsson, L. (1986). An empirical study of borderline personality disorder and psychiatric suicides. *Journal of Nervous and Mental Disease, 174,* 328–331.

Kupfer, D. J., Kraemer, H. C., & Bartko, J. J. (1994). Documenting and reporting the study results of a randomized clinical trial (spicy meatballs, not pabulum). In R. F. Prien & D. S. Robinson (Eds.), *Clinical evaluation of psychotropic drugs: Principles and guidelines* (pp. 237–260). New York: Raven Press.

Kuypers, J. A., & Bengtson, V. L. (1973). Social breakdown and competence. *Human Development, 16,* 181–201.

Leckman, J. F., Sholomskas, D., Thompson, D., Belanger, A., & Weissman, M. M. (1982). Best estimate of lifetime diagnosis: A methodological study. *Archives of General Psychiatry, 39,* 879–883.

Leenaars, A. A. (1988). *Suicide notes.* New York: Human Sciences Press.

LeSage, A. D., Boyer, R., Grunberg, F., Vanier, C., Morisette, R., Menard-Buteau, C., & Loyer, M. (1994). Suicide and mental disorders: A case-control study of young men. *American Journal of Psychiatry, 151,* 1063–1068.

Lester, D. (1971). MMPI scores of old and young completed suicides. *Psychological Reports, 28,* 146.

Lester, D. (1991). Completed suicide in the gifted: A late comment on "suicide among gifted women." *Journal of Abnormal Psychology, 100,* 604–606.

Levinson, D. J., Darrow, C. D., Klein E., Levinson, M. H., & McKee, B. (1978). *The seasons of a man's life.* New York: Knopf.

Lewin, D. I. (1996). Meta-analysis: A new standard or clinical fool's gold? *Journal of NIH Research, 8,* 30–31.

Lin, N., Woelfel, M. W., & Light, S. C. (1985). The buffering effect of social support subsequent to an important life event. *Journal of Health and Social Behavior, 26,* 247–263.

Linehan, M. M. (1986). Suicidal people: One population or two? *Annals of the New York Academy of Sciences, 487,* 16–33.

Links, P. S., Mitton, J. E., & Steiner, M. (1990). Predicting outcome of borderline personality disorder. *Comprehensive Psychiatry, 31,* 490–498.

Litman, R. E., Curphey, T., Shneidman, E. S., Farberow, N. L., & Tabachnik, N. (1963). Investigations of equivocal suicides. *Journal of the American Medical Association, 184,* 924–929.

MacMahon, B., & Pugh, T. F. (1965). Suicide in the widowed. *American Journal of Epidemiology, 81,* 23–31.

Magnusson, D. (1990). Personality development from an interactional perspective. In L. A. Pervin (Ed.), *Handbook of personality: Theory and research* (pp. 193–222). New York: Guilford Press.

Maltsberger, J. T., & Buie, D. H. (1974). Countertransference hate in the treatment of suicidal patients. *Archives of General Psychiatry, 30,* 625–633.

Mann, J. J., Stanley, M., McBride, P. A., & McEwen, B. S. (1986). Increased serotonin$_2$ and ß-adrenergic receptor binding in the frontal cortices of suicide victims. *Archives of General Psychiatry, 43,* 954–959.

Maris, R. W. (1981). *Pathways to suicide.* Baltimore: Johns Hopkins University Press.

Maris, R. W., Berman, A. L., Maltsberger, J. T., & Yufit, R. I. (1992). (Eds.). *Assessment and prediction of suicide.* New York: Guilford Press.

Markus, H., & Oyserman, D. (1989). Gender and thought: The role of the self-concept. In M. Crawford & M. Hamilton (Eds.), *Gender and thought* (pp. 100–127). New York: Springer-Verlag.

Martin, R. L., Cloninger, C. R., Guze, S. B., & Clayton, P. J. (1985). Mortality in a follow-up of 500 psychiatric outpatients: Cause-specific mortality. *Archives of General Psychiatry, 42,* 58–66.

Marttunen, M. J., Aro, H. M., Henriksson, M. M., & Lönnqvist, J. K. (1991). Mental disorders in adolescent suicide: *DSM-III-R* Axes I and II diagnoses in suicides among 13- to 19-year-olds in Finland. *Archives of General Psychiatry, 48,* 834–839.

Marttunen, M. J., Aro, H. M., Henriksson, M. M., & Lönnqvist, J. K. (1994). Antisocial behavior in adolescent suicide. *Acta Psychiatrica Scandinavica, 89,* 167–173.

Masling, J. (1960). The influence of situational and interpersonal variables in projective testing. *Psychological Bulletin, 57,* 65–85.

Masling, J. (1986). Orality, pathology, and interpersonal behavior. In J. Masling (Ed.), *Empirical studies of psychoanalytical theories* (Vol. 2, pp. 73–106). Hillsdale, NJ: Erlbaum.

Masling, J. M., Johnson, C., & Saturansky, C. (1974). Oral imagery, accuracy of perceiving others, and performance in Peace Corps training. *Journal of Personality and Social Psychology, 30,* 414–419.

McGinnis, J. M., & Foege, W. H. (1993). Actual causes of death in the United States. *Journal of the American Medical Association, 270,* 2207–2212.

McIntosh, J. (1992). Epidemiology of suicide in the elderly. *Suicide and Life-Threatening Behavior, 22,* 15–35.

McIntosh, J. L., Santos, J. F., Hubbard, R. W., & Overholser, J. C. (1994). *Elder suicide: Research, theory, and treatment.* Washington, DC: American Psychological Association.

Menninger, K. (1985). *Man against himself.* New York: Harcourt Brace Jovanovich. (Original work published 1938)

Miles, C. P. (1977). Conditions predisposing to suicide: A review. *Journal of Nervous and Mental Disease, 164,* 231–246.

Miller, J. B. (1976). *Toward a new psychology of women.* Boston: Beacon Press.

Miller, M. (1978). Geriatric suicide: The Arizona study. *The Gerontologist, 18,* 488–495.

Modestin, J., & Wurmle, O. (1989). Role of modelling in inpatient suicide: A lack of supporting evidence. *British Journal of Psychiatry, 155,* 511–514.

Monk, M. (1987). Epidemiology of suicide. *Epidemiologic Reviews, 9,* 51–69.

Murphy, G. E. (1992). *Suicide in alcoholism.* New York: Oxford University Press.

Murphy, G. E., & Robins, E. (1967). Social factors in suicide. *Journal of the American Medical Association, 199,* 303–308.

Murphy, J. M., Monson, R. R., Olivier, D. C., Sobol, A. M., & Leighton, A. H. (1987). Affective disorders and mortality. *Archives of General Psychiatry, 44,* 473–480.

Murray H. A. (1981). *Endeavors in psychology: Selections from the personology of Henry A. Murray.* New York: Harper & Row.

National Center for Health Statistics. (1994). *Advance report of final mortality statistics* [Monthly vital statistics report]. Hyattsville, MD: United States Public Health Service.

Nielsen, B., Wang, A. G., & Bille-Brahe, U. (1990). Attempted suicide in Denmark: IV. A five-year follow-up. *Acta Psychiatrica Scandinavia, 81,* 250–254.

Nuland, S. B. (1994). *How we die: Reflections on life's final chapter.* New York: Knopf.

Paffenbarger, R. S., & Asnes, D. P. (1966). Chronic disease in former college students: III. Precursors of suicide in early and middle life. *American Journal of Public Health, 56,* 1026–1036.

Paffenbarger, R. S., King, S. H., & Wing, A. L. (1969). Chronic disease in former college students: IX. Characteristics in youth that predispose to suicide and accidental deaths in later life. *American Journal of Public Health, 59,* 900–908.

Paffenbarger, R. S., Lee, I.-M., & Leung, R. (1994). Physical activity and personal characteristics associated with depression and suicide in American college men. *Acta Psychiatrica Scandinavia Supplement, 377*, 16–22.

Paris, J., Nowlis, D., & Brown, R. (1987). Long-term follow-up of borderline patients in a general hospital. *Comprehensive Psychiatry, 28*, 530–535.

Pearson, J. L., Simonsick, E. M., & Phillips, C. L. (1993, November). *Prospective data on elderly suicides: Findings from the Established Populations for Epidemiologic Studies of the Elderly.* Poster presented at the annual convention of the Gerontological Society of America, New Orleans, LA.

Perry, J. C. (1989). Personality disorders, suicide and self-destructive behavior. In D. Jacobs & H. N. Brown (Eds.), *Suicide: Understanding and responding* (pp. 157–171). Madison, CT: International Universities Press.

Pokorny, A. D. (1960). Characteristics of forty-four patients who subsequently committed suicide. *A.M.A. Archives of General Psychiatry, 2*, 92–101.

Pokorny, A. D. (1983). Prediction of suicide in psychiatric patients. *Archives of General Psychiatry, 40*, 249–257.

Radloff, L. S. (1977). The CES-D Scale: self-report depression scale for research in the general population. *Applied Psychological Measurement, 1*, 385–401.

Rado, S. (1956). *Psychoanalysis and behavior: Collected papers.* New York: Grune & Stratton.

Rao, U., Weissman, M., Martin, J. E., & Hammond, R. W. (1993). Childhood depression and risk of suicide: A preliminary report of a longitudinal study. *Journal of the American Academy of Child and Adolescent Psychiatry, 32*, 21–27.

Rich, C. L., Fowler, R. C., Fogarty, L. A., & Young, D. (1988). San Diego Suicide Study: III. Relationships between diagnoses and stressors. *Archives of General Psychiatry, 45*, 589–594.

Rich, C. L., Ricketts, J. E., Fowler, R. C., & Young, D. (1988). Some differences between men and women who commit suicide. *American Journal of Psychiatry, 145*, 718–722.

Rich, C. L., & Runeson, B. S. (1992). Similarities in diagnostic comorbidity between suicide among young people in Sweden and the United States. *Acta Psychiatrica Scandinavica, 86*, 335–339.

Rich, C. L., Young, D., & Fowler, R. C. (1986). San Diego Suicide Study: I. Young vs. old subjects. *Archives of General Psychiatry, 43*, 577–582.

Richters, J. E. (1992). Depressed mothers as informants about their children: A critical review of the evidence for distortion. *Psychological Bulletin, 112*, 485–499.

Riso, L. P., Klein, D. N., Anderson, R. L., Ouimette, P. C., & Lizardi, H. (1994). Concordance between patients and informants on the Personality Disorder Examination. *American Journal of Psychiatry, 151*, 568–573.

Robins, C. J. (1990). Congruence of personality and life events in depression. *Journal of Abnormal Psychology, 99*, 393–397.

Robins, E. (1981). *The final months.* New York: Oxford University Press.

Robins, E., Murphy, G. E., Wilkinson, R. H., Gassner, S., & Kayes, J. (1959). Some clinical considerations in the prevention of suicide based on a study of 134 successful suicides. *American Journal of Public Health, 49*, 888–889.

Rockett, I. R. H., & Smith, G. S. (1993). Covert suicide among elderly Japanese females: Questioning unintentional drownings. *Social Science and Medicine, 36*, 1467–1472.

Romanov, K., Hatakka, M., Keskinen, E., Laaksonen, H., Kaprio, J., Rose, R. J., & Koskenvuo, M. (1994). Self-reported hostility and suicidal acts, accidents, and accidental deaths: A prospective study of 21,443 adults aged 25 to 59. *Psychosomatic Medicine, 56*, 328–336.

Rosenthal, R. (1991). Meta-analysis: A review. *Psychosomatic Medicine, 53*, 247–271.

Ross, R. K., Bernstein, L., Trent, L., Henderson, B. E., & Paganini-Hill, A. (1990). A prospective study of risk factors for traumatic deaths in a retirement community. *Preventive Medicine, 19*, 323–334.

Runeson, B. (1989). Mental disorders in youth suicide. *Acta Psychiatrica Scandinavica, 79*, 490–497.

Runeson, B., & Beskow, J. (1991). Borderline personality disorder in young Swedish suicides. *Journal of Nervous and Mental Disease, 179*, 153–156.

Runyan, W. M. (1983). Idiographic goals and methods in the study of lives. *Journal of Personality, 51*, 413–437.

Rydin E., Åsberg, M., Edman, G., & Schalling, D. (1990). Violent and nonviolent suicide attempts—A controlled Rorschach study. *Acta Psychiatrica Scandinavica, 82*, 30–39.

Sadavoy, J., & Fogel, B. (1992). Personality disorders in old age. In J. E. Birren, R. B. Sloane, & G. D. Cohen (Eds.), *Handbook of mental health and aging* (pp. 433–463). San Diego, CA: Academic Press.

Sainsbury, P. (1986). Depression, suicide, and suicide prevention. In A. Roy (Ed.), *Suicide* (pp. 54–78). Baltimore: Williams & Wilkins.

Sapolsky, R. M. (1992). *Stress, the aging brain, and the mechanisms of neuron death.* Cambridge, MA: MIT Press.

Schmideberg, M. (1936). A note on suicide. *International Journal of Psycho-Analysis, 17*, 1–5.

Seiden, R. H. (1966). Campus tragedy: A study of student suicide. *Journal of Abnormal Psychology, 71*, 386–399.

Shaffer, D., Garland, A., Gould, M., Fisher, P., & Trautman, P. (1988). Preventing teenage suicide: A critical review. *Journal of the American Academy of Child and Adolescent Psychiatry, 27*, 675–687.

Shaffer, J. W., Perlin, S., Schmidt, C. W., & Himelfarb, M. (1972). Assessment in absentia: New directions in the psychological autopsy. *Johns Hopkins Medical Journal, 130*, 308–316.

Shafii, M., Carrigan, S., Whittinghill, J. R., & Derrick, A. (1985). Psychological autopsy of completed suicide. *American Journal of Psychiatry, 142*, 1061–1064.

Shafii, M., Steltz-Lenarsky, J., McCue-Derrick, A., Beckner, C., & Whittinghill, J. R. (1988). Comorbidity of mental disorders in the post-mortem diagnosis of completed suicide in children and adolescents. *Journal of Affective Disorders, 15*, 227–233.

Shedler, J., Mayman, M., & Manis, M. (1993) The *illusion* of mental health. *American Psychologist, 48*, 1117–1131.

Shneidman, E. S. (1971). Perturbation and lethality as predictors of suicide in a gifted group. *Life-Threatening Behavior, 1*, 23–45.

Shneidman, E. S., & Farberow, N. L. (1961). Sample investigations of equivocal suicidal deaths. In N. L. Farberow & E. S. Shneidman (Eds.), *The cry for help* (pp. 118–128). New York: McGraw-Hill.

Stanley, M., & Mann, J. J. (1983). Increased serotonin-2 binding sites in frontal cortex of suicide victims. *Lancet, 1*(8318), 214–216.

Stanley, M., Mann, J. J., & Cohen, L. S. (1986). Serotonin and serotonergic receptors in suicide. *Annals of the New York Academy of Sciences, 487*, 122–127.

Stanley, M., Virgilio, J., & Gershon, S. (1982). Tritiated imipramine binding sites are decreased in the frontal cortex of suicides. *Science, 216*, 1337–1339.

Steer, R. A., Beck, A. T., Garrison, B., & Lester, D. (1988). Eventual suicide in interrupted and uninterrupted attempters: A challenge to the cry-for-help hypothesis. *Suicide and Life-Threatening Behavior, 18*, 119–127.

Stengel, E., & Cook, N. G. (with Kreeger, I. S.). (1958). *Attempted suicide: Its social significance and effects.* London: Oxford University Press.

Stokes, H. S. (1974). *The life and death of Yukio Mishima.* New York: Farrar, Straus & Giroux.

Stone, M., Hurt, S. W., & Stone, D. K. (1987). The PI 500: Long-term follow-up of borderline patients meeting *DSM-II* criteria: Global outcome. *Journal of Personality Disorders, 1*, 291–298.

Talbot, N. L. (1995). Uncovering shame in psychotherapy supervision. *American Journal of Psychotherapy, 49*, 338–349.

Thomas, C. B. (1971). Suicide among us: II. Habits of nervous tension as potential predictors. *Johns Hopkins Medical Journal, 129*, 190–201.

Tomlinson-Keasey, C., Warren, L. W., & Elliott, J. E. (1986). Suicide among gifted women. *Journal of Abnormal Psychology, 95*, 123–130.

U.S. Department of Commerce, Economics and Statistics Administration, Bureau of the Census. (1995). *Sixty-five plus in the United States* (Bureau of Census statistical brief). Washington, DC: U.S. Government Printing Office.

von Andics, M. (1938). *Über Sinn und Sinnlosigkeit des Lebens* [About the meaning and meaninglessness of life]. Vienna: Gerold & Company.

Warshauer, M. E., & Monk, M. (1978). Problems in suicide statistics for whites and blacks. *American Journal of Public Health, 68*, 383–388.

Weissman, M. M. (1993). The epidemiology of personality disorders: A 1990 update. *Journal of Personality Disorders, 7*(Suppl.), 44–62.

Widiger, T. A., & Shea, M. T. (1991). Differentiation of Axis I and Axis II disorders. *Journal of Abnormal Psychology, 100*, 399–406.

Young, M. A., Fogg, L. F., Scheftner, W. A., & Fawcett, J. A. (1994). Interactions in risk factors in predicting suicide. *American Journal of Psychiatry, 151*, 434–435.

Younger, S. C., Clark, D. C., Oehmig-Lindroth, R., & Stein, R. J. (1990). Availability of knowledgeable informants for a psychological autopsy study of suicides committed by elderly people. *Journal of the American Geriatrics Society, 38,* 1169–1175.

Zilboorg, G. (1936). Suicide among civilized and primitive races. *American Journal of Psychiatry, 92,* 1347–1369.

Zilboorg, G. (1937). Considerations on suicide, with particular reference to the young. *American Journal of Orthopsychiatry, 7,* 15–31.

Zung, W. W. K. (1965). A self-rating depression scale. *Archives of General Psychiatry, 12,* 63–70.

Author Index

Numbers in italics refer to listings in reference sections.

Subject Index

About the Editors

Joseph M. Masling is Emeritus Professor of Psychology at the State University of New York (SUNY) at Buffalo. He received his PhD in clinical psychology from Ohio State University in 1952; he was director of clinical training at Syracuse University (1959–1964) and chairperson of the Department of Psychology at SUNY–Buffalo (1969–1972). Masling has written numerous articles on interpersonal and situational variables influencing projective tests and has published widely on the empirical study of psychoanalytic concepts. He edited the first three volumes of the series Empirical Studies of Psychoanalytic Theories (1983, 1986, 1990) and coedited (with Robert F. Bornstein) Volume 4, *Psychoanalytic Perspectives on Psychopathology* (1993) and Volume 5, *Empirical Perspectives on Object Relations Theory* (1994).

Robert F. Bornstein is Professor of Psychology at Gettysburg College. He received his PhD in clinical psychology from the State University of New York at Buffalo in 1986. Bornstein has written many articles on perception without awareness and has published extensively on the antecedents, correlates, and consequences of dependent personality traits. He edited *Perception Without Awareness: Cognitive, Clinical and Social Perspectives* (1992), coedited (with Joseph M. Masling) *Psychoanalytic Perspectives on Psychopathology* (1993) and *Empirical Perspectives on Object Relations Theory* (1994), and is the author of *The Dependent Personality* (1993), a comprehensive review of the empirical literature on dependency.